THE THEOLOGY
OF
DIETRICH BONHOEFFER

ERNST FEIL

THE THEOLOGY
OF
DIETRICH BONHOEFFER

Translated by Martin Rumscheidt

Fortress Press　　　　　　　　　　Minneapolis

THE THEOLOGY OF DIETRICH BONHOEFFER

Fortress Press ex libris publication 2007

This book is a translation of a revised version of *Die Theologie Dietrich Bonhoeffers. Hermeneutik—Christologie—Weltverständnis* (Munich and Mainz: Chr. Kaiser and Matthias Grünewald, 1971), copyright 1971 by Chr. Kaiser Verlag, Munich. It is based on the third German edition (second edition in the German Democratic Republic) as extensively condensed and revised by the author himself specifically for this English edition.

English translation copyright © 1985 Fortress Press, an imprint of Augsburg Fortress. All rights reserved. Except for brief quotations in critical articles or reviews, no part of this book may be reproduced in any manner without prior written permission from the publisher. Visit http://www.augsburgfortress.org/copyrights/contact.asp or write to Permissions, Augsburg Fortress, Box 1209, Minneapolis, MN 55440.

ISBN: 978-0-8006-6240-0
The Library of Congress has catalogued the original publications as follows:

Library of Congress Cataloging-in-Publication Data

Feil, Ernst.
    The theology of Dietrich Bonhoeffer.

    Rev. translation of: Die theologie Dietrich Bonhoeffers.
      Bibliography: p.
      Includes index.
      1. Bonhoeffer, Dietrich, 1906-1945. I. Title.
    BX4827.B57F4413   1985   230'.044'0924   84-47919
    ISBN 0-8006-0696-5

The paper used in this publication meets the minimum requirements of American National Standard for Information Sciences—Permanence of Paper for Printed Library Materials, ANSIZ329.48-1984.

Manufactured in the U.S.A.

Contents

Translator's Preface	xi
Author's Preface	xv
Introduction	xix
What Does This Study Seek to Accomplish?	xix
The Ecumenical Aspect of This Work	xx
The Procedure and Method of This Work	xxi

Part One
Bonhoeffer's Hermeneutical Point of Departure: Theology in the Service of Christian Praxis

1. Historical Survey of Bonhoeffer's Understanding of Theology	3
The Difficulty of Bonhoeffer Interpretations	3
Bonhoeffer's Understanding of Theology as Scholarly Activity in His Earliest Writings	5
Mystery as Leitmotif	5
The Concrete-Ecclesiological Point of Departure in *Sanctorum Communio*	6
The Impasse of the Idealistic Point of Departure in Theology	6
Overcoming the Impasse Through the Ecclesiological Point of Departure	7
The Dialectical Point of Departure in *Act and Being*	9
Overcoming the Difference Between Act and Being as a Theological Task	10

CONTENTS

    The Impasse of the Transcendental and the Ontological Outlooks   11
    The Dialectic of Faith and Church as Solution   11
    Theology as Ecclesiastical Cognition   14

The Perception of Theology as a Scholarly Activity in Bonhoeffer's Later Writings   16
    Academic Studies   17
    Theology as an a posteriori Construction   17
    Christology as Scholarly Discipline   18

The Influence of Ecumenism and the Church Struggle on the Problem of Theology   20
    Thinking in the Service of Action   20
    The Bond of Theology to the Church's Decisions   22
    Excursus: The Relation to the Roman Catholic Church   25

2. Systematic Summary of the Hermeneutical Implications of Bonhoeffer's Theology   27

Faith as *fides directa in mysterium*   27
    The Mystery   27
    Actus Directus and *Actus Reflectus*   28

The Concept of Reality   29
    Reality: Concept and Counter-Concepts   30
    The Concept of Possibility   30
    Abstraction and Idea   32

Reality as Concrete Reality   37
    God the *Concretissimum*   37
    Concrete and Contingent Revelation   39
    The Binding Force of the Empirical Church   40
    The Concrete Command   41
    The Sermon as Concrete Proclamation   44

The Consequences for Bonhoeffer's Hermeneutics   46
    The Problem of Language   46
    The Sacrament as the Concreteness of Proclamation   48
    The Hermeneutical Function of Action   49

Conclusion   52

CONTENTS

Part Two
Jesus Christ the Center [*Mitte*] and Mediator [*Mittler*]

3. Historical Survey of Bonhoeffer's Christology	59
The Meaning of Christology for Bonhoeffer's View of the World	59
The Foundation of Christology	61
The Ecclesiocentric Outlook in *Sanctorum Communio*	61
The Absence of an Explicit Christology in the Outlook of *Sanctorum Communio*	61
The Ecclesiological Character of the Expression "Christ Existing as the Church" [*Gemeinde*]	62
The Christocentric Outlook in *Act and Being*	64
Christ as Boundary	64
The Intentionality of the *Actus Directus* Toward Christ	65
Mediation [*Vermittlung*] Through Christ	66
Basic Structure of the Early Christology	67
Christological Statements Preceding the Christology Lectures	67
Christ—God's Way to People	68
Increasing Concentration on Jesus Christ	69
The Connection Between Middle [*Mitte*] and Boundary	72
The Lectures on Christology	74
Jesus Christ: Mediator [*Mittler*] and Center [*Mitte*]	74
The Christological Concentration of the Middle Period	76
The Road to *The Cost of Discipleship*	76
The Christology of *The Cost of Discipleship*	78
The Cancellation of Immediacy [*Unmittelbarkeit*] by the Mediator [*Mittler*]	79
The Deputyship of Christ	80
"The Image of Christ"	81
The Relation to the World in Bonhoeffer's Late Christology	82

CONTENTS

The Transition to *Ethics*	82
The Christology of *Ethics*	84
Connecting Links to Earlier Statements on Ethics and Christology	84
Strictest Concentration on Jesus Christ	86
The Subject of History	88
Jesus Christ in *Letters and Papers from Prison*	90
The Question of God	90
The "Being-for-Others" of Jesus	92
Concluding Summary of the Christology	95

Part Three
Religionless Christianity in a World Come of Age

4. Historical Survey of Bonhoeffer's Understanding of the World	99
Preamble	99
The Question of the World: Its Background and Starting Point	100
Introduction to the Problems Relating to the Theme of "the World"	100
The Background to and the First Statement of the Traditional Problem of Religion	102
Early Studies in the Subject of Religion	102
Religion as the Subject of the First Lectures	104
Early Developments of a Positive Understanding of the World	107
The Beginning of the Development at Barcelona	107
The Primarily Negative Aspect	108
The Primarily Positive Aspect	110
Bonhoeffer's 1932 Discussion of the World: First Summit	114
The Cross as the Salvation of the World	114
The Relation to the World of the Church and of Christians	116
The Relation of Church and State	120
The Declining Significance for Bonhoeffer of the Subject of "World"	123
The Detached View of the World of the Middle Period	125

CONTENTS

The Transition to *The Cost of Discipleship*	125
The Understanding of the World in *The Cost of Discipleship*	128
The Break with the World	129
Indications of the 360-Degree Turn	135
Other Statements About the World from This Period	136
The Dialectical Understanding of the World of the Last Period	138
The Approach to *Ethics*	138
The Understanding of the World in *Ethics*	141
The Form of Christ and the Conformation of the World	141
The Dialectics of Ultimate and Penultimate	143
The Natural and the Penultimate	144
The Rejection of Thinking in Two Spheres	146
Liberation for True Worldliness	147
The Religionless Understanding of the World in *Letters and Papers from Prison*	152
Bonhoeffer's Personal "Yes to the Earth"	153
The Transition to the Second Period in Prison	155
The Subject Matter of Bonhoeffer's Last Letters in Light of His Theology to That Time	156
5. Systematic Synopsis of Bonhoeffer's Understanding of the World	**160**
Bonhoeffer's Concept of Religion and Its Meaning for the Problem of Religionless Christianity	160
Barth's Concept of Religion	162
Religion as a Preliminary Step	162
Religion as Radical Contrast	163
The Suspension of Religion	165
The Development of Bonhoeffer's Concept of Religion	167
Systematic Critique of the Religious Understanding of the World	167
Religion as a Historically Conditioned and Transient Form of Expression	172

CONTENTS

The Origin and Meaning of the Reflections on the World Come of Age	178
The Influence of Wilhelm Dilthey on the Prison Letters	178
God's Absence and Presence in a World Come of Age	185
Religionless Christianity and Non-Religious Interpretation	192
The Relation Between Religionless Christianity and Non-Religious Interpretation	192
The Meaning of Non-Religious Interpretation	194
Religionless Christianity as a Form of "Worldly-Universal" Christianity	195
Epilogue	203
Notes	206
Index of Subjects	242
Index of Names	244

Translator's Preface

Ernst Feil's major study of Dietrich Bonhoeffer's theology gives testimony in a variety of ways to the truth that in theological scholarship, too, everything has its season. Indeed, it is as if the cyclical pattern of the seasons of the year had its counterpart in the manner in which the work of theologians moves into the field.

Not many really knew Dietrich Bonhoeffer although he had used his diverse gifts in the service of the church. And when his life, bearing the signs of exile, ended in martyrdom and death by a tyrant's *fiat*, it seemed that those few alone would treasure this theologian's thinking. Certainly Eberhard Bethge did not anticipate that publishing Bonhoeffer's remarkable prison letters, excerpted at that, would significantly change the remembrance of Bonhoeffer by the theological world. Still, Bethge knew what he was doing: the possibility did exist that church and theology would both perceive *and* respond creatively to the signs of the times and grasp what that "man of vision, man of courage" had given at such great cost. It was possible that, working with Bonhoeffer's legacy, those who had known him could assist the generations of World War II in perceiving both God's judgment and promise of something new and preventing a return to "the fleshpots of Egypt." A world that seems to have changed intellectually on the one hand and irrevocably crossed thresholds of morality on the other might find Bonhoeffer's questions and hunches useful for moving forward and shaping the times.

We know how the story went: the excitement with Bonhoeffer led to what I called the seasons in theological scholarship. The interest in *Letters and Papers from Prison* quickly spread to all his work and soon the explorations into his later ideas were joined with the first full-length descriptions and interpretations of that thinking in its entirety. John Godsey, Kenneth Hamilton, William Kuhns, John Phillips, James Woelfel, to name only a few in the English-speaking world, Heinrich Ott, Hanfried Müller, Rainer Mayer in the German-speaking world, and

René Marlé in the French-speaking world published significant overviews from differing perspectives. The extensive study of Bonhoeffer in doctoral dissertations, elicited in part by the growing body of literature just referred to, followed quickly and seems to be only now abating. Alongside these two modes of study were countless articles enriching, but also obscuring, the view of Bonhoeffer's life and thought. In many ways the body of literature on Bonhoeffer has become too large to be grasped by one interpreter alone. (Manfred Kwiran listed 774 titles in the category of "secondary literature" in his *Index to Literature on Barth, Bonhoeffer and Bultmann,* published in 1977. An updated edition would not only include the items he missed but would add an estimated 200 titles that have appeared since 1977.)

A new "season" sets in when a fresh attempt is made to synthesize the thought of the one who is the subject matter of this research. Usually the two foci of life and thought, biography and theology, are creatively brought to bear upon each other. And something new often comes upon the scene, works which, though not exhaustive or conclusive, are seminal, studies which can only be ignored at the price of obscurantism.

I believe that Feil's study is such a seminal, "later season" work. When Eberhard Bethge reviewed the German edition, which was published in 1971, his critique was that it should have appeared earlier! Feil regards this book as the theological complement to Bethge's biography. It is not clear whether Bethge would agree with this perception; what seems quite clear, however, is that he welcomed the book as a highly necessary and successful corrective to much of Bonhoeffer scholarship.

In 1976 Professor Geffrey Kelly, one of those indispensable persons of the International Bonhoeffer Society, described what gives this book its value: "Feil's systematic, penetrating analysis and ordering of Bonhoeffer's complete writings seen in the general perspective of an underlying . . . unity and in the particular depths which reveal that unity is, indeed, awesome." (See his review of the German edition in *Union Seminary Quarterly Review,* Vol. 31, No. 4, 283–86; the cited passage is from 285–86.) Feil's attention to the whole of Bonhoeffer's corpus is constant and firm; it never slackens even when a particular idea is traced to its antecedents, such as the idea of the world come of age and its antecedents in the writings of Dilthey. The importance of Feil's work in the literature on Bonhoeffer derives both from the clear answers he gives and the sharp questions that precisely those answers raise. Those questions cover also much of what in the years between 1960 and 1970 called itself the analysis and interpretation of Bonhoeffer for our time. What was called radical Christianity in that decade may well be in for a thorough reassessment *if* it called itself radical in reliance on Bonhoeffer's late theological reflections. However true it is that authors, once they have uttered their thoughts in public, no longer have exclusive claim on the meaning of those thoughts, the unity of Bonhoeffer's thought demonstrated by Feil here may not only rule out some "interpretations" of Bonhoeffer made at that time but also show them to be not at all radical, or at least not as radical as Bonhoeffer was himself. This recovery of Bonhoeffer's own radical stance also makes Feil's study important.

We come to see not only that many people related their thinking to Bonhoeffer but that he, too, was thus related to others. Just as Feil enables his readers to assess critically how others appropriated Bonhoeffer for their own endeavors or even how they interpreted him, so he elicits critical response from them to his own description of those on whom Bonhoeffer relied to develop and advance his theological position. Even though the strong personal relation between Bonhoeffer and Karl Barth is widely known due to the significant stimulation the former received from the thought of the latter, the discussion of Barth in Bonhoeffer studies has, with only a few exceptions, suffered from a curious phenomenon: Bonhoeffer's *indeed* radical theology stands out so radically because it is contrasted with a bland picture of a Barth who it is said could not effectively shake off liberalism. There are several "later season" studies that show a Barth with whom Bonhoeffer studies have to deal. The seminal works on Barth by Eberhard Busch, Helmut Gollwitzer and Friedrich-Wilhelm Marquardt are shaping the study of Barth in a similar way to that of Bethge and indeed this study by Feil on Bonhoeffer. But until this issue is seriously reckoned with by those who study Bonhoeffer and Barth this aspect of the interpretation of either theologian and of the history of recent theology is not properly treated.

A much sharper question has to be raised, however, about the state of existing Bonhoeffer translations. While urging readers of this book to read Paul Lehmann's unambiguous comments under the heading of "Bonhoeffer: Real and Counterfeit" (*Union Seminary Quarterly Review*, Vol. 21, No. 3, 364–69), I limit the reference to the openly acknowledged sad state of affairs concerning almost all the translations. "A former colleague of mine, upon his return from a series of speaking engagements, was wont, ever and again, to remark: 'it is not my traducers who bother me; it is my introducers.' Just so—Dietrich Bonhoeffer, from the perspective of the nearer presence of God into which from our vantage he has been untimely called, must ever and again be saying to himself: 'it is not my critics who bother me; it is my commentators and translators' " (364). It is as if a praiseworthy felicity to mellifluous English had more often than not overridden what is utterly essential and, in a scholarly environment, even more praiseworthy: felicity to the original text. (A similar judgment could be made about the translation of Karl Barth's second edition of the *Römerbrief*.)

The translator acknowledges with gratitude the assistance he received from several persons in preparing the text of this translation, but to

TRANSLATOR'S PREFACE

name some of them directly is not to declare that the responsibility for the final text is jointly shared by them and the translator; he alone bears that responsibility. Granger Ryan, John Bollier and Paul MacGlasson, but especially Wendy Duschenes gave freely of their time and energy when it was needed. Norman Hjelm gave truly extraordinary help to the entire translation project. Finally the translator expresses profound gratitude to Barbara Rumscheidt who not only prepared the manuscript for the publisher but also arranged life at our home in such a way that this translation could be prepared at all.

Atlantic School of Theology
Halifax, Nova Scotia

MARTIN RUMSCHEIDT

Author's Preface

Christ and the world come of age—this is the theme of Bonhoeffer's life and theology. Bonhoeffer was haunted by the question of how Christ could become Lord also to the religionless. He was convinced that this could not be achieved by making people religious once again. Instead, he looked for a new form of Christianity in which people could have faith, be religionless, and be of age. For Bonhoeffer was certain that the time of religion was up.

It is not surprising that these ideas received wide attention; they are, after all, the ideas of a prisoner who had offered resistance as a Christian to Hitler and paid with his life for that. But Bonhoeffer's ideas are open to misunderstanding and have often been misunderstood. Several very diverse theological orientations, among them theologies inspired by Marxist thought and theologies of the death of God, have laid claim to Bonhoeffer. Marxist-inspired theologies have claimed Bonhoeffer because of his farewell to religion and his advocacy of the world's having come of age. Death of God theologies have claimed him because of his declaration that the time of religion is up. Some theologians followed Bonhoeffer's way for a limited time only and, like Harvey Cox, have parted company with him. It seemed to them that a more religious practice of Christianity was preferable to Bonhoeffer's proposal of a faith "religionless" and "of age."

In this situation it is urgent to understand what Bonhoeffer really had in mind, for only then can one answer the question of whether his ideas are still of use or whether one should revert to the religion which Bonhoeffer had so clearly rejected.

This book seeks to explain Bonhoeffer's view of Christian faith lived in a religionless world. An attempt is made, therefore, to interpret the ideas Bonhoeffer expressed in his prison correspondence, ideas he was not able to develop to their completion, in light of his entire theology. As a result of that attempt a view of what Bonhoeffer meant by religion is presented, which to date has not been challenged. From the perspective of this view of religion the contours provided by his letters and other writings of the faith which is of age are filled out. It is not surprising that, given Bonhoeffer's predisposition, this new faith could not be given shape in the realm of theory, but had to be sought in the realm of practice.

The interpretation of Bonhoeffer proposed in this book has not been negated by several studies which have appeared after this book was first published in 1971. This claim is true especially in relation to the study of Tom Day, *Dietrich Bonhoeffer on Christian Community and Common Sense* (Lewiston: The Edwin Mellen Press, 1982), which was written from the perspective of a Marxist-oriented theology, and in relation to the study of Tiemo R. Peters, *Die Präsenz des Politischen in der Theologie Dietrich Bonhoeffers* (Munich and Mainz: Chr. Kaiser Verlag and Matthias Grünewald Verlag, 1976), which was written from the perspective of political theology. The study presented in the pages to follow seeks to avoid making an interpretation of Bonhoeffer that is based on a prior point of departure. Hanfried Müller's work, *Von der Kirche zur Welt*, was the first to develop an interpretation of Bonhoeffer based on such a prior position; Müller set out to legitimate his own Marxist position through the theological statements which Bonhoeffer made in the final period of his life.

It is my concern to make Bonhoeffer's theology understandable from within its own perimeter. We cannot learn from Bonhoeffer when we see our own presuppositions confirmed by him nor can we repudiate what he said approaching him from our presuppositions. The more significant he and his work become in countries whose political situations challenge Christian faith in a special way, the more serious must be the effort to discern Bonhoeffer's real intention.

This study was written between 1966 and 1969 and was preceded by several long preliminary explorations in Bonhoeffer's thought. Abbreviations were made in the English text, notably in the historical reflections of part one, sections 1-3, and in the christology of Bonhoeffer, part two, sections 1-3; the endnotes particularly were shortened. No changes were made in passages of essential content; on the contrary, they now emerge more clearly. Readers are referred to the third edition of the German text, published in 1979, for detailed argumentation and citations. Reference could be made only in endnotes to studies on Bonhoeffer which appeared at the time of first publication of this book or since then, but I have no reason yet to alter my thesis substantially. Nor do I see any need to include in this work the conclusions presented by Clifford Green, since his work has now been published (*The Sociality of Christ and Humanity: Dietrich Bonhoeffer's Early Theology, 1927-1933* [Missoula: Scholars Press, 1975]).

AUTHOR'S PREFACE

There are many whom I must thank for the completion of this book and now for its translation. Eberhard Bethge and Ulrich Kabitz, who is associated with Christian Kaiser Verlag in Munich, gave persistent support in the preparation of this study. I want to name Johann Baptist Metz whose assistant I was when I began the work for this book. My gratitude is extended particularly to Clifford Green and Geffrey B. Kelly without whose determination the translation of this study would not have been undertaken. I must not fail to mention with appreciation Albert H. Lueders and Norman A. Hjelm of Fortress Press and Martin Rumscheidt who assumed the labor of translation. Finally I want to refer with gratitude to the personal community which came into being among the many people who seek to understand Bonhoeffer.

Munich, January 1983   ERNST FEIL

Introduction

WHAT DOES THIS STUDY SEEK TO ACCOMPLISH?

The subject of the world has attracted increasing attention in recent theology. Hitherto, the world was not really a matter for systematic reflection in Roman Catholic theology, since all that was necessary had been said in the doctrine of creation. From the middle of the nineteenth century up to Karl Barth, Protestant theology was shaped to a large extent by a latent acosmic perspective. Worldlessness was either given a neutral interpretation, the world being simply of no significance for faith and theology, or was said to be central to the program of theology. The word 'world' carried a negative connotation, a fact to which the debate about secularism after World War I gives eloquent testimony. But neither a neutrally understood nonworldliness of faith nor a desecularization postulated with polemical intent against secularization could become an adequate answer to the urgent question of the world.

Christian theology entered into a different relationship to the specifically modern subject of the world only after the Second World War. Using the ideas of Dietrich Bonhoeffer and Friedrich Gogarten, theologians shifted from a rejection of worldliness toward a positive engaging of the question.

The purpose of this work is to further the discussion about "the world" by investigating the contribution that Dietrich Bonhoeffer brought to it. There are two reasons for pursuing such a question in Bonhoeffer's writings.[1] First, Bonhoeffer personally confronted the world and declared himself in solidarity with it to such an extent that he deeply compromised himself; *as a Christian* he became a conspirator. Because he had renounced in *practice* a false dichotomy, he no longer separated his being-a-Christian and his being-in-the-world into distinct spheres. Second, he devoted his attention to the world in his *theory*, which meant that he became something of a state's witness for a theology of the world. His theological understanding of the world has not been presented systematically and, even in the most important texts, remains incomplete. For that reason it is urgent to analyze in detail his theological understanding of the world.

We shall attempt to elucidate Bonhoeffer's understanding of the world in order that he may no longer be regarded as the herald of a religionless Christianity in the sense of an actual elimination of Christianity. The opposite view, namely, that Bonhoeffer transmitted an unaltered, traditional Christianity, must also be rejected. For him, a practical *relation to the world* and a theoretical *understanding of the world* were inseparable. Indeed, toward the end of his life he placed his theology at the service of the worldly sector. The discussion about Bonhoeffer has rightly emphasized again and again that knowledge of his life is required for an understanding of his thought.[2] This mutuality of life and thought, practice and theory, and faith and theology gave shape to his life and work from the very beginning. Practice became more important for Bonhoeffer than theory; as a consequence, ethics was strongly integrated into dogmatics. His progress from teaching at the university through activity in the church to political engagement deepened his theological reflection. The question about the world now became more central.

Bonhoeffer could, therefore, no longer proceed on the assumption that the question about the world was of no special importance. Rather, it had become a fundamental feature of systematic theology. In other words, a full understanding of this subject requires that the whole of Bonhoeffer's theology be taken into consideration even though his thoughts on this subject are found chiefly in his late, incomplete, works.

In this regard Hanfried Müller's enquiry as to whether Bonhoeffer's development occurred in "qualitative leaps" or in a homogeneous unfolding is worthy of consideration.[3] In our examination of Bonhoeffer it has become more and more apparent that his theology does represent a sustained unity. In later life Bonhoeffer himself recognized this progression in his thought. Therefore, the only defensible view, in our judgment, is to interpret his unpolished assertions about the world, which had never been meant for publication, in connection with his whole work. It is important to realize that his final theological reflections about religionless Christianity arose from the center of his theology, having their antecedents in much earlier ideas and projects.

THE ECUMENICAL ASPECT OF THIS WORK

The point of departure in this study of Bonhoeffer is the Catholic understanding of faith, but only one of several possibilities of reflection arising from that understanding is to be considered. With regard to Bonhoeffer's theological considerations of the world, it is impossible to sustain denominational differences (as if Bonhoeffer's theology of the world were a specifically Protestant one to which a specifically Catholic response could be given). Theological interpretations of Christian life in the world differ widely but those distinctions are not always caused by differences between denominations. They can also be quite in agreement without thereby suggesting that denominational differences have been overcome.

This denominational question brings into focus the necessity for readers of Bonhoeffer to accept the man as he understood himself and as he lived, namely as a Protestant Christian and theologian. It is illegitimate for Catholics to claim him directly for their cause;[4] but it is equally wrong for Protestants to reject Bonhoeffer, with the argument that he "Romanizes" the Protestant religion, and thus to dispense with the imperative of truly recognizing Bonhoeffer's denominational position.[5]

THE PROCEDURE AND METHOD OF THIS WORK

A description of Bonhoeffer's theology of the world would be substantively one-sided and not well founded if his christology were not presented in at least its main features. Bonhoeffer's statement, "Henceforward one can speak neither of God nor of the world without speaking of Jesus Christ," (E, 194) significantly depicts his belief that the relation to God and the world is mediated through Jesus Christ. Thus Bonhoeffer's understanding of the world can only be legitimately apprehended within the framework of christology.

Bonhoeffer's christological endeavors, however, were related to his assertions about theological scholarship in which he, describing his own theological work, reflected upon the relation of faith and theology. Closely tied to christological statements, these assertions allowed him to give precision to his hermeneutical starting point. It is necessary to describe initially the presuppositions of Bonhoeffer's theology in order to present, subsequently, the true aim of this study—the illumination of Bonhoeffer's theological understanding of the world.

Bonhoeffer's theology itself leads to the division of our work into three parts. His understanding of the world cannot be depicted adequately unless his christology is shown clearly at first; his christology, however, demands that his understanding of theology be clarified. Thus, the three parts are mutually connected. The analysis of Bonhoeffer's christology is placed in the middle section of this critical work; but christology also forms the center of his thinking.

Because there are particular difficulties connected with the interpretation of Bonhoeffer, each of the three parts requires a historical trajectory through his work before systematic summations are ventured in part one and part three.

PART ONE

BONHOEFFER'S HERMENEUTICAL POINT OF DEPARTURE: THEOLOGY IN THE SERVICE OF CHRISTIAN PRAXIS

1
Historical Survey of Bonhoeffer's Understanding of Theology

THE DIFFICULTY OF BONHOEFFER INTERPRETATIONS

Dietrich Bonhoeffer's theological understanding of the world cannot be analyzed unless the hermeneutical difficulty that presents itself to every study of his theology is clarified first. The initial difficulty is that his work is so varied as far as the genre of texts is concerned. Next to his academic studies, *Sanctorum Communio* and *Act and Being*, there are the more spiritually oriented works, *The Cost of Discipleship* and *Life Together;* and there are, finally, the posthumously published fragments entitled *Ethics* and *Letters and Papers from Prison*. These books are augmented by a variety of texts: letters, addresses, catechetical studies, essays, memoranda, lectures, and, not least, the sermons to which Bonhoeffer devoted himself passionately. But all texts lead again and again to those last letters from prison which stimulated all the interest in Bonhoeffer and without which little notice would be paid today to the earlier writings.

The variety of the texts raises the question for interpreters as to what extent the writings together form the basis for a scholarly analysis. It may well appear questionable to make diverse texts the working foundation for a theological investigation. For that reason *Letters and Papers from Prison* is considered more often as a breviary of spiritual life than as a scholarly text. If one builds an argument on the basis of those letters one becomes open to the charge of over-interpreting Bonhoeffer.[1] If on the other hand the central assertions of *Letters and Papers from Prison* are regarded as theologically very relevant despite the fact that they have not been developed in detail, then one fashions the key to interpretation from Bonhoeffer's biography and supports this procedure with the claim that a consideration of both his life and work together is requisite to an understanding of him.[2] But this only transforms the problem, for how is one to interpret Bonhoeffer's life: primarily as a uniform development or as a development in which far-reaching changes took place? The interpretations of the fragmentary statements of *Letters and Papers from Prison* depend on the determination of these questions. Yet mere reference to Bonhoeffer's own comments concerning those fragments is not enough (LPP, 219, 297).

In view of this difficult situation it comes as no surprise that there are various reasons why people made use of Bonhoeffer's posthumous works. Karl Barth considered *Letters and Papers from Prison* to be of importance but saw no way in which to interpret the letters.[3] Moltmann based his studies of Bonhoeffer chiefly on *Ethics*,[4] Pfeiffer unambiguously on the early Bonhoeffer, such that the later works were of secondary value in terms of evidence and were no longer of prime importance to the theologian. Müller assumed what in this respect was a quite justified, sharply critical counterposition, by interpreting Bonhoeffer beyond Bonhoeffer (KzW, 13). But Müller brought a new question into the discussion by speaking of Bonhoeffer's life and work as unfolding in "qualitative leaps" (KzW, 9, 31–33).[5] That is the decisive term for Bonhoeffer interpretation. The possibility of making an unambiguous interpretation is quite slim if one cannot determine whether one is dealing with a work marked by qualitative leaps or by a continuous unfolding of its development. Were it the former, the fragmentary nature of Bonhoeffer's final statements would radically narrow the basis on which to decide what in those assertions must be interpreted in connection with his earlier works and what has to be eliminated as reactionary; that is to say, what in those earlier works seems to augur future thoughts and what seems to be superseded. Such a conclusion would finally have to be made independently and could not be drawn from Bonhoeffer's work itself.[6]

Eberhard Bethge has rightly warned us not to divide Bonhoeffer's life and theology into various phases and, in so doing, dissolve the dialectics of church and world.[7] Many Bonhoeffer interpreters support him in that.[8] Nor should Bonhoeffer be appropriated eclectically, something that happens easily if one bases oneself only on the later works or even on *Letters and Papers from Prison* alone.[9] This must be made clear in relation to the understanding of the world in Dietrich Bonhoeffer, as the whole difficulty connected with the study of Bonhoeffer will also emerge. For Bonhoeffer addressed the question of the world quite early in his 1928 sermons in Barcelona, only to give the topic intensive discussion in 1932. In *Ethics* and *Letters and Papers from Prison*, written between 1939 and 1944, he reflected on this matter with great clarity. As these sources were never meant for publication and were not completed, the problem of hermeneutics becomes most acute, for without those texts a study of Bonhoeffer's understanding of the world would be possible in only a very limited fashion.

BONHOEFFER'S UNDERSTANDING OF THEOLOGY AS SCHOLARLY ACTIVITY IN HIS EARLIEST WRITINGS

There is little sense in presenting a general hermeneutic from which the presuppositions for an understanding of Bonhoeffer may be derived. Instead we shall attempt to develop the hermeneutical presuppositions for our work from Bonhoeffer himself. In entering upon this task it is useful to state how he perceived theology and, thereby, clarify his position on the relation of human life and thought and his understanding of reality.

It will become clear in the course of our presentation that, by developing the hermeneutical presuppositions in this way, we do not proceed arbitrarily but follow the inner structure of theological argumentation as it appears in Bonhoeffer himself. He was convinced that he came out of a tradition which, on account of a false (idealistic) hermeneutic, could not define the relation of praxis and theory. This is why he searched indirectly throughout his life for a hermeneutic which would overcome the false one. His immediate preoccupation, of course, was increasingly with the reality, which his words were meant only to interpret and to mediate, and with the praxis which he sought to bring about. This concern is indicated by the fact that, beginning with *Act and Being*, Bonhoeffer again and again focused his attention on the distinction between *actus directus* and *actus reflectus*, between faith and reflection or, more generally, between life and thought.

Mystery as Leitmotif

The distinction between believing and thinking grew out of the experience of the poverty of thinking vis-à-vis believing. Bonhoeffer's reflection moves outwards from the center, from the mystery of a faith that is beyond complete rational comprehension, and to that center his reflection seeks to return. It is the center which necessitates the distinction in theory between faith and reason, *actus directus* and *actus reflectus*.

The central significance of mystery was spelled out by Bonhoeffer in a passage which we would like to place as a leitmotif before the hermeneutical reflections to follow:

> Mystery [*Geheimnis*] is something *uncanny* [*unheimlich*] because we are not *at home* [*daheim*] in it, because it tells of a manner of *being at home* [*Daheimsein*] different from ours. To live without mystery means that one knows nothing of the mystery of one's life, of other people's lives, of the world. It means to walk past the hiddenness of our selves, of others' selves, and of the world. It means to be always on the surface. It means that one takes the world seriously only to the extent that it can be subject to calculation and use; it means that one never departs from the sphere of calculation and use. We do not want to be told that *mystery is the root of everything comprehensible, clear, and revealed*. . . . But mystery does not mean

> *merely that one does not know something.* The most distant star is not the deepest mystery; on the contrary, the closer something comes to us and the better we know it, the more mysterious it becomes. The deepest mystery is not the person farthest away but precisely the one closest to us. . . . God lives in mystery. His being is mystery to us, mystery from eternity to eternity. Mystery, because it speaks of a *home [Heimat]* in which we are—not yet—*at home [daheim]*. (GS V, 516–18)

It took the directness of preaching for Bonhoeffer to state clearly that mystery is the root of everything comprehensible. The mystery which is close to us was also the original point of departure for Bonhoeffer's theology, although that was not explicitly stated.

THE CONCRETE–ECCLESIOLOGICAL POINT OF DEPARTURE IN *SANCTORUM COMMUNIO*

The Impasse of the Idealistic Point of Departure in Theology

The community of saints, or the "reality of the church" (SC, 87), was the subject matter of Bonhoeffer's doctoral dissertation. Such a reality was to be comprehended theologically, but Bonhoeffer found the available conceptual tools of the "metaphysical scheme" (SC, 26) unsuitable for his perception of the church as an empirically real community of believers:

> We must reject the derivation of the social from the epistemological category as a metabasis eis allo genos. *From the purely transcendental category of the universal we can never reach the real existence of alien subjects.* How then do we reach the alien subjects? By knowledge there is no way at all, just as there is no way by pure knowledge to God. (SC, 28)

This was the task Bonhoeffer faced. The initial step was to overcome the prevalence of epistemology and its necessarily concomitant individualism. Due to the premise of its metaphysics of cognition, idealism includes individualism because it cannot comprehend the other person; that is to say, it can only comprehend the other person as *something* other (SC, 28). Instead, idealism leans toward a metaphysics of spirit, which does not show persons in their concreteness and actual contingency because it "absorbs" persons into generality (SC, 26).

What was the theological consequence of such an idealistic scheme in Bonhoeffer's view? The individualism inherent in such a perspective causes not only the elimination of the true thou but also God, the "impenetrable thou" (SC, 34), to be completely missed. Bonhoeffer therefore felt compelled to overcome the starting point of idealism by means of a concept of person that would not by its very nature rule out but rather fundamentally embrace the sociality of people. By means of such a concept both the isolation of people and the subject–object dichotomy of idealism were to be overcome positively. The subject–object scheme allowed no possibility to comprehend the other person; theologically it was especially unsuitable because God could not be expressed through it. According to Bonhoeffer it was a mistake, however unavoidable in idealism, to assume that something has been said about God with the concept of transcendence as cognitive theory uses it (SC, 33).

Because thought relates everything to the subject and, consequently, qualifies another subject, in this case God, as object (as a result of which the subject is hopelessly isolated, since there is no genuine thou) idealism has no true boundaries. In idealism the boundary, which is "between obligation and being," does not lie at the edges where "the boundary of the human as a whole" lies but, instead, right through the middle of persons (SC, 29). "But with Kant's 'You can, for you ought' it moved from ethical transcendence to the immanence of a philosophy of mind. . . . The real barrier was not acknowledged. This is possible only in the ethical sphere" (SC, 29).

The concepts of transcendence and boundary are connected. By attempting to overcome transcendence in the epistemological sense, Bonhoeffer sought to regain the possibility of a real, that is, ethical delimitation of the subject: "Statements concerning the transcendence of the thou in fact say nothing about epistemological transcendence. It is a purely ethical transcendence which is experienced only by the one who makes a decision, which can never be demonstrated to someone outside" (SC, 33). This can be overcome through the acknowledgment of the other person. "So the thou-form is to be defined as the other who places me before an ethical decision. With this I–thou relationship as the basic Christian relation the epistemological subject–object relationship has been left behind in principle" (SC, 33).

The three aspects just mentioned belong together since they mutually condition and give rise to one another: (1) idealism represents an individualism which diffuses the concretely encountered person into generality; (2) from this derives a false notion of transcendence which can show no real boundary; (3) the basic structure of this starting point, the subject–object scheme, is also the basis on which one completely misses both the other and transcendence.

Overcoming the Impasse Through the Ecclesiological Point of Departure

Bonhoeffer directed his efforts against the position just outlined. He saw its essence in transcendental as well as idealistic thinking:

> Since the aim of our inquiry is to understand a particular concept of community, namely, the *sanctorum communio*, we must, in order to grasp it fully, investigate its particular concept of the person. Concretely this means that we must study the *Christian concept of the person*. In understanding the meaning of person and community we shall also have said something decisive about the concept of God. For the *concepts of person*,

community, and God have an essential and indissoluble relation to one another. Where a concept of God is formed, it is formed in relation to person and personal community. In principle, the nature of the Christian concept of community can be reached as well from the concept of God as from the concept of the person. (SC, 22)

This states the primary concern of Bonhoeffer. The central concept is ethical transcendence, given in the thou who is to be acknowledged (SC, 29, 31–34). This thou is the thou of both the neighbor and God (SC, 36–37). The thou alone provides a *real boundary* through which deadly isolation is lifted and *genuine sociality* established. This is true because the thou of the neighbor and the thou of God belong together. "Social community is in essence given with community with God. The latter is not what leads to the former. Community with God is not without social community, nor is social community without community with God."[10] This is one of the central theses of *Sanctorum Communio,* although it is not sufficiently explained there.

The basis for Bonhoeffer's argument is the facticity of the church. His incisive axiom was that "the nature of the church can be understood only from within, *cum ira studio* [SC, 20], and never from a disinterested standpoint"; or later, in cognitive terms: *"Only from reality can we deduce necessity in dogmatics"* (SC, 97). When studying the church we learn nothing from a general concept such as that of religion, since it does not include the community (SC, 93–97), for the "Christian *concept of the church* is reached only by way of the concept of revelation" (SC, 97). Only with that concept of the church can one correctly understand the *concept of God,* for which reason it would be commendable to begin dogmatics with the doctrine of the church and not with that of God (SC, 97).

On the basis of the *sanctorum communio* alone it is possible to include socio-philosophical considerations in theology (SC, 86). All theological statements "in the logic of a complete dogmatics" (SC, 41) arise for Bonhoeffer basically from the concept of the church. At the heart of the theology of *Sanctorum Communio* there is, dominating all, the concrete church.

The claim of the church to be the church of God is, therefore, the premise of theology, which is for that reason referred to as "the fact of Christ or the 'word' " (SC, 88). This claim is presupposed and no longer defended, for indeed, it is no longer susceptible of further defense (SC, 89).

If this premise is in no need of defense, it follows for theology as a scholarly activity that faith "is not a possible method of arriving at scientific knowledge, but as the faith which accepts the claim made in revelation, it is the given premise for positive theological knowledge" (SC, 89). This suggests that it is different from necessary knowledge.

It would be completely wrong, too, to establish from faith in Christ faith in the church as a conceptual necessity. *What is conceptually necessary is not for that reason real. Rather there is no relation to Christ in which the relation to the church is not necessarily presupposed. Thus logically the church presupposes its basis within itself;* it can be judged only through itself, like all revelations. It presupposes what is to be found. Before one can begin to talk about the church there must be knowledge and acknowledgement of its reality. . . . Only they who are already in the church can admit that these theological methods are justified; but being there they will have abandoned the objective outside position. (SC, 89)

This shows quite clearly Bonhoeffer's direction of thought, even though what he said was problematic. He wanted to concede the status of given reality and to regard it seriously, but he thought that he could accomplish that only by giving priority to concrete, actual, contingent, and ethical matters rather than to abstract, necessary, absolute (in the epistemological sense), and metaphysical questions.

In summing up one might say that Bonhoeffer's premise concerns a concrete believing existence in the church, from which is deduced the systematically compelling significance of the empirical church for theology. From this follows, at least for *Sanctorum Communio,* that ecclesiology has priority in principle. Comprehending the empirical church in a systematic way is theology's urgent task. Sociological categories are of help here since, changed now through their association with faith, they alone can grasp the sociality which had been obscured by the traditional epistemological starting point.

Our question about Bonhoeffer's understanding of scholarship has received an initial indirect answer through the elucidation of his premise in *Sanctorum Communio.* In the latter work priority over knowledge and thought is assigned to the concreteness of the empirical church. All thinking must set out from and be judged by existence in decision; all thinking must subordinate itself to that facticity. One cannot presuppose a general concept of any kind on the basis of which revelation and church are examined and understood. "We are speaking not of religious community, but of the empirical church as the *sanctorum communio* present in its actual embodiment" (SC, 180). Because theology can deduce necessity only from reality (SC, 97), it must be regarded as an "empirical discipline," a "discipline of facts," before it can be viewed as a "discipline of essences."

THE DIALECTICAL POINT OF DEPARTURE
IN *ACT AND BEING*[11]

Bonhoeffer's dissertation provided an initial, indirect answer to the question of what theology meant to him as a scholarly discipline. *Act and Being,* the work which qualified him for habilitation at the University of Berlin in 1930, provides an explicit answer. While seeking to achieve clarity in epistemology, Bonhoeffer set out to discern the anthropology which every epistemology implies (AB, 14). In *Act and Being* Bonhoeffer did not simply draw conclusions from *Sanctorum Communio*.[12] Indeed, he tried to do more than give an explanation of his dissertation after the fact (KzW, 36). For the later work is a certain expansion of the perspective outlined in *Sanctorum Communio*. On the basis of the point of departure of *Sanctorum Communio*, namely, the concrete church, Bonhoeffer wanted to overcome the dichotomy of a theology of act and a theology of being. In *Act and Being* the systematic developments emanated from a different point of orientation which indicates a certain distancing from *Sanctorum Communio*. This is shown by the noticeable reduction in the use of the phrase "Christ existing as community," an expression used so frequently in the earlier work that it had become almost a catchphrase.[13] Instead there now appeared the crucial, oft-repeated distinction between *actus directus*, or *fides directa*, and *actus reflectus*.[14] Bonhoeffer adopted this distinction from the dogmatics of Protestant orthodoxy and broadened it at the same time. It remained part of his thinking even into his latest letters (LPP, 373).

We create a problem for ourselves by not only citing this distinction between *actus directus* and *actus reflectus* but by using it to give structure to our discussion. The distinction signals a unity. In our quest for theology as a scholarly discipline we have to deal primarily with the *actus reflectus*, whereas the *actus directus* is part of christology. For that reason we shall discuss the *actus directus* extensively only in part two of our study, and here explore the *actus reflectus*.

Overcoming the Difference Between Act and Being as a Theological Task

In *Act and Being* Bonhoeffer sought to discern "the interrelation of belief as act and revelation as being" (AB, 12). The work set out to overcome the difference between a transcendental and an ontological starting point of theology. According to Bonhoeffer this difference can be overcome only through the understanding of the church as a unity of act and being. For in the church there is both genuine act and genuine being. Genuine act is faith, an act by its very nature and purely intentional because it is specifically directed toward Christ. Genuine being is there because it is "being in . . . ," "being in Christ." The church as a unity of act and being is constituted by revelation, that is, by actual proclamation (AB, 117). Revelation makes possible and brings about genuine sociality *and* individuality and, consequently, genuine "being in community" on the part of those who believe in Christ. In order to solve the problem posed by this idea Bonhoeffer made use of the distinction between *actus directus* and *actus reflectus*. The *actus directus*, which is pure "being directed toward . . . ," is a matter of being *conscious*, because it is a spiritual act. (Being conscious, it is to be noted, is not meant in a psychological sense.) It follows, for Bonhoeffer, that it can also be a matter of *being* conscious (AB, 13)—that is to say, *actus reflectus*. Direct consciousness, *actus directus*, or faith that "abides in itself," however, is not adequately amenable to reflection:

> In the act of belief, which Christ himself creates within me, inasmuch as he gives me the Holy Spirit who hears and believes within me, he also proves himself the free Lord of my existence. Christ "is" only in faith, yet he "is" master of my faith. (AB, 141)

In this sentence Bonhoeffer's main concern is stated. In the act of faith *cor curvum in se,* the state of being enclosed without exit is broken open.

The Impasse of the Transcendental and the Ontological Outlooks

The state of being enclosed in ourselves, from which there is no exit, is overcome through Christ. In order to demonstrate this assertion, Bonhoeffer subjected the philosophical act-and-being problem to a critical analysis in which the I-enclosedness of thought without Christ would be shown. His conclusion was that in a system with a transcendental starting point, reason [*Vernunft*] remains in its own limits and all attempts "to surpass itself or prescribe its own limitations" fail so that there are no bounds set for reason from beyond itself (AB, 31). In the ontological system the attempt of thought to open the concept of being to the transcendental fails equally, and is left with only an illusory transcendence (AB, 69). Whether thought declares the mode of being of human existence to the act, as in transcendental systems, or whether thought insists on "the primacy of being over consciousness" (AB, 49), as in ontological systems, genuine transcendence is achieved in neither case. Indeed, it is inevitable that "both—the act as foundation of being, and being as foundation of act—evolve into the I-enclosed system in which the 'I' understands itself from itself, can place itself in truth" (AB, 70). Neither act as foundation of being nor being as foundation of act can break open the *cor curvum in se* as Bonhoeffer stated it, following Luther:[15] "Thought is as little able as good works to deliver the *cor curvum in se* from itself" (AB, 72). Only a real "beyond" signifies boundary, transcendence, truth, and reality; but that "beyond" is not to be found in humanity itself.

The Dialectic of Faith and Church as Solution

Only in the "act of encounter with God" (AB, 97) is a solution to be found; through that encounter alone is existence placed into truth and into decision. Solely at the boundary, experienced and *affirmed* in faith, does the insufficiency of human thought become manifest. For in revelation alone human thought, which again and again seeks an I-enclosed system, is set free from such an enclosure and, at the same time, from the deadly isolation out of which there is no escape for those without faith. Even thought placed into truth, that is to say, theology, remains enclosed within itself if left to its own resources. A system which is no longer I-enclosed is only an eschatological possibility:

> From God to reality, not from reality to God, goes the path of theology. Accordingly the will to refrain from a system must fail in its purpose; thought stays within itself, in sin as in grace. The true system thus remains an eschatological possibility. . . . But for that reason any system of humankind which *is* not eternally in truth is an untrue system and must be broken in pieces so that the true system may become possible. It is the preaching of the word that brings about this breakage through faith. And so we come to the problem of theology, preaching and faith. . . . (AB, 89)

There can only be a true system through the demolition by faith of an untrue system; even theology must allow itself to be disturbed anew by preaching and faith.

Here the relation becomes apparent between transcendence, eschatologically present reality, and sociality, a primary aspect of Bonhoeffer's theology. Humans and their thought become truly open to the neighbor only as the *cor curvum in se* and the resulting I-enclosedness of thought are broken open. "Existence in this sense [existence which undergoes impact from beyond itself] is existence in social relation, existence in relation to Christ" (AB, 127). In this way Bonhoeffer eliminated at the very outset every form of individualism or subjectivism, for revelation always encounters the person and creates community at the same time.

Through the concretizing of the idea of revelation in the idea of church the problem of act and being "receives its final clarification by taking the shape of the dialectic of faith and church" (AB, 124). The unity of act and being is presented as the dialectic of faith and church inasmuch as the person is at one and the same time individual and humanity (AB, 130). According to Bonhoeffer, the difference between transcendentalism and ontology is overcome through this theological–sociological category: "When the sociological category is thus introduced, the problem of act and being—and also the problem of knowledge—is presented in a wholly fresh light" (AB, 122).

This "sociological category" makes it possible for thinking to proceed. On the basis of the unity of faith and community, thinking about faith can only be ecclesial knowledge; hence, theology *qua* reflected knowledge is not existential knowledge. How existential knowledge and systematic knowledge fit together is something, according to Bonhoeffer, which an act-theology, as found for example in Karl Barth, cannot make clear (AB, 96). In such an act-theology these two types of knowledge are separated by a chasm which can be described as the distinction between religion and faith (AB, 94). For Bonhoeffer there can be scholarship only where there are concepts of being: "A science [*Wissenschaft*], the essence of which is its knowing [*wissen*], not its asking, must be passionately interested in concepts of being; what *mode* of being is apposite here must remain for the present an unanswered question" (AB, 97).

If theology can exist as such at all, contrary to an understanding of revelation strictly as an act (as transcendental) (AB, 97), it is because God has bound himself freely, because he can be grasped in his word in the church. This "bondage" does away with God being act-like in nature, God being an ungraspable transcendence, and for that reason it is no longer human autonomy which takes possession of God in knowledge: "Humans cannot transplant themselves into the existential situation from where they could speak of God, for they are unable to place themselves into truth" (AB, 93). Contrary to Barth, therefore, Bonhoeffer's concept of revelation was conceived strictly in historical terms which meant that faith could be considered once again in its intentionality: "The essence of the *actus directus* does not lie in its timelessness but in its intentionality towards Christ, which is not repeatable at all, because it is freely given by God. This is as much as to say that its essence is expressed by its manner of touching upon existence—by which we mean the totality of historical, temporal *Existenz*" (AB, 103). The unity of act and being is given, therefore, only in the church. This cannot be demonstrated philosophically since the real contingency of revelation would otherwise not be observed. God's action can be demonstrated only through itself: this was Bonhoeffer's irreducible presupposition.

For Bonhoeffer the theological–sociological category of the church provided the unity of act and being. God's action alone can cause it to be historical reality so that it must be presupposed prior to every reflection upon it. But it must be recalled that "the church is regarded as constituted by the present proclamation, within the communion, for the communion, of Christ's death and resurrection" (AB, 119). Only in this manner is the contingency of revelation guarded as something coming toward us, something in the future. It must not be overlooked that the church awaits the return of the heavenly Christ as the community founded by his death and resurrection (AB, 121, n.2). The church, understood by Bonhoeffer as "personal community" (AB, 140), or as "community of persons" (AB, 137), and borne entirely by Christ (AB, 121), makes possible the resolution of the difference between act and being.

It follows that faith, always to be met within the church, "encounters a being which is prior to the act" (AB, 128), so that the concepts of being deduced from the concept of church "are always formed with reference to the act of faith" (AB, 129).

This dialectic of faith and church (AB, 130) turns out to be the precondition for theology as a scholarly discipline [*Wissenschaft*] in Bonhoeffer's thought.

Theology as Ecclesiastical Cognition

Since the reality of revelation, as a socially structured reality, was the precondition for theology, the problem of cognition posed itself for Bonhoeffer differently from the way he saw it posed for theologians before him. This is shown by the fact that he could not adopt Barth's point of departure in which concrete reference to Christ and, consequently, real history were not sufficiently manifest. Over against that viewpoint Bonhoeffer postulated "a concept of cognition envisaged in a sociological category" corresponding to three "distinct sociological functions of the church" (AB, 137). Bonhoeffer distinguished between three different ways of knowing: "Knowing as a *believer*, knowing in *preaching*, and *theological* knowledge, of which the first may be called *existential* and the others *'ecclesiastical cognition'* " (AB, 137). Here knowing as a believer corresponds to the *actus directus* (AB, 141, 137, 31), knowing in preaching and theological knowledge to the *actus reflectus* (AB, 135, 141). On account of the unity of act and being, that is, the dialectic of faith and church, this concept of cognition, seen in terms of sociological category and being in itself dialectical, can surpass the hitherto individualistic concept of knowledge.

The *actus reflectus*, or ecclesiastical knowledge, has two forms: preaching and theology. A sermon is reflection, too. But it must contain "no uncertainty here, no not-knowing," because in preaching "Christ causes himself to be declared the 'subject' of the spoken words"; a sermon takes place "in the strength of Christ, the strength of the faith of the community" (AB, 142).[16] The preacher's act of faith is not and cannot be the ultimate foundation of the sermon, for the preached word is given qualification by the preaching office which is itself socially structured.

We may now perceive Bonhoeffer's understanding of theology through his statement that "theology is a function of the church, for the church is not without preaching, nor preaching without remembrance, but theology is the memory of the church" (AB, 143). This statement declares that theology has a boundary, for it is known that what theology asserts, it cannot establish. The verbal statement, "your sins are forgiven," does not bring about forgiveness; rather, it is Christ himself who can do this. It is this mystery alone which has its happening in the church, and which creates the church, on which theology reflects. In doing this the church has no other way of escaping its urge to justify itself but by remaining firmly located in the community.

Theology itself cannot be an existential confession because there is absolutely no reflection in faith as such. Reflection in this sense turns out to be an obliteration (AB, 147). It is for this reason that in faith alone there is "no longer the self-imposed extreme of the self-transparent I" (AB, 149).

Theology is, therefore, fundamentally retrospective; it is something which remembers, something oriented toward the past. Its subject matter is "the word that was spoken" just as the subject matter of faith is "the living word of Christ" and that of preaching is "the word to be spoken now and declared to the community" (AB, 148). Theology is aware of its retrospective orientation because it reflects on the coming, yet already present, salvation and has for that reason its own boundary clearly in mind. Since theology, being the function and remembrance of the church (AB, 143), thinks upon the direct reference to Christ, or the *actus directus*, it is no longer

> system, autonomous self-understanding. Only in the church itself, where the word of Christ is held in remembrance and his living person is active, is it understood that a theology meaning to serve the concrete church is in reality subserving, as autonomous thought, the *nomos* of Christ. Where a theological self-understanding is concerned, it is no longer a case of "self-understanding which has been placed into truth"—*that* it is in faith—but of "reflective thought in the service of the church." If one may adopt Luther's dictum, the theologian's rubric is *Reflecte fortiter, sed fortius fide et gaude in Christo.* (AB, 150; "reflect boldly but believe and rejoice in Christ more boldly still")

We may summarize our preliminary results in this way: For Bonhoeffer theology is "positive science" (AB, 144), that is to say, a discipline which has a definite subject matter, "the remembered happenings of the Christian community, the Bible, preaching and sacrament, prayer, confession, the word of the Christ-person which is preserved as entity in the historical church" (AB, 143). Since theology is also thought, it seeks to give rise to a system, but it will be theology only when that desire is again and again thwarted. Theology is an endeavor to obtain knowledge that arises out of the recollection that theology is directed toward Christ. Theological knowledge necessarily falls behind the act of faith: "The representation of God which I have in my consciousness is not God himself. God is only in the act of faith" (AB, 92). Theology knows that it cannot make creative assertions but that it makes general statements, whereas the community knows that those statements "are meaningless without their confirmation by Christ" (AB, 145). Faith can never be verified (AB, 147, 94); it can only be reflected upon (AB, 149). Theology knows that dogma, in the specific sense of a statement of the church's teaching "on which preaching builds, is 'judged' by preaching" (AB, 145, 151). Bonhoeffer sees a judging and a directing function for preaching over theology.

The task of theology, therefore, is to think upon the mystery that has come into history as real boundary and transcendence. This is not to belittle or to reduce the scope of thought and of theology but to indicate its true place.

THE PERCEPTION OF THEOLOGY AS A SCHOLARLY ACTIVITY IN BONHOEFFER'S LATER WRITINGS

Bonhoeffer explicitly discussed the scholarly nature of theology in only one of his works, namely, his *Habilitationsschrift*. He did not, however, lose sight of the urgency of this matter, as evidenced by the fact that he considered writing a hermeneutic long before this became a popular topic.[17] It is above all in his non-religious interpretation of biblical concepts that he followed up, at least implicitly, the question about the reflection of Christian faith and its relation to its specific historical situation.

To some extent, after his student years Bonhoeffer discontinued his epistemological explorations. As a consequence of his having embraced a theology that favored praxis over theory, his attention shifted instead to the life of the church. But attention to epistemological problems was not totally absent in his writings. In the latest of his thematic works, *"Theologie und Gemeinde,"* dating from 1940, he said: "*Faith* comes from the preaching of God's word alone and it requires no theology, but right preaching is in need of confession and theology. Faith that has come about through preaching seeks its confirmation again in the Scriptures and in the confessions of the church and, therefore, itself does theology" (GS III, 423). Faith, preaching, and theology figure one next to the other in this work as they had in *Act and Being*. Preaching and theology belong together and, according to Bonhoeffer, there is no distinction in principle between a "theology of the community" and a "theology of the pastors" (GS III, 423). He leaves no doubt that theology is necessary but that it has an explicitly subservient function and is, therefore, a "corrective" (GS III, 425). Reflection is necessary in order to keep faith and obedience pure. "Theology is a resource, a weapon, and not an end in itself" (GS III, 423). Such assertions give evidence of a certain continuity with his earlier epistemological statements, but they also reveal the influence of the struggle against the pernicious threat to the church from the distorted gospel disseminated by the only church the state recognized, that of the German Christians.

ACADEMIC STUDIES

Before the period of the Church Struggle, when all attention was focused on crucial issues, Bonhoeffer was a member of university and seminary faculties. While at that vocation his contemplation of theology as a scholarly discipline underwent a certain clarification. In his inaugural lecture about "the question of man" Bonhoeffer discussed the difference between theology and philosophy.[18]

Theology as an a posteriori Construction

In some of the lectures Bonhoeffer delivered during his year of study in the United States he described the task of theology as that of depicting the human sense of being grasped. There he emphasized for the first time that theological thinking implies a circularity[19] inasmuch as it ponders revelation while presupposing it and claiming that this same revelation is the sole truth. The fact that theology "is not a construction a priori but a posteriori" (GS III, 102)[20] distinguishes it fundamentally from philosophy, as Bonhoeffer declared in his lecture of 1931, "Concerning the Christian Idea of God."[21] Unlike philosophy, theology has for its premise the church, "the reality of God" (GS III, 101), or, finally, the revelation of God in Christ (GS III, 111). On account of this premise theology is basically concrete. In contrast, closed thinking is a circle, the center of which is the ego which subordinates other humans and God to itself (GS III, 101) and, therefore, comes short of the reality of other humans and of God. This circle is broken open only by faith (GS III, 102). Faith bases itself on the answer which God gave "in his own word in Jesus Christ" (GS III, 104). At issue is God's action in history: not an idea, not even the idea of God (GS III, 104–6; cf. NRS, 362). Thus Bonhoeffer concluded that there is "no Christian philosophy, . . . philosophy remains profane science" (NRS, 372). The way to the knowledge of God is through action (GS III, 107). That proclamation holds true even when theological thinking makes use of, or relies upon, philosophical thought-forms. The essential difference between theology and philosophy, which Bonhoeffer stated more clearly in his North American lectures than in *Act and Being,* can be expressed in this way:

> Theology and philosophy are executed in reflection, into which God does not enter. Philosophy essentially remains in reflection; man knows himself and God only in reflection. Theology at least knows of an act of God, which tears man out of this reflection in an *actus directus* towards God. (NRS, 372)

Bonhoeffer's treatment of the problem of theodicy makes his views clear. Thinking in terms of a theodicy seeks to justify God in the world, whereas for Christian thinking it is God who justifies the world and has done so in Christ. Philosophical thinking can perhaps deduce an absolute cause from a philosophical cosmology and can then call that cause "God"; theodicy may solve the problem of evil, but neither assertion reaches God. We can know God as creator only through revelation, for God alone can make known to people who he is, and what he has done. Only through faith in God is the name "God" not an idea, not an aspect of human autonomy. Faith alone reaches God because God, who creates faith through Jesus Christ, permits himself to be found through faith which is directed toward Christ.

After his return to Germany, Bonhoeffer had occasion to reflect on methodology. Lecturing on "The Nature of the Church," Bonhoeffer stated that in current Roman Catholicism, and in fact since Augustine, the church has been the brackets around the *loci,* or the doctrines of theology. If these brackets were removed, theology would become something independent, reducing the church to a theological sub-specialty. When the latter occurred in Protestant orthodoxy, according to Bonhoeffer, theology assumed the place formerly occupied by the church. At that point theology was placed before the brackets that now enclosed the church—indeed a fateful exchange! Bonhoeffer believed, instead, that the church must be both presupposition and subject matter of dogmatics; consequently, the method of dogmatics would have to be descriptive and not analytical or synthetic (GS V, 235).

Christology as Scholarly Discipline

During the summer semester of 1933 Bonhoeffer lectured on christology.[22] The task of christology is to express God's inexpressible mystery, to make comprehensible the incomprehensibility of Christ's person. Speaking and comprehending have special meaning, however, as "the spoken word is the inexpressible. . . . To speak of Christ means to keep silent; to keep silent about Christ means to speak" (C, 27). Bonhoeffer went on to say that "*critical christology* has as its objective the delimiting of what must be placed within the category of the incomprehensible" (C, 74). It should be pointed out, however, that theology is not the stereotypical exclamation that the mystery of God is ineffable; rather, theology is the reflection upon the mystery of God present in history in and for its time. Since the incarnation is the revelation of that mystery in history, christology as a scholarly discipline has special significance.

The lectures not only take up the concerns of *Act and Being* but also foreshadow certain important insights later found in *Letters and Papers from Prison.* In Jesus Christ we encounter the distant nearness of God in such a way that he is both the absolute and unavoidable center. It follows from this understanding that the *logos* is not an idea but instead a human person. That this is true and that transcendence is manifested in this person, is not subject to proof (C, 28). Against reason the *logos* is "counter-*logos*," showing reason its boundaries. We cannot ask *how* that is possible; we can only ask, "Who are you?" But we cannot ourselves answer the *who* question; indeed, "the question must already have been answered before it could be stated correctly. This takes us further: the christological question can be posed in scholarly fashion only in the setting of the church" (C, 31). Only in the church is the presupposition made that the claims of the *logos* are justified. The sheer fact of the existence of Jesus on earth as testimony to himself is "the backbone of every theology. The 'truth' of the revelation of God in Christ cannot be established or disputed in the terms of scholarly discipline" (C, 32).

The theological point of departure that shows itself quite clearly in these lectures allowed Bonhoeffer to pursue a certain direction in christology within which he could bring the problem of the historical Jesus and the biblical Christ closer to a solution. What he proposed evaded being classified as a "christology from above" or a "christology from below." Bonhoeffer structured the lecture course in such a way that even before raising the question of the historical Christ it was evident that he set out from the reality of Christ present now. Faith in Christ as the faith of the community as well as the faith in the community is presupposed. Historically no proof can be established; "One cannot get behind the belief in the Christ as Lord" (C, 70). It is, rather, the task of critical or negative christology to allow belief in the mystery to stand and to rule out all inadequate thought-forms (C, 74). One can speak of this mystery only in a contradictory and paradoxical manner, as was done in the Chalcedonian Definition, according to Bonhoeffer (C, 88). Human thinking and the forms it takes do not give rise to knowledge: "Only from the fact itself can one know who God is" (C, 102).

When theology has its foundation in faith, the problem of whether or not "history can bear the dogmatic statements" may be solved (C, 71). This is because history cannot provide faith with compelling evidence or, for that matter, with compelling counter-evidence. On account of the fact that God's word became historical through Jesus Christ, belief in Jesus as the Christ is the only possible way of finding access to the Jesus of history. Only faith can discern that Christ is the "center of history" (C, 64). Here Bonhoeffer's thinking in academe about theology as a scholarly discipline comes to an end. It can be synthesized into two assertions: (1) the church is the brackets around theology; (2) christology is the "scholarly discipline" per se; "As *logo-logy*, christology alone makes scholarship possible" (C, 33).

THE INFLUENCE OF ECUMENISM AND THE CHURCH STRUGGLE ON THE PROBLEM OF THEOLOGY

We have already referred to an essay of 1940, "Theologie und Gemeinde," in which Bonhoeffer maintained that theology was a resource, a weapon, and not an end in itself. While being used as a resource until the onset of the Church Struggle, theology quickly became more and more of a weapon as the threat to the church intensified. Bonhoeffer's almost unique stance in the struggle is characterized by the fact that ecumenical work and the church's fight, two seemingly disparate concerns, became for him the same concern not only in his daily life but also in his theological reflection. Bonhoeffer began his ecumenical work in the World Alliance of the Churches, a group whose focus was the practical life of churches. He was to become its youth secretary. Later he joined the Alliance's Life and Work section. This orientation was more akin to his theology, for in his view the real decisions about ecumenism, concerning the issue of whether or not the church is ecumenical, were made in the church's practice and in the Alliance's Life and Work section, not in the church's theory nor in the Alliance's Faith and Order section. Not until the establishment of the Confessing Church at the Synods of Barmen and Dahlem in 1934 was there a clear alternative as to which church was the true church in Germany. Up until then, the often bitterly disputed issue centered around the safeguarding of the true gospel which was frequently relegated to the background, especially in relation to the Aryan Clauses which people seldom opposed with every available means.[23] In his insistence on praxis Bonhoeffer could not accept the superficial activities which sought to achieve political or ecclesiastical results by means of accommodation to the times. For him praxis meant discipleship in the empirically real church. There is no doubt that discipleship became instantly very complicated after the events of 1933. Less than ever before could the churches of the Reformation revert to familiar, theologically well-conceived positions.[24] The church had to practice theology in that very situation and in that way prepare for the decision required there. Such a decision, however, touched the very center of Christian faith; Bonhoeffer believed "that the struggle over the government of the church is in fact *the* question, which has inevitably arisen out of the history of the church, the question of the possibility of a 'protestant' church for us."[25] Bonhoeffer was in the very midst of this discussion; he was not only able, but also compelled to verify his views about the relationship of life and thought, of faith and theology.

Thinking in the Service of Action

Bonhoeffer's statement that "acquired knowledge cannot be divorced from the existence in which it is acquired" (CD, 43) was based very much on his own experience. Yet we must not conclude from this that in his practical commitment was an implied condemnation of thinking. On the contrary, he warned expressly against despising theology,[26] since the preeminence of faith and church can only be weakened by a disregard of theology. The emancipation of theology from the tutelage of the church, brought about allegedly in the interest of theology, is equally ineffectual for the advancement of theology.

Bonhoeffer realized that thinking can only prepare and give clarity to action but it can never replace it. Thinking does not spare us the step into the dark. For that reason, he repudiated the idea that Scripture gives "us such clear instructions that it absolves us from acting in faith. We want to see the way before we go along it" (WF, 176). Later he was to put it like this: it is not true that "if we weigh in advance the possibilities of any action, it will happen automatically" (LPP, 298). In light of the experiences of the Church Struggle it is obvious what he meant. The experiences of the years 1932–1933 gave rise to this conviction. The verse from Scripture, "we know not what we ought to do; we lift our eyes to thee," played an important role for him in those days.[27]

If the result of action cannot be weighed in advance in our thinking and if, consequently, experience cannot be had prior to action, humans cannot foresee whether responsible action is ultimately righteous action. On the other hand, "all ideological action carries its own justification within itself from the outset in its guiding principle" (GS III, 461 and E, 234). Thus, Bonhoeffer was not worried that, for example, the Lutheran and Reformed churches came to an accord in a really untheological manner, namely, through

> the "guidance" of God (Union, Confessing Church) and the recognition of what is given objectively in the sacraments. Christ is more important than our thoughts about him and his presence. . . . It seems to me that churches have united not primarily theologically, but through decisions of faith, in the sense that I have mentioned. That is a very dangerous statement, isn't it! One can do anything with it! But have we in the Confessing Church not in fact done just that? (TP, 71)

Bonhoeffer himself acted in this manner as can be seen from a letter in which he advised his friends in Pomerania on the matter of the instruction, given by the church courts, that members of the Confessing Church seek legal status. When asked what should be done, Bonhoeffer wrote: "There are so many reasons, and theologians can prove anything. Everything will depend on whether God gives us his testimony afresh in our hearts. Jesus Christ alone can lead the way" (WF, 171). Yes, to practice theology was necessary, but not a theology that sought to have things its own way; instead, one that oriented itself according to the belief in God in Jesus Christ as held in the church. Bonhoeffer considered theology an important means for faith to confirm itself, but here, too, with dependence on the church: "For theology is the church's self-understanding of its own nature on the basis of its understanding of the revelation in Christ" (NRS, 158).

A "self-understanding" had to come about, however, if the rise of the ecumenical movement was to be a genuine change in and out of faith rather than a simple peripheral association for common action.

> If the ecumenical movement stems from a new self-understanding of the church of Christ, it must and will produce a theology. If it does not succeed in this, that will be evidence that it is nothing but a new and up-to-date improvement in church organization. No one requires a theology of such an organization, but simply definite action in a concrete task. (NRS, 158)

The problem of the specific, concrete command arose with urgency for Bonhoeffer in the context of his theological reflection on the ecumenical movement. Keeping such concreteness steadily in view allows theology to be responsible theology, one which can be practiced from within only, and never from the outside, from the place of the onlooker. To one church the task has been given to proclaim to the whole world the word of God in Jesus Christ. From that task ecumenism arises by necessity. This movement needs a theology for its self-understanding, but there will be such proclamation only if it comes together with a theology.

The ecumenical movement is, therefore, an event taking place in and between the various denominations. This movement is independent of theology, cannot be generated by theology and exists before theology exists. It is a question about the church and only when this movement is church or leads toward the creation of empirical church is it more than a program of ecclesiastical policy around which one gathers "for common tactical and practical action or for unauthoritative theological conversation" (NRS, 331). Thus the ecumenical problem stands and falls with the question about what is confessed and its truth.

The Bond of Theology to the Church's Decisions

"The German Church Struggle marks the second great stage in the history of the ecumenical movement and will in a decisive way be normative for its future" (NRS, 326). That was true because the Church Struggle was fought vicariously for the whole ecumenical movement. "In this encounter the ecumenical movement and the Confessing Church ask each other for their reason of existence" (NRS, 328). The Confessing Church confronted the ecumenical movement with the question of confession and witness and, therefore, asked it whether or not it was church. The ecumenical movement then confronted the Confessing Church with the question concerning the seriousness of its witness. That one enquired of the other as to whether or not it was church implies acceptance of the assertion that "there can only be a church as a Confessing Church, i.e. as a church which confesses itself to be for its Lord and against its enemies" (NRS, 335). Here, "enemies" refers explicitly to the members of the German Christian Church. Confession is much more than only a theological issue because it has to do with the authority in which the church definitely must make a decision.

If the ecumenical movement is regarded simply as a problem of theology, as is often the case, "there is the very great danger . . . that just this theological conversation, necessary as it is in itself, will be used to obscure the real situation. . . . With the question of the Confessing Church we have already gone beyond the stage, necessary in itself, of theological conversation. The Confessing Church knows of the fatal ambivalence of any conversation and presses for a clear church decision" (NRS, 333). That the nature of theology is to be servile, as Bonhoeffer had stated earlier in his writings, and that the bond of theology is to the church, are made concrete in this assertion. Within these strictures alone is theology guarded against becoming a game, or worse, a useful tool with which to circumvent the truth. The Church Struggle raised the question of the church as well for the ecumenical movement, since the church of the German Christians had betrayed the true gospel.[28] That church was not church at all. Thus Bonhoeffer believed that the ecumenical movement could no longer remain in communion with the German Christian Church but only with the Confessing Church, which alone could claim to be the Protestant Church in Germany.[29] On account of the Church Struggle, Protestant Christianity in Germany and, consequently, in the whole world was confronted with the question of truth; here there could be no half-measures: "The concept of half-truth completely destroys the concept of truth" (GS I, 181).[30] Thus, the situation was that of the *status confessionis*.

Bonhoeffer's remarks about the need of the church to come to a decision on the truth of the confession constitute the high point of his argument concerning the relation of church and theology.[31] On that decision depends true doctrine. But the decision of the church cannot be attained by force of logic or theology. Bonhoeffer called attention to differences separating schools and differences separating churches (WF, 84).[32] The difference between what separates schools and what separates churches comes to light only in relation to the church's decision about confession.

A decision of that kind, going beyond theology, was made at Barmen and Dahlem. Such a decision must never be reversed "because we can no longer go back behind the word of God" (WF, 87). And because the church was obligated to, and did, make a definite decision, Bonhoeffer concluded: "*Extra ecclesiam nulla salus* (There is no salvation outside the church). . . . Whoever knowingly cuts himself off from the Confessing Church in Germany cuts himself off from salvation" (WF, 93). The decision about salvation, however, is not one within the power of the church.

Bonhoeffer conceded that the church has the final word on the decision about the confession to which its members are bound. This raises the question of authority, ministry, discipline and heresy. The early church's assertion that "outside the church there is no salvation" was taken for granted by Bonhoeffer.[33] But it must not be understood univocally, that is to say as something capable of adequate demonstration and, thus, to be applied in a rigoristic manner. It is possible that God listens more gladly to the curses of the godless than to the prayers of the pious, that one may well be a Christian unconsciously (LPP, 373). But the assertion is not simply reversible, becoming the ultimately spiritualistic phrase that where salvation is, there is the church. Church is always also the empirically observable, visible church. In it alone it is both possible and necessary to find the truth through hearing, discipleship and decision. Such a decision alone, *made in and by the church*, can, and at times even must, declare clearly whether an assertion of belief or a theological opinion is the *church's true testimony* or *heresy*.

To sum up one may say that in the Church Struggle the issue for Bonhoeffer was the church coming to decide whether the state church, the church of the German Christians, was heretical or not, and whether it was church or not. He urged that a Protestant council be convened at which this decision, aided by theology, could be made with authority. This shows his firm conviction that within the faithful hearing of the proclamation handed on to the church a conciliar decision is not mere human opinion but the word which God vouchsafes. Founded on that word the church does not go astray even without earthly safeguards because it has for its basis the promise of God himself. The confession in which that word is given expression can only be a confession of the church, and the separation of true from false teaching can be made only by means of such a communal confession in an actual situation. Thus, Bonhoeffer could not give up the notion of heresy, which was for him not a theoretical but a very concrete, situation-related notion. Theology itself is historical: it is quite attached to the situation in which it is exercised and its aim cannot be to be true perennially, but here and now only. It has as its basis discipleship and its task is to give expression to that discipleship in whatever it is asked to do, without in so doing justifying that discipleship.

Excursus: The Relation to the Roman Catholic Church

In the context of these thoughts on the importance of church decision Bonhoeffer also spoke about the matter of the *una sancta* (TP, 71). At the height of the Church Struggle he said that the Confessing Church was not making a witness against Rome (NRS, 338). A little later he reminded his readers that the difference between what separates schools and what separates churches must be regarded in its historical variations. Bonhoeffer put it in this remarkable way: "The article which divides the churches today may no longer be divisive tomorrow" (WF, 82).[34] The separation of churches is bound up with church decisions and can be caused by them, even if they hold in common certain confessional material. "The Lutheran Confessional writings were of the view that there was confessional material common to both the Lutheran and the Roman Church" (WF, 81). Despite agreement on the doctrines of God, the Trinity, and on christology, an agreement which Luther reckoned as a common basis, it was the doctrine of justification over which unity broke apart during the Reformation. Bonhoeffer considered that if a rapprochement of churches could come about through historical changes, as could their separation, and if such rapprochement could come about quite untheologically, then there is no reason why this could not be true in "the Catholic question" (WF, 71). Recalling earlier assertions, Bonhoeffer concluded that "the Lutheran–Reformed controversies, and to some extent the Roman Catholic–Protestant ones are now unreal. They may at times be revived with passion, but they no longer carry conviction. There is no proof of this, and we must simply take it that it is so" (LPP, 382). In his situation Bonhoeffer was not directly confronted with endeavors also to unite with the Roman Catholic Church, but his view, located at the heart of the practice of his theology, has unquestionably contributed to the rapprochement. In prison he read the church fathers and commented that "in some ways they are more relevant to our times than the Reformers, and at the same time they provide a basis for talks between Protestants and Roman Catholics" (LPP, 135). Perhaps Bonhoeffer's theology itself could become a basis for those talks.

A union with the Roman Catholic Church might be broached, in Bonhoeffer's view, not in a theological but in a practical way; that is to say, not by means of theological consensus but through a practical union. That assumption already relativized denominational opposition and reduced it to a certain extent. Bonhoeffer refused to become fixed in denominational fronts: "We are not concerned with the terms Catholic or Protestant, but with the word of God" (DB, 43). Bonhoeffer was quite sure that there was a greater proximity to Roman Catholicism in the earliest Protestantism than there was for several participants in the ecumenical movement, one to another (NRS, 178). Throughout his life Bonhoeffer had a special interest in Rome.[35]

Precisely because he may very well have been tempted to convert to Roman Catholicism,[36] but did not do so, Bonhoeffer must be taken ever more seriously as a Protestant Christian and theologian and, thus, be spared the dubious charge of being a "Catholicizer." It would seem better to take the far-reaching consequences of that visit to Rome in 1924 as seriously as did Karl Barth.[37]

2
Systematic Summary of the Hermeneutical Implications of Bonhoeffer's Theology

In the preceding section on Bonhoeffer's hermeneutical point of departure we analyzed his understanding of theology as a discipline in relation to theological epistemology. We concentrated on the historical development of how Bonhoeffer understood this matter.

What must be shown now, in a systematic fashion, are the hermeneutical implications of his theology. It goes without saying that they are found implicitly in the foregoing discussion, situated in their contexts and related to the challenges and predicaments within which they had arisen and to which they were addressed. Now these hermeneutical implications are to be spelled out explicitly in order to support adequately the proposition that Bonhoeffer's theology is indeed a unity.

FAITH AS FIDES DIRECTA IN MYSTERIUM

The Mystery

Something Bonhoeffer said in a sermon about mystery is to guide our interpretations in the discussion about hermeneutics. It is not an isolated comment. His circular letter for Christmas 1939 reiterated the point, clearly relating it to the question of theology as a discipline, and explicitly confirming the connection we established to that sermon preached in London on 27 May 1934:

> "God revealed in the flesh," the God-man Jesus Christ, is the holy mystery which theology is appointed to guard. What a mistake to think that it is the task of theology to unravel God's mystery, to bring it down to the flat, ordinary human wisdom of experience and reason! It is the task of theology solely to preserve God's wonder as wonder, to understand, to defend, to glorify God's mystery as mystery! This and nothing else was the intention of the ancient church when it fought with unflagging zeal over the mystery of the Trinity and the person of Jesus Christ. How superficial and flippant, especially of theologians, to send theology to the knacker's yard, to make

out that one is not a theologian and doesn't want to be, and in so doing to ridicule one's own ministry and ordination and in the end to have, and to advocate, a bad theology instead of a good one! But of course, where in our theological classes were we shown and taught the mystery of God in the flesh, the birth of Jesus Christ, the God-man and Savior, as the unfathomable mystery of God? Where do we hear it preached?

A little further on are echoes of ideas that Bonhoeffer had discussed in his christology lectures:

> The ancient church meditated on the question of Christ for several centuries. It imprisoned reason in obedience to Jesus Christ, and in harsh, conflicting sentences gave living witness to the mystery of the person of Jesus Christ. It did not give way to the modern pretence that this mystery could only be felt or experienced, for it knew the corruption and self-deception of all human feeling and experience. Nor, of course, did it think that this mystery could be thought out logically, but by being unafraid to express the ultimate conceptual paradoxes, it bore witness to, and glorified, the mystery as a mystery against all natural reason. (TP, 28).

Recourse to mystery is no trick to make theological arguments unassailable; indeed, they are themselves subject to the vulnerability which arises precisely from the fact that the mystery about which Christian faith speaks cannot be plumbed by reason nor legitimated by arguments. Of this mystery one can only speak in hints.[38]

Actus Directus and *Actus Reflectus*

The distinction between faith and theology, between *actus directus* and *actus reflectus,* is closely related to Bonhoeffer's insistence that the mystery of both be left untouched and stated as such. Mystery is the all-bearing center of faith and theology; for that reason, the distinction between the two is synonymous to the distinction between *fides directa* and *fides reflecta* (LPP, 373).[39] Faith is a part of mystery and cannot be transformed into knowledge. As *actus directus* faith is the same as discipleship and is, therefore, not primarily something intellectual.[40]

Bonhoeffer took up anew the distinction he had made in *Act and Being* between *actus directus* and *actus reflectus,* a distinction he borrowed from early Protestant baptismal theology. It occurs in an important text on baptism, dating from 1942, and later in his prison letters.[41] His added comment in one of those letters, "I wonder whether this doesn't raise a far-reaching problem," shows that Bonhoeffer did not consider his thoughts on that distinction to have solved the matter; on the contrary, he perceived an urgent task. The problem of "unconscious Christianity," raised in that same letter, had already occupied him in *Ethics.*[42] Clearly the distinction between *actus directus* and *actus reflectus* is broadened generally in Bonhoeffer's later writings. In citing Luther's statement that "perhaps God would rather hear the curses of the ungodly than the alleluias of the pious,"[43] Bonhoeffer referred to the example he had used in *Act and Being* to clarify that distinction. A few years later he was to use that same example again in his lectures (GS V, 265). This distinction had been especially important to him during his university years.

This explicit correlation in the terminology used in both the late and early writings of Bonhoeffer enables us to conclude that one of the basic concepts of his whole theology is depicted in the distinction between *actus directus* and *actus reflectus*. It also indicates one of the basic lines of his theology, for in addition to these explicit correlations there are implicit ones, thus allowing us, when viewing them together, to reinforce our conviction that *Act and Being* lays the ground not only for *The Cost of Discipleship* but also for *Ethics*. In *Act and Being* Bonhoeffer says, "And so it is only in the believing in Christ that I know that I believe, which is to say that here and now I do not know it and in reflection on the believing I know nothing" (AB, 95). Without using such terminology, this assertion is repeated in *The Cost of Discipleship,* confirming that the distinction is one of that work's basic tenets: "Thus faith, which is the mainspring of Christian prayer, excludes all reflection and premeditation" (CD, 146). The disciple does not enter into such reflection but in everything follows Christ. In *Ethics* Bonhoeffer made this distinction a basic concept, adding that we cannot know whether we are good or evil: "That we finally do not know whether we are good or evil and are, therefore, dependent on grace is part and parcel of responsible, historical action. . . . The responsible person lives by God's grace into whose hands his or her action is placed."[44] This sets the responsible person apart from the one who acts according to ideology. "When the deed is performed with a responsible weighing up of all the personal and objective circumstances and in the awareness that God has become human and that it is *God* who has become human, then this deed is delivered up solely to God at the moment of its performance" (E, 235). Reminiscent of the texts from *Act and Being* just cited, but with a shift in accent, is Bonhoeffer's statement that "the knowledge of Jesus is entirely transformed into action, without any reflection upon the human self" (E, 34).

The distinction between *actus directus* and *actus reflectus* is, in other words, an essential indication of how Bonhoeffer understands things. The distinction is clearly present in his entire work and therefore it is no exaggeration to say that it is also at the very center of his theology.

THE CONCEPT OF REALITY

The claim that the distinction of *actus directus* and *actus reflectus* is at the very center of Bonhoeffer's theology is supported by the connection Bonhoeffer establishes between that distinction on the one hand and the concept of reality so essential to his thought. The citation from *Ethics* just given implicitly mentions this distinction and points to the final reality of God's incarnation in Jesus Christ. Bonhoeffer's concept of reality and the distinction that he maintained are understandable only in relation to his christology. If the *actus directus* is focused on Christ, then reality is borne by him. The understanding of reality that we alone regard as valid, in our unmysterious lives, is an illusion and, therefore, represents the loss of actual reality. Our illusionary reality cannot be corrected by actual reality. Only in faith focused on Christ, a faith that is not directly amenable to reflection but which appears in this world in the form of the cross, is it appropriate and not presumptuous to declare that the world "is now really better understood than it understands itself, namely, on the basis of the gospel and in the light of Christ" (LPP, 329).

Reality is a theological concept for Bonhoeffer predicated upon God and the world. According to Bonhoeffer, it is not possible to define reality but only to give hints about it, a characteristic common among basic universal concepts (E, 217).

In order to describe Bonhoeffer's concept of reality more accurately it is necessary to point out that it is clearly differentiated from a positivistic-empirical concept of reality that comprehends no mystery.[45] Bonhoeffer remarked "that the concept which underlies the positivistic ethic is the meretricious concept of the empirically verifiable, which implies denial of the origin of this reality in the ultimate reality, in God" (E, 194).[46] Over against that, Bonhoeffer stated that reality is

> the reality of God as the ultimate reality without and within everything that is. It speaks of the reality of the world as it is, which possesses reality solely through the reality of God. Christian belief deduces that the reality of God is not in itself merely an idea from the fact that this reality of God has manifested and revealed itself in the midst of the real world. (E, 194)

Initially, and most importantly, reality means God, God in Jesus Christ, who alone is the real one (E, 228).[47] God is ultimate reality and only in him does all reality rest.

> It is from the real one, whose name is Jesus Christ, that all factual reality derives its ultimate foundation and its ultimate annulment, its justification and its ultimate contradiction, its ultimate affirmation and its ultimate negation. To attempt to understand reality without the real one is to live in an abstraction to which the responsible person must never fall victim; it is to fail to make contact with reality in life. . . . (E, 228)

REALITY: CONCEPT AND COUNTER-CONCEPTS

The Concept of Possibility

That the concept of reality covers a large territory is evident from the last quotation. In order to explain the concept of reality more clearly it is useful to consider its counter-concepts. The first among those to be mentioned is the concept of "the possible" or "possibility." According to Bonhoeffer this concept necessarily arises in our thinking and is to be traced back theologically to human sin. In sin, humankind stole the knowledge of good and evil, with the consequence, for humankind, that "instead of knowing itself solely in the reality of being chosen and loved by God, humankind must now know itself in the possibility of choosing and of being the origin of good and evil" (E, 19).[48]

Long before he wrote that, Bonhoeffer had already asserted that "our limit is in the middle of our existence, not on the edge. The limit which we look for on the edge is the limit of our condition, of our technology, of our possibilities. The limit in the middle is the limit of our reality, of our true existence" (CF, 52). Being-in-reality was the human condition before the fall. "For this reason Adam cannot know or think evil and death. But he knows his limit because he knows God," and this is "knowledge issuing from freedom of the creature, knowledge in . . . ignorance" (CF, 52).

These ideas are echoed in *Ethics*. Being-in-possibility means to be in disunion. In Christ alone human action is beyond question, it "is no longer one possibility among many, but the one thing, the important thing, the will of God. Knowledge can therefore no longer intervene and impede us, and now quite literally no time can be lost in delaying action, rendering it doubtful and judging it. The judgment remains hidden not only from other people, but even from the forum of a person's own knowledge. The situation is quite clear: knowing of Jesus people can no longer know of their own goodness" (E, 35). In Christ one can be the person "one really is. Now there is no more pretense, no more hypocrisy or self-violence, no more compulsion to be something other, better or more ideal than whatever one is. God loves the real human being. God became a real human being" (E, 81).

The area of concrete human action is the focus of Bonhoeffer's juxtaposition of reality and possibility. This is expressed in the poem "Stations on the Road to Freedom," in the second verse: *"Nicht im Möglichen schweben, das Wirkliche tapfer ergreifen"* (LPP, 371).[49]

From the outset Bonhoeffer attacked the category of possibility.[50] In *Sanctorum Communio* he changed the normal formula of "potential–actual" to "real–actual" (NRS, 63). "It is only upon the basis of concrete revelation that we can overcome the empty concept and potentiality and arrive at the real community relationships," and "only from reality can we deduce necessity in dogmatics" (SC, 91, 97).

Corresponding to the prevalence of ethical transcendence the category of "real" is also an ethical category for Bonhoeffer (SC, 138). "On the epistemological and metaphysical path one never reaches the reality of the other. Reality cannot be derived, it is simply given, to be acknowledged, to be rejected, but never to be established by proofs, and it is given only to the moral person as a whole" (SC, 35). For that reason ethical transcendence alone is real limit (SC, 29).

In *Act and Being* the polemic against the category of possibility is intensified. "Faith is not in itself a human possibility . . . but a contingent advent of revelation in reality. Neither is sin a human possibility, not even of fallen creatures, nor even an absolute possibility: it too is a happening reality" (AB, 100). The reason for this sharp rejection of possibility is that human beings in their possibility cannot be the precondition for revelation, salvation or guilt. Thus Heidegger's concept of existence, derived from the human and not from revelation, was, for Bonhoeffer, theologically unusable (AB, 100). To the contrary, Bonhoeffer maintained, "But faith is a God-given reality" (AB, 138).

Bonhoeffer summarized his ideas by saying that *"the concept of possibility has no place in theology and therefore in theological anthropology"* (NRS, 64). The most important reason for that is that human beings who understand themselves on the basis of their possibilities and, consequently, in the light of their reflections, do not understand themselves in relation to God, and thus are without revelation, without a genuine "from beyond," without a real limit. The *actus directus* toward Jesus Christ, which alone provides true self-knowledge, is broken in its immediacy and then God is no more than an idea (NRS, 65; GS III, 88).

To conclude, the concept of reality is one which, according to Bonhoeffer, is understood adequately only in a theological sense. In faith alone is reality manifest. "We can be 'in reality' and 'in truth' only through God. True reality is reality seen through the truth of the word of God, so that whoever is in reality is also in truth, and vice versa" (AB, 88).[51] The reality of existence of human beings is one that lies "outside the bounds of their own peculiar potentialities" (AB, 148). It is founded in Jesus Christ (AB, 148).[52]

Abstraction and Idea

Next to the concept of possibility, and closely related to it, are two other important counter-concepts: "abstraction" and "idea." By juxtaposing the latter concepts, reality is given the strengthening feature of concreteness:

> If God were merely a religious idea there would be nothing to prevent us from discerning behind this allegedly "ultimate" reality, a still more final reality, the twilight of the gods and the death of the gods. The claim of this ultimate reality is satisfied only in so far as it is revelation, that is to say, the self-witness of the living God. (E, 189)

It is abstraction when we take no account of God and his revelation as ultimate reality, for in so doing we turn toward an idea, a religious idea, to be precise, instead of toward God. But this does not lead to reality;

rather, it obstructs reality. Reality is "not the real in the abstract, the real which is detached from the reality of God, but the real which possesses reality only in God" (E, 190). There is no reality without God and his will.

> The will of God, however, is nothing other than the becoming real of the reality of Christ with us and in our world. The will of God, therefore, is not an idea, still demanding to become real; it is a reality already in the self-revelation of God in Jesus Christ. Nor is the will of God simply identical with what is in being, which would mean that it would be fulfilled by submissive acquiescence in things as they are. It is, on the contrary, a reality whose purpose is to become real ever anew in what is in being and against what is in being. The will of God is already fulfilled by God himself, by his reconciliation of the world with himself in Christ. It would be a most hazardous relapse into abstract thought if one were to wish to disregard the reality of this fulfilment and to replace it with a fulfilment of one's own. (E, 212)

These few texts indicate already the opposition between reality and abstraction, reality and idea, in Bonhoeffer's thinking. What becomes more manifest than in the opposition between reality and possibility is the fact that these pairs of concepts and counter-concepts are not really on the same level, that they are in fact not opposites or antitheses. Rather, the reality of God excludes all possibility, all potentiality; the *real one* alone overcomes idea and abstraction. The world, created for Christ, is to be understood from God in Jesus Christ since from God comes its reality. "Because the world has its being 'through Christ' and 'for Christ' (Col. 1) every consideration of the human 'per se' or of the world and its order 'per se' is an abstraction" (GS I, 358). This indicates why Bonhoeffer considered it an abstraction not to view God as reality, and why he regarded all philosophy principally as abstraction. Were philosophy derived from faith instead of from the human being, it would be theology. But this is where, theologically speaking, the abstraction lies. One must not overlook the theological basis on which Bonhoeffer rejects philosophy as abstraction. Otherwise one does not do justice to his critique of philosophy.

Let us consider the concept "abstract" in detail. It is to be found throughout Bonhoeffer's entire work. Already in *Sanctorum Communio* he said that "idealism has no conception of movement. The movement of the dialectic of mind is abstract and metaphysical, whereas the movement of ethics is concrete" (SC, 31). For that reason, idealism has no understanding of the concrete person and history. In this statement, "abstract" is used in the same context in which it would later appear as a central concept: ethics and metaphysics are juxtaposed; metaphysics is abstract, and ethics is concrete. In his address on ethics, delivered at Barcelona soon after the publication of *Sanctorum Communio*, Bonhoeffer used the term "unconcrete" in relation to the situation in which one does not begin with what is concretely given in that situation and with the decision demanded by that situation, but with "norms and principles" or "ideas and principles" (NRS, 39–48). The whole address is a strong attack on so-called Christian ethics, if it is conceived of as a collection of "Christian norms and principles." Reiterated is what Bonhoeffer had said in an earlier address about Jesus Christ, namely, that Christianity is basically amoral and a-religious, by which he means to say, in exaggerated terms, that there are no specifically and exclusively Christian "principles and norms" (NRS, 40). "Now it follows from all this that ethical problems of content can never be discussed in a Christian light" (NRS, 45). Bonhoeffer repeats this comment in *The Cost of Discipleship* and adds, "To follow in his steps is something which is void of all content. It gives no intelligible program for a way of life, no goal or ideal to strive after" (CD, 49). In this context he speaks of ideas of Christ and, as in the address on ethics, of "the law": "There is ethics only in the completion of the act, not in the letter of the law" (NRS, 45), or as one might add, in the principle, in the idea. All of these items are abstractions for Bonhoeffer.

The use of the term "abstract" in *Act and Being* points in the same direction as these arguments even though the question of ethics is not the issue, or at least not directly. Criticizing Bultmann's use of Heidegger's philosophy, Bonhoeffer said that "the phenomenological definition of existence according to its existential structure as 'historical,' as 'care,' as 'being unto death,' is for revelation no less an abstraction and hypothesis than a merely biological definition of the human, inasmuch as the human is thought of in each instance apart from the event of revelation" (AB, 75).[53] For Bonhoeffer there can be no disregarding of revelation which, understood theologically, is what gives reality to existence, and creates real existence in the first place.

Abstraction is spoken of in another significant context. "The concept of the absolute individual is an abstraction with no corresponding reality," Bonhoeffer wrote, adding that "dialectical theology thinks individualistically, i.e., in constant abstractions" (AB, 130, 146). In order not to do so himself Bonhoeffer emphasized the sociality that is found concretely in the church, in the real, empirical community. Those who take no account of it, showing thereby that they have fundamentally no understanding for concrete, empirical history, practice theology in the abstract.[54] An abstraction which takes no account of human sociality is a sign of religious interpretation, for to make a religious interpretation "means to speak on the one hand metaphysically, and on the other hand individualistically" (LPP, 286). The charge of positivism of revelation is rightly made against Barth because "in the non-religious interpretation of theological concepts he gave no *concrete* guidance" (LPP, 328). It is no coincidence that Barth is said to have given no *concrete* guidance, or, in other words, that he remained in abstractions.[55]

SYSTEMATIC SUMMARY OF THE HERMENEUTICAL IMPLICATIONS

The term "abstract" sounds a fundamental note in *Act and Being* which continues to be of decisive significance right up to the prison letters.

In *Ethics* Bonhoeffer claimed that it is abstraction to take no account of Jesus Christ (E, 188–91). That is why the name of Jesus Christ must not be allowed to be reduced "to a mere abstract concept. This name must always be understood in the full concrete significance of the historical reality of a living human being" (E, 51). The reference to history is important. "In every section of their history people are simply and entirely the ones taken upon himself by Christ" (E, 86). Individualism does not ensue from this, for it would in itself be an abstraction (E, 87). Bonhoeffer, resuming the important argument of *Act and Being*, here turns sharply against individualism: it is an abstraction and a double one at that, to measure the isolated individual by the absolute standard of good or evil per se. "In this abstraction from life the ethical is reduced to a static basic formula which forcibly detaches humans from the historicity of their existence and transposes them into the vacuum of the purely private and the purely ideal" (E, 215). Ethics must not deteriorate into abstraction, nor seek its salvation in general norms or principles. That means that ethics must take account of Jesus Christ, for to "attempt to understand reality without the real one [namely, Jesus Christ] is to live in an abstraction" (E, 228). Ethics must set out neither from God nor from the human being per se, for "there is no human being *per se,* just as there is no God *per se;* both of those are empty abstractions" (E, 221). Ethics has to address human beings in the concrete, historical and social situation which is given in and through Jesus Christ. Therefore, "since God became human in Christ all thought about humans without Christ has been a barren abstraction" (E, 110). In Jesus Christ alone is true reality: "All concepts of reality which do not take account of him are abstraction" (E, 194).

To sum up, one may say that Bonhoeffer considered there to be two kinds of abstractions. First, abstraction is the attempt on the part of thought to find the once-and-for-all-real, to abstract from reality norms and principles as essential truths and to seek to master reality deductively on the basis of them. Second, abstraction is our thinking about reality which cannot be mastered in thought; we cannot dispense with abstraction in this sense but must not confuse it with reality. Indeed, theology is also an abstraction: "It does not provide rules for life but records revelation in terms of abstractions while the church, on the other hand, must preach, that is to say, proclaim concretely" (GS V, 307).[56] Theology is reflection and cannot become a concrete, authoritative voice, nor must it seek to replace such a voice. If, however, abstraction, reflection, the *actus reflectus* remain bound to reality, which they do not transcend, that is to say behind which they cannot go, then they are not superfluous but become comprehensible in their limitations and usefulness. Bonhoeffer is clear about this to the very end: "Knowledge and experience that were gained, and of which one did not become conscious till later, are only abstractions of reality, of life actually lived" (LPP, 3). Still, they form a part of responsible life where they give clarity to the past in the service of new and daring deeds in the future. We avoid false abstraction only when our thinking, the *actus reflectus,* is related again and again to life as we really live it. This protects our thinking from the absolutizing separation of actual reality from Jesus Christ, in whom reality is based, by whom it is borne and in relation to whom it is, consequently, to be understood.

Whether one has grasped reality or lives in abstraction is determined in relation to Christ. To live in an abstraction means to confuse reality with an *idea.* In Christ alone we are protected against such confusion.

> He is the word in the form of the address to people, but the word of people is word in the form of idea. Address and idea are the basic structures of the word. But they exclude each other. Human thought is dominated by the form of the word as idea. The idea rests in itself and is related to itself; its validity holds throughout space and time. When Christ is called the word of God today, it is usually with this sense of the idea. An idea is generally accessible, it lies ready at hand. People can freely appropriate what they choose from it. Christ as idea is timeless truth, the idea of God embodied in Jesus, available to anyone at any time. (C, 50)[57]

Bonhoeffer consistently opposed the understanding that made Christ into an idea and into the proclaimer of an idea of a timeless God; such an understanding squeezed Christ out of history and reduced him to an abstraction. That God became a human being is not something to be "derived from an idea of God, . . . it is not permissible to slip in once again a speculative idea of God which derives the incarnation from the necessity of an idea of God" (C, 105).[58] Bonhoeffer also noted that "If we speak of Jesus Christ as God, we may not say of him that he is the representative of an idea of God, which possesses the characteristics of omniscience and omnipotence (there is no such thing as this abstract divine nature!); rather, we must speak of his weakness, his manger, his cross. This man is no abstract God" (C, 104; cf. C, 27). Bonhoeffer persisted in his arguments about the incarnation of God in history with an impressive consistency in order to rule out an understanding of God as an idea. "A Christianity without the living Christ is inevitably Christianity without discipleship, and Christianity without discipleship is always Christianity without Christ. It remains an abstract idea, a myth" (CD, 50; cf. CD, 35). History and idea are mutually exclusive. Bonhoeffer had already made this point in his lecture on Jesus Christ, delivered in Barcelona: one cannot come to history when one begins with the philosophy of idealism, because it seeks to create a system and because it discerns reality from the position of an abstract, intellectual norm. But it is impossible to measure history in the light of an idea because, in that way, history becomes relativized by the idea (GS V, 193).[59]

Bonhoeffer was opposed throughout his life to general ideas and abstractions.[60] One cannot act in correspondence with reality on the basis of ideas.[61] Bonhoeffer believed that World War 1 caused the breakdown of faith in the idea. He said in his important radio talk of 1933, entitled "The Leader and the Individual in the Younger Generation," that the chaos of the war had made it plain that "the idea divorced from reality [has] gone bankrupt" (NRS, 194).

From start to finish Bonhoeffer spoke out against abstraction and idea, against general, forever valid eternal truths, principles, norms, law, ideals, and ideology toward which, were they given predominance, our thinking would necessarily lean.[62] What is attained through all these categories is not real transcendence but only apparent transcendence, not real existence but only a self-governed life out of self-centeredness; no real boundaries and no real "beyond" are given in these categories. To know and to grasp reality is what Bonhoeffer wished: reality in which God is really God, the world is really the world, and humans are really humans. In order to state this more clearly, Bonhoeffer changed the term "reality" to "concrete reality."

REALITY AS CONCRETE REALITY

God the *Concretissimum*

When considering God it is especially important not to confuse reality with an idea. Instead of succumbing to an idea of God it is imperative to experience the real God. In an important letter from about the year 1931, Bonhoeffer expressed this point in moving words:

> Is our time up and will the gospel be given to another people, proclaimed perhaps in quite different words and deeds? What do you think about the perennial nature of Christianity in the light of the world-situation and our own way of living? It becomes more and more incomprehensible that "the city will not be destroyed" for the sake of one righteous inhabitant. I am now chaplain at the Technical Institute: how am I to preach such things to these people? Who still believes it? This invisibility will destroy us. If we cannot see in our personal lives that Christ was present then let us see it at least in India. But this insane and persistent being thrown back to the invisible God himself—nobody can take that forever. (GS I, 61)

Bonhoeffer had been asked about the visibility of God in our personal lives. That question of being thrown back to the invisible God became in fact a concern which he dealt with all his life. The significance of that letter of 1931 lies in the fact that it already contains hints about religionless Christianity and non-religious interpretation. Here Bonhoeffer wondered about the proclamation of the gospel in "quite different words and deeds"; in later communications this phrase was inverted to read, "in quite different deeds and words" (LPP, 299-300). Referring to India several times in that letter, Bonhoeffer hoped to see that "Christ was present" there.[63] It was in such an experience that he hoped to overcome the invisibility of God.

The distress about God's invisibility is found already behind passages in *Sanctorum Communio*. He traced back to that invisibility what appear to be inconclusive arguments against idealism. "God is impenetrable thou, and his metaphysical personality . . . does not affect what we have said about his being as I" (SC, 34-35). God is not knowable in his "I," that is, as person. The attempt to conceive of him as spirit and to comprehend him on that basis must, therefore, fail. God cannot be known (*erkennen*); he can only be acknowledged (*anerkennen*).

The point of the struggle against idealism and the abstraction accompanying it is that real understanding might be achieved or, more accurately, there might be experience of the reality of God and, in consequence, a real concept of God. In philosophy God is thought of as the world's cause and not as its creator, but the real God is precisely what matters (GS III, 87-88). "Every human attempt to discover God, to unveil his secret reality, is hopeless because of God's being personality. All such attempts remain in the sphere of the idea. Personality as reality is beyond idea" (GS III, 104).[64] Thus only God can say who he is.

It is for that reason that Bonhoeffer put such emphasis on the assertion, "God alone is the *concretissimum*."[65] Bonhoeffer did not mean the God who is God always and everywhere. These adjectives Bonhoeffer regarded as descriptive of the idea of God. The true God is instead the one who is God here and now: "God is 'always' *God* to us *'today'*" (NRS, 162). What matters is not that God is always and everywhere, nor God's eternity, nor even that God is eternal; what matters is the God who is God here and today, the God who is concrete.

This God cannot be grasped in thought. "One cannot simply reflect about God on one's own, one has to beseech him. Only when we seek him does he answer" (GS III, 26-27). We can only seek him if we already know him, namely through his granting us knowledge of himself, something which must be left to his will. "If it is I who determine where God is to be I will always find there a God who somehow resembles me, who pleases me, who is akin to my being. But if it is God who determines where he wants to be it will most likely be in a place which is not akin immediately to my being, which does not please me. That place, however, is the cross of Christ" (GS III, 27-28).[66] With that mention of the cross comes the answer to the question provoked by the invisibility of God, an answer, it is true, not in the intellectual but in the factual-historical sense. "Only from the fact itself can one know who God is"

(C, 102). One cannot even begin with the idea of the holy, in order to come to God. On that road one always discovers oneself instead of God; one cannot come to God on one's own but only when he calls.

The correct understanding of God cannot lie in the concept of God as "the one who is":

> Primarily, God is not the sheer Is: he "is" the just one, "is" the holy one, he "is" love. Theological concepts of being must have precisely this as their ontological premise, that the Is can in no way be detached from the concrete definition. Any formalistic attempt to fall back on "something of a more general nature," supposedly discoverable behind the specific conditions of divinity, must serve to obliterate the Christian idea of revelation. The contingency of God's revelation in law and message is changed into a general theory of being with occasional modifications. (AB, 68)

One must keep Bonhoeffer's intensive search for the concrete God clearly before one's eyes in order not to forget God himself over the significance which Bonhoeffer attaches to Jesus Christ for faith and theology. God is the *concretissimum,* but we experience and know that precisely in and through Jesus Christ. The invisibility of God in this world is overcome through faith in the cross. And the cross is about God, about God in history (GS III, 104–6).[67]

General statements cannot describe God even though all theological assertions have to generalize; a statement such as "God is love" is, theologically speaking, ultimately not a truth about God because God is at the same time a God of wrath. "Therefore every statement concerning God's essence must contain both of these contradictory aspects in order to give room to the reality of God" (GS III, 103). The metaphysical identification of love, omnipotence and the like with God does not mediate true knowledge of God. Only the concrete manifestations of God's historical action "give room to the reality of God," something that must be stated in paradoxes if it is to be put into words at all.

Bonhoeffer sought God as the *concretissimum;* to him God was both concrete reality and the mystery that is close to us. In God there is true reality which transcends what is alleged to be reality understood positivistically.

Concrete and Contingent Revelation

All reality which deserves to be called concrete, and therefore genuine, reality depends on this concrete reality of God. Thus, revelation is "concrete revelation"; it is "contingent revelation" (SC, 91; cf. AB, 15, 79). The characterization of revelation in those terms stresses that revelation is historical. This concrete, contingent revelation occurred in Jesus Christ who, as God's word, truly entered into empirical, contingent history. Bonhoeffer remarked in his christology lectures that in Jesus Christ "the Counter-Logos appeared in history, no longer as an idea, but as 'word' become flesh" (C, 30). He went on to say that "Christ as word in the sense of address is not timeless truth. It is truth spoken into the concrete moment" (C, 50). It is therefore impossible to find access appropriate to him via our human *logos*. It is also impossible, on account of God's incarnation in Jesus Christ, to speak of Christ as "the representative of an idea of God" (C, 104). Precisely because it is personal this reality can only be acknowledged and only within such acknowledgment can it be comprehended.

An outstanding characteristic of this concrete reality is that it is actual here and today, or rather today and here. For word, too, is word only when it is not general truth. " 'Thou shalt love thy neighbor as thyself' is in itself so general that it needs to be made as concrete as possible if I am to hear what it means for me here and now. And only as a concrete saying is it the word of God to me" (NRS, 162). This here and now is a feature, in other words, of God's reality, a feature of the reality of Christ.

Concreteness is a characteristic also of the word Christ addresses to us: "Insofar as Christ commands, he makes very concrete commands" (GS I, 64).[68] Even as early as 1932 Bonhoeffer was already very concerned with what "encounters me here and now in all my reality" (NRS, 161), with what is of significance to me today and here, with what is concrete, just as God is concrete because he "is 'always' God to us *'today'* " (NRS, 162). Bonhoeffer anticipated what was to occupy him again in *Ethics* and *Letters and Papers from Prison,* namely, how "Christ takes form among us here and now," adding the question, "What do we mean by 'among us,' 'now' and 'here'?" (E, 85–86). In the later work the question was put in these words: Who really is Christ for us today (LPP, 279)? The answer Bonhoeffer gave in *Ethics* is this: "The 'among us', the 'now' and 'here' is therefore the region of our decisions and encounters" (E, 86–87), which to ignore would mean to lapse into abstraction (E, 87).[69]

The Binding Force of the Empirical Church

Having emphasized the concreteness and contingency of revelation in Jesus Christ, it follows naturally that Bonhoeffer laid great stress on the absolute binding force of the concrete, empirical church. The basis for this stress is found already in *Sanctorum Communio* and not only in the section developing the predicament of "authority and freedom in the empirical church." Through the recognition that it has a concrete and binding authority the empirical church obtains the form of an institution competent to make final decisions. Bonhoeffer stated that the church's authority, deriving from God's word, is relative because the church is obliged to orient itself according to that word. It is absolutely necessary that there be vigilance against the distortion of authority through totalitarian ways; still there is no doubt that a church which has no authority founded on and bound to God's word in Christ is no church at all, for it cannot watch over the purity of God's word with any power. That means that opposition to the church's authority can arise only in closest attachment to the church if it is not to be irresponsible willfulness (SC, 175). Here, too, the irreducible sociality of the church is manifest. The church is the community of those who hear God's word and follow it; in that community alone is there right witness and the truth of the confession. For it is the word of God that came into the world in Christ and calls individuals, who have become lonesome on account of sin (SC, 71; CF, 58, 90), out of their lonesomeness and into the community anew (CD, 84–91, 209). It is that word which at one and the same time creates the church and is only found in the church. In proclaiming the word the church must call for obedience to the word. To preach that word is the church's commission. The basic reason why the church's authority is derived authority is that God's word must be made known in the church, too, as a word with power, that is, as a word that awakens and calls for obedience. Only when the church pays heed to this two-sided character of the word is the church's call for obedience to itself not a violent usurpation but an act of humble submission to the word.

The word of the church, however, must be concrete if it is truly to be a word calling for obedience. For that reason Bonhoeffer repeatedly called for the convocation of a council to arbitrate situations for which, in his view, such a concrete word seemed necessary. A council of that sort would make authoritative declarations on matters of true faith or, more accurately, would give witness to true faith and would speak authoritatively about heresy.[70] There was never any doubt in Bonhoeffer's mind about the need for doctrinal authority and discipline, both of which must be exercised on the basis of conciliar decisions. Examples of such binding, concrete conciliar decisions of the empirical church were the confessional statements of Barmen and Dahlem.[71] What had often been urged actually took place there: the church said something concrete (NRS, 137). Bonhoeffer regretted deeply that the ecumenical movement did not see itself as a church in such a sense and did not have the courage to speak concretely about the true faith.[72]

The Concrete Command

Two specific subjects illustrate Bonhoeffer's preoccupation with concreteness: the command, which in his conviction can only be concrete command; and preaching. It should not be surprising, then, that he dedicated intensive attention to them both.

Let us first consider his thoughts about the concrete command. The command applies to people only when it is related to their situations and when it determines them. Only then can the command be heeded. This command is not one that is discernible in a general way; it cannot be set forth with a generally binding force. Only the concrete reality of a given situation demanding decision can be said to have binding force. Command is truly command to me only in situations shaped by the presence of my fellow human beings. "Reality is the sacrament of command," as Bonhoeffer put it in an earlier address (NRS, 164).[73] He had already said, "What the sacrament is for the preaching of the Gospel, the knowledge of firm reality is for the preaching of the sacrament" (NRS, 164). This inner connection between concrete deeds, concrete situation and the word of God is the basic condition not only for the relation of gospel and sacrament but also for that of command and the believer's life. Only in the relation of command and situation does command become command; otherwise it is an abstract principle or norm. A command has to be concrete or it is no command.[74]

The basis for the concrete command declared by the church, which is sinful and subject to error, is laid in the "faith in the promise of forgiveness of sins which applies also to the church" (NRS, 164). The christological foundation of the command is indicated here; there is no command that is not a command of Christ: *"The commandment cannot stem from anywhere but the origin of promise and fulfilment, from Christ"* (NRS, 166).

If for some reason the church is not in a position to declare this concrete, definite command it must exercise a qualified silence which is "essentially different from ignoring things and passing them over without qualification" (SC, 174). Bonhoeffer later called specifically for such qualified silence when he demanded that people dissociate themselves from the resolutions which ecumenical gatherings pass with such ease.

> No good at all can come from acting before the world and oneself as though we knew the truth, when in reality we do not. This truth is too important for that, and it would be a betrayal of this truth if the church were to hide itself behind resolutions and pious so-called Christian principles. . . . Qualified silence might perhaps be more appropriate for the church today than talk which is very unqualified. (NRS, 160)

When the confrontation with the German Christian Church arose the time for silence was, of course, over; Bonhoeffer tried unsuccessfully to persuade the church to say the definite things it was constrained to say.

Whether or not one has to do with Christian ethics is determined by God's concrete command. It was this matter of concreteness that caused Bonhoeffer to return again and again to ethics. His repeated insistence on the nonexistence of Christian ethics may be explained in this way: there exists no ethics that is Christian, an ethics which is based not on general, human principles and norms but on specifically Christian ones. When Bonhoeffer spoke of Christian ethics he meant concrete ethics. "The point of departure for Christian ethics is not the reality of one's own self, or the reality of the world; nor is it the reality of values and

SYSTEMATIC SUMMARY OF THE HERMENEUTICAL IMPLICATIONS

standards. It is the reality of God as he reveals himself in Jesus Christ" (E, 189–90).[75] Thus, Bonhoeffer made the general assertion that

> ethical discourse cannot be conducted in a vacuum, in the abstract, but only in a concrete context. Ethical discourse, therefore, is not a system of propositions which are correct in themselves, a system which is available for anyone to apply at any time and in any place, but it is inseparably linked with particular persons, times and places. This limitation does not mean that the ethical loses any of its significance, but it is precisely from this that it derives its warrant, its weight; whereas whenever it is not restricted in this way, whenever it is available for general application, it is enfeebled to the point of impotence. (E, 271)

From this statement it is quite clear what the categories "here" and "today" mean for concrete reality; general statements or a system give no access to reality. "The wise are aware of the limited receptiveness of reality for principles; for they know that reality is not built upon principles but that it rests upon the living and creating God" (E, 69). In other words, wisdom is not transforming principles into reality but submitting to God's command which is concrete. "The commandment of God is the total and concrete claim laid on people by the merciful and holy God in Jesus Christ" (E, 277). Bonhoeffer's teaching on the mandates, so important for his ethics, rests on this foundation.

The aim of this ethics, which is Christian because it is concrete, is that "the reality of God should show itself everywhere to be the ultimate reality" (E, 188). The concern of Christian life is not to enforce Christian principles and norms but to live discipleship, to become conformed to the figure of Jesus Christ. In discipleship alone *"the realization among God's creatures of the revelational reality of God in Christ"* takes place (E, 190).

Bonhoeffer's understanding of command can be summarized in the following statement, the sentiment of which is rooted deeply in his theology.

> God's commandment, revealed in Jesus Christ, embraces the whole of life. It does not only keep watch on the untransgressible frontier of life, like the ethical, but it is at the same time the center and fulness of life. It is not only obligation but also permission. It does not only forbid, but it also sets free for life; it sets free for unreflected doing. (E, 280)

The context to which the question of God's concrete command points is delineated by the question of transcendence, in the Bonhoefferian sense of ethical transcendence as the center of life, and by the question of *actus directus* and *actus reflectus*. The concrete form, that is to say, the ethical form of what is commonly understood as doctrine, is for Bonhoeffer contingent, historical command of God which, because it concerns the situation of human beings, is concrete. The ethical, perhaps one could even say the practical side of faith, normally interpreted in cognitive terms, is called the promise and command of God.[76] For that reason it is to be seen as a theology of ethics rather than as a theology of dogma.

The Sermon as Concrete Proclamation

The concrete revelation in Jesus Christ is present in the witness of the empirical church as the community of those who believe in Jesus Christ. It was in connection with revelation that Bonhoeffer paid as much attention to the concreteness of the command as he paid to the question of preaching. Contrary to theology the sermon is concrete. "Theology does not provide rules for life. It records revelation in terms of abstraction while the church, on the other hand, must preach, that is to say, proclaim concretely" (GS V, 307). It is no coincidence that the assertion "God is the *concretissimum*" appears in the context of his homiletics. A sign of a sermon's concreteness is its very social structure.[77] It is not addressed to each individual gathered but always to the concrete gathered community only in which, *through preaching,* Christ's authoritative claim on his community comes to fulfillment. The concreteness of preaching is founded in the incarnation (BWP, 126). But the proclaimed word is "no new incarnation, but the Incarnate One who bears the sins of the world" (BWP, 127).[78] The presence of Christ demands that preaching be in touch with the present,[79] and that the prerequisites for hearing it remain available, thereby preventing that "the summons to the preaching . . . for some quite extraneous reason no longer be obeyed" (E, 140).[80] The presence of Christ demands that preaching itself be assessed correctly and appropriately.

It is no coincidence that concrete preaching was the context in which Bonhoeffer differentiated the various concepts of ministry.[81] "The concrete function of the empirical church is the divine service of preaching the word and of administering the sacraments" (SC, 155–56). The concreteness of preaching also relates to the fact that preaching, rather than being teaching, is the proclamation of God's word.[82] Bonhoeffer wrote in an early letter that the problem of concreteness in preaching was occupying him much at the time (GS I, 34). Thus he had a particular interest in the sermon. This is also the most likely reason why his work at the preachers' seminary at Finkenwalde was so fulfilling to him (WF, 259). With this in mind it is appropriate to characterize Bonhoeffer's direction as leading from lectern to pulpit.[83] The concreteness of faith is not established by theology; the theology of justification does not itself justify (AB, 145).

The concreteness belonging to the sermon is not its own but is the gift bestowed by Christ who is present in the sermon, for "preaching can never apprehend this central point but can only be apprehended by it, by Christ" (NRS, 38). That is why the sermon must not seek to impart worldly wisdom (GS II, 165). What must be emphasized here is that

SYSTEMATIC SUMMARY OF THE HERMENEUTICAL IMPLICATIONS

concreteness does not mean addressing oneself to issues of the day. Preaching which does that loses concreteness.[84] "Only where Christ is preached is God present. Without him the sermon is at best nothing more than empty doctrine" (BWP, 133).

It would be wrong to think that because the sacrament is preaching made visible there are two different kinds of concreteness. It is senseless to hold the concreteness of preaching and of the sacrament one against the other, just as it is senseless to hold the presence of Christ in the sacrament versus the presence of Christ in preaching. But without the sacrament the word is in danger of becoming general and noncommittal, which means becoming unreal (C, 52). It is particularly the preaching of justification and forgiveness, which is the central matter of preaching, that is in need of the concrete discipline of personal confession in order that it does not dissolve into generalities but instead becomes preaching in which forgiveness really occurs (SC, 241, n. 137).[85] The sacrament is concrete because it is a visible action in which salvation in the world and for the world, as inculcated by preaching, is made real in symbols.

It was Bonhoeffer's concern in all his theological work to make the concrete visible and to assist in its acknowledgment. Here lies the basic cause for his rigorous opposition to the philosophy of idealism as he perceived it.

The concept "concrete" may serve, therefore, as a guide through Bonhoeffer's theology. Concrete reality, as represented by the concrete real God, the concrete historical incarnation of God's word in Jesus Christ, the concrete empirical church, and the concrete reality of the world made real in and for Christ, is in every instance the basis on which theology makes its deliberations; the latter are a posteriori, but are nevertheless appropriate on account of that.

It should be apparent that in Bonhoeffer's view theology is not in danger only when it is practiced in the believing community and when it makes its deliberations about faith a posteriori; for in so doing, it in fact receives its clarity and relevance. He knew of the point where our thoughts and correlative insights have their boundaries and where we must become prepared to make decisions in darkness, even in the darkness of guilt.[86] We have noted that he attempted again and again in the ecumenical gatherings during the Church Struggle to have the church make such a decision, but, when he saw that this would not happen, he made a personal decision.

In our summation of the hermeneutical implications of Bonhoeffer's theology we emphasized especially the concepts "reality" and "concrete." The purpose here was to show that something impossible was undertaken in the attempt to explicate Bonhoeffer's hermeneutical point of departure. Basic concepts were, for him, concrete concepts in themselves; his theology is in this aspect also an ethically oriented theology.

THE CONSEQUENCES FOR BONHOEFFER'S HERMENEUTICS

The Problem of Language

The character of Bonhoeffer's theology as an ethical theology manifests itself, not least, in his somewhat scattered hermeneutical assertions. He never completed his plan to write a hermeneutics.[87] Instead, one may conclude, he set out to work on *Ethics*. That he turned to ethics instead of hermeneutics is due to his theological point of departure. Even his concern for a non-religious interpretation of theological terms is misinterpreted if it is seen in isolation and taken primarily as a task of hermeneutics.[88]

One can assess Bonhoeffer's views about hermeneutics above all from his views about language. Language is the chief medium of the development of hermeneutics. When confronted with the problem of language Bonhoeffer faced great difficulties precisely because language carries so much weight "in the Protestant church, the church of the preaching of God's Word" (GS III, 41). The creation of new words, however, is no solution to empty phrases:

> A radical cure such as the deletion of the words cross, sin, grace, etc. from our vocabulary is of no avail. For one, the cross is not replaceable with the guillotine because Jesus died on a cross. Secondly, the word "feeding trough" might do for a while instead of "manger" but after the third or fourth time it would sound just as flat. (GS III, 42)

Bonhoeffer preferred to leave the language of the Bible intact: "The simple language of the Bible should, in my judgment, be kept. . . . It all depends on the depth from which it comes and in what surroundings it is found" (GS III, 43). The depth from which the words come determines whether the word is genuine, full, or empty. That is why Bonhoeffer placed such a value on silence. "The word which comes to expression out of a long silence weighs more than the same word uttered by the mouth of a loquacious person" (GS III, 42). Silence is the soil where Christian speaking roots itself. This conviction led Bonhoeffer to make his assertions, to which we have already referred, about the "qualified silence" of the church. We add an important statement from the introduction to his lecture on christology:

> Teaching about Christ begins with silence. "Be still, for that is the absolute," writes Kierkegaard. . . . The silence of the church is silence before the word. Insofar as the church proclaims the word, it falls down silently in truth before the inexpressible. . . . The spoken word is the inexpressible. . . . To speak of Christ means to keep silent; to keep silent about Christ means to speak. When the church speaks rightly out of a proper silence, then Christ is proclaimed. (C, 27)

SYSTEMATIC SUMMARY OF THE HERMENEUTICAL IMPLICATIONS

The task of theology, therefore, is to think about this word that came out of silence.

In distinguishing between existential and systematic knowledge Bonhoeffer spelled out the difference between the word and a theological statement. The price to be paid for systematic knowledge is existentiality, for it is given up when existential knowledge, the "truth for me," becomes systematic knowledge (AB, 96). But what matters is existential knowledge. Correspondingly Bonhoeffer warned against confusing ontological statements with the testimony to be proclaimed:

> If we take the statement that Christ is risen and present as an ontological proposition, it inevitably dissolves the unity of the Scriptures. . . . It is exalted into a theological principle. . . . The proclamation of the scriptural testimony is of an absolutely different character. The assertion that Christ is risen and present, when taken strictly as testimony given in the Scriptures, is true only as a word of the Scriptures. This word is the object of our faith. (CD, 206)

Scripture is not the only testimony to be proclaimed; the word of the church, too, is testimony in this sense, for the church is to make this testimony known. This conviction, expressed in his statement, "Those who knowingly cut themselves off from the Confessing Church in Germany cut themselves off from salvation" (WF, 93–94) brought Bonhoeffer into deep controversy.

> Insofar then as this statement is not an existential expression of the faith of the true church but is intended as a theoretical truth about the saved and the lost, insofar as it is anything but an offer of grace, the means of salvation, it is reprehensible, for then a statement of faith is made a speculative statement. (WF, 93–94)

Theology must resist the false attempt to become a closed system which seemingly grasps the truth. For the subject of theology is the mystery to which silence is appropriate, the silence out of which language concerning the mystery may alone arise. That is why the only possibility left for theology is to use formulations in contradiction and paradox, as was done at the Council of Chalcedon, for that is how structures of thought are broken down and space is created for the mystery (C, 88).[89] Theological formulations must be contradictory and paradoxical in order that statements of theology are not regarded as statements of ontology. "In the Chalcedonian Definition, an unequivocal, positive, direct statement about Jesus Christ is superseded and split into two contradictory, opposing statements" (C, 102).

In Bonhoeffer's thinking this paradoxical nature of the formulations is always firmly related to the reality of Jesus Christ. This is why he rejected the "how" question, which inescapably leads to dualism, and preferred the "who" question in which, alone, the paradoxical unity can be given expression: "Who are you? Speak for yourself! The question, 'who are you?' is the question of dethroned and distraught reason; but it is also the question of faith: 'Who are you? Are you God himself?' " (C, 30). Another kind of paradox emerges here, namely, the incognito of God in history, the "incognito of the Incarnation" (C, 38). Concerning this hiddenness of God in history Bonhoeffer had remarked earlier that the paradoxical essence of God becomes manifest to the believer in our justification (GS III, 108–9). Space is created for this reality of God only through "contradictory aspects" (GS III, 103), such as the love and the wrath of God. One can trace this insistence right up to the prison letters where we find the statement that "God is beyond in the midst of our life" (LPP, 282). Seen from the human perspective our language about God is equivocal. Dialectical statements express this situation most adequately since they protect the freedom of God and the mystery of predestination (GS V, 221).

Bonhoeffer spoke of dialectics in this context more frequently in his earlier than in his later writings. The terminology was influenced by Karl Barth's dialectical theology. It would be more appropriate to call it paradoxical theology. It is important for us to keep in mind that, from the outset, Bonhoeffer wanted to overcome the constrictions of Barth's dialectics which appeared to him to be marked by a strongly logical character (NRS, 33). He set out, therefore, to find other ways of expressing God's reality. Throughout his work one discovers dialectical, or, better, paradoxical formulations, such as the reference to the transcendence of God in the midst of our lives. Bonhoeffer saw the danger of dialectical theology in the fact that it began with a "theology of the word of God," or with revelation. Bonhoeffer attempted to begin with God's reality in history, from Jesus Christ. By itself the word was again in danger of becoming an abstract word, one that was general, that had no binding power and, consequently, was empty.[90]

The Sacrament as the Concreteness of Proclamation

The word is firmly related to reality. This becomes clear when one considers the contingency of the word on the sacrament. In the sacrament proclamation becomes concrete, definite (NRS, 163). Bonhoeffer believed that the sacrament had to go together with the word (CD, 215).[91] It is not necessary now to present a detailed exposition of Bonhoeffer's doctrine of the sacraments;[92] it is sufficient to show what emphasis Bonhoeffer placed on them. The sacraments are the activity of the congregation, an activity in which nature is drawn into the mediation of salvation, and thereby is grasping humans in their nature. There is no sacrament of individuals but only that of the actually assembled people of God. It pleased God "to 'tie' his grace to Christ—and that means to word and sacrament" (TP, 157). For Bonhoeffer there was no doubt that "the physical presence of Christ as he preached was itself already a sacrament" (TP, 158).

Bonhoeffer did not wish to reduce the word; he knew that the word has complete authority only if it is the word that is Christ, and that cultic acts cannot render it any greater (BWP, 129). Because the word has its source in the incarnation of Jesus Christ (BWP, 125) and because God's word entered into nature and history (C, 52–53, 62), the word alone is never adequate on its own for Bonhoeffer; it needs to be complemented by the materialization that the gathered congregation provides. Word and sacrament are one; they cannot be placed in opposition (C, 57; cf. TP, 158). One must not emphasize one of these elements more than the other, nor should the value of the sacraments be misjudged. "The community of the sacrament is the community of believers who have been won by the word. The unbeliever, too, has access to the word, but not to the sacrament" (WF, 152). Why not? What consequences arise for theological hermeneutics from such an anthropology which is equally implied in the idea of arcane discipline?

The hermeneutical significance of Bonhoeffer's doctrine of the sacraments lies in the fact that the spoken word cannot be the sole issue of concern for the community; the sacrament must also be present, for God's incarnate word takes form in sermon and sacrament. Wherever God becomes incarnate and because God became incarnate it is not only God's word we must deal with, but God's presence in nature and history, as Bonhoeffer said in the christology lectures: we must deal with God's reality in the reality of the world, as he said later in *Ethics* (E, 194). The event of God taking form in the world is what occurs in the activity of the community. Arcane discipline, after all, is part of religionless Christianity.

The Hermeneutical Function of Action

Bonhoeffer's thesis of the sacrament as the concreteness of proclamation is not the only area where his attempt to circumvent the isolation of the word is apparent. It shows itself also in the way he relates word and action. The word must never lose its contact with reality which, being personal, has the character of event and, therefore, implies action. Bonhoeffer was convinced that action, which he knew to be inevitably equivocal, was still the unequivocal word. An action that is done is an action of a person. The person in whom I have faith interprets the action, as Bonhoeffer put it, following Luther (C, 37). Through such interpretation alone the word becomes unequivocal, yet the incognito, the hiddenness of the historical situation is not lifted by the action. Again and again Bonhoeffer made reference to this relation of word and action, or, better, of action and word. Action itself has a hermeneutical function; a word without action is no complete word any more; instead it is the word's deflation and, consequently, its destruction. The relation of sacrament and word is, in theological terms, the clearest special case of the general relation between the *actus directus* and the *actus reflectus*. And here the structure of the relation between ethical and dogmatic theology becomes apparent.

In his lecture on the Christian idea of God Bonhoeffer expressed most forcefully that action has a hermeneutical function. Replying to the question of how we can know anything of God if our thinking stays within its own boundaries, Bonhoeffer stated: "The pathway to this knowledge is action" (GS III, 107). For Bonhoeffer that action is faith. Faith as action, however, is not an autonomous action of humans (E, 43). In that action which is faith, we hand ourselves over to God without any reflection (E, 35). Faith includes listening to God, a listening which is a following after God. Listening is justified solely as the basis on which action is initiated. Listening must not be separated from action because action would otherwise be forgotten in the listening and then the listening itself "is forgotten as that which it essentially is, namely, as that which points solely and entirely towards action" (E, 45). For this reason knowledge which mediates God's word is dependent, for Bonhoeffer, upon obedience, and not vice versa: "From obedience derives knowledge and not obedience from right knowledge. Through obedience to the word we are guided into all truth" (GS IV, 354). What that means for the churches is that "the actual doing of what had been commanded constitutes the church and not the religious formulae, the dogmas" (GS III, 331). What Bonhoeffer had said specifically in relation to Holy Communion has, therefore, general application: "Right thoughts only come from right practice" (TP, 38). Of course, right thoughts must be present, too, in order to keep practice right: "So right thought comes from right usage and in its turn leads on to right usage of the sacrament" (TP, 42).

Action has a constitutive meaning for the rightness of thinking and receives from it help for its own rightness. The primary and original testimony of faith, therefore, is action which initially interprets itself. "Should action become a force to be reckoned with the world will begin asking for a testimony in words also" (GS V, 259).[93] Action possesses an illuminating power directed both into the church and its internal life and outward toward the non-believer. For that reason Bonhoeffer repeatedly urged that the message of faith be not only taught, interpreted and then applied but that it be put into action.[94] Such action is not blind and irrational but something that one dares to go into and that leads into the uncertain. This distinguishes genuine responsible action from ideological self-justifying action (E, 234). Responsible action cannot justify itself: "A historical decision cannot be entirely resolved into ethical terms; there remains a residuum, the venture of action," (E, 344). Such daring, such venture cannot be anticipated by reflection (E, 27).[95] One cannot see the road before one has set out on it (WF, 43). We are able to set out on the road and walk it through Christ alone (E, 51–52).

That action has a hermeneutical function is confirmed by Bonhoeffer's thoughts about intellectual honesty which, at first glance, would seem to be about the intellectual dimension. But the intellectual honesty, of which he speaks in his prison letters, is more than a matter of knowledge; it is an action—ultimate honesty is repentance (LPP, 360). In *Ethics* is a comment in which intellectual honesty is related to action, that is to say, in which the orientation and contingency of intellectual honesty are explained in the context of action: "If intellectual honesty is not the last word that is to be said about things, and if intellectual clarity if often achieved at the expense of insight into reality, this can still never again exempt us from the inner obligation to make clean and honest use of reason. We cannot now go back to the days before Lessing and Lichtenberg" (E, 97–98). Indeed, we cannot return to pre-Enlightenment times. But it is quite inapposite to reverse the intention of that assertion and to rely on reason and assume that reason can grasp reality in its depth. The only thing which will have any legitimacy in the future is thinking which implies action and prepares for renewed action (LPP, 298). This idea has great significance for theological understanding. After all, Christ did not come "so that we might understand him but that we should cling to him" (GS IV, 77). Here is the idea of discipleship. Discipleship is obedience to God in what one does. Faith and obedience are, therefore, also ethical categories,[96] and the discipleship of the community is visible action (CD, 106). Such action Christ alone can make real. "There is really no action without Jesus Christ" (E, 43). And this action can be undertaken only in intellectual honesty which is itself action oriented. That is why Bonhoeffer was not concerned with the relation of faith and reason, except, of course, when faith is understood from the point of view of practice and ethics rather than of the theory of cognition. The problem to which he addresses himself was that of the relation of doing and thinking.[97]

There is one more aspect to which attention must be drawn. It has already been touched on several times in this section but has not yet been explicitly stated. If action is understood as discipleship, it is always social action, an action in and for the community. An individual is never a disciple qua individual. Bonhoeffer's efforts to establish a community where discipleship was to be quite concretely exercised, were significant precisely because of the understanding that only in the practice of such communal life would new insights be gained.

This analysis confirms what had already been mentioned in the summary of the conceptual discussion regarding "concrete reality": for Bonhoeffer the word, be it the word of proclamation or of reflection, must be based in or must lead to action; for him thinking is a thinking that follows upon something; thinking is something a posteriori, for the sake of action. This means that hermeneutics finds reality and justification only in the context of an ethics of which it is a constituent part. This will be dealt with in part three where, in relation to non-religious interpretation, it will be shown that the interpretation is a secondary but by no means unimportant aspect of religionless Christianity. All attempts to find theological understanding must be borne by the fulfillment of faith on the part of the community, and must serve it.

CONCLUSION

The analysis of Bonhoeffer's understanding of theology as a scholarly discipline and of the structure of his theology arose from the quite extrinsic need to have Bonhoeffer himself provide the basis upon which to found our interpretation of his theology. Given the diverging interpretations of that work to date, that basis was by no means easily discernible.

This examination of Bonhoeffer's hermeneutical point of departure, designed to clarify the presuppositions of the entire study, has already led us quite deeply into his work. His conception of theology as well as the basic features of his own theology have clearly shown, in two ways, the presuppositions for a study of Bonhoeffer: his thoughts clarify how one should set out to interpret Bonhoeffer vis-à-vis other such attempts, and they open up the understanding of his theology.

In summing up the results of the first section of this study we may note, initially, that it is quite justified to regard Bonhoeffer's life and work as a theological unity, as Eberhard Bethge convincingly did in his biography of Bonhoeffer. It follows from this premise that Bonhoeffer's theology should also be regarded as a unity. It is necessary to describe that unity in a more explicit way. The discussion to date depicts the unity of Bonhoeffer's theology as a dialectical procursus which developed by qualitative leaps,[98] or as a collapse of the theological system which does not, however, imply a break in theology itself,[99] or as a continuous development.[100]

In relation to the structure and numerous other details of his theology it was shown that between 1930 and 1933 Bonhoeffer took up his earlier theological intentions quite concretely. During this time Bonhoeffer worked out concretely his earlier commitment (*Ansatz*) which he had pursued throughout his life. It would be a mistake to believe that Bonhoeffer's commitment led him to a repetition of his efforts; rather, it allowed him to respond to the demands and tasks of the actual moment. Thus, one must not look for certain axioms or even a system occupying a primary place in Bonhoeffer's interests. Instead, one must realize that Bonhoeffer made use of concepts in a sweeping manner, as shall be seen

SYSTEMATIC SUMMARY OF THE HERMENEUTICAL IMPLICATIONS

in relation to the concept of religion or "positivism of revelation." Nothing is to be gained by attempting to subject Bonhoeffer's work to an analysis of concepts in the hope of understanding his ideas. Bonhoeffer knew only too well that one cannot accurately conceptualize important concepts, such as life and world. For that reason he cannot be understood primarily in the cognitive categories; indeed, the opposite is the case. In the course of his life he devoted himself, both in practice and in theory, more and more relentlessly to the concrete, historical reality of faith and the world, that is to say, of faith in the world. He did so in a way that cannot simply be copied—for that is not how life and thought are mediated. Herein lies what is paradigmatic in Bonhoeffer: he both experienced and thought about discipleship as the heart of faith in its nonmanipulative character and therefore turned ever anew to the action of discipleship.

It became apparent that there is a strong connection between Bonhoeffer's early and late theological statements by virtue of the way he linked theology to concrete faith. The majority of Bonhoeffer interpreters support the view that his theology is a unity in the sense of having ongoing development; they have, therefore, attempted to discern the basic theme of this theology.[101] These matters will be explored further on, particularly in relation to an analysis of "religionless Christianity in a world come of age."

It is only in the context of such a unity that one may speak, as did Eberhard Bethge, of three distinct periods in Bonhoeffer's work.[102] Bonhoeffer's two visits to the United States in 1930–31 and 1939 are, broadly speaking, the external demarcation points between the three periods. The time between 1930 and 1932 was of far deeper influence on him than was his short visit in 1939 although, in its clarity and impact, the later visit had such readily noticeable repercussions on his future.

Bonhoeffer himself perceived of his life as a unity; in a letter to Eberhard Bethge he wrote that he never changed direction except under the influence of his first impressions abroad and under the first conscious impact of his father's personality. "It was then that I turned from phraseology to reality. . . . Self-development is, of course, a different matter. Neither of us has really had a break in our lives" (LPP, 275).

If one is mindful of what the word reality meant for Bonhoeffer one will truly understand his comment about having turned from phraseology to reality and proceeding from then on in an unbroken development. That is why there is limited scope for answering affirmatively the question of whether there is a point in the prison letters where Bonhoeffer breaks off his thinking in order to venture into a new theology, namely the theology of religionless Christianity and non-religious interpretation. Bonhoeffer did not consider these terms, however surprising they appeared even to him, to be radically new. That matter shall be taken up later in this study. The "new" insight was not new for Bonhoeffer in the sense of a break, but in the sense of a deeper experience and a deeper understanding of the ever changing historical tradition. Bonhoeffer wrote: "In the traditional words and acts we suspect that there may be something quite new and revolutionary, though we cannot as yet grasp or express it" (LPP, 300). These new experiences became his final theological preoccupation. Still, in all these new reflections he saw himself explicitly committed to the heritage of his theological past, including the theology of liberalism to which he had at times shown strong opposition.[103] The continued engagement with discipleship was the basis on which Bonhoeffer subsequently developed his theology. For this reason such a sustained engagement, open to tradition, and the reflection upon it, itself borne by a consistent and unchanged theological structure, brought something new, something that had not been there before, which did not arise from his personal development but from the far-reaching changes of the times.[104] Since Bonhoeffer's impressions of those changes remained quite rudimentary, what he said materially about them cannot be regarded as more than initial probings.

The study of Bonhoeffer begins therefore with the presupposition that he represents a unity. It is initially a unity of his *life* within which there was development and unfolding. But his theology is also a unity; the points of departure and basic structure of reflection remain the same throughout his work, which thus gives expression to what was concretely happening around it. To the end of Bonhoeffer's life, the theologian consistently gave priority to action, even if the consequences were dire, a pattern which thought cannot reproduce for itself.

Bearing the consequences meant that Bonhoeffer's life and his theology remained fragmentary just as everything human must finally remain so. As early as 1928 he wrote that "in the world there is never anything wholly complete" (GS V, 438). Although Bonhoeffer's generation, shaped by its historical situation, experienced life as something fragmentary in a particular sense, one must not regard Bonhoeffer's untimely death as a merely external catastrophe.[105] One hopes that in relation to Bonhoeffer the answer will be positive to the question of whether or not "we should be able to discern from the fragment of our life how the whole was arranged and planned, and what material it consists of" (LPP, 219).

The questions posed at the outset of this study are now answered sufficiently in relation to the foundation of the work. Because Bonhoeffer's thought grew out of life and his theology is an attempt to think upon faith lived out concretely, quite varied texts are useful for our progress. One may regard it as a distinct advantage that Bonhoeffer said many things in letters in a way so much more directly and less carefully balanced than would have been the case had he explained them in a schol-

SYSTEMATIC SUMMARY OF THE HERMENEUTICAL IMPLICATIONS

arly treatise. That the task of reporting from letters demands discretion on our part is beyond question.

The issue of the fragmentary character of his legacy has also been answered.[106] If Bonhoeffer's life is a unity, as we maintain, then one can attempt to understand what Bonhoeffer's final fragmentary statements mean in light of what he had said and done earlier. Long before he gave such eloquent and striking expression to those "new" thoughts there was a certain anticipation of them in his words. Bonhoeffer wanted to consolidate these ideas into a cohesive position which he tried all his life to make concrete. He returned home from the United States in 1939 in order to participate in this new departure. For that reason Bonhoeffer's whole theology is to be drawn upon for an understanding of the theological assertions he made in prison. The prospect of understanding those assertions is made possible through the study of both his early and late statements, allowing them to cast light upon one another.

PART TWO

JESUS CHRIST THE CENTER [*MITTE*] AND MEDIATOR [*MITTLER*]

3
Historical Survey of Bonhoeffer's Christology

THE MEANING OF CHRISTOLOGY FOR BONHOEFFER'S VIEW OF THE WORLD

The preceding part of this study, devoted to an analysis of the hermeneutical point of departure in Bonhoeffer's theology, is preparatory to the real aim of this work: to elucidate Dietrich Bonhoeffer's view of the world. In part one it was frequently necessary to consider Bonhoeffer's christology because, in his theology, the *actus reflectus* was inseparably bound to the *actus directus,* or faith directed toward Christ. In order to provide both foundation and core to part one, it is necessary to describe the fundamentals of Bonhoeffer's christology.

Christology is indispensable in relation to part three. One cannot present Bonhoeffer's view of the world adequately without including his christology. Bonhoeffer spoke of Jesus Christ repeatedly in *Letters and Papers from Prison,* particularly in connection with the world come of age: "Let me just summarize briefly what I'm concerned about—the claim of a world that has come of age by Jesus Christ" (LPP, 343). His primary question concerned the nature of Christianity, or "what Christianity really is, or indeed who Christ really is, for us today" (LPP, 279). Bonhoeffer later affirmed that "the question is: Christ and the world that has come of age" (LPP, 327). These statements alone warn against presenting Bonhoeffer's theology of the world without the inclusion of his christology, or, to speak concretely, against seeking to experience and comprehend the world without Jesus Christ. The relationship between Christ and the world which Bonhoeffer established in the prison letters would have provided sufficient reason for us seriously to consider his christology in the context of the view of that world that he presented. But those texts are the capstone, so to speak, of Bonhoeffer's theology; earlier assertions of his point toward the substance of and are provided with a basis by those texts. The validity of this statement can be shown in reference to *Ethics.*

JESUS CHRIST THE CENTER [*MITTE*] AND MEDIATOR [*MITTLER*]

In Jesus Christ the reality of God entered into the reality of this world. The place where the answer is given, both to the question concerning the reality of God and to the question concerning the reality of the world, is designated solely and alone by the name Jesus Christ. . . . Henceforward one can speak neither of God nor of the world without speaking of Jesus Christ. (E, 194)

A similar statement is found already in *The Cost of Discipleship,* where Bonhoeffer says of Christ: "*He is the Mediator* [*Mittler*], not only between God and human beings, but between one human being and another, between people and reality" (CD, 85). In cognitive terminology this becomes: "We cannot rightly acknowledge the gifts of God unless we acknowledge the Mediator [*Mittler*] for whose sake alone they are given to us" (CD, 88).

Yet long before that was written, Bonhoeffer had already explained the matter in his lectures on christology in this way: "Nothing can be known either of God or the human until God has become human in Jesus Christ" (C, 101). Jesus Christ is claimed to be "truly the center of human existence, the center of history and . . . the center of nature." (CD, 65).

Jesus Christ is in the midst of the world as the world's center; he is the mediator [*Mittler*] to God, to the world and to true worldliness. He is the center because he is God's mediator. In Bonhoeffer's understanding there is no immediacy any more to God or the neighbor or the world. Real transcendence is given to us in Christ who, as the boundary, is also the center [*Mitte*]. That being true a theology of the world can only be an indirect theology which is mediated by Christ; an immediate understanding of the world is theologically impossible. According to Bonhoeffer, faith directed toward Christ is the only immediacy there is.

It is appropriate that a study of Bonhoeffer's christology should occupy the middle section of this work. This section is linked with part one and has methodological import but it also lays a foundation for part three and has, for that reason, material relevance. Thinking about the Christian's engagement in discipleship in the world is to be undertaken only in faith in Christ. That very venture, however, surrenders itself directly to Christ himself, without any precaution and reflection. Jesus Christ is the foundation that supports thinking about discipleship. It follows that part two is by necessity in the middle. At one and the same time its import is formal and material, methodological and substantial.

It must be noted that Bonhoeffer did not assume that christology occupied such a central place in his theology. He frequently chose to begin with ecclesiology, only later to reshape things christologically and to give them deeper meaning on account of that. That ecclesiology becomes more profound when shaped by christology becomes quite apparent when *Act and Being* is compared to *Sanctorum Communio*. Another way, perhaps, of understanding this transformation is to recall that a year after he lectured on ecclesiology Bonhoeffer gave his course on christology. Eberhard Bethge has rightly reminded us that Bonhoeffer grounded preaching in ecclesiology during the first course at Finkenwalde, but, beginning with the second course and without revoking that argument, he prefaced it with a chapter showing how preaching is grounded in the incarnation (DB, 362).

THE FOUNDATION OF CHRISTOLOGY

In order to describe Bonhoeffer's christology we need to return once again to his earlier works, which have been analyzed, so far, by the concern with theological theory. Yet there is a certain divergence in those analyses which we shall look at now in relation to christology.

THE ECCLESIOCENTRIC OUTLOOK IN *SANCTORUM COMMUNIO*

Bonhoeffer's theology begins with and emanates from the church. Through the church Bonhoeffer attempted to have access to reality which would not only be theologically appropriate but also theologically binding. Such an access is established when one affirms the concrete presupposition "being in the church," and develops one's arguments on that basis *cum ira et studio* (SC, 20). The church is the presupposition, the subject matter, and the core of theological work.

In the context of theological statements about the church, Bonhoeffer referred back to Christ. Some very important insights are expressed in these assertions, of which the following statement is seminal: "Thus Christ is the sole foundation upon which the edifice of the church rests" (SC, 112).[1] Bonhoeffer assumed, therefore, that every ecclesiology has an implicit christology. "Communion with God exists only through Christ, but Christ is present only in his church, hence there is communion with God only in the church" (SC, 116).[2] Generally speaking, one can say that "Christ bears within him the new life-principle of his church" (SC, 107; cf. 112-13).

The Absence of an Explicit Christology in the Outlook of *Sanctorum Communio*

The foundation of Bonhoeffer's dissertation contains several obvious differences from that of his *Habilitationsschrift*. There is at first the development of the Christian concept of the person. We have already referred to the fact that, in order to overcome the subject-object scheme of idealism, Bonhoeffer introduced the I-thou scheme in which, alone, a real boundary becomes manifest (SC, 32,44). When the "I" finds its boundary in the "thou" real transcendence is attained as ethical transcendence. It is significant that Bonhoeffer did not speak of Jesus Christ in his endeavor to find a proper concept of transcendence or boundary. In addition to that, he extended the I–thou scheme quite unexpectedly into an I–thou–I–God scheme, in order to show that the impenetrableness of the other "thou" related directly to God, since "God is impenetrable Thou" (SC, 34). Thus, every human being is a "thou," "*real, absolute and holy,* like the divine Thou" (SC, 36). It follows, then, that the neighbor is called "the divine Thou" (SC, 37). There is no mention of Jesus Christ in this context, either.

If one puts all the assertions about the concept of person together and relates them to a theological view of the church, one cannot but be struck by the absence of any reference to Christ's mediation. It is difficult to understand why there is no explication of the significance of Jesus Christ for our concept of person in the very midst of Bonhoeffer's endeavor to discern "the reality of the church of Christ which is given in the revelation of Christ" (SC, 20), and to develop "the Christian concept of the person and the concept of basic social relations" (SC, 22). It seems that Bonhoeffer made things more difficult for himself by developing a concept of person in which the neighbor becomes a "thou" through God or the Holy Spirit, and the true boundary is established by the "thou" of God or the neighbor, instead of his developing it on the basis of Jesus Christ, the sole mediator.

Finally, we note that in the further development of *Sanctorum Communio* faith is said to be directed primarily toward God: "Faith, by its nature, is solely orientation upon God" (SC, 140). In addition, Bonhoeffer asserted that the individual faces God single and in solitude (SC, 128). Such formulations were quite out of the question for Bonhoeffer in his later work.

One may conclude that the discussion of Jesus Christ was not as critical for the theology of *Sanctorum Communio* as it was in Bonhoeffer's later works. In spite of the christological statements found in the dissertation one can declare that the point of departure for *Sanctorum Communio* was not shaped by christology:[3] the "thou" is the neighbor or God, but not Jesus Christ (SC, 52; cf. 202).

The Ecclesiological Character of the Expression "Christ Existing as the Church" [*Gemeinde*]

One might object that the expression "Christ existing as the church," which is central to *Sanctorum Communio,* indicates that Bonhoeffer's ecclesiological reflections were thoroughly founded on christology. Yet neither the use nor the meaning of the phrase manifests an explicitly christological intention.

The expression appears in the dissertation in the context of an examination of the New Testament view of the church. In that discussion the christological impulse predominates. The phrase is meant to show, as one can see from the context in which it is mentioned for the first time, that the church is a collective person: humankind "is 'Adam,' a collective person, who can be superseded only by the collective person, 'Christ existing as the church'" (SC, 84–85; cf. 203).

The subsequent use of the expression strikes us as being quite eloquent.[4] In his lectures on christology Bonhoeffer explained the matter much more carefully and with a more christological concentration: "This Christ existing as church is the whole person, the one who is exalted and who is humiliated" (C, 59).[5] No longer a formula, but simply a formulation, the expression appears, for what seems to be the last time, in *The Cost of Discipleship,* where it is used in a less rigorous but more concrete manner: "Through [the Holy] Spirit, the crucified and risen Lord exists as the church, as the 'new human being.' It is just as true to say that his Body is the new humanity as to say that he is God incarnate dwelling in eternity" (CD, 218).

In referring back to the expression "Christ existing as church" in Bonhoeffer's dissertation, it seems appropriate to conclude that the issue for him was not so much the concrete Christ who entered history as it was the concept of the church as collective person. Even if Bonhoeffer had wanted to repudiate idealism with the phrase "Christ existing as church," a modification of Hegel's conception,[6] his manner of stating the case was not yet sufficiently free of that tradition.

In making his case, Bonhoeffer repeated the term like a refrain, and used it to define what the church is in the categories of sociology. It would seem, however, that the community is established directly through God's will: "God, as he seeks to make his will prevail, gives himself to people's hearts and creates community, that is, he provides himself as the means to his own end" (SC, 181).

The reason why the church was not understood sufficiently as something historical in *Sanctorum Communio* presumably has to do with this understanding of such a directness to God.[7] Bonhoeffer's neglect of history in that dissertation resulted in the charge that he did not regard history seriously,[8] a charge which certainly is not justified in relation to his later theology.[9] Later in his life, Bonhoeffer would no longer have said, for instance, "Christ was man and God, he stood both in and beyond history" (SC, 219 n.1). There is no doubt, however, that even in this early work Bonhoeffer sought to do justice to God's activity in history.[10] He was not prepared, therefore, to develop general concepts which would formally comprehend reality, but only concepts which arose from genuine dialectics (SC, 39).

We may summarize our examination of *Sanctorum Communio* by

saying that a positive impression remains that Bonhoeffer attempted to grasp the reality of the church in terms of an empirical community and to interpret transcendence as something ethical, since "the problem of reality can be solved only from the ethical standpoint" (SC, 52). He never gave up this intention. His enduring merit is established by the fact that he never ceased to insist that the empirical church has binding force. Yet there is also the negative impression that Bonhoeffer did not satisfactorily realize his desire to overcome the constraints of the idealistic tradition by his introduction of the sociological category. If he had not changed his argument after that dissertation we would not need to speak explicitly and directly of Jesus Christ in order to be able to speak about the world; instead we would have to speak about the church, since *"in the local church . . . a piece of the world is organized purely out of the sanctorum communio"* (SC, 159).

THE CHRISTOCENTRIC OUTLOOK IN *ACT AND BEING*

Christ as Boundary

The first important indication that a change in Bonhoeffer's outlook had occurred in relation to *Sanctorum Communio* is given in the question of the boundary, of transcendence. Whereas the "thou" of the neighbor or of God constituted the true boundary, it is now clearly Christ who is the boundary: "There are bounds only to concrete human beings as a whole, and their name is Christ" (AB, 32). Bonhoeffer made this statement in the context of his discussion of the transcendental endeavor of philosophy but it applies equally to the ontological endeavor (AB, 72). That is why one can say generally of both that "existence either is or is not actually encountered by revelation, and this happens to it, as a concrete, psychological whole, on the 'borderline' which no longer passes through humans as such, or can be drawn by them, but is Christ himself" (AB, 80).

Christ is the boundary: clearly a change in Bonhoeffer's perspective had taken place. He did not state this explicitly himself but one cannot fail to notice it. Influenced by the I–thou scheme he spoke of the "thou" of the neighbor and the "thou" of God as the unmediated boundaries in *Sanctorum Communio*. In *Act and Being, Christ* is explicitly put into that place. It is no longer God or the Holy Spirit who came to the concrete "thou" (SC, 36); Christ is now at the center: "God gives himself in Christ to his communion, and to each individual as member of that communion. This he does in such a way that the active subject in the communion, of both the annunciation and the believing of the word, is Christ" (AB, 121–22). Bonhoeffer also put it like this: "It is only from the person of Christ that other persons acquire for us the character of personhood" (AB, 124).

The Intentionality of the *Actus Directus* Toward Christ

That a change occurred in the *Habilitationsschrift* becomes completely clear only when one looks at the statements about *actus directus*. As already noted,[11] the *actus directus* makes the *actus reflectus* possible in the first place and sustains it by giving it content. The *actus directus* is "founded in and directed toward Christ" (AB, 103; cf. 169,177). In the *actus directus* toward Christ, the perennially self-enclosed *cor curvum in se* (AB, 89, 28–29, 72) is opened up together with our reflection. It is important to note that the *cor curvum in se* is overcome because the neighbor has become a "thou" in Christ (AB, 124); in Christ alone there is "existence in the social reference" (AB, 140). Faith comes into being only through the claim of Christ, a claim which places people into community; such faith is directed primarily toward Christ (AB, 95) and no longer primarily toward God, as Bonhoeffer had said hitherto.

The *actus directus* is directed toward Christ. This by no means self-evident statement shows that Bonhoeffer's orientation in *Act and Being* is clearly christological. Why is the *actus directus* not directed toward God? In relation to Christ existence is affected in its *historical* dimension. That Bonhoeffer understood the *actus directus* as directed toward Christ and not, as the theological tradition would have suggested, toward God[12] has quite obviously to do with the fact that a thematic understanding of history was more clearly behind *Act and Being* than *Sanctorum Communio*. The problem with that theological tradition is that God and thinking, God and epistemological transcendence, are too closely aligned to it. The attempt to circumvent this position must by necessity be radical and consistent. To be directed toward Christ is something Christ alone can cause to happen, and in such a directedness alone is existence really affected.

Bonhoeffer developed a historical concept of existence in this work: historical existence is existence affected by Christ. "Existence in this sense is existence in social context with reference to Christ, knowing itself accepted or rejected in its historical totality" (AB, 127). In other words, historical existence is the social existence given in the contingent revelation in Christ.

> This is no more than the formal definition, as we may call it, of being in Christ. But in its historical actuality this being is similarly determined by both past and future. It is from this point that we may begin to see clearly the concrete mode of being shared by being directed to Christ and being with the communion. (AB, 177)

JESUS CHRIST THE CENTER [*MITTE*] AND MEDIATOR [*MITTLER*]

Mediation [*Vermittlung*] Through Christ

The place of Christ is stated differently in *Act and Being* than in *Sanctorum Communio*. This is confirmed by Bonhoeffer's use of a theological affirmation which has crucial importance in his later theology. He had referred for the first time, even though tenuously, to the absolute mediation through Christ. Jesus had been called "the Mediator of our reconciliation" in *Sanctorum Communio* (SC, 103), but there, still, was the notion of immediacy to God. In *Act and Being,* however, Bonhoeffer put the matter in paradigmatic form: "If conscience made a direct line of communication between humans and God, it would circumvent God's self-obligation to the mediating word, hence exclude Christ and the church" (AB, 160). Bonhoeffer elucidated this further by saying that "it is probably no idle coincidence that Holl both defines Luther's religion as one of conscience and admits a possibility of finding, in the first commandment, God without Christ" (AB, 160). What Bonhoeffer calls "God's obligation to the mediating word" has become event in the word of God incarnate. But God does not give up his freedom in his self-obligation. "God is not free *of* human beings but *for* them. Christ is the word of his freedom. God *is there,* which is to say: not in eternal non-objectivity but (to put it very tentatively) 'haveable,' graspable in his word within the church" (AB, 90–91). Mediation through Christ is fundamental: "In the existential event of revelation the existential structure of existence is attacked and transmuted. There is here no second mediator, not even the existential structure of existence. For revelation, the ontic–existential and the ontological–existential structures coincide" (AB, 75). This gives emphasis also to Christ's place as mediator.

This more sharply defined place of Christ has an effect on the relation of Christ to the world. It is also stated tenuously at first. Christ is one who stands outside of the world and yet as such he is not at all that which makes the external world extrinsic (AB, 139). Personal–social reality and, consequently, ethical–historical reality also are based on the quality of the Christ-person that causes him to stand outside.

> And so it is that through the extrinsicality of the Christ-person the *external world* takes on fresh meaning. But even the external world, as mediator of the spirit of Christ (here including the empirical church), should not be classified in the sphere of "there is." "There is" presupposes the position of the *detached* observer, which with regard to the being of revelation is inapplicable even to the external world, i.e., creation, since the being of revelation is the very basis of my being a person. (AB, 139–40).

One has the impression of hearing for the first time ideas about reality that were to be stated in *Ethics*. "Reality is first and last not lifeless; but it is the *real one,* the incarnate God" (E, 228). In being affected by Christ the world cannot be objectified, even though it naturally remains a being (*ein Seiendes*); the world cannot be separated from its relation to Christ for it is reality determined by him.

An examination of Bonhoeffer's *Habilitationsschrift* yields the following conclusions. Jesus Christ is now seen as the boundary, genuine extrinsicality. The *actus directus* is directed toward him, for which reason he is the sole mediator to God as well as to the neighbor and the external world. We may say even now, in anticipation of further study, that Christ is at the center.[13] Center refers to the middle between God and human beings, and also to the self-obligation of God to the contingent, historical revelation in Jesus Christ. The center is not a self-sufficient center; it is a center the significance of which can be stated only in the paradox that it mediates without thereby ceasing to be the true center.

This gives a christological rendering of the intentions of Bonhoeffer in *Sanctorum Communio;* being-in-the-communion is complemented by faith directed toward Christ.

In light of this conclusion one can speak of the argument of *Act and Being* as christological because Jesus Christ is now the center from which theology is developed. For Bonhoeffer a theology that is christocentric is one that is bound to the event of God's becoming human in Jesus Christ, the absolute mediator. Every feasible theology is christology for Bonhoeffer, and, since Christ is both man and humankind and exists not for himself or the individual but for all, every such theology is also ecclesiology. Rather than leading away from God this is the only way to reach him.

BASIC STRUCTURE OF THE EARLY CHRISTOLOGY

CHRISTOLOGICAL STATEMENTS PRECEDING THE CHRISTOLOGY LECTURES

The christological statements of Bonhoeffer's first two works have been compared, here, in order to find the place of christology in each. We must now look at Bonhoeffer's address, given at Barcelona, in which he explicitly entered the christological discussion for the first time. It is particularly important because he combined this concentration on Jesus Christ with a discussion of the problematic of history. In this way the address complements the equally important one of his about Christian ethics.

It is significant that a prominent feature of Bonhoeffer's later theology, particularly found in *Ethics,* is still absent at this stage. What is yet to be discussed is the relation of concrete ethics and of the concreteness derived from christology. Yet both emerge at Barcelona: an ethics which is not an ethics of principle and a christology which cannot be conceptualized in terms of ideas.

JESUS CHRIST THE CENTER [MITTE] AND MEDIATOR [MITTLER]

Christ—God's Way to People

Jesus Christ lays a singular claim on every human being by calling for a decision of belief or non-belief. That is what Bonhoeffer wanted to show in the address.

> Christ has become the subject of concern of the church or of certain people's attachment to the church; he is not the subject of concern of life. For the psyche of the nineteenth and twentieth centuries religion became a cosy parlour to which one was quite pleased to withdraw for a few hours. . . . One thing is clear: we shall understand Christ only when we are prepared to decide about him in a harsh either–or. He did not go to the cross to decorate or beautify our life. . . . We shall not understand him if we make room for him in one sphere of our life only; we shall understand him, rather, if we orient our life by him alone. . . . The religion of Christ is not a delicacy served after the bread, it is bread itself or nothing at all. (GS V, 134–35).

This was the first time that Bonhoeffer stated that Jesus Christ cannot be restricted to only one sphere; that idea became important again in the prison letters. Christ cannot be compared to anyone; he is no great ethical thinker. Christianity is not completely original in all its details and even our knowledge of Jesus Christ is historically meager. *"Vita Jesu scribi non potest"* (GS V, 138). The New Testament shows little interest in the psychology of Jesus. "Everything that has to do with his person as personality, such as its fascinating or repulsive features, is utterly unimportant for Jesus compared to the one thing: the decision to do God's will" (GS V, 143).

And yet, the either–or which Jesus desires is not a divisive one. What he wants is shown in his deeds: "He cares for children and for those of morally and socially low estate, the inferior ones" (GS V, 145). Paying heed to children and sinners or social outcasts appears full of contradiction; however,

> the solution, or, more accurately, the paradox lies in the utterly new understanding Jesus has of God. He who is utterly superior to the world and absolutely transcendent, he who is far removed from and wholly other to the world, he to whom humans and their nature are totally unlike and who is forever unattainable to human thinking and willing: he desires only one thing from us, namely, that we are nothing before him. (GS V, 147)

Bonhoeffer expanded this statement by noting that, if no more is demanded than that we are nothing before God, then no morality and no religion is demanded either in which God is quite distant no matter how close he is said to be. If we are "those who only hear, those who only receive, that is to say, if God seems utterly distant through un-religion and immorality, then he is really closest to us" (GS V, 148). This argument reflects back on Bonhoeffer's understanding of religion and morality in which he found aspects of human hubris; yet it is questionable whether one should conclude from that that "the Christian message is basically amoral and a-religious, however paradoxical that may sound" (GS V, 149). One must remember that Bonhoeffer intended to convey in that statement that there was no way for us to proceed to God on our own. "Ethics, religion, and church have to do with the way from us to God; Christ, however, speaks solely of God's way to us and of nothing else" (GS V, 149). A positive function is served by that "move against ethics, religion, and church, the things we claim to know before God, against humanism and mysticism in their euphoria about culture and the divinisation of the creature," for only when people have been deprived of the highest good that they possessed can they perceive "how Christianity reinstates all such goods in their essentially restricted and relative rights" (GS V, 152). The cross of Christ is the basis upon which all of these things are reinstated in their relative rights. "The idea of Christianity is God's way to people and the cross is that idea's visible manifestation" (GS V, 152). Only in view of the cross can one assert that "God's way to people leads back to God" (GS V, 153–54). Bonhoeffer concluded that "Christ does not bring a new religion," and a new ethic, as one might well add, "but he brings God" (GS V, 154).

As Bonhoeffer's theology developed, its basic orientation was shaped more and more by this fundamental insight. His more pronounced attention to christology provided him with the basis on which a critique of the church could be made. Bonhoeffer spoke of an impulse within Christian faith that is hostile to the church. The argument he presents is not an argument against the church as such; it is an argument in favor of the church because it speaks of and warns against the inherent danger of the church becoming self-sufficient and providing its own justification.

The beginning of Bonhoeffer's christology shows that the christological nuances of *Act and Being* were no accident. It should be pointed out that practical demands caused Bonhoeffer to state christology with more precision, for he had to instruct a congregation in the basic themes of Christian faith in only a few lectures. As we shall see again, christology was a highly practical issue for Bonhoeffer.

Increasing Concentration on Jesus Christ

In the address given at Barcelona and in *Act and Being,* Bonhoeffer brought incarnation and history into relation with one another. This is confirmed by his work in the United States which, of course, followed directly upon his habilitation. In his address "Concerning the Christian Idea of God,"[14] Bonhoeffer juxtaposed idea and history. God is "person," he said, and, in view of the freedom of the person, history is the only sphere in which one can speak of the person. "The only place where 'oneness' might occur is history" (GS III, 104). God himself has answered the question of God "in his own word in Jesus Christ" (GS III, 104). "God entered history and no human attempt can grasp him beyond this history" (GS III, 105). But revelation in history means "revelation in hiddenness," and, consequently, it "is an ever new challenge to man" (GS III, 105). If it is seen from the perspective of the realm of ideas, history became clearly "a symbol, transparent to the eternal spirit" (GS III, 105). Christianity sets itself against this and, in doing so, "gives us a new conception of history" (GS III, 105). This conception does not render what is given into "the transient bearer of eternal values and ideas," but is taken seriously in its uniqueness, for the attitude it brings toward the given "is not one of interpretation but one of decision. . . . That decision is made in the encounter with Christ" (GS III, 106).

Revelation in history is at the same time revelation in hiddenness. This hiddenness is made manifest in the cross of Christ. In the last of his American addresses, in which he also dealt with the meaning of God's coming into history for the world (NRS, 361–72), Bonhoeffer said, as if to sum up his christology: "Thus only through Christ do we see the creator and preserver and the Lord *of* the world and *in* the world. Only through Christ do we see the world in God's hands" (GS III, 126).[15] As God's word in history Christ shows us God as the Lord of and in the world. The relation between Jesus Christ and history, which Bonhoeffer made in this address, leads to a theological understanding of the world.

In these thoughts Christ has moved more and more noticeably into the foreground of faith and theology. In his courses at the university in Berlin Bonhoeffer continued in this direction. Even in the very first course he taught, on the history of systematic theology in the twentieth century, Bonhoeffer raised the question of Jesus Christ at important junctures, particularly in the final section entitled *"Wo stehen wir?"* ["Where do we stand?"].[16] Bonhoeffer was not content to build upon the concept of the church but hoped that renewed attention to christology would yield better fruit, although he did not see that hope adequately realized in any of the christologies of his contemporaries. Karl Barth, too, came in for criticism from Bonhoeffer because he stood in the way of a concrete ethics, even though he was rightly opposed to an ethics of principles. Bonhoeffer asked, how can the concrete Christ be proclaimed (GS V, 226)? In asking this, Bonhoeffer combined for the first time the question of concrete ethics with that of Christ, who can be made known concretely only in concrete situations. In the same manner ethics can be said to be real ethics, and, in consequence, Christian ethics, only when it is concrete ethics rather than an ethics of principles. In this view Bonhoeffer now no longer separates christology and ethics as he had still done in the address at Barcelona.

The next course Bonhoeffer gave concerned the nature of the church. Preceding the actual discussion of ecclesiology is a foundational section on Christ.[17] There had been no reference to Christ in the foundational sections of *Sanctorum Communio*. Only after the christological discussion in the course on ecclesiology did Bonhoeffer reintroduce the expression "Christ existing as church," and stress the identity of Christ and community (church) which must however be clearly distinguished from their identification. At the same time he emphasized more strongly that Christ and community also stand over and against each other (*das Gegenüber von Christus und Gemeinde*), thereby releasing the phrase "Christ existing as church" from some of its constriction.

Of special significance is the fact that Bonhoeffer addressed the problem of the church being worldly and Christian. The solution is found in Christ, for the church is "part of the world's reality," and "like Christ has become world" (GS V, 270). Genuine worldliness can renounce everything but the word of Christ (GS V, 270). In this context Bonhoeffer spoke of the arcane character of confession (GS V, 259). This is the first unambiguous reference to arcane discipline, and it is no coincidence that the question of worldliness is discussed at the same time.

In relation to the arcane character of confession Bonhoeffer made a critical comment about the Apostles' Creed, saying that Adolf von Harnack's question was far from being answered (GS V, 258). The manuscript does not make clear exactly what that question was all about; it probably had to do with Bonhoeffer's critique of the Creed in which, according to him, the earthly life of Jesus had such meager reference.[18] There appears to be a reminiscence of that idea in *The Cost of Discipleship*. Speaking about Jesus, Bonhoeffer said, "We hear the words of One who is on his way to the cross, whose whole life is summed up in the Apostles' Creed by the one word 'suffered'" (CD, 51).[19]

While lecturing on the nature of the church Bonhoeffer also conducted a seminar entitled "Is there a Christian ethic?" There he raised the matter of the orders of preservation.[20] This concept has been used polemically against the concept of orders of creation which can be considered as a theological concept without any relation to Jesus Christ at all.[21] But that is precisely what must not be done. In order to avoid this error, which some may have made unintentionally, Bonhoeffer counseled that orders of creation be substituted by orders of preservation. The difference between the two phrases is "that in the light of the concept of orders of creation, certain ordinances and features of the world were regarded as valuable, original, 'very good' in themselves, whereas the concept of orders of preservation meant that each feature was only a feature preserved by God, in grace and anger, in view of the revelation in Jesus Christ. Any order under the preservation of God should be directed toward Christ and only preserved for his sake" (NRS, 180).[22] The repudiation of the concept of orders of creation, which was under much discussion in those days and often hotly disputed, demonstrates that all of Bonhoeffer's theological arguments were grounded in christology, at least in the sense that there can be no theological argument independent of Christ.

At first Bonhoeffer had made use of concepts that had been derived from a real, historical dialectics; they had as yet no christological accent. In his *Habilitationsschrift* he went beyond this and attacked "ontological categories primarily derived from creation," a polemic he was to continue in his addresses given in the United States. Here he conceived of the problem more broadly: faith in God as the creator is dependent upon Christ, but the world is also preserved in orientation toward Christ. Through the "world of the new order of God" given in Christ, we are not only directed toward Christ but "we also understand the whole world order of fallen creation as directed solely towards Christ, towards the new creation" (NRS, 166).

Bonhoeffer's next course was entitled "Creation and Fall." Here, too, the presentation of the world in orientation toward Christ was affirmed.[23] The notion of the world being preserved for the sake of Christ recurs in Bonhoeffer's later work. God preserves for the sake of his Son who has redeemed us and who will come again.[24] Here the eschatological component of the concept of the orders of preservation is expressed. In *The Cost of Discipleship* the concept is broadened to include even those who follow Christ (CD, 244). There is a passage in *Life Together* which sums up the christological structure of the order of preservation: "The fellowship acknowledges that all earthly gifts are given to it only for Christ's sake, as this whole world is sustained [preserved] only for the sake of Jesus Christ, his word, and his message" (LT, 167).

What is significant for us in this context is that Bonhoeffer related the preservation of the world to Jesus Christ particularly at a time (the year was 1932) when there was so much interest in the idea. Even then a christological view of the world was emerging; creation was regarded historically as fallen creation, preserved after the fall only for the sake of and in orientation toward Christ. It is interesting that Bonhoeffer drew upon the New Testament texts, which speak of creation through Christ and for his sake, for the first time at Finkenwalde while dealing with creation in the preparation of *The Cost of Discipleship*.[25]

The Connection Between Middle [*Mitte*] and Boundary

The course on creation and fall followed the one on ecclesiology and preceded the christology course. It is the course on creation and fall, however, which shows how rapidly and consciously Bonhoeffer's theology became centered in christology. A decisive advance in his christological reflection took place in that course. Up until that time he had been concerned with the question of boundary, with real extrinsicality and that boundary had been Christ. Now, however, the concept of middle came to the fore; or, more precisely, the concept of the boundary, far from being rejected, became connected to the concept of the middle. *Creation and Fall* thus began with an idea which led to the assertion, made in the prison letters, that God is transcendent in the midst of our life. The course was to be "a theological exegesis of Genesis 1–3."[26] That Christ is the middle is to be seen from Bonhoeffer's comment about beginning and end: "The new is the real end of the old; Christ is the new. Christ is the end of the old. He is not the continuation of the old; he is not its aim, nor is he a consummation upon the line of the old; he is the end and therefore the new" (CF, 9). The question of the beginning led Bonhoeffer to raise the matter of the thinking that cannot have its beginning in itself. Our thinking is without a beginning; it is "the thinking of those who must go to Christ to know of God" (CF, 11–12). Therefore, it is "a circle. We think in a circle. . . . We exist in a circle. . . . The decisive point is that thinking takes this circle for the infinite and original reality only to entangle itself in a vicious circle" (CF, 12). Something that Bonhoeffer had said all along is repeated here: the vicious circle is nothing other than the cognitive form of the *cor curvum in se*. These thoughts about the beginning lead to the idea of the middle in which we live without knowing the beginning (CF, 12). It would appear that Bonhoeffer related those in the middle directly to God (CF, 21–22); but he also referred to Christ, asserting "that we can know about the human of the beginning only if we start from Christ" (CF, 36). We are those "who live in the middle through Christ" (CF, 37).

Christ is related to the material world (CF, 46) as he is to history, "but as those who only live and have a history through Christ, our imagination cannot help us to know about the beginning. We can only know about it from the new middle, from Christ" (CF, 57). Before that, however, Bonhoeffer had connected boundary and middle: "*the boundary of humans is in the middle of their existence*, not on the edge. The limit which we look for on the edge is the limit of their condition, . . . technology, . . . possibilities. The limit in the middle is the limit of their *reality*, of their *true existence*" (CF, 52).

It was Adam's sin, his fatal sin, to have taken that middle. Christ's cross cancels that sin; that is why it stands in the middle: "The stem of the cross becomes the staff of life, and in the midst of the world life is set up anew upon the cursed ground. In the middle of the world the spring of life wells up on the wood of the cross" (CF, 93). Here we find the concrete-historical context of the statement about the middle.

These comments of Bonhoeffer, by no means systematic, provide an interesting view of the growing relation of the two hitherto unrelated concepts of boundary or transcendence and center. There is for the first time a coming together of Christ and center, allowing the connection of center and boundary which is made possible and real through Christ.

The assertion in which center and boundary are said to be identical and in which no mention is made of Christ is valid only in relation to the state before the fall. But now, after the fall, Christ's cross is the center, once lost but now found again, of each human being as well as of humankind as a whole. This connection of boundary and center refers us directly to the christology lectures, to which we now turn.

THE LECTURES ON CHRISTOLOGY

Jesus Christ: Mediator [*Mittler*] and Center [*Mitte*]

These lectures were the last ones that Bonhoeffer gave. They may be regarded as the fruit of his theological endeavors up to that point and the foundation of his subsequent practical work and its diverse ramifications (DB, 164).

The first christological statement reads as follows: "Jesus is the Christ present as the Crucified and as the risen one" (C, 43). Before speaking of the historical Christ, Bonhoeffer first dealt with the present Christ, Christ *pro me,* in his historical and vicarious actuality.

Three interrelated aspects are of special significance in relation to the present Christ: history, sociality, and boundary, which is also the center.

History was much more for Bonhoeffer than the mere listing of facts (*Historie*). The latter is the search for and discovery of past events and is of peripheral importance as it offers no real *extra nos,* no transcendence or limit. Faith alone can bring that *extra nos.* "The historical nature of Jesus has two aspects, that of history and that of faith" (C, 74). Faith creates access to Jesus Christ. "Faith is where the search for certainty out of visible evidence is given up. There it is faith in God and not in the world" (C, 110).

For Bonhoeffer Jesus Christ is present and, as the one present, is historical. This presence is itself historical presence, presence "in the incognito of history, in the flesh" (C, 38). Christ is present "in his person" (C, 45); that is to say, he is totally human, even as the risen one, and he is God at the same time. *How* that can be is beyond answering unless one asks *who* he is (C, 45). The first christological statement, that Jesus is the Christ present as the crucified and the risen one, is qualified in the sense that "his presence [is to] be understood in space and time, here and now" (C, 43).

The presence of Christ in the "now" and, following from that, in the "here" is essential for the being of the church (C, 43). This leads us to the aspect of sociality. For something to be ecclesiological is for it to be dependent on the presence of Jesus Christ. This person, Jesus Christ, is present in the church as word, as sacrament, and as community (C, 48).

This threefold presence is itself historical presence, presence in history.

Bonhoeffer's discussion begins with the presence of Christ as word. The word of preaching "happens in history. . . . Its character as address requires the community" (C, 50). Having a connection to the community, the concrete word of preaching is a historical word. One must not overlook this close connection between history and sociality. How important sociality was for Bonhoeffer can be discerned from the fact that he regarded sociality as a constitutive factor of truth, especially of the truth of preaching. "Truth is . . . something that happens between two. Truth happens only in community" (C, 50).[27] Is not such an understanding more to the point than the one, commonly held, that contends that truth is *adaequatio rei et intellectus*? Besides being present in preaching, the latter comprising concrete word (C, 50), Christ "is present in the sphere of tangible nature" (C, 57), in the sacrament. But here, too, sociality is of constitutive importance: "In the sacrament, Christ is by our side as creature, among us, brother with brother" (C, 57). This applies so much more to the presence of Christ as community.[28]

The present Christ "stands *pro me*. He stands there in my place, where I should stand, but cannot. He stands on the boundary of my existence, beyond my existence, yet for me" (C, 60). Here we touch on the third aspect, that of boundary, which is also the center. "At this place stands Christ, [in the center] between me and me, the old and the new existence. Thus Christ is at one and the same time my boundary and my rediscovered center. He is the center, between 'I' and 'I,' and between 'I' and God" (C, 60). These remarks are followed by statements considered basic to Bonhoeffer's theology:

> It is the nature of the person of Christ to be in the center, both spatially and temporally. The one who is present in word, sacrament and community is in the center of human existence, of history, and of nature. It belongs to the structure of his person to be in the center. When we turn the question "Where?" back into the question "Who?" we get the answer. Christ is the mediator as the one who exists *pro me*. (C, 60)

All of Bonhoeffer's comments about history, sociality and center hinge on the presupposition that Christ is *pro me* as Christ. Toward the conclusion of the christology course Bonhoeffer introduced a significant variation of that assertion: "Of this man, we say: 'This is God for us'" (C, 103). What is significant here is that Bonhoeffer quietly changed the *pro me* into *pro nobis*, "for us" (C, 110), thereby laying the groundwork for his christological expression, "Christ—the one for others," which emerged in his final letters. The aspect of sociality comes to full expression only in that change; the vicarious nature of Jesus Christ is itself understood in social categories, for it is not only for me but also for us.

Bonhoeffer's central themes were by now securely anchored in christology and thus related to one another. Bonhoeffer had brought together many separate aspects of his theology: the problem of sociality which was present in *Sanctorum Communio* where it was related to the question of boundary, or transcendence; the characterization of Christ as boundary, as given in *Act and Being*; the connection of boundary and middle established in *Creation and Fall*; and the emphasis on the concrete command and concrete history in relation to Jesus Christ, as seen in the addresses given in Barcelona and the United States. He was now able to say that Jesus Christ is for me, for us, present in word, sacrament, and community as one who is historical, manifesting himself through that presence as the center [*Mitte*] of existence, history, and nature, and as mediator [*Mittler*], who stands in our place. Bringing these aspects together, the lectures speak of Christ as mediator and center, the one in and through the other. In mediating, Christ is the center; in being the center, Christ mediates.

THE CHRISTOLOGICAL CONCENTRATION OF THE MIDDLE PERIOD

The short summary of the christology course has probably shown sufficiently that these lectures were the completion as well as the climax of Bonhoeffer's efforts up to that time to make Jesus Christ the center of theology. We shall now give an overview of further developments in his christology.

THE ROAD TO *THE COST OF DISCIPLESHIP*

At first glance it seems that Bonhoeffer was fully occupied with the affairs of the church and, as a consequence, absorbed in ecclesiology. Indeed, he identified himself decisively with the church. During the Church Struggle he did not respond predominantly to the challenge of National Socialism, although he did respond to it. The discussion in which he fervently engaged himself was not one of politics, or even church politics, but rather it concerned the question about the only true church in Germany. For him the Church Struggle was not a matter of defending or recapturing lost positions; it was both less and more: the challenge, in the midst of extreme danger, just to find the form of the church that was true to its commission.

Before the Church Struggle broke out Bonhoeffer had hoped that there would be a "great reorganization of the churches" (GS I, 37). Believing that the empirical church could not be given up, he attempted with all his strength to reform it. That the situation was not promising became quite clear to him during a visit by Karl Barth to Berlin in 1932 (GS I, 30).[29] Bonhoeffer's attacks on the "violet church" and "Dibelius-theology," marked by their bitter irony, did not arise from an occasional, momentary anger.[30] When the Church Struggle began and the first opposition arose in the church, Bonhoeffer made it plain, prophetically, that a second phase of the struggle would follow the first in which a quite different dimension would have to be reached. He pointed to the Sermon on the Mount, relating to it the question of discipleship: "To follow Jesus Christ—what that is I would really like to know—is not explained exhaustively in our understanding of faith" (GS I, 40).[31]

According to Bonhoeffer, the meaning of the Church Struggle resided in the need that "*we* become converted, rather than Hitler" (GS I, 42–43). He saw the Church Struggle as a challenge to the church to become converted. After the hopeful beginnings made at Barmen and Dahlem the Confessing Church also fell hopelessly behind, for which reason Bonhoeffer paid no direct attention to it during the last period of his life.[32] Yet his theology then was not hostile to the church and was certainly not divorced from it; it was a church theology of a church in and for a world come of age. "The church is the church only when it exists for others" (LPP, 382). It is especially important for our present discussion to note that it is a mistake to suggest that Bonhoeffer reverted to the ecclesiology of his early period in his endeavors on behalf of the church during the Church Struggle.[33] Instead it is the christological intensification of his position in *Sanctorum Communio* that one perceives here. One has to be quite careful when speaking of the extension of earlier ecclesiological views in the context of the henceforth consistently maintained christology.

The sermons Bonhoeffer preached in London show in some measure that the christological orientation had gained momentum.[34] The christocentric emphasis is more apparent, however, in the sermons and Bible studies from Finkenwalde.[35] His second homiletics of Finkenwalde is based on christology.[36] In the same manner several important studies from the Church Struggle period are grounded in christology.[37] Finally, the text of Bonhoeffer's sermon about mystery, which was used above as the leitmotif at the beginning of this study, speaks of Jesus Christ as the unrecognized mystery of God in the world, thus conceiving of mystery in terms of christology (GS V, 518).

This christological emphasis does not suggest that Bonhoeffer made Jesus Christ the means for the defense of the church, that he used christology in order to consolidate his ecclesiology. Throughout the Church Struggle he was not interested in the church as an end in itself (GS II, 538), but in the concrete message which it must proclaim to the whole world, the message based on and resulting from the incarnation of God. Bonhoeffer's theme is the obedient hearing of the Sermon on the Mount, not the salvation of the church. In that context alone did he concern himself with the church because he saw it in grave danger.

Because of its weak premise, that is to say, because it had established a reciprocal arrangement with the world in the manner in which Cultural Protestantism had done, the church was being overpowered by a counter-church. In order to help the church overcome this threat and find its real self again, Bonhoeffer turned again and again to the Sermon on the Mount, in which discipleship of Christ became concrete for him. He was convinced that there would have to be great faith, much prayer, and suffering in order that God would again side with the church and that the church would discover how little it had followed the Sermon on the Mount (NRS, 147). Bonhoeffer was convinced that "the whole issue will come to a head in relation to the Sermon on the Mount" (GS I, 40).[38] He was certain that clarity and integrity would come to him only at that time when he "really starts taking the Sermon on the Mount seriously" (GS III, 25).[39]

It was therefore no accident that the Sermon on the Mount was the chief topic of *The Cost of Discipleship*. Bonhoeffer had been interested in it for a long time.[40] Even after completing the book and realizing that it was, to some extent, one-sided, Bonhoeffer thought that it dealt with what he had intended (LPP, 157, 369). The words he wrote on the occasion of the founding of the Community of Brethren in 1935 surely apply also to him: "The aim is not the seclusion of a monastery, but a place of the deepest concentration for service outside" (WF, 31).

THE CHRISTOLOGY OF *THE COST OF DISCIPLESHIP*

This book is of no little significance for the study of Bonhoeffer's christology. Not much attention has been paid to this fact; indeed, the book is regarded much more as a contribution to his ecclesiology. The central concern of the work is determined by christology; at its center is the Sermon on the Mount, in relation to which the reality of discipleship is determined. Bonhoeffer wanted to say something concrete in a very concrete situation and it is with that endeavor in mind that *The Cost of Discipleship* can be understood. Given that desire for concreteness it is not surprising that there is this christological basis. The work opens with the question: "What is his [Jesus'] will for us today?" (CD, 29). The concreteness with which Bonhoeffer was concerned must not be confused with the actuality of day-to-day matters, as he stated emphatically. The issue, in these times of "revival of church life" (!), is much more lofty: it is "Jesus himself" (CD, 29).[41]

"Costly grace," the phrase which caused much sensation, is itself christologically conceived. It is "the Incarnation of God" (CD, 37). "Cheap grace," the opposite of costly grace, is "grace without Jesus Christ, living and incarnate" (CD, 36). Grace, therefore, is the incarnation of Jesus Christ and the offer of discipleship; as such, grace is personal and must be interpreted in that light.

The Cancellation of Immediacy [*Unmittelbarkeit*] by the Mediator [*Mittler*]

Discipleship is contingent upon Christ's call, but Christ's call is without any mediation. When Christ calls, only he and his call are present without any mediation. Doctrine, principle, system, and reflection do not mediate (CD, 35). "The disciple always looks only to his master, never to Christ *and* the world. He does not enter upon such reflections at all but follows, in everything, after Christ alone" (CD, 154).[42] That eliminates any other mediation, such that there exists no other immediacy, no other directness of contact, except that with Christ. Immediacy is a lie; "to think otherwise is to deceive ourselves" (CD, 86). "Christ has delivered them [the people] from immediacy with the world, and brought them into immediacy with himself" (CD, 84). Nowhere else in Bonhoeffer's work is Christ referred to as a mediator with such force. It follows positively from this mediatorship that Christ "*is the Mediator, not only between God and people, but between people themselves, between them and reality. Since the world was created through him and unto him (John 1:3; 1 Cor. 8:6; Heb. 1:2), he is the sole Mediator in the world. Since his coming people have no immediate relationship of their own any more to anything, neither to God nor to the world; Christ wants to be the mediator*" (CD, 85). This, we believe, is the heart of *The Cost of Discipleship*. First, mediation between God and people is affirmed. How exclusive that mediation was in Bonhoeffer's view is shown by his statement that there is not even direct prayer to God: "Not even prayer affords direct access to the Father. Only through Jesus Christ can we find the Father in prayer. . . . He is the one and only Mediator of our prayers" (CD, 145). Second, mediation between people is affirmed; this will be made more explicit later.

Third, there is mediation between people and the world. "For the disciples the only 'God-given realities' are those they receive from Christ" (CD, 87). Here Bonhoeffer's repudiation of orders of creation is grounded in discipleship. It is significant that in this book Bonhoeffer for the first time made use of New Testament passages dealing with a christological view of creation, thereby affirming that the world was not only preserved after the fall for the sake of and in orientation toward Christ, but was also created through and in direction toward him. From "the beginning, [Christ] was the mediator of creation" (CD, 212). Bonhoeffer did not remove the christological statements about creation from their concrete relation with the incarnation; "by virtue of his incarnation, [Christ] has come between me and the facts and conditions of the world. I can no longer turn back. He is in the center. By calling us he has cut us off from all immediacy with those facts and conditions. He wants to be the medium; through him alone all things shall come to pass" (CD, 85).

Christ is the center of existence, of history, and of nature; this affirmation of the christology course is reiterated in *The Cost of Discipleship*. Jesus Christ, it says there, is the center to whom, alone, there is immediacy. This immediacy to him is the sole mediation to God, the neighbor, and the world which was created through and in orientation toward him alone and preserved for his sake.

Bonhoeffer was quite aware that this repudiation of any other mediation was an affront to natural reason. He saw it as "a stumbling block for natural reason; it makes frantic efforts to pry this hard sequence apart, to interpose something, to explain the matter. By hook or by crook something must be found that would become the intermediary, something psychological or historical" (CD, 48). But our natural reason and this desire of ours to find that "something" remains unfulfilled; it is not possible any more to account for the call to discipleship and the response to it. "The absolute, direct, and unaccountable authority of Jesus" alone accounts for that order (CD, 48). The mediatorship of Jesus Christ, the reality of which cannot be established by independent argument, is based on the incarnation of the Son of God, who alone calls us to follow him (CD, 49).

The Deputyship of Christ

An understanding of the increasing intensification of Bonhoeffer's stress on Jesus Christ as center and mediator requires a close look at the notion of deputyship and, arising from it, the mediation between neighbors. Through this mediation alone does community come about. "Between father and son, husband and wife, the individual and the nation, stands Christ the mediator, whether they are able to recognize him or not. We cannot establish direct contact with our neighbors except through him, through his word, and through our following him" (CD, 86). Because Jesus Christ is the sole mediator he alone also establishes the new community (CD, 90). That is why the love of God and the love of the neighbor cannot be separated. "The Incarnation is the ultimate reason why the service of God cannot be divorced from the service of the neighbor" (CD, 117). The community established by Christ is the community of those who have obeyed his call; since he is human and also humankind at one and the same time he always does what he does as himself and for the neighbor. "He therefore suffers vicariously for the world" (CD, 81).

"Christ is 'for us,' not only in word and in his attitude toward us, but in his bodily life" (CD, 216). The consequence of the deputyship of Christ is that we become his deputies: "We do vicariously for [him] what [he] cannot do for [himself]" (CD, 134; cf. CD, 136). We continue his suffering in this world and face opposition in his stead. This is where Bonhoeffer spoke of martyrdom: it is not self-imposed (CD, 50), it is not self-sought (CD, 192); to be a martyr only comes from having obediently followed Christ even to death (CD, 273).

Bonhoeffer had already raised the matter of deputyship in *Sanctorum Communio*, as well as in his courses on the nature of the church and on christology. In *The Cost of Discipleship* deputyship again became a major concern. This book is a station on the road to Bonhoeffer's *Ethics*, because of the exploration of this important concept.

When Bonhoeffer spoke of the church in *The Cost of Discipleship* he did so in a christocentric context. The church is not a proper and independent medium between Christ and us which Christ grants to us; it is the community of those who have their center and mediator in Christ. That is why the statements about the church in the second part of *The Cost of Discipleship* are neither a distortion, caused by inadmissible sacramentalizing, nor a withdrawing of the statements made in the first part,[43] even though not all of the individual assertions are convincing in themselves. The sacramental nature of the church is rather the consequence of the incarnation: "Because of the presence of the body of Christ alone there are sacraments" (CD, 214).

In this work Bonhoeffer spoke about the church as church, especially in the context of the relationship of the disciples to the world. Eventually he saw the need to correct some of the things he had said. But it was the christocentrism of this work which became the center and foundation upon which his subsequent thoughts about the world were to rest. The ecclesiological affirmation of *The Cost of Discipleship* must be placed into the framework of this christocentrism.

"The Image of Christ"

The remarkable conclusion of this book, "The Image of Christ," is symbolic of the orientation toward Christ. At the center of attention was the call which the hearer would obey with deeds, and was the mutual correlation of hearing and obeying. It is surprising, therefore, that at the end of the book there should be language about image, about seeing and unmediated contemplation:

> The image of Jesus Christ, which his disciples have always before their eyes and in the light of which all other images are screened from their sight, penetrates into the depths of their being, fills them, reshapes them, so that they come to be more and more like their Master. The image of Jesus Christ impresses itself in daily communion on the image of the disciple. The disciple cannot contemplate the image of the Son in cold detachment; this image radiates transforming power. If we surrender ourselves to Jesus Christ, we cannot help bearing his image ourselves. We become the sons of God, we stand side by side with Christ, the unseen brother in the same form, bearing the image of God. (CD, 269).

God responds to our opposition to him in sin by restoring his image in us; he sets his image in Christ against the image of "the god [we] have invented for [ourselves]" (CD, 270), the image of which is the falsification of the image God had intended. Because we cannot give ourselves what we have lost, God himself has become the image which we were meant to be: "As we can no longer be like the image of God, God must become like the image of us" (CD, 270). By laying aside his divine form, the Son of God comes in the form of a servant. Jesus Christ, the one rejected and forsaken, is "God in the form of humans . . . , [the] human being in the new image of God" (CD, 271). But the disciples "must first be conformed to the image of the Suffering Servant who was obedient to the death [on] the cross" (CD, 272) in order that they may also bear the image of his glory. These sentences foreshadow the passages in *Ethics* in which Bonhoeffer dealt with our being conformed to him who was crucified and raised from the dead.

The disciple, in other words, not only hears but also sees. "The disciple looks solely at him whom he follows" (CD, 275). To be a disciple of Jesus Christ, which is accomplished by hearing and seeing, means to be directed toward God. Bonhoeffer asserts this at the very end of the book, saying that the disciple "has been called to be the 'imitator of God.' The follower of Jesus is the imitator of God. 'Be ye therefore imitators of God, as beloved children' (Eph. 5.1.)" (CD, 275). Discipleship leads to God, its true end, but only with and through Christ, who is the sole center and mediator, does the disciple reach God.

The further development of Bonhoeffer's christology in *The Cost of Discipleship* is to be seen in the understanding of the deputyship of Christ and the exclusive immediacy to him.

In speaking of Christ as mediator who comes to us from outside, *extra nos*, and who alone is of immediacy to us, *Life Together* stays within the framework of *The Cost of Discipleship* (LT, 23, 54). In Christ, "God's presence and help have been demonstrated for us," so that now "we are the reverent listeners and participants in God's action in the sacred story, the history of the Christ on earth" (LT, 54).

THE RELATION TO THE WORLD IN BONHOEFFER'S LATE CHRISTOLOGY

THE TRANSITION TO *ETHICS*

Soon after the completion of *Life Together* a new phase in Bonhoeffer's thinking began, not so much in relation to his views of christology, strictly speaking, as to the assertions that he made about the world, which were born out of christology.

There is a glimpse into this new phase in a letter which is of much importance to our considerations. On 22 January 1939, Bonhoeffer wrote to Theodor Litt, asserting that the relation of Christians to the world is a positive one, and explicitly grounding that relation in Jesus Christ. Indicating what is "the ultimate source of the Christian faith for its relation to the world," Bonhoeffer cited the name of Jesus Christ.[44] What is important for our study of Bonhoeffer is that it is the name of Jesus Christ which is the source of the Christian's relation to the world and not God and his command of creation.

Bonhoeffer further explicated his point by stating that our task to serve this world cannot have human guilt for its basis because it could easily become the very basis for the refusal to serve this world. The fact of God's incarnation alone is the basis of that task; solely within it are we to seek the basis for a positive relation to the world and for our service.

> Christians affirm that "the unconditional is indeed enclosed in the conditional" . . . that in sovereign freedom of grace the "otherworldly" has entered into the "this worldly." For that reason, the believer is not divided but discovers God and the human in one, in that one place here in this world. And that is also why from now on the love of God and the love of neighbor are inseparably bound one to the other. (GS III, 32)

To deny the world is to become culpable, since God became human. Weakness is therefore the mask, or, better, the form, of God's strength in the world. Because God lets himself be found on the cross alone "we cannot rid ourselves of human beings and the world" (GS III, 32). For Bonhoeffer, all Protestant understanding of history is rooted in this conviction, and in it resides its clarity.

There is a "Christian understanding of the world" in and through Jesus Christ;[45] it is provided clearly and unambiguously through him. Through Jesus Christ, Christians have been turned toward the world even though they know precisely, because God is present in Jesus Christ, that the world is ending.

The recourse to Jesus Christ and his cross permits Bonhoeffer to work out a comprehensive Christian understanding of the world. Christology is the bridge, therefore, which connects the theological assertions of *The Cost of Discipleship* and the other studies of that time with *Ethics*.[46] This is affirmed in Bonhoeffer's circular letter for Christmas 1939, from which the comment about mystery prefacing our methodological reflections on Bonhoeffer's theology was taken. The remark is christologically phrased: "'God revealed in the flesh,' the God-man Jesus Christ, [that] is the holy mystery" (TP, 28; cf. TP, 31–32). His reference to Chalcedon is no accident; in "the person of Christ . . . God and humanity [are] united, 'without confusion, without change, without division, without separation,' as the Chalcedonian definition put it in a supreme paradox, and at the same time in a most reverent preservation of the mystery of the person of the Mediator" (TP, 28).[47] What matters to us here is that Jesus Christ is also called mediator in this context. Bonhoeffer gives emphasis to the point by quoting a statement by Friedrich Oetinger which is characteristic of Bonhoeffer's theology itself: "The end of the ways of God is bodiliness" (TP, 33).[48] This statement makes sense only in view of the existence of Jesus Christ, who is the mystery of God in history.

THE CHRISTOLOGY OF *ETHICS*

The particular significance of *Ethics* does not lie only in the fact that it contains Bonhoeffer's last extensive theological studies but also in the realization that he gave it his special attention. He regarded it as something like a testament: "I sometimes feel as if my life were more or less over, and as if all I had to do now were to finish my *Ethics*" (LPP, 163). Analysis is difficult since only fragments of it are extant, all of which were written intermittently during Bonhoeffer's work in the conspiracy against Hitler. This led to the view that *Ethics* represents the beginning of a new phase in his theology.[49]

In the pages of this work essential ideas of Bonhoeffer's earlier theology are taken up and developed further. Christology, too, is continuously sharpened. For that reason, *Ethics* provides important evidence for our contention that there is continuity in the structure and central ideas of Bonhoeffer's theology and that all of these ideas are increasingly grounded in christology.

Connecting Links to Earlier Statements on Ethics and Christology

Before we look at the christology of *Ethics,* the continuity of Bonhoeffer's theology is to be sketched in terms of the course of the question of ethics as raised by him. Similarly, the christological concentration is to be traced in terms of the relation between the question of ethics and christology. As early as *Sanctorum Communio* Bonhoeffer was interested in ethics. This may be seen in his concern with ethical transcendence, in which the ethical turn of his theology is only too apparent.[50] After that time Bonhoeffer continued to pursue the problem of ethics. His address in Barcelona is a case in point. We have already mentioned that ethics and christology stand side by side only there, although Bonhoeffer did say that "the way of love in Christ, the way of the cross" (NRS, 41) was the only way of God to people. Later, however, he said, contrary to the formulations in *The Cost of Discipleship,* that "Jesus places people immediately [sic] under God" (NRS, 43). The corresponding immediacy is stated in Bonhoeffer's summation of "the significance of all Jesus' ethical commandments": "You stand before the face of God, God's grace rules over you; you are at the disposal of others in the world and for them you must act and work. So be mindful in your actions that you are acting under God's eyes" (NRS, 42-43). The Christian's relation to God and the world is placed one next to the other and without mediation.

Ethics continued to be a central concern for Bonhoeffer. It was important to him, for example, to touch on "the problems of ethics" during his first visit with Karl Barth (NRS, 121). Bonhoeffer's reflections on the concreteness of the command are part of ethics.[51] But here christology is already the manifest foundation for ethics; the seminar Bonhoeffer conducted in the summer of 1932 makes that quite plain. The question of the orders of preservation was drawn into ethics and given a christological basis. The question of the Sermon on the Mount, which had raised itself for Bonhoeffer already in Barcelona and which had assumed sharp contours in 1932, links his thoughts to *The Cost of Discipleship* because it is a question about a Christian ethics, and an ethics "without content." In that sense *The Cost of Discipleship* itself is an ethics. Discipleship is no ethical blueprint, no general wisdom about life and the world; it is rather a direct following after Jesus Christ. The connection established between christology and ethics in the treatment of the Sermon on the Mount in *The Cost of Discipleship* makes that book a connecting link with *Ethics*.

It can be shown that *Ethics* not only occupies a central place in Bonhoeffer's theology as a whole, but that it also embraces important ideas from his earlier work and reflects upon them anew.

In order to substantiate that claim, let us look at the question of "the knowledge of good and evil." Bonhoeffer used it to open the first of the fragments which comprise *Ethics*. The same issue also arose in *The Cost of Discipleship*,[52] and already before that in *Creation and Fall*; the question of the knowledge of good and evil was seen as a sign of the disunion caused by sin and related to shame and conscience.[53] In both instances Jesus Christ is mentioned; he heals the disunion insofar as the knowledge of good and evil becomes knowledge of Christ as the origin of reconciliation (E, 33; CF, 53-57). The statement, "The knowledge of Jesus is entirely transformed into action, without any reflection upon one's self" (E, 34-35), reiterates, without actually using the specific terminology, the distinction between *actus directus* and *actus reflectus* in *The Cost of Discipleship* and *Act and Being*. The notion of conformity also takes up earlier views.[54]

The subject of "deputyship" demonstrates very usefully the connection with the earlier work of Bonhoeffer. Since God became human in Jesus Christ and since humankind was accepted by God in the incarnation, "there is no relation to people without a relation to God, and no relation to God without a relation to people, and it is only our relation to Jesus Christ which provides the basis for our relation to people and to

God" (E, 221; cf. 336–37). The encounter with the neighbor is mediated through Jesus Christ; this earlier assertion is repeated again in this work.[55] Given that mediation, deputyship is one of the central characteristics of the life made possible by Jesus Christ. "In view of the incarnation of God, to live as a human being before God can mean only to exist not for oneself but for God and for other human beings" (E, 297). It is the task of the community, the church, to make this deputyship its own (E, 300–301, 83). Founded on Jesus Christ, the deputyship of the community is fulfilled in two ways. The community stands at the place where the world should stand:

> To this extent it serves as deputy for the world and exists for the sake of the world. On the other hand, the world achieves its own fulfillment at the point at which the congregation stands. The congregation is the 'new creation,' the 'new creature,' the goal of the ways of God on earth. The congregation stands in this twofold relation of deputyship entirely in the fellowship and disciplehood of its Lord, who was Christ precisely in this, that he existed not for his own sake but wholly for the sake of the world. (E, 301)

Because of Christ's deputyship, humankind receives new community in the incarnation. The "disunion with God, with people, with things, and with oneself" (E 20), which resulted from sin, is healed. The church is the place where this healing occurs. This takes up the aspect of sociality: the new humanity is constituted in Christ who at one and the same time is human being and humanity (E, 225). In Christ, therefore, the isolation of the (sinful) human being is overcome, since both God and our neighbor encounter us in him.[56]

Strictest Concentration on Jesus Christ

It is in the concentration on Jesus Christ that the continuity of Bonhoeffer's theology is particularly apparent. Bonhoeffer sought to concentrate all ideas and statements on Jesus Christ in the strictest possible manner without reducing this name to a mere abstract concept. "This name must always be understood in the full concrete significance of historical reality" (E, 51). In this concentration "our only criterion is the living Christ himself" (E, 42). The basic note of the specific christology of *Ethics* is found in this statement: "The more exclusively we acknowledge and confess Christ as our Lord, the more fully the wide range of his dominion will be disclosed to us" (E, 58).

Concentration on Jesus Christ can be found in all parts of *Ethics*. Next to the references chosen from the first fragment we will deal paradigmatically with two passages which are designed in a particularly christological fashion. The foundation of the subject of "ethics as formation" is Jesus Christ: "Whoever sees Jesus Christ does indeed see God and the world in one" (E, 70). Bonhoeffer developed the assertion, "Ecce homo!—Behold the man!" (E, 70), in terms of the following exclamations: "Behold the God who has become a human being" (E, 71); "Behold the human being judged by God" (E, 75); and, "Behold the human being who has been taken to Himself by God, sentenced and executed and awakened by God to a new life. Behold the Risen one" (E, 78). Humans obtain the form which is essentially proper to them only from the form of Jesus Christ (E, 82).

In the final approach of *Ethics* Bonhoeffer referred to Jesus Christ with emphasis and in a manner which can in no way be called stereotypical. Jesus Christ is *"the eternal Son with the Father for all eternity,"* the mediator of creation (E, 296). He is also *"the crucified Reconciler"* (E, 297) whose cross makes plain that the whole world has become godless by its rejection of Jesus Christ (E, 297). But the cross is also "the setting free for life before God in the midst of a godless world" (E, 297), for through Jesus Christ alone does the world become "a world which in its godlessness is reconciled with God" (E, 298). Finally, Jesus Christ is *"the risen and exalted Lord,"* the living Lord (E, 298).

Against the background of the basic christological conception of the individual sections of *Ethics*, one has to interpret the statements which we cited at the beginning of Part Two. "In Jesus Christ the reality of God entered into the reality of this world," so that "henceforward one can speak neither of God nor of the world without speaking of Jesus Christ" (E, 194). One cannot leave Jesus Christ aside since in him God and the world are bound together, God and the world are reconciled. The place where God and the reality of the world can be seen together without the danger of falsely mixing them is "in the midst of history" (E, 69, 198). Bonhoeffer maintained that Christ is the mediator of creation (E, 337), for which reason there is no more immediacy to God. But in *Ethics* Christ is not perceived exclusively as the mediator of creation but also as the mediator of reconciliation to the world which is preserved in orientation toward him. The circular structure of mediatorship is apparent: it is mediation of creation and reconciliation. "The figure of the Reconciler, of the God-Man Jesus Christ, comes between God and the world and fills the center of all history. In this figure the secret of the world is laid bare, and in this figure there is revealed the secret of God" (E, 70). The revelation of God and the world in Jesus Christ must not be torn apart again, for it has its reality in the historical oneness of God and the world which became event in Jesus Christ. In him, the mediator and the center, God and the world are *one* reality, namely, God's reality in the reality of the world. "There are not two realities, but only one reality, and that is the reality of God, which has become manifest in Christ in the reality of the world. Sharing in Christ we stand at once in both the reality of God and the reality of the world" (E, 197).[57] The correlates which are bound to each other and mediated through Christ are not God and the church, but God and the world; "It is only in the midst of the world that Christ is Christ" (E, 206). The consequence for Christianity of Christ's being the center of and for the world is that it "is not now something which lies beyond the human element," but "requires to be in the midst of the human element" (E, 296–97). Christian faith asserts that the "reality of God has manifested and revealed itself in the midst of the real world" (E, 194). Again and again Bonhoeffer emphasized in *Ethics* that Christ is the middle between God and the world, found in the midst of the world. Therefore, Jesus Christ has a very special significance, as we shall see later when we deal with our specific subject, the problem of the world.[58] Only then will the full meaning of the christology of *Ethics* become clear.

The Subject of History

Several of the subjects in *Ethics* should be treated explicitly. History is one such topic: it is frequently discussed and is of much importance, but it also has a special relation to christology.

In the context of the problem of concreteness, Bonhoeffer stated that Jesus Christ is present "here and now" (E, 85), that is to say, in history and in the world. Bonhoeffer was careful to add, in most places, a temporal qualification such as "henceforward" (E, 194) or "now" (E, 219) to those crucial statements which stress the relation of God and world through Jesus Christ. All of these qualifications testify to the historical dimension in the statements about the world. Access to God and the world is mediated through Jesus Christ alone, and therefore it is historical. Incarnation and cross do not abolish history but in fact truly constitute it; in Jesus Christ "history becomes a serious matter without being canonized. . . . History does not become a transient vehicle, but through the life and death of Jesus Christ it does for the first time become truly temporal. It is precisely in its temporality that it is history with God's consent" (E, 89).

Every ethical endeavor and statement is, therefore, a historical endeavor and statement (E, 214). But history is the only way to God because God first came to people. After his address on christology in Barcelona, Bonhoeffer continued to stress that this movement was the primary one. "The way of Jesus Christ, . . . leads not from the world to God but from God to the world" (E, 356).

If the reality of the world became truly reality by being accepted by Jesus Christ, it follows that reality is personal, that "*reality* is first and last not lifeless, but . . . is the real one, the incarnate God" (E, 228).

Summing up, one can state with Bonhoeffer that the problem of Christian ethics is "the relation of reality and realization, past and present, history and event (faith), or, to replace the equivocal concept by the unambiguous name, the relation of Jesus Christ and the Holy Spirit" (E, 190).

In light of the foregoing it is difficult to see how Bonhoeffer can be said to have no sensibility for history and, related to that, for eschatology.[59] A brief glance at the whole of Bonhoeffer's work is necessary in order to reject that charge while providing a summary of his understanding of history.

In a seminar given at university Bonhoeffer had already spoken of God as the one who had entered into history, thereby rendering himself incognito.[60] In other words, Bonhoeffer maintained that history is marked by that incognito which is characteristic of it alone.[61] In *Sanctorum Communio* Bonhoeffer reflected on history and eschatology. Then in Barcelona he related christology to the subject of history. In his lectures on christology Bonhoeffer called Christ the center of history. The subject of history and eschatology can be traced from *Act and Being*, to the addresses given in the United States, to Bonhoeffer's academic courses. In the middle period of Bonhoeffer's work this subject is less visible, only to come very much to the fore again in *Ethics*.

If one were to maintain that, in his concern for concreteness in the commandment, Bonhoeffer neglected history and the future while remaining preoccupied with the here and now, one would only have to look again at his concurrent concern for the orders of preservation—they are defined eschatologically. The world is preserved after the Fall in orientation toward Christ who will come again.[62]

The eschatological aspect of Bonhoeffer's thinking is clearly depicted throughout his entire work and not only in the final chapters of *Sanctorum Communio* and *Act and Being*.

Christians "understand their present being as determined from two sides. First and decisively by their future, which is Christ alone, but, second, by their past, which is Adam, and which must ever be surrounded in the death of Christ" (NRS, 67).[63] God, the *concretissimum* in the present, is also not depicted in language which is static and bound to the now. In fact, Bonhoeffer stated in this context what he meant by "the present": "The fact that something is 'present toward' us means that the present *is defined from without* and not from within. . . . The present is primarily defined not by the past, but by the future, and this future is Christ, it is the Holy Ghost" (NRS, 311).[64]

In the prison letters too there are clear signs of Bonhoeffer's preoccupation with history and eschatology. The latter was not in the forefront of his reflections at that time because he was especially concerned with the future of the world after the impending catastrophe. To have busied oneself with an (ahistorical) eschatology would have amounted to flight from the world and apocalypticism.[65] He once remarked that the younger generation of blacks in the United States is turning its back on the faith of the older generation because, "with its strong eschatological orientation, [it] seems to them to be a hindrance to the progress of their race and their rights" (NRS, 112).⁶⁶ Such a flight from thisworldliness, from one's present, Bonhoeffer denied himself, knowing it would lead merely to an imaginary beyond.

JESUS CHRIST IN *LETTERS AND PAPERS FROM PRISON*

Our historical survey of Bonhoeffer's christology is to be brought to a close with a resume of his statements about Jesus Christ in his prison letters, keeping in mind that he perceived his incarceration as something "for the cause of Christ" (LPP, 129).

The Question of God

Given the circumstances, it is understandable that the question, "Who is God?" (LPP, 381), is very urgent.⁶⁷ Bonhoeffer regarded his fate as God-given, since, quite naturally, "God still reigns" (LPP, 384). It was Bonhoeffer's prayer that "God in his mercy lead us through these times; but above all, . . . to himself" (LPP, 370). Bonhoeffer was sure that "through every event, however untoward, there is access to God" (LPP, 167). Therefore, "we ought . . . to love . . . God in our *lives*" (LPP, 168), not on the other side of our lives, for "God is in the facts themselves" (LPP, 191). God no longer meets us "as 'Thou,' but also 'disguised' in the 'It,'" so that the question becomes, "How are we to find the 'Thou' in this 'It' (i.e. fate)?" (LPP, 217). Of course, the events of this world or the world itself are not God himself, nor is God satisfied when we have found him in our lives. Instead the world is in God's hands: "We realize more clearly than formerly that the world lies under the wrath and grace of God" (LPP, 297).

Bonhoeffer tried to let God be seen as the transcendent one in the total range of thisworldliness and to understand his transcendence as one which is not determined by us and our insights. That is why he was opposed to all attempts to work God into the process of the world, and to such concepts as God "the working hypothesis" (LPP, 325, 360, 381), "the stop-gap" (LPP, 311, 312, 381)⁶⁸ and *deus ex machina* (LPP, 282, 341, 361).⁶⁹ Bonhoeffer objected to every concept of God which used God to deny the limits of our knowledge by locating God in the gaps and beyond the limits of our current insight, a conception which is akin to a metaphysical *horror vacui*, for, with every advance of knowledge, "God is being pushed back . . . , and is therefore continually in retreat" (LPP, 311).⁷⁰

Bonhoeffer was equally opposed to the God of "tutelage" (LPP, 326), who is just as much a deity invented by humans. A concept of God which portrays God as the one who redresses our being under tutelage triumphs by once again constricting us. Consequently such a concept fails to achieve its aim; our weakness is not overcome.

To define transcendence as that which lies beyond our powers of insight (LPP, 341), or "on the far side drawn by the boundary of death" (LPP, 336), is to lose all real transcendence. That also holds true for the traditional doctrine of God which speaks of God as "the Almighty," etc. In his "Outline for a Book" Bonhoeffer wrote: "Who is God? Not in the first place an abstract belief in God, in his omnipotence etc. That is not a genuine experience of God, but a partial extension of the world" (LPP, 381).

"I should like to speak of God not on the boundaries but at the center, not in weaknesses but in strength; and therefore not in death and guilt but in our life and goodness. . . . The transcendence of epistemological theory has nothing to do with the transcendence of God. God is beyond in the midst of our life" (LPP, 282; cf. LPP, 312, 341, 344–45). Bonhoeffer made the same point in the formulation, God "must be recognized at the center of life" (LPP, 312), although he could not accept that this was a statement in strictly cognitive terms. This becomes evident in the development of the idea in which Bonhoeffer cited God's revelation in Jesus Christ as the reason why we recognize God in the midst of life: "He [Jesus Christ] is the center of life" (LPP, 282). And we know from Christ what transcendence is, for he "takes hold of us at the center of our lives" (LPP, 337). Within the context of the question of God as raised in the prison letters, Jesus Christ is again said to be the center, the center of our lives; in the center of life alone is God to be recognized.

For Bonhoeffer God is always "God in Jesus Christ." The most important text for that claim is the following:

> And we cannot be honest unless we recognize that we have to live in this world *etsi deus non daretur*. And this is just what we do recognize—before God! God himself compels us to recognize it. So our coming of age leads us to a true recognition of our situation before God. God would have us know that we must live as people who manage our lives without him. The God who is with us is the God who forsakes us (Mark 15.34). The God who lets us live in the world without the working hypothesis of God is the God before whom we stand continually. Before God and with God we live without God. God lets himself be pushed out of the world onto the cross. He is weak and powerless in the world, and that is precisely the way, the only way, in which he is with us and helps us. But Matt. 8.17 makes it quite clear that Christ helps us, not by virtue of his omnipotence, but by virtue of his weakness and suffering. (LPP, 360–61).

This is testimony to the God of whom Bonhoeffer wanted to give testimony, God in Jesus Christ who is not the God of religion but "the God of the Bible" (LPP, 361). What is significant is that we must live in this world *etsi deus non daretur*, "even if there were no God" (LPP, 359). What must not be overlooked is that Bonhoeffer made use of a formulation in the conjunctive; it occurred first in the discussion of Hugo Grotius's teaching on natural law and was used again, but in order to generalize a point. To change the conjunctive into the indicative is to distort the statements of Bonhoeffer![71]

One of the last of the extant letters shows that Bonhoeffer derived true knowledge of God from the earthly Jesus, the historical Jesus Christ. Bonhoeffer cited the scriptural text 2 Cor. 1:20, "He is the 'Yes' pronounced upon God's promises, every one of them. That is why, when we give glory to God, it is through Christ Jesus that we say 'Amen'" (N.E.B.), and he continued by saying that

> the key to everything is the "in him." All that we may rightly expect from God, and ask him for, is to be found in Jesus Christ. The God of Jesus Christ has nothing to do with what God, as we imagine him, could do and ought to do. . . . But the truth is that if this earth was good enough for the man Jesus Christ, if such a man as Jesus lived, then, and only then, has life a meaning for us. (LPP, 391)

The life and death of Jesus mediates to us the knowledge of the God of Jesus Christ as opposed to the God of our imagination. "In Jesus God has said 'Yes' and 'Amen'" to our life, to us, and that "is the firm ground on which we stand" (LPP, 391). It is of profound meaning for the earth that it bore the man Jesus Christ.

It is through Jesus alone, therefore, that we may live at one and the same time with God, before God, and in this world without God. In Jesus the invisibility of God which wears us down, and the isolated otherworldliness which is identical with it, are not changed into clear apperception and thisworldliness, for that would be tantamount to removing the mystery. Instead, they are encompassed by the image, which the disciples behold, and by the proximity in which alone transcendence is given. This can be the only meaning of the statement "The beyond is not what is infinitely remote, but what is nearest at hand" (LPP, 376).

The "Being-for-Others" of Jesus

What has been said so far shows that Bonhoeffer certainly did not intend to do away with faith in God as the transcendent one, but that he attempted, instead, to interpret his transcendence as closeness. This is confirmed by the specific development of christology in the prison letters which begins with the question of "what Christianity really is, or indeed who Christ really is, for us today" (LPP, 279). Bonhoeffer wanted to show that "Christ is no longer an object of religion, but something quite different, really the Lord of the world" (LPP, 281). In light of the fact that Bonhoeffer interlaced his statements about Jesus Christ with statements about the world, it is clear that these two subjects cannot be separated any more.

"Incarnation, crucifixion, and resurrection of Jesus Christ" (LPP, 286, 381) are inseparable, in Bonhoeffer's view; that is very important for christology. Only after having given up every attempt to isolate a theology of the cross from a theology of glory is it legitimate to assert that special weight is to be given to the cross in its deep thisworldliness.[72] Bonhoeffer insisted that the cross must not be made into "an abstract principle" (LPP, 374); only when it is not a principle but a concrete act of Jesus will we understand why Paul speaks of the formula "Christ our hope" in the sense of a "hope based on absolute certainty" (LPP, 373). In the cross lies the answer to the question of who God is because there, in a "reversal of all human life," we experience that "Jesus is there only for others" (LPP, 381). Here is the central systematic affirmation of Bonhoeffer's last letters. "His [Jesus'] 'being there for others' is the experience of transcendence. It is only this 'being there for others,'" this freedom from himself given in him, "that is the ground of omnipotence, omniscience, and omnipresence" (LPP, 381).[73]

These statements about God are not metaphysical but, rather, concrete statements which are rooted in the experience of real transcendence given in Jesus as the one who is for others.

In this context Bonhoeffer took up again the idea of deputyship which had appeared in the concept of *pro nobis* from the christology course to *Ethics*.[74] Yet he made a significant change: here he used the phrase "for others," substituting "*pro aliis*" for "*pro nobis*" (LPP, 381).[75] The way of discipleship, in which "Christ is formed, becomes known, in this 'for others'" (LPP, 359).[76] He had earlier said that "It is not with the beyond that we are concerned, but with this world as created and preserved, subject to laws, reconciled, and restored. What is above this world is, in the gospel, intended to exist *for* this world" (LPP, 286). The message of the gospel is clearly applied, in these words, to the whole world; even if it points beyond this world that message is there for the world. The intention of this directive is a variation of the statements concerning the deputyship of Christ who, as God in human form, is not "in the Greek divine-human form of 'the human per se,' but 'the one who is for others' and therefore the Crucified, the one who lives out of the transcendent" (LPP, 381).

Another important aspect of christology is the relation of the Old and New Testaments. Bonhoeffer had spoken of the world as being created and preserved, subject to laws, reconciled, and restored; it is legitimate to regard this statement as a reminiscence of his earlier words about the orders of preservation. It is remarkable that, at this point, Bonhoeffer no longer spoke alternately of orders of creation and orders of preservation but, instead, that he simply placed the terms "created" and "preserved" next to one another. One must not interpret this, however, in the sense of a disjunction. There are two places where Bonhoeffer saw the two terms together: he said that he understood what he had said "in the biblical sense of the creation and the incarnation" (LPP, 286), and that he was searching for a worldly interpretation "in the sense of the Old Testament and of John 1.14" (LPP, 286).

Up to this point Bonhoeffer had read the Old Testament as the book of Christ[77] and, in repeatedly describing Christ as the one who prays the Psalms, he had related the Old Testament to Christ.[78] But in his prison writings there is a significant difference. The Old Testament became, for Bonhoeffer, the advocate of that "profound thisworldliness" (LPP, 369) in which one learns to have faith. Bonhoeffer warned against the desire to take one's thoughts and feelings too quickly and too directly from the New Testament (LPP, 157). From his reading of the Old Testament he had come to learn that "it is only when one knows the unutterability of the name of God that one can utter the name of Jesus Christ" (LPP, 157). The two testaments belong one to the other, for, as he added significantly, "it is one and the same God" (LPP, 157).[79] Bonhoeffer's tendency was not only to discover Christ in the Old Testament; instead he was also interested in clearly relating the New Testament to the world on the basis of the teachings of the Old Testament. The Old Testament now had the function of protecting "the penultimate" instead of being "an 'earlier stage' of religion" (LPP, 157). Just as the Old Testament must be read in the light of the New Testament (LPP, 163, 282), so Christ is not to be separated from the Old Testament (LPP, 336).

From this interrelatedness of the two testaments Bonhoeffer drew certain conclusions about a proper relation to the world and a proper hope in the resurrection. He opposed the false eschatology of the redemption myths of antiquity, the focus of which lies beyond the boundary of death, as representing something alien to the Old Testament which speaks of redemption as "historical, i.e., on this side of death" (LPP, 336).[80] The New Testament does not abrogate the concept of "this side of death" but instead emphasizes it; if one does not ignore the Old Testament the danger of dissipating the eschatology of the New Testament is met (LPP, 336).

The relation of the two testaments is found in none other than Christ. In this relation alone, or in the christologically-based union of the penultimate and the ultimate, does that "polyphony" exist (LPP, 303, 305) that eschews "shallow and banal thisworldliness" but grants the "profound thisworldliness" (LPP, 369) which Bonhoeffer had described in the terminology of reality, particularly in *Ethics*. By polyphony of life he meant the act of loving God and his eternity with one's whole heart without thereby infringing upon or weakening earthly love. *Cantus firmus* and counterpoint are "'undivided and yet distinct' in the words of the Chalcedonian Definition" (LPP, 303). Is the image of polyphony not "a musical reflection of this Christological fact" (LPP, 303)? It signifies the "many different dimensions of life at the same time; we make room in ourselves, to some extent, for God and the whole world" (LPP, 310).

Not to do away with the Old Testament because of the New permits life to remain "multi-dimensional and polyphonous" (LPP, 311). Such multi-dimensionality is to be found in Christ alone, since in it we experience transcendence in the midst of our lives (LPP, 311).

Bonhoeffer's reading of the Song of Songs shows his specifically christological way of interpreting the Old Testament. The Song was for him an "ordinary love song" which is "probably the best 'christological' exposition" (LPP, 315). He no longer looked primarily at Christ in the Old Testament but, with Christ, at the world, at thisworldliness.

Bonhoeffer considered the Old and New Testaments to belong one to the other because of a circular relation which is founded on and borne by Christ.

We may conclude our comments about *Letters and Papers from Prison* with this remark: On the foundation of Jesus Christ as the "one for others," Bonhoeffer developed a view of transcendence and an understanding of the world in which the two elements were inseparable.

CONCLUDING SUMMARY OF THE CHRISTOLOGY

The subject of part two of this work was Bonhoeffer's christology. Our analysis supported the conclusion of the first part that his entire theology represents a unity in the sense of a continuous development. It also showed that Bonhoeffer's christological views rightly occupy the middle between his hermeneutics, examined in part one, and his theological understanding of the world, the subject of part three. At the beginning of part two there was considerable preoccupation with the questions of theory that formed the substance of part one, but as the analysis proceeded the material aspect of christology became central, a development that is parallel to Bonhoeffer's own increasing preoccupation with praxis. His efforts were concentrated more and more on concrete discipleship, eventually leading, in his third period, to his embracing the world; part three will pay full attention to this matter. The view of Jesus Christ that emerged for Bonhoeffer was that of the center and mediator between God and world.

We may conclude that the first signs of the centrality of Jesus Christ in Bonhoeffer's theology are to be found in *Act and Being*. This emphasis differentiates to a certain extent the basis of *Sanctorum Communio* from that of the works that follow. From *Act and Being* onward there was a steady development of christology as the point of departure for his theological endeavors. In addition, our analysis of christology has demonstrated that it is eminently justifiable to regard christology as the guiding principle of Bonhoeffer's theology.

We are convinced that Bonhoeffer did not abandon the concerns that

JESUS CHRIST THE CENTER [*MITTE*] AND MEDIATOR [*MITTLER*]

he raised in *Sanctorum Communio,* such as the questions of transcendence, sociality and concreteness; but he no longer answered those questions on the basis of the point of departure on which he had attempted to answer them in that book. Bonhoeffer's new point of departure becomes plain only in his *Habilitationsschrift*; later on it is elaborated with more sharpness and in a more concrete way, but it is never abandoned again. The new foundation is discerned best in relation to the problem of transcendence which had been raised in *Sanctorum Communio* and, beginning with *Act and Being* and especially the christology lectures, had been related to Jesus Christ. From then on Jesus Christ was understood by Bonhoeffer as "Christ for us." That term received a new dimension in the prison letters: "being for us" became "being for others," and only through that dimension could there be a true overcoming of the *cor curvum in se*. That dimension brought with it, also, a turning toward the world, about which part three will speak.

Finally, we must eliminate a possible misunderstanding on our part. Having demonstrated that Bonhoeffer's christology is the foundation and heart of his theology and having called his whole theology a christocentric one, we must not conclude that he fell victim to a christological constriction, a charge that one could possibly make against Karl Barth.[81] Such incrimination is not justified in relation to Bonhoeffer, since a christocentric theology for him was the attempt to speak of the mystery, something we can only do in contradictions and paradoxes.

PART THREE

RELIGIONLESS CHRISTIANITY IN A WORLD COME OF AGE

4
Historical Survey of Bonhoeffer's Understanding of the World

PREAMBLE

Our analysis of Bonhoeffer's late christology could not help raising the topic of "the world." The question arises as to whether Bonhoeffer dealt with it earlier, and if so, how. The first section of part three attempts to answer this by providing a historical survey of Bonhoeffer's understanding of the world; the second section will be given to the systematic summary of that understanding in terms of the central assertions of the *Letters and Papers from Prison*.

Before we set out on these tasks we must remind ourselves that, according to Bonhoeffer, a general concept of the world cannot be evolved. That is because "the 'world' is . . . *the sphere of concrete responsibility* which is given to us in and through Jesus Christ. It is not some general concept from which it is possible to derive a self-contained system" (E, 233). Bonhoeffer was concerned with the Christian's life in the world and, consequently, with the world which remains *world* because "it is the world which is loved, condemned and reconciled in Christ" (E, 232). The Christian and the secular are not opposed to each other in principle but must not be understood as forming a unity either (E, 232).

These statements bring into view two essential matters. The first is that the question of the world cannot be construed as a theoretical one and that it cannot be answered on the basis of a theory. It can be raised only in the context of the existing relation Christians have to the world within their concrete praxis with the view of achieving clarity about that relation. The second is that the question of the world cannot be separated from Jesus Christ.

The significance of what has been discussed up to this point for the understanding of the world becomes clear in these two inseparable aspects. But the discussion of Bonhoeffer's hermeneutical point of departure and christology also belongs to part three because they are integrative elements, so to speak, and must not be excluded from a study of Bonhoeffer's understanding of the world. Christology is not only the presupposition for the hermeneutical starting point but is also the very condition for theological statements about the world, given the thematic assertion that "henceforward one can speak neither of God nor of the world without speaking of Jesus Christ" (E, 194).

The presence of the word "and" in the phrase "Christ and the world come of age" does not indicate that Christ and world are to be placed one next to the other externally and that the world is to be perceived as a heterogeneous, secondary, or peripheral addition. Rather, the word "and" shows the unity which is Jesus Christ himself, since the separate realities of God and the world are brought together in him; for in his person the reality of God has entered the reality of the world. According to Bonhoeffer there can be no direct doctrine of God; it is Christ alone who mediates access to God. In the same way there can be no direct theological doctrine of the world; there can only be indirect theological reflection about the world, reflection which is mediated through Jesus Christ, and that is christological, christocentric reflection.

THE QUESTION OF THE WORLD: ITS BACKGROUND AND STARTING POINT

INTRODUCTION TO THE PROBLEMS RELATING TO THE THEME OF "THE WORLD"

> I am amazed that I not only live without the Bible but actually can live without it for days. I would not regard it as an act of obedience but one of autosuggestion were I to force myself [to read it daily]. . . . Whenever I open the Bible again it is always new to me and gladsome as never before and all I want is to preach. I know that I need only open my own books to hear everything that could be said against that. . . . But I sense how the resistance against everything "religious" is growing in me, often to the point of an instinctive revulsion—something that is surely not good. I am not of a religious nature. But I just have to think about God, about Christ and I value very much integrity, life, freedom and mercy. It is their religious garbs that I find so discomforting. Do you know what I mean? These are not new thoughts and insights, but since I believe that something in me is about to burst I let things fly and do not try to muzzle them. It is in such a sense also that I understand my current activities in the worldly sector. (GS II, 420)[1]

These words were written in a letter two years before Bonhoeffer began his intensive reflections about the world, contained now in his prison letters. One has to regard what he said as a manifestation of the experiences and thoughts they gave rise to which occupied Bonhoeffer so much during the last years of his life. He sought to have religious Christianity give way to worldly Christianity. Bonhoeffer's activity in the "worldly sector," as he succinctly put it, had shown him that he had to abandon the predominant form of Christian faith. The alternative was not religion or world; indeed, "religious" and "worldly" are antithetical adjectives of faith and its interpretation.[2]

Clearly, Bonhoeffer's concept of religion must be explained in order that his understanding of the world may be comprehended. But this must be done from not only the systematic but also the historical perspective, because Bonhoeffer did not make explicit inquiries about the world from the very outset. It seems that he could raise this question and come closer to an answer only when the danger of another understanding of the world had been checked: the danger of the "religious understanding of the world." On the surface that understanding was close to actual fact, however, quite different from Bonhoeffer's understanding. According to him the religious understanding was predominant in Pietism and especially in Cultural Protestantism and its thought structure, liberal theology. An indication that this was true is the fact that he followed his statement about Christ and the world that has come of age with an explicit reference to liberal theology (LPP, 327). He sought to overcome this negative inheritance in an at times polemical manner.

One of the chief characteristics of this inadequate understanding of the world was the fact that religion had become a province, a reserve of the world. This manifested itself in two ways: God was relegated to the beyond and one either saw radical flight from the world as one's way to God, or one lived in this world, radically open to it but independent of all relations to God. Behind both ways of solving the issue lurks a schema of interpretation operating in terms of locality and spatiality. The attempt is to assign a space to God by either separating God and the world and settling God where the world ends, or leaving to God a specified but limited space in the world. This means, of course, that one relates God once again to the world's space. Bonhoeffer said clearly that both positions, however much they appear to be opposite, are in fact the two sides of the same thing, for both have in common the idea that *there is no faith in God's kingdom,* his kingdom on earth.[3]

The spatiality which Bonhoeffer opposed again and again is, of course, to be understood in the first instance as a metaphorical term. Yet his critique is particularly trenchant when the initial attempts of theologians to remain conscious of the metaphorical dimension failed and an unmetaphorical spatial conception emerged, such as vulgar images of the beyond or a false view of "the two realms."

The chief task for the theology of his generation was, in Bonhoeffer's view, to overcome religion as something which either separates or identifies faith and the world. When faith and the world are not properly related one to the other, faith easily falls captive to the world and that is what theology has to oppose. The decisive breakthrough in that task came in the work of Karl Barth which, in actual fact, began the critical destruction. Bonhoeffer followed him in his own engagement of traditional faith and its theology. And yet, from the beginning, Bonhoeffer opposed the reputed radicality of Barth whenever Barth rejected the world and history as theologically of no account, or even as anti-divine, leaving them outside the scope of faith.[4] In this sense Barth went only one step forward, at least as far as Bonhoeffer, in his knowledge of him, was concerned; he did not take the second step which the first one had necessitated (LPP, 328). Barth structured dialectical theology against the captivity of Christian faith to the world, but at the price of the theoretical worldlessness of faith which marked the theology following Schleiermacher. The worldlessness of faith that emerged in Albrecht Ritschl's work came to full bloom in Wilhelm Herrmann, Ritschl's pupil and Barth's teacher.[5] It was this acosmism that Barth was unable to overcome theologically, at least in the years following the appearance of the revised edition of *Römerbrief*.

THE BACKGROUND TO AND THE FIRST STATEMENT OF THE TRADITIONAL PROBLEM OF RELIGION

Early Studies in the Subject of Religion

Bonhoeffer's engagement of religion as a false attempt to illumine the relationship between God and world goes back a long way. It is especially apparent in the first course he taught in Berlin, which he devoted, significantly enough, to the theology of the twentieth century.[6] What he could not readily do in the seminars and papers of his student days he did directly in this course, which culminated in the question "Where do we stand?" The roots of this engagement, the key concept of which is religion, reach down into an even earlier stage in his life; his preoccupation with Schleiermacher is to be seen as one of the most important of those roots. While still at school he read Schleiermacher's *Speeches on Religion* which he later studied systematically at university.[7]

In order to understand Bonhoeffer's concerns here, it seems appropriate to recall what led Schleiermacher to compose the famous speeches. He set out to provide a theological response to the philosophical attempts of Kant and Hegel to illumine the relationship between God and the world. The peace established in Schleiermacher's work between theology and philosophy, however, resulted in the complete dismissal of what had hitherto been called religion, itself a heavily loaded concept. According to Schleiermacher, religion had the same subject as metaphysics and ethics, namely, the universe and the relation that human beings have to it.[8] If religion has the same subject as have ethics and metaphysics, then the difference between them can consist only in the relations of human being to that subject, as the nature of religion involves neither thinking nor acting, but intuition and feeling (*Speeches*, 59).

Religion seeks to regard the universe as it is. Religion is reverent attention and submission, in childlike passivity, to be stirred and filled by the universe's immediate influences (*Speeches*, 59). This characteristic of religion allows it to stand independently and autonomously next to metaphysics and ethics. It is not surprising that Schleiermacher again and again opposed the intermingling of religion with metaphysics and ethics, an action that seemed legitimate because the subject of all three was the same (*Speeches*, 276).

Schleiermacher tried, therefore, to describe the nature of religion, both in connection with and in contradistinction to metaphysics and ethics. In doing so he believed that the autonomy and status of religion were safeguarded, and that the status of religion had indeed been reestablished. Summing up, Schleiermacher defined religion as follows: "Practice is art, speculation is science, religion is sense and taste for the Infinite" (*Speeches*, 278).

One has to ask, however, at what cost Schleiermacher sought to constitute religion as something autonomous next to metaphysics and ethics. The consequence of envisaging this conception of religion was that religion became partial in a twofold way, namely, in relation to the power which gives rise to it and in relation to its juxtaposition with metaphysics and ethics. By setting religion apart from them and by assigning it special access to the mutually shared subject, religion was robbed in a very deep sense of its independence, which itself had been conceived of much too superficially. Religion now became ordered toward the universe and, thus, finally toward the world while at the same time losing its universality. By setting religion off from other human ways of relating to the universe, including, of course, the integration into the natural patterns of life embodied in those ways, religion became limited to a particular space. Eliminated was the question about God and about Jesus Christ as the sole mediator as it would have destroyed Schleiermacher's concept (*Speeches*, 59). To this separation of God and world, of religion and state, corresponds the complete subjection of religion, in the partiality mentioned above, to the world into which it fits without a gap.

It is not difficult to see that Bonhoeffer had to deal with Schleiermacher's views even when that theologian was not specifically referred to. Again and again he had reason to take a stand against liberal theology, which in the end meant against Schleiermacher.

Another reason for Bonhoeffer's sustained interest in religion was his preoccupation with Friedrich Naumann's much discussed letters about religion, which he had studied quite thoroughly while still at school.[9] After that time, the understanding of religion as something partial disquieted him. Naumann, who was himself actively engaged in the world and demanding the same from others, could sustain that engagement only on the basis of a radical separation of faith and world. He saw no problem in the fact that many were "indeed merchants with their right hand and benefactors of the poor with their left,"[10] and that they practiced directly the general morality of business while at the same time working as Christians for the abolition of the distress which that system of business creates. Bonhoeffer was very dissatisfied with the resulting total separation of human life and Christian faith, of citizens' duties and the Sermon on the Mount, as well as with the seemingly necessary and peculiar mixture of life and faith which corresponds to that separation. He rejected equally the idea, arising from that separation, that faith had to do only with purely natural life. He did not believe that such a misconstrued "doctrine of the two kingdoms," as Naumann proposed it, could solve the dilemma; or that one could justly claim Luther as one's authority for such an interpretation.[11] Bonhoeffer sharply rejected the inwardness which Naumann's position forced on his concept of religion,[12] but he neither could nor wished to accuse Naumann of trying "to evade the fact" (NRS, 309). Bonhoeffer could only conclude that Naumann's endeavors to respond as a Christian to the new times and the completely changed understanding of the world[13] had failed.[14]

Religion as the Subject of the First Lectures

Having read Schleiermacher and Naumann quite early, Bonhoeffer was familiar with the subject of religion; this familiarity informs his first course of lectures. These lectures, being Bonhoeffer's assessment of the relation between faith and reason, church and state or world, were given over to a discussion of religion, most likely because of the force of the problem that beset religion in the literature which he had read on the subject and his own intense interest in that very problem.[15]

The critical discussion of the tradition he had inherited took place under the influence of Karl Barth's critique, as the conclusion of the course shows.[16] Barth, however, did not do away with that tradition; if he had done so, Bonhoeffer would not have given so much of his attention to it. Nor did Barth's proposed solution seem adequate; even then Bonhoeffer already raised, albeit implicitly, the charge of positivism of revelation (GS V, 226). This course of lectures, seeking to do justice to the contemporary situation, was governed by the question of religion and the insistence on christology which is either missing or falsely understood in religion. Beginning with Paul Tillich's book, *The Religious Situation,* Bonhoeffer gave a brief overview of society at the turn of the century, a society to which he himself belonged, only to proceed directly to the subject of religion. Of very great significance is his concept that in the post-Copernican world the word *religio* smothered the word "faith" or gave it a new meaning (GS V, 185). The concept "religion" obtained its current meaning, in other words, only in modern times.

Bonhoeffer then pursued the question of religion in detail through several distinct approaches. Again and again the conclusion emerged that religion completely fits itself into existing social conditions, be it as the suitable pedagogy, instruction for the upbringing of good citizens of the state, or as a humanly advanced phenomenon of culture, or, finally, as something of scholarly merit (GS V, 185).

In the course of this discussion many names are cited of people who were directly or indirectly influential in the contemporary situation. Next to Schleiermacher, Bonhoeffer referred briefly to Kant and Hegel, who, beyond doubt, had provided fundamental positions especially for the discussion of religion with which Bonhoeffer had to deal. It is remarkable that the Berlin theologians, his teachers, with the sole exception of Adolf von Harnack, carried very little weight in his analyses. Obviously Bonhoeffer knew that he had to be more attentive to a different approach to religion, and while he by no means committed himself to it, he took it seriously enough to deal with it quite intensively. Thus, next to Naumann, he referred especially to Ernst Troeltsch. It is interesting that he showed far greater respect for him than, for example, for Reinhold Seeberg, even though Troeltsch had set out to build on the religious a priori[17] and thus represented a quite developed subjectivism. Yet next to and unrelated to that subjectivism stood Troeltsch's rigorous historical research, with which he sought to interpret history and on the basis of which he rejected all claims to absoluteness on the part of Christianity.

Next to the concrete approach to the world, which Bonhoeffer had inherited from his parents and gained through his experiences in the United States, there was the strong theological impulse from Naumann and Troeltsch to address the question of the world. Yet it was in them that he perceived the impasse of the chasm between culture and Christianity. Neither of these theologians had been able to overcome this impasse. That they did not misjudge or conceal this fact seems to be the reason why Bonhoeffer held them in deep respect, as can be seen even in *Letters and Papers from Prison.* There he noted that the strength of liberal theology "was that it did not try to put the clock back, and that it genuinely accepted the battle (Troeltsch), even though this ended with its defeat" (LPP, 327). Bonhoeffer did not remain silent about the weakness of that theology: "It conceded to the world the right to determine

Christ's place in the world; in the conflict between the church and the world it accepted the comparatively easy terms of peace that the world dictated" (LPP, 327). It almost seems to be a late reminiscence and summation of this first lecture course when Bonhoeffer writes that "Barth was the first to realize the mistake that all these attempts (which were all, in fact, still sailing, though unintentionally, in the channel of liberal theology) were making in leaving clear a space for religion in the world or against the world" (LPP, 328). With Barth began the attack in the name of God against the religion which is in the service of humankind and which is one sphere next to others in life (GS V, 218).

In *Sanctorum Communio* Bonhoeffer had discussed false conceptions of transcendence; these ideas are seen as a part of religion, as a false conception of the relation of God to the world. Bonhoeffer saw such a false conception of transcendence in Tillich's attempt to perceive of transcendence as "the expansion of perspectives" (GS V, 217), or to speak of the boundary as the place where or beyond which we sense ourselves to be affirmed by God (GS V, 223). Both views are characteristic of religion.

In summing up it may be said that the relation between faith and culture or society, or to put it more inclusively, between God and world, which is distorted by religion, was a subject that occupied Bonhoeffer deeply throughout his life and right up to his final days. It is no surprise, therefore, that he spoke negatively several times even in his early works about the absence of an adequate christology. But such absence goes with the kind of religion which seeks to reconcile Christianity and human society. But this reconciliation is proposed apart from Jesus Christ in whom the opposition of faith and world is overcome, to which the Chalcedonian Creed and its formulation of the oneness and the distinction of God and the world in Jesus Christ give witness. Bonhoeffer spoke appreciatively of Barth, who had criticized religion by appealing to God's word, although he had not given a concrete enough conception of God's relation to the world. Only when religion is no longer made "the precondition of faith," Bonhoeffer maintained, "will liberal theology be overcome (and even Barth is still influenced by it, though negatively), and at the same time its question be genuinely taken up and answered" (LPP, 329). But that is what Bonhoeffer had tried to do already in 1931–32. But he did not get beyond the formulation of the question. The reason for this is obvious: Cultural Protestantism still dominated the scene; its view of the relation to the world had gained primacy. Faith could not possibly agree with such a view because in it Christianity was assigned a place apart from life while, in what only sounded contradictory, being taken up completely in the world. Was Bonhoeffer wrong in stressing this aspect of Christianity when he stated that Overbeck and Nietzsche had rightly denounced the marriage of Christianity and culture as a betrayal (GS V, 210)? Yet his early assessments of the state of things showed clearly where the impasse of the tradition lay. A comment made late in the prison letters shows that it had been a constructive impulse that had prompted him to solve his own question about liberal theology (LPP, 378).

Appearing initially to be an assessment, only, of where theological matters stood at the time, this first lecture course in Berlin was also, at a deeper level, an outline of the problem to which his work would later address itself. The problem was depicted negatively in the concept "religion." But this concept also provided the background and the point of departure from and against which Bonhoeffer launched his work. The error he depicted lay in the fact that the Christianity he observed was either subject to the world from the outset or took flight from it, failing in both instances to get away from the world (E, 200). Against that error Barth had rightly pitted his dialectical theology as a theology of protest. Under his influence, Bonhoeffer tried to assimilate theologically the positive elements of Cultural Protestantism. This intention is behind the theme of "Christ and the world come of age."

EARLY DEVELOPMENTS OF A POSITIVE UNDERSTANDING OF THE WORLD

THE BEGINNING OF THE DEVELOPMENT AT BARCELONA

In the last period of his life, Bonhoeffer sought to accept the world without God precisely as the world whose Lord is really and properly Jesus Christ. That seemed to be the way toward overcoming in a positive fashion the religious understanding of the world which he had abandoned long ago. The question before us is whether Bonhoeffer, having abandoned the religious understanding, developed a positive, albeit indirect, understanding of the world, mediated through Jesus Christ. The answer is that this was not really accomplished.

Clearly, Bonhoeffer did not initially neglect the question of the world completely nor did he answer it in an unequivocally negative fashion. By virtue of his ancestry and disposition he was open to the world; this openness was the personal background of his theological reflections, especially in this matter. His relationship to the world was disrupted quite early, however. The uncritical affirmation of the world, so characteristic of the nineteenth and early twentieth centuries, had been deeply shaken, though not to the extent of resulting in a one-sided negation of the world. For that reason Bonhoeffer's relationship to the world can never be depicted in dichotomous alternatives. One may summarize his objections to the relation to the world of Cultural Protestantism and of Karl Barth in the following, perhaps simplified, manner. Even though diametrically opposed, both fall into this alternative: either faith is regarded as something partial to the world, causing it to be taken up completely into religion in the hope of eliminating the tension between faith and the world, or the tension between faith and the world is radicalized to the point where they are completely opposed to each other. In the end the latter direction turns out to be less radical than living with the tension between faith and world, based on the reconciliation achieved already in the incarnation.

An examination of the question of the world in Bonhoeffer's early publications shows that the question as such is not raised in them and is certainly not answered. In *Sanctorum Communio* the world is spoken of as the world encountered by revelation or as the world which revelation is seeking to transform (SC, 184); it is asserted that in Christ "the reconciliation and justification of the world" is real (SC, 105). Only in the context of eschatology does Bonhoeffer say that church and world must not be viewed as antagonists, that "the kingdom of Christ has become the kingdom of God . . . in all the world" (SC, 199). On one occasion only, in an excursus, is there talk of the "two concepts of the world . . . the one seeing the world as good, as created, the other seeing it as evil, made bad by the evil will" (SC, 63).

In *Act and Being,* also, the subject of the world is not in the forefront. The reason for this lies chiefly in the aim of that work, which is the removal of a difference in the method of theology. In the one-sided positions of transcendentalism and ontology the world is seen chiefly as related to or given shape by humans; or, to put it theologically, as created by them (AB, 29). That world is closed in on itself; it is, therefore, a narrow world. Only faith, permitting the world to be regarded as God's creation, can break open that narrowness (AB, 174). Bonhoeffer concluded his study with the assertion that those who look away from themselves to the revelation of God, to Christ, are borne out of the narrowness of the world into the breadth of heaven (AB, 184). The world is not the focus of Bonhoeffer's attention in these reflections. Even when Christ is spoken of as the mediator to the world, in the sense of the external world (AB, 139), one has the impression that this was meant to be an assertion of christology. The implications of that comment for the understanding of the world are not developed at all in that work.[18]

The Primarily Negative Aspect

Bonhoeffer's interest in the world surfaced not only in his work of 1932, but also in his sermons delivered in Barcelona. It is no coincidence that his practical engagement gave rise to his concerns about the world or to his christology. To be sure, there is by no means a unified conception of the world in these theologically and linguistically still immature sermons delivered in Barcelona. The world is not yet unequivocally thought of as being accepted in Jesus Christ, i.e., the world to which the Christian is committed because of that acceptance. There prevails instead a strangely divided and primarily negative view of the world.

One sees this especially in a sermon on the text of 1 John 2:17: "The world is passing away with all its allurements, but he who does God's will stands forevermore" (GS V, 452–57). This sermon serves as an example for the chiefly negative view of the world in the sermons of Barcelona since it speaks of "the transitoriness of the world" (GS V, 454); "the wicked world" (GS V, 454); and, finally, the world which is "vain" (GS V, 453), because it is subject to a certain fate, namely, time (GS V, 453). This is equivalent to death, and death, in the face of everything else, the penultimate, is the ultimate in this world (GS V, 455); the world is a "world of death" (GS V, 454).

Against the world of death Bonhoeffer placed the cross, "the sign of eternity" bathed "in the light of God's sun and grace" (GS V, 455–56). There stands the cross "in all transitoriness and darkness"; Christ hangs on it, his arms spread out as if to embrace the whole world. Those who cling to the cross will be lifted out of time, to become eternal. Here God and world, time and eternity, are utterly separated for the sake of a drastic juxtaposition. This juxtaposition is resolved only in appearance toward the end of the sermon, where it is said that Christians are in this world, having been "placed into it" (GS V, 457) by God. This placement in the world changes the hearers of the sermon from "people of death into people of eternity" (GS V, 457). But here, too, the process which led to the cross, finding there its visible, empirical climax, has no real consequences for the world. It is remarkable that at no place in this sermon did Bonhoeffer speak of the resurrection; eschatological hope is not discussed as being a hope for an already existing reality *in* the world and *for* the world but as being a hope for the eschatological eternity. That eternity, however, is unmediated and, hence, abstract and purely otherworldly. Bonhoeffer illustrated this clearly at the conclusion of the sermon where he spoke of the boundaries, the end of the world which "is the beginning of something new, of eternity" (GS V, 455), before which death, the ultimate in this world, becomes something penultimate. Precisely such a view leaves the world entirely on its own; it is a world fallen away from God, and a unholy one, not part of the salvation which, it is true, is also its very judgment. In this view the world is not the newly created world, made new in the hiddenness of Jesus Christ's death and resurrection. Hope for eternity has no longer anything to do with the world. To this world, unholy and excluded from salvation, there corresponds a worldless and unhistorical salvation. Matching this negative conception of time is a view of eternity separated from time, untouched by and unrelated to time. God's hand takes the hearers of this sermon out of the world and history into an eternity beyond.

This separation of salvation and world, with its negative effect on the world, is found repeatedly in the other sermons. They counsel that one keep oneself pure from the world (GS V, 450), not to look to the world but to God (GS V, 460–62). They speak of grace as "an event beyond the world" which "seeks to draw us away from our world to the one beyond" (GS V, 460), and since we live "in the world where we must exercise renunciation" (GS V, 462) we look to the cross "and call out, over the noises of the world, 'we shall not let you go lest you bless us.'" May we not regard the alienating comment from Bonhoeffer's farewell sermon in Barcelona as the summation of the understanding of the world which he was later to reject: "My peace has set me free from the world, strengthened me against it and made me ready for the other world (GS V, 481)?

The Primarily Positive Aspect

There is another view of the relation of faith to the world, other than this negative and undialectically formulated one, which, to some extent, seems to have carried over into *The Cost of Discipleship*. This other view appears in subordinate clauses, as it were, in the sermons referred to just now. One may note, for example, Bonhoeffer's remark that to see God also means "to recognize him in one's own life, in the world" (GS V, 451), or that "God desires to have dealings with the world" (GS V, 461). One also perceives this view in the call to God "come into our world," or the reference to God as "the God of the world" (GS V, 474). These statements, however, do not yet lead to a positive view of the world; yet they cause us to keep the question open as to whether Bonhoeffer really wanted to put forth an unambiguously and directly negative view of the world. Clearly these remarks would not be sufficient for the development of a dialectical understanding of world and history or time.

An understanding of the world which shows the positive significance of the world for faith is expressed in a sermon on Rom. 12:11c entitled "Meet the Demands of the Hour."[19] Here Bonhoeffer explicitly and insistently commended his hearers to the world, and, in this way, prefigured the understanding of the world which triumphed in his last works.

"The basic question of every Christian is clearly the question for eternity: how do I attain to eternity here in the midst of time?" (GS V, 463). This question, corresponding completely to the purport of the sermons considered so far, takes up the matter of time and, as we shall see, the world. In those sermons Bonhoeffer would have answered this question about attaining to eternity by stating that one must stay "away from time, become unconcerned about whatever happens here, live solely in eternity"; this statement instead appears in the sermon "Meet the Demands of the Hour" in the form of an objection which Bonhoeffer raised against himself and then responded to critically (GS V, 463). The critique is elicited by the text of the sermon and phrased in God's call to us: "You want to find eternity, then meet the demands of the hour" (GS V, 463). This call from God must strike us "as a tremendous contradiction" (GS V, 463); in explaining this idea Bonhoeffer broadened the temporal antithesis of eternity–time into the more comprehensive one of God–world. "If you seek that which does not pass away, attend to that which does; if you seek that which is eternal, attend to that which is temporal; *if you seek God, attend to the world*" (GS V, 463–64). There is no reference yet to Jesus Christ as the ground for finding God in the world and eternity in time. The argumentation proceeds still immediately from God, for God wants "to be found in time, as we find his will in Jesus Christ" (GS V, 464). The introduction of Jesus Christ at this point is metaphorical to a large extent. He is spoken of only in the sermon's trinitarian statements, which sound almost like formulae and doxological additions without any real impact on the sermon itself or its structure. What is important and a sign of things to come in Bonhoeffer's work is the remark, "We encounter God's holy presence in the midst of our time" (GS V, 466).

This immediacy to God expresses itself also in the fact that the problem of history and christology are not yet brought together. Ranke's statement that "every moment is in immediate relation to God" (*jeder Augenblick ist unmittelbar zu Gott*) is twice repeated by Bonhoeffer. He had already cited it in *Sanctorum Communio* (SC, 198), and did so again in the letters which make up *Letters and Papers from Prison* (LPP, 230). Bonhoeffer explained Ranke's statement in this sermon, saying that it points us "to the present" in which alone "a piece of eternity is concealed" (GS V, 464); the present alone is "the one truly significant hour" (GS V, 465) of all world history. That is what the scriptural admonition "Meet the demands of the hour" means. The hour is the same as the present; to flee from this hour is, therefore, to flee from God.

This sermon speaks of an understanding of the world which, despite its references to need and misery and, consequently, to the boundaries of human existence and the world, is different from the one we discerned in the sermons which chiefly warned against the world. In time itself, and in the world, God is to be found like clear water in the depth of a well. However hazardous that simile of Bonhoeffer may be, it does show something other than an unambiguous rejection of the world; "If you seek God, attend to the world" (GS V, 464). By meeting the demands of the hour, *their hour*, the present, Christians become "people of the hour in the deepest sense" (GS V, 465), people who open themselves wholly to the political, economic, moral, and religious needs of the present;[20]

"Everywhere there is the call: enter into the needs of the present" (GS V, 465). Christians, who may not turn away from "the events of modern times" (GS V, 466), are reminded in those words clearly of the *responsibility* they bear for meeting the demands of the hour. The term "responsibility" signals what is for Bonhoeffer an important concept from the history of ideas.

We touch that history again in another basic concept of Bonhoeffer's theology, namely, the idea of solidarity. "We have to understand anew what is the solidarity of humankind" (GS V, 466). God seeks precisely those who are in solidarity with the world. Bonhoeffer expanded this statement by saying that God seeks earthly–worldly people, and "not ghosts who shun the earth," because "God loved the earth and made us from it, he made the earth to be our mother, he who is our father" (GS V, 467),[21] a comment reminiscent of Nietzsche's appeal for faithfulness to the earth. We are not angels but human beings, and that is what we are to be. Whether it is felicitous to speak "of our spiteful position on earth" (GS V, 467) is another matter; it is clearly unfortunate that Bonhoeffer referred to the earth as our mother. The earth is not depicted here as having a function directly related to salvation; the reference means, rather, that humans have an ongoing dependency on the earth, caused and maintained by God, so that they may find him on it: a relation to God is found only in a relation to the world. Bonhoeffer explicated this by referring to Antaeus, the giant, as a (pagan) symbol for his understanding of the world. This reference could be an indication of Bonhoeffer's endeavors, behind which certainly was a personal concern to encourage Christians "to get their feet firmly planted on the earth" (GS V, 468). Several times Bonhoeffer urged people of our times to "put some ground under their feet,"[22] but above all he urged Christians to do so because they have been called and placed into a critical relation to the world by the message of faith. Yet they are Christians only when they stand firmly on the earth; they can only be true Christians *in* the world.

In summary, we may say with Bonhoeffer that people "are saved in the midst of the world, for only in the world can God be loved; only in the world can sacrifice be made to him; in the world means in relation to the neighbor. You who give yourself wholly to the neighbor, give yourself to God" (GS V, 472). To turn toward the world and thereby to the neighbor is to turn toward God, because God allows himself to be found in the world and in the neighbor only.

The contradictory and inadequate view of the world manifest in these sermons governs equally the lectures Bonhoeffer gave toward the end of his stay in Barcelona. In the first of these lectures Bonhoeffer called upon his hearers "to bring so much love to our present age, to our species, as to enter into solidarity with it both in need and in hope" (GS

V, 116). Yet one does not have the impression that Bonhoeffer had found his way out of the constrictions and boundaries of "religion." The remainder of the lecture does not speak of the world. The second lecture, which is important to christology, makes no mention of "the world." Only in the third lecture, concerning Christian ethics, does the subject emerge. Toward the end a clear warning is issued against Christians deserting the world; this appears even though it does not really correspond to the preceding discussion (GS V, 175). Bonhoeffer failed to make clear on what Christians are to base their turning toward the world, which he had said was not only possible but necessary. His concluding comments show, however, that behind the question concerning the concreteness of the ethical claim, which is the issue of this lecture, there is the question concerning the world. Christians "remain bound to the earth when they wish to come to God," but they "have to experience the paradox that the world does not offer us a choice between good and evil, but between evil and evil, and that God leads them to himself also through evil" (GS V, 178). The picture of the giant Antaeus, which follows that point, and the consequences that are drawn from it, do not seem congruent with this negative aspect. "Those who want to leave the earth and get away from the cares of the present, lose the power which through everlasting, mysterious forces still holds them" (GS V, 179). Here Bonhoeffer added the already cited phrase of the earth as mother who delivers those who remain faithful to her into the arms of God, our father; "This is the Christians' song of songs about the earth and her cares" (GS V, 179). Yet the relation to the earth must be given up. This is to be regarded as something quite positive, even if individual statements very much recall a false doctrine of the two realms.

A concluding glance at the extant texts from the period at Barcelona leaves an ambiguous impression also in relation to Bonhoeffer's understanding of the world. His comments about the world are primarily negative. Still, he warned emphatically against every form of flight from the world. A contradiction remains between the view of the world as wicked, one in which there is only evil, on the one hand; and the insistence, on the other, that only by standing firmly on the earth does one have the power to come to God. The exclamation, therefore, "Remain true to the earth," drawn most likely from Bonhoeffer's rich knowledge of Nietzsche, has no theological foundation here. The picture of Antaeus, the giant, remains pagan; it has the appearance of Titanism and is open in its form here to an interpretation much more in the sense of Albert Camus's *The Myth of Sisyphus* than in the form of Christian faith. Only later, when this matter became founded in christology, was there a basis for the constructive force of a positive turning toward the world.

BONHOEFFER'S 1932 DISCUSSION OF THE WORLD: FIRST SUMMIT

"Our world depart, your kingdom come" (GS V, 180). This is how Bonhoeffer ended his lecture on ethics in Barcelona. The phrase "Your kingdom come also to us" represents a remarkable change in the ending of an address which may be regarded as the culmination of Bonhoeffer's efforts in 1932 to formulate his understanding of the world.[23] The issue for Bonhoeffer, then, was no longer the departing of the world but the coming of God's kingdom to the earth.

One cannot precisely pinpoint when Bonhoeffer raised the question about the world anew and in a deeper way in 1932, a year so full of meaning for him. This topic had been almost completely absent in the intervening years since his first, still largely unclear, efforts of Barcelona. There may be external reasons for this absence; nevertheless, it is an indirect indication that the question concerning the world had no priority for Bonhoeffer.[24] The concentration on Jesus did not lead to a similar intensification in the theological exploration of this topic but instead kept it in the background. In 1932 the question of the world emerged almost unannounced together with Bonhoeffer's polemic on the one hand against Dibelius's church and ecclesiology, and with his efforts on the other in relation to the concrete commandment. The topic was anticipated in the stock-taking which concluded his first course of lectures in the winter semester of 1931–32 and its repudiation of a religious understanding of the world; one may understand that section of the course as Bonhoeffer's prelude to the discussion of a theme he now focuses on clearly: the understanding of the world. In contrast to the two extremes of flight from and bondage to the world, both of which are typically religious for Bonhoeffer, he sought to discern the reality and fulfillment of God's kingdom on earth in a non-religious or secular manner without, however, expressing that reality in such terminology. Bonhoeffer's statements about the world were first made in sermons, as in Barcelona,[25] but were later reflected upon in addresses, an essay, and in some parts of his course on the nature of the church.[26] Compared to what Bonhoeffer had said on the subject in Barcelona, these statements manifest a considerably more nuanced view of the world, an occurrence that was to happen a second time in Bonhoeffer's later theology. For this reason, the statements of this period may be regarded as the first "summit" in his efforts to develop an understanding of the world.

The Cross as the Salvation of the World

Bonhoeffer's sermon for the Sunday *Exaudi* begins with a reference to "God's faithfulness to the world" (GS I, 133-39). The world is defined as the world which God "has created a second time," except that the works of this second creation, namely, the cross and resurrection of

Christ, are different from those of the first (GS I, 137). The world made new in cross and resurrection, where only the cross is visible, is the world really touched by cross and resurrection. But one must not separate the cross from the resurrection or vice versa (GS I, 137). The basic difference between the sermons of 1932 and those of Barcelona lies in the relevance the cross is said to have for the world.[27] The cross is no longer a simple sign of salvation which is said to be a salvation in another world; rather, it is what brings about salvation in the world and for the world. This accent gives those sermons of 1932 an orientation related more concretely to the incarnation and the economy of salvation.

This is confirmed by the sermon, delivered four weeks later, in which Bonhoeffer's words about the world are more explicit than those in the sermon for the Sunday *Exaudi*. The text on which the later sermon is based, Col. 3:1–4, which includes the verse "Let your thoughts dwell on that higher realm, not on this earthly life," would quite likely suggest a view of the world close to the one which predominated in Bonhoeffer's thoughts in Barcelona. After talking about the suspicions harbored against Christians by those who let their thoughts dwell on the realm of the earth, the sermon utters a biblical "woe" on those Christians who bury their talent and, subsequently, will be rejected as worthless servants. Bonhoeffer continues that, in the end, "one would have to say to the *godless* of this world: you good and faithful servants . . ." (GS IV, 69). For it may well be that the godless, with their motto "Remain faithful to the earth," do exactly what Christians, excusing themselves by insisting that they dwell on that which is above, fail to do altogether.[28] Yet it is precisely Christians who should have a more objective, that is to say, a more adequate and intense relation to the world because they are hidden with Christ in God (Col. 3:3), and have thus gained a distance from the world which makes possible a proximity so much the greater. This relation to the world must be operative, and therefore not primarily speculative, for "Christ did not come into the world so that we may comprehend him but that we may cling to him, that we allow ourselves simply to be drawn by him into the event of the resurrection" (GS IV, 77). This "into" may well be opposed to the "out of" of the sermons of Barcelona. Cross and resurrection are the works in which our world is created anew; they do not tear Christians away from the world but rather place them squarely into it. Bonhoeffer wanted to repudiate all flight and estrangement from the world as being ultimately unchristian; he wanted to make plain the whole range of responsibility for the world precisely on the part of Christians. They may not flee "out of the homelessness of the world" into the church or seek a false "shelteredness in God" (GS IV, 72).

A third sermon on this subject stresses that we are not to flee from the world but to perceive "the call of Christ in it," and hence to know ourselves to be responsible to the world (NRS, 182–89). The church is reminded that Christians do not believe in the world, "not even in the world that is capable of development and improvement," but solely in God (NRS, 183). What truly touches the world is the cross alone; before it alone the world trembles. This articulation is followed by the appeal "And now plant the cross into this world out of joint. Christ is not far from the world, not in a distant region of our world. He went into the lowest depths of our world, his cross is in the midst of the world" (NRS, 187). Universality and not partiality, relatedness to and not flight from the world are the characteristics that express the significance of the cross. The cross does not remove people from the world but, standing in the midst of the world and pointing toward itself, the cross directs people into the very midst of the world. Christians are to perceive their responsibility for the world under the cross. The sermon ends with the engaging question, "Europe, the world, would be conquered a second time by Christ. Are we ready?" (NRS, 189). The cross, the imperative for service to the world, is the exhortation of the gospel.

It was the question of the relation between *church and world*[29] which chiefly shaped the affirmations of these sermons;[30] the church is commissioned to proclaim the word of Jesus Christ to the whole world. In order to state that word as a concrete word, the church, for its part, must pay heed to the world; it can proclaim the word to the world only while existing in the world, the world which is preserved in orientation toward Christ and to which he has already come.[31] Two aspects attracted Bonhoeffer's special interest: the basic question of the relation of church and world and the more specific one of the Christian's relation to the world.

The Relation to the World of the Church and of Christians

Bonhoeffer rejected the kind of church which "became world, without the world at the same time becoming church," and which is familiar with and bears only the anxieties of the *petite bourgeoisie* and no longer those of "the people who direct the economy, the intellectuals, the enemies of the church, the revolutionaries" (GS V, 231). Bonhoeffer desired instead a church which "is a bit of the world, a lost, godless world under the curse, a complacent, evil world" but also "a bit of the world qualified by God's revealing, gracious word" (NRS, 153). The church, therefore, may not place itself above the profane and let itself become separated from the world as a kind of "exceptional luminary" (GS V, 234). The church stands in solidarity with the sinful world. It "knows better what is world," and commits itself today to the pledge "to be worldly," thereby becoming "free from the world. . . . Because it takes its divine origin (*Göttlichkeit*) seriously the church takes seriously that it is committed to the world (*Weltlichkeit*). For herein consists its Christian nature (*Christlichkeit*)" (GS V, 271–72). Precisely in this approach lies the church's true worldliness, as that worldliness is its ability to renounce everything except Christ and the forgiveness of sins (GS V, 270). The most plausible meaning of the above quotation is that in the liberation from sin granted through Christ, bondage to the world (of sin) is overcome, albeit covertly, and true worldliness is genuinely brought into being in place of bondage to the world. The basis of the church's "worldliness" is Jesus Christ's lordship of the world, in which the church is given a definite relation to the world. "It is not a holy, sacred part of the world which belongs to Christ, but the whole world" (NRS, 161).[32] We may perceive this rather explicit statement about the universality of the incarnation as an anticipation of Bonhoeffer's late theology. The church is not a sphere set apart by God and for God but the sphere of the message and salvation for the entire world to which this message is addressed (NRS, 164). The world, as the world of Christ, is itself related to salvation. In view of Christ, the distinction between profane and sacred does not stand up; for that reason the church is not to be separated from the profane. There is, to be sure, an inner sphere of the church consisting of the arcane, the assembly of the believers in which the confession of faith has its place; but in relation to the world action is the primary confession in response to which "the world will seek to hear also the confession in words" (GS V, 259). Yet this hidden aspect, the arcane, must not remove the church from the world. Christ is not excluded from the world nor is the world excluded from the church (NRS, 161). "The church is not a consecrated sanctuary, but the world, called by God to God" (NRS, 154). Consequently, the church is not cordoned off from but stays always in relation to the world; it remains always a world in discipleship, and therefore remains worldly without ever being allowed to become "worldlike" (GS V, 271). The church is truly church only when it is related and open to the world; it is not the church when it is in bondage to the world.

Next to these fundamental assertions about the relation of church and world are more detailed and practical considerations about the understanding of Christians of the world and their relation to it. Bonhoeffer contrasts this relation to the world with the two extremes of provinciality [*Hinterweltlertum*] and secularism. The latter are characterized either by a relation to God without or even against the world or by a relation to the world without or even against God.

> We are provincial (otherworldly)—ever since we hit upon the dubious trick of being religious, yes, even "Christian," at the expense of the earth. . . . One leaps over the present. One disdains the earth; one is better than it. After all, besides the temporal defeats one has one's eternal victories, and they are so easily achieved. (PB, 28)

In these words Bonhoeffer described the "religion of provinciality [*Hinterweltlertum*]" which "cannot bear having the world so near" (PB, 29).

In contrast to provinciality, which involves denying the world, secularism stands for a position bound to the world. It exercises "the Christian renunciation of God as Lord of the earth" (PB, 30) so that one may stand up victoriously for God's business on earth in the combat between world and church, between worldliness and religion. In order that one may stand up in that way, "faith is compelled to harden into religious habit and into morality, and the church must become an organ for effecting religious and moral reconstruction" (PB, 30).

Bonhoeffer rejected both of these positions as being, in the long run, merely the two sides of the same thing.

> They who evade the earth do not find God. They find only another world: their own, better, more beautiful, more peaceful world. They find a world beyond, to be sure, but one that is not God's world, that world which is dawning in this world. They who evade the earth in order to find God, find only themselves. They who evade God in order to find the earth do not find God's earth; they find only the jolly battleground of a war which they incite themselves, a war between the good people and the bad, the pious and the blasphemous—in short, they find themselves. (PB, 32)

Secularism and provinciality are quite clearly rejected here as religious positions. Their place is filled instead by the only appropriate position, which Bonhoeffer labeled "non-religious," for those who truly believe in "God's kingdom on earth." They are the people who walk on this earth which bears them, and who love this earth. Such people alone are not weak provincials, for "Christ does not will or intend this weakness; instead, he makes people strong. He does not lead them in the provincialism of religious flight from this world; rather, he gives them back to the earth as its loyal children" (BP, 29). They are given back to the earth by Christ, strong and yet weak, weak and yet strong; with their being in this position, describable only in paradoxes, we are to see the proper relation of the faithful to the earth. Bonhoeffer spoke of it in the following manner, without any initial reservations:

> Whoever loves God . . . loves him as Lord of the earth as it is; and whoever loves the earth loves it as God's earth. Whoever loves God's kingdom, loves it wholly as *God's* kingdom, but loves it also as God's *kingdom on earth*. And that because the King of the kingdom is the Creator and Preserver of the earth, who has blessed the earth, and who created us out of it. (PB, 32)

It becomes clear from the following twofold "but" that these assertions concern the primordial state.

> But—God has cursed the blessed earth; we live on the cursed ground that bears thorns and thistles. But—it is to this cursed earth that Christ has come; the flesh Christ bore was taken from this ground; on this ground the

Tree of the Curse has stood. And it is this second "but" that establishes the kingdom of Christ as God's kingdom here on the cursed ground. Thus the kingdom of Christ is a kingdom that, coming from above, is sunk down into the cursed ground. (PB, 32)

In this Barthian phrase, "from above," every form of autonomy for the earth is repudiated; and yet the "from above" is not a peripheral or merely external ascription, thrust onto the earth from on high, as it appeared to Bonhoeffer in Karl Barth's work. Bonhoeffer rather saw this kingdom of God as having been really sunk down into the cursed ground. Even though it is eschatologically hidden, God's kingdom, being Christ's kingdom, is truly in the world, and not somehow above it.

That has a specific consequence for the faithful who believe in God's kingdom on earth: they neither can nor want to bypass or relinquish the earth. For "the earth wants us to take it seriously. It will not let us escape, either into the provincialism of pious blessedness nor into the thisworldliness of secular utopias. Instead it comes right out and shows us how it is enslaved in finitude. Its enslavement is our enslavement as well; with it we too are subjugated" (PB, 35). We are not meant to be concerned about the things which are beyond the world; no, "the kingdom comes *to us*" and it does so "where the church perseveres in solidarity with the world and expects the kingdom solely from God" (PB, 35-36). Solidarity with the world is demanded particularly in those times especially marked by grief and pain. "The hour in which we today pray for God's kingdom is the hour of utmost togetherness with the world" (PB, 33). Thus, solidarity with the world is more directly solidarity with the present. The congregation may not disassociate itself from the world but must behold in the resurrection the very coming of God's kingdom to us on earth, coming into our world (PB, 36). God's kingdom is not a kingdom "found only in an eternal beyond"; the issue is not "the strengthening of the church" or "the Christianizing of culture, politics, and education" but the coming of the kingdom, brought about by God alone, the kingdom which "is meant for the earth, . . . the earth that stands under the curse" (PB, 37-38).[33]

Bonhoeffer made it quite plain in this context that one's own personal blessedness is not what the coming of the kingdom is all about. "Our question today is not about God and the individual, but God and humankind" (PB, 38). In sociality alone, that is to say, in the community of the faithful, and, concurrently, in solidarity with all people does God's kingdom become reality. For "God wants us to honor him on earth; he wants us to honor him in our brother and sister—and nowhere else" (PB, 45). Christ "died as the sacrifice for the brother and sisterhood of the world" (GS III, 269). Discipleship is the way to make God's kingdom real. "His kingdom must go the same way he goes" (PB, 39). Precisely in that way does the earth become wholly affirmed.

Bonhoeffer concretely answered the question "How does God's kingdom come to us?" in this way:

> The answer is that it comes in exactly the same way that God himself comes, namely, in breaking through the law of death, in the resurrection, in the miracle; and yet, at the same time, in the "Yes" to the earth, in his entering into its orders, its communities, its history. Both ways belong inextricably together. (PB, 39)

This sentence contains what appears to be the heart of Bonhoeffer's understanding of the world as conceived in 1932; it is expressed in the "and" which ties together the "breaking through" and the "affirmation" of the world and so brings together the two aspects of the understanding of the world from the period of Barcelona. This "and" is actually lost again, as we shall see when we discuss *The Cost of Discipleship*.

The Relation of Church and State

In order to discern more clearly the earthly, albeit hidden, form of "God's kingdom on earth," Bonhoeffer addressed the relation of church and state within the overall context of his concrete reflections on the relation of faith and world. In doing so, he raised an issue which had created much hardship for the Protestant church after 1918. Even though his comments are not completely satisfactory, a fact which in light of that hardship is hardly surprising, they are nonetheless remarkable as far as the relation of church and state and the concrete relation of faith and world are concerned.

By "the kingdom of God on earth" Bonhoeffer meant the duality of church and state.[34] This subject occupied him on more than one occasion in 1932–33.[35] It emerged also in *Ethics,* especially in the sections concerning the mandates (E, 207). Clearly, the subject was profoundly significant for Bonhoeffer.

"The kingdom of God exists in our world exclusively in the duality of church and state" (PB, 40). The state no longer faces a state church or a territorial church but one founded on God's word without any claims to absolute or absolutistic domination over the state. In fact, "the kingdom of Christ becomes a reality only when these two are genuinely related to each other and yet mutually limit one another" (PB, 44).[36]

Bonhoeffer conceded to the state a certain autonomy vis-à-vis the church, for "the kingdom of God assumes form *in the state* insofar as the state acknowledges and maintains the order of the preservation of life" (PB, 40), "insofar as here the orders of existing communities are maintained with authority and responsibility" (PB, 42). The state concerns itself with the order of the preservation of the world; through the state God acts in the world (GS V, 273). The function of the state is neither Christian nor godless; it is responsible and objective. Only when the state opposes God's word, and acts against it, may one oppose and act against the state.

God's kingdom is made known appropriately on earth only in the duality and mutual delimitation of church and state and the consequent "tension of coexistence, which in this world must never be coalescence" (PB, 43).

> The kingdom of Christ is God's kingdom, but God's kingdom in the form appointed for us. It does not appear as one visible, powerful empire, nor yet as the "new" kingdom of the world; on the contrary, it manifests itself as the kingdom of the other world that has entered completely into the discord and contradiction of this world. It appears as the powerless, defenseless gospel of the resurrection, of the miracle; and, at the very same time, as the state that possesses authority and power and maintains order. (PB, 44)

What follows from this duality of Christ's kingdom is that the church's proclamation of the concrete commandment for the world is at the same time "necessarily 'political,' i.e., it is directed at the order of politics by which people are governed"; but because the church only delimits politics in this way, it is "eminently political and apolitical at the same time" (NRS, 156).

Bonhoeffer elaborated the meaning of that statement a year later when the dispute with the state over the Jewish question came to a head for the first time: "The church cannot in the first place exert direct political action, for the church does not pretend to have any knowledge of the necessary course of history" (NRS, 223). The church does not advance and direct independent initiatives for history, for "history is not made by the church, but by the state" (NRS, 222). "The action of the state remains free from the church's intervention" (NRS, 222). But since the church alone testifies "to the penetration of history by God in Christ," then it is only the church, which makes no history, that can know what history is; "only the church, which bears witness to the coming of God in history, knows what history, and therefore what the state, is" (NRS, 223). The church cannot give the state any substantive instructions for political action, yet it has the obligation to "ask the state whether its action can be justified as legitimate action of the state" (NRS, 223). Whenever the state violates its obligation to secure the orders of preservation, and thus acts against itself—the Aryan Clause being such a violation—the church must interfere. Such interference in the affairs of state cannot consist of merely giving aid to the victims of state action (NRS, 225), but must, in the extreme case, be "direct political action" (NRS, 225) by the church,[37] action in which the church assigns limits to the state and in so doing acknowledges the rights of the state (NRS, 226). Just as the church limits the state so does the state limit the church, namely, whenever the church "desires to be a state within the state and a political power," which is just as improper as the opposite case, whenever the state "desires to use the church as one of its tools" (GS II, 114).[38]

The relation between church and state, as Bonhoeffer saw it, is necessarily one of tension as there exists between them both mutuality and difference. Bonhoeffer's lectures on christology show how this relation of tension is founded, for the dialectics of church and state are traced back to Christ himself: "Christ is present to us in the forms both of church and state" (C, 63). There is no support in Bonhoeffer's by no means unambiguous comment for the conclusion that he envisaged the church triumphing over the state: "The relationship of church and state since the cross is new. There is a state, in the proper sense, only when there is a church" (C, 63), for both are dependent on Christ and have nothing to do but his will. If the church is both center and boundary of the state it cannot derive any claim for domination over the state from that very fact. "The state is God's 'rule with his left hand,'" as Bonhoeffer noted with reliance on Luther. "So long as Christ was on earth, he was the kingdom of God. When he was crucified the kingdom broke up into one ruled by God's right hand and one ruled by his left hand. Now, it can only be recognized in a twofold form, as church and as state" (C, 64).

One must view all of these statements in light of Christ, or more accurately, in light of the cross of Jesus Christ. Bonhoeffer attempted to portray for Christians a relation of church and state which would no longer be framed in the conceptuality of the authority of the state but which would not at the same time render the state insignificant for them. For "Christ as center of history is the mediator between state and God in the form of the church" (C, 64). This is true only in light of what Bonhoeffer immediately went on to say: "As the center of history Christ is the mediator between this church and God. Christ is also the center of this church. Only as a church of which Christ is the center can the church be the center of history" (C, 64). This concentration on Christ removes every trace of apparent self-glory from that statement about the church.

The significance of the discussion about the state lies in the fact that Bonhoeffer tried to describe, at a threatening time of transition and with a sharp eye for the troubles looming ahead, how the church might remain independent without becoming autonomous. It was to be a position *in the middle between state–church and church–state*. The church can be only political–apolitical in one. When the state goes against God's word the church must inform the state in a political manner of its limits, while, at the same time and in an apolitical fashion, the church cannot independently know what the state must do in actual reality. The church possesses no substantive knowledge about what the tasks of the state are; it obtains such knowledge only by accepting the state and worldly reality. The church for its part achieves concreteness, given solely in Christ and his acceptance of the world, only when it enters into the world—into given situations, and into the state; that is to say, when the church enters into the world which Christ has made his own and which is being preserved for him, and when the church enters into the state which has the responsibility to preserve the orders of the world. Clearly the world and the state have a reciprocal significance for the church, for concreteness is achieved only in the world.

These early statements and their ambiguous repudiation of a falsely perceived doctrine of the two kingdoms show that in theory Bonhoeffer had laid the groundwork for his later political–apolitical stance. In his concerns with God's kingdom on earth one may already see why it is "the cause of Christ" for which he became a political conspirator, and why holding out "in this boundary situation" (LPP, 129) was not really a *boundary* situation, in the sense of a situation at the extreme periphery, but was much more a *limiting* situation. Bonhoeffer saw himself called upon as a Christian to inform the state of its limits in order that the state could see clearly what constituted its place and task. With such limitation alone is the state truly state rather than being depraved, just as the church is truly church only when it permits itself to be limited by the state as the protector of the worldly orders of preservation.

The Declining Significance for Bonhoeffer of the Subject of "World"

Whereas Bonhoeffer was intensely preoccupied with the subject of faith and world, in general, and the subject of church and state as a particular aspect of that general theme, the lectures on creation and fall, given mostly in 1932–33, and the subsequent ones on christology, show a noticeable decline in the endeavor to forge an understanding of the world. The reason for this may well be that both of these courses focused on narrower theological *loci*.

In "Creation and Fall," the context of which is Bonhoeffer's paraphrase of the opening chapters of Genesis, the world is mentioned only indirectly and does not seem to have any particular significance. The world referred to is the old world, the world under sin; the fall is "not simply a *moral lapse*" but "affects the whole of the created world" (CF, 77). Since then humankind lives "in the destroyed world, between the curse and the promise of God" (CF, 85). The curse of God is that humankind *must* live in the fallen world; that they *may* live in it in his promise (CF, 84). On account of the promise still contained in God's curse the world is not destroyed but becomes "the world of the *preservation of life*" (CF, 86). God's original blessing on the world has become void, it is true, the blessing in which the "total empirical existence . . . creatureliness . . . worldliness . . . earthliness" of humankind were blessed (CF, 40). Sin disturbed the relation between humankind and the world inasmuch as people, belonging wholly to the world and yet free *from* it, are now under the domination of the world (CF, 38). The cross of Christ is the way out of this bondage, bringing salvation to this enslaved existence, the cross "on which God himself had to suffer and die" (CF, 94), and through which the world, robbed of its center, received a true center again.

The subject "world" receded even more in the course on christology. Bonhoeffer was concerned with the reality of the incarnation in history and, therefore, in the world, as opposed to its dissolution in idealism. The significance for the world of Christ's being "the center of human existence, the center of history, and . . . the center of nature" is expressed in very broad terminology: "The mediator as fulfiller of the law and liberator of creation is all this for the whole of human existence. He is the same who is intercessor and *pro me,* and who is himself the end of the old world and the beginning of the new world of God" (C, 65).

The statements about faith and world, church and state may rightly be called the first peak in Bonhoeffer's preoccupation with the subject of world. The fact that both Christianness and worldliness are grounded in the incarnation, and are both said to converge toward Christ, and the mutual divergence of the tasks of faith and world, allows Christianness and worldliness to be perceived clearly for the first time in their interrelation and difference. Given the dispute about church and state in the Third Reich it is quite understandable that the ecclesiological aspect was so strongly emphasized by Bonhoeffer. He had hoped to encourage the church as church to become conscious of its responsibility for the state and, at the same time, of its independence from it. The mutual separation and relation of both constrained the church to show reticence toward the state in worldly issues, but also forbade such reticence when the state was seen to be betraying its duties. Even though he insisted that the church could not meddle politically in the affairs of state and, naturally, that the state could not involve itself in the matters of the church, Bonhoeffer did not in any way suggest that the church remain apolitical. It would appear that this position has to this day not gained sufficient support; rather an (allegedly) Lutheran position of maintaining total political abstinence on the part of the church has established a doctrine of the two kingdoms that allows church and state to slide into an existence in which they live side by side but where, in truth, they tend to become completely identified one with the other as in the position of the German Christians.

This thought-provoking reflection on the relation of church and state may well be of significance beyond the special situation in which it originated. Bonhoeffer certainly did not seek the self-preservation of the church, but he was anxious to guard the state against self-destruction, on the one hand, and the church against a complete incorporation into the state, on the other. Thus, Bonhoeffer spoke of the relation of church and state in such a way that the untenable consequences of the prevailing position of the church toward the state and that of the state toward the church were overcome precisely when the church was the defenseless victim of the authorities, to the detriment of both parties.

In the span of six months Bonhoeffer worked out a concrete relation and understanding of the world which sought to remain in the middle between flight from and bondage to the world. This understanding of the world is grounded in the incarnation; on account of the cross the true proclamation of salvation for the world exists only in utter solidarity with the world. The dimension of the theology of the cross is clearly manifest. It rules out a triumphalistic interpretation of the statement that the whole world is the preserve of the one church of Christ. The Christian's progress on the ridge between flight from and bondage to the world suggests a non-religiousness even though it is stated more negatively than positively. Later the positive aspect was called "deep thisworldliness," by which was meant a multidimensional understanding of the world. The first draft of the Bethel confession stated that since faith and the world have come apart on account of sin (GS II, 97), and since the world is restored solely in Christ (GS II, 102), Christians should "obediently receive this world from the hand of the God revealed in Christ, take his cross upon them and carry it in the power of the promise that God will in the end of all things create a new heaven and a new earth" (GS II, 108). On that basis, therefore, the confession goes against the false teaching that "so tears the world of hope and our world apart, that the latter has nothing to do with the former" (GS II, 118–19). The world of hope, that is, the "world of the resurrection," and "our world" are therefore neither to be identified nor to be separated. "It is our world which is made new, the world on which stood the cross of Christ" (GS II, 118).[39]

THE DETACHED VIEW OF THE WORLD OF THE MIDDLE PERIOD

THE TRANSITION TO *THE COST OF DISCIPLESHIP*

We have already noted that Bonhoeffer did not succeed in conceptualizing the relation of the believer to the world and to the state in a practice-oriented theory. This may well be the reason why the question of the world receded in his writings. It seems as though Bonhoeffer retreated in order to reexamine or to consolidate his foundations and to draw new conclusions from them. The few statements about the world from his London days, made again later in sermons, reflect a predominantly negative view of the world.

The following text makes plain, however, that even that negative view did not arise from indifference toward the world, but rather from a fascination with it, and from the fear of turning unreservedly toward it:

> It is said of the great poet of the Italian Renaissance, Petrarch, that he once looked down from a mountain in Upper Italy into the countryside in full bloom and that he was overcome by the feeling: God, how beautiful, how beautiful is this world—but that in the very next moment he made the sign of the cross and took hold of his breviary in order to pray. That is the one who is frightened in the face of the world's beauty, who flees from it full of fear, not wanting to love this world with its glory more than the one who created it, not wanting to love the creature more than the creator. (GS V, 511)[40]

One would have to look at the understanding of the world which Bonhoeffer developed in *The Cost of Discipleship* against this background. The latter work is one of strong concentration and trenchant development.

It is no accident that the cross is very much in the foreground of the sermons given in London. Facing a danger that was more than theoretical, Bonhoeffer sought orientation in the cross. He stated that the cross is "the sign of the fulfillment of this world"; it shows that "this world is ripe for demolition, more than ripe" (GS V, 560). In light of such a comment it would appear that Bonhoeffer set the world over against faith in a one-sided, negative manner, even when he had previously stated that the cross is God's action in the world "on which the whole world lives ever since" (GS V, 556). Without making absolute the juxtaposition of faith and the world in Bonhoeffer, an absolute juxtaposition is still implied in what he said about "poor humankind" a little later. Poor humankind "wants to learn from us, come to have faith again, to love, to hope; let us not withhold it from humankind. Let us shout out to one another on Reformation Day: have faith, hope, and above all love, and you will overcome the world" (GS V, 560). To say that the world has been overcome is justified, indeed, but it does not state the fact that the world is overcome precisely because it is itself redeemed. The demise of the world was for Bonhoeffer too isolated a sign of its fulfillment; and its humiliation, too isolated a potential sign of its healing, corresponding to God's own humiliation in the world. For "God's throne in this world is not on the thrones of humankind but in the abysses and the depths of people, it is in the manger" (GS V, 502). Is this not "religious" language, that is, speech concerning God and salvation as seen at the boundaries of life?

The address Bonhoeffer delivered at Fanö shows very clearly the juxtaposition of faith and world, church and state. It contains his most intensive appeal for peace, based on what Eberhard Bethge called

Bonhoeffer's "christological ecclesiology" (DB, 311).[41] "Peace ought to prevail because Christ is in the world, i.e., peace ought to prevail because there is a church of Christ on account of which alone the whole world still lives" (GS I, 217). The conclusion of the address shows that the world is more the wicked one, and hostile to Christ; the "raging world" must hear the church's word of peace. Even if one takes into consideration the appellative nature of these words and the situation in which they were spoken, a deep gap still remains between church and world, a gap which is not based entirely on that situation; otherwise Bonhoeffer would have had to argue in a similar way later in his life. There can be no doubt that in comparison to the statements about the world of 1932 a different note is sounded here.

From its outset Bonhoeffer's sojourn at Finkenwalde, which followed that at London, was marked by the character of *The Cost Of Discipleship*. Writing to his brother-in-law in 1936, Bonhoeffer asked, "How do I live a Christian life in the real world?" (GS III, 26). Quite obviously he was concerned with the "Christian life" only, that is, with the Sermon on the Mount, which is also referred to in that letter, and not with "the real world," even though one may assume that his concern with the Christian life was for the sake of service to the real world.

Bonhoeffer's sermon outline about the cross according to Gal. 6:14 makes this plain. There, Bonhoeffer summed up the assertion "The world is crucified to me" in the lapidary phrase "it is damned and dead," in order to elaborate the counterassertion "I am crucified to the world."

> To be crucified to the world does mean to have a part in his cross. Because I have really been crucified with Christ by God, by his—God's—judgment, I can suffer Christ's suffering with him. This takes place in faith and faith is carrying the cross after him. Discipleship, following after Christ, is to be crucified by the world. (GS IV, 215)

Here discipleship is clearly juxtaposed to the world. At the end of the outline Bonhoeffer went beyond this juxtaposition. After referring to the significance of Christians bearing the cross he declared, "The final glory is not that the world will be judged and sentenced but that Christ shows mercy to the world and makes peace through his cross which is the cross also of the congregation. Our glory is the peace of the cross, the salvation of God" (GS IV, 216). Yet the emphasis of what Bonhoeffer said at that time was on the idea that we "live in the world of the cross" (GS IV, 192), which is preserved only for the sake of the preached word.[42] "Christ will be Lord over the earth . . . which rejected him and from which he rose" (GS IV, 185). One wonders whether the preposition "from" in that statement indicates that the resurrection is to be understood as a distancing from the world. The statement uses the words "the ultimate" (GS IV, 185); the world is in fact a "lost world" (GS IV, 198 n.

2). The world is a shackle for Christians; it is too constricted for them (GS IV, 226). Even though there are other statements besides the many critical ones of this nature which speak of the hiddenness of God in this world (GS IV, 398), they do not carry enough weight to be the foundation for the believer's relation to the world.

The relation of church and state is determined in a similar, one-sidedly negative way: "Friendship between the church and the world is not normal, but abnormal" (NRS, 324).[43] The issue in this dispute between church and state is the attempt to assure that the church has "a place in the world" (WF, 42), since the church is but a piece of the newly-created world. The boundaries of the church are not set by the church itself but by the world which distinguishes itself from the church (WF, 79). Thus, the church is *in* but not *of* the world (WF, 107).

"He enters *into* the world" (GS III, 300) was Bonhoeffer's remark about Christ the crucified. Because God enters into the world there is a different prefix now before the "worldliness of the Psalter" (GS III, 301), and yet the break between Christianity and the world predominates. This cannot be summarized any more clearly than in Bonhoeffer's second draft for a catechism: "The world is all that about me which stands under the power and the curse of godlessness. The world is all that which seeks to draw my heart away from God. I live in the midst of that world" (GS III, 346). The congregation, however, "lives as a stranger who moves about in his homeland. The congregation makes use of the goods of the world only to meet its needs. Its heart is not with the world but in heaven" (GS III, 361). This ambiguously negative assertion may well represent a recourse to the isolated, negative aspect of the view of the world that was apparent already in Barcelona. Even if it is true that there can be no unbroken relation for the Christian to the world, one still needs to ask whether a direct flight from the world is not the only consequence of the assertions just cited.[44] The warning against flight from the world, issued in 1932, does not counterbalance these assertions at all. For that reason one may regard the period of *The Cost of Discipleship* as a time of cloistered separation for Bonhoeffer, corresponding to his understanding of the biography of Luther, a man who left the world behind and entered the monastery (NRS, 323).

THE UNDERSTANDING OF THE WORLD IN
THE COST OF DISCIPLESHIP

We have said that, given Bonhoeffer's distance from the world apparent in this book, this period of its composition corresponded to Luther's time in the monastery. This is confirmed by a comment that Bonhoeffer made some time later: "I thought I could acquire faith by trying to live a holy life, or something like it. I suppose I wrote *The Cost of Discipleship* as the end of that path. Today I can see the dangers of that book, though I still stand by what I wrote" (LPP, 369).

If this personal testimony is salient to the point it would follow that Bonhoeffer viewed his experiences of that period in a critical way, but he did not renounce them. Although he regarded the view of the world put forth in *The Cost of Discipleship* as not comprehensive enough, he did not denounce it as being entirely false. This view, in fact, represents an aspect of his later reflections, as may be seen in his comment in *Letters and Papers from Prison* that the reality which he tried to grasp in the concept of "the penultimate and the ultimate" was just hinted at in chapter one of *The Cost of Discipleship*, but was never completely followed up (LPP, 157).

The fact that Bonhoeffer repeatedly referred to Luther's entry into and subsequent departure from the monastery shows that he was quite fascinated by it, which also suggests that his interest is of some significance for an understanding of Bonhoeffer himself. Quite early Bonhoeffer said, "It was hard for Luther to make this personal and fundamental separation from the monastery" (GS III, 130). While working on *The Cost of Discipleship* he made reference to this topic several times and incorporated an extensive presentation of it into the final version (CD, 39). In *Ethics* he returned to the topic once again (E, 255). Yet even in *The Cost of Discipleship* Bonhoeffer had wanted to express something to the effect that "Luther lived a thisworldly life in this sense" (LPP, 369), as we shall soon see, but that he had perceived thisworldliness to be still too much from the perspective of the monastery.

The various layers, or, better, stages of Bonhoeffer's understanding of the world as depicted in *The Cost of Discipleship* seem to be graphically manifested in his analysis and interpretation of the fundamental decisions that Luther had made about his own life. Luther's entry into the monastery was a departure from the world in the sense of a renunciation of the evil and malicious world. But because Luther had renounced everything, and not just his own pious subjectivity, the monastery itself became, for Luther, world as self-justified world. Luther's return to the world constituted a sharp attack on the world, a decisive hand-to-hand struggle with the world as the wicked world; it was decisive because a complete renunciation of his own subjectivity was also required. In *The Cost of Discipleship* the world is always portrayed in a negative light as representing the counter-position to discipleship. The relation to the world of Christians is seen primarily as one of defensiveness, although it is also seen as one of aggression; it is chiefly negative, and rarely constructive and constitutive. This relation must now be described in detail.

The Break with the World

Initially the world is said to be "evil" (CD, 150), "malicious" (CD, 129), and "sinful" (CD, 245). In sin humankind "has made itself god . . . [and] ruled in solitude as creator-god in God-forsaken, subjugated world" (CD, 270). This widely held conviction in Christian theology, accessible, to be sure, in faith only, receives a particular emphasis in *The Cost of Discipleship*. To put it bluntly, the monastery, or as we may also say, the church, is no more than the world (CD, 40)[45] if it considers grace to be a principle (CD, 42) or a presupposition rather than the answer (CD, 42) of justification; for here the "costly grace" offered initially by God is corrupted into "cheap grace." Under the motto, "The world remains the world and we go on being sinners 'even in the best life' " (CD, 35), Bonhoeffer stated the imperatives of the life under cheap grace: "The world has been justified by grace. . . . Therefore, let [Christians] live like the rest of the world" (CD, 36). Let Christians renounce the extraordinary for the sake of the world, and for the sake of grace, and let them remain content with "having to live in the worldly fashion," comforting themselves "in their worldliness" with the grace that accomplishes all (CD, 36). These statements, which use the terms "living in worldly fashion" and "worldliness" in a clearly negative sense,[46] show plainly that to live in cheapened grace is no more than to live in the malicious, sinful, and lost world hostile to God.

Bonhoeffer adduced a historical basis for the worldliness of Christians: "As Christianity spread, and the church became more secularized, this realization of the costliness of grace gradually faded. The world was Christianized, and grace became common property of a Christian world" (CD, 38). Luther's way into the monastery represented the separation from the world as a secularized church, but his leaving everything behind "except his pious self" made obvious that this form of discipleship was the "ultimate spiritual self-assertion of the 'religious' " (CD, 39). Luther concluded that he had to leave the monastery and return to the world "not because the world in itself was good and holy, but because even the cloister was only a part of the world" (CD, 40). Grace was cheapened as a consequence of the abolition of the catechumenate of baptism, the arcane discipline which "enabled a strict watch to be kept over the frontier between the church and the world and over costly grace" (CD, 45). It is therefore part of discipleship that the boundary between faith and world not be blurred, for otherwise a reduction occurs which, under the guise of grace, hides the fact that it is only the world one deals with. The secularization of the church (CD, 38) is more difficult to discern than the worldliness of the world, since the whole world "has been made 'Christian' under the influence of this grace," but at the cost "of secularizing Christianity as never before" (CD, 42). Following the end of hostilities "between Christian life and the life of bourgeois-worldly vocation," the former consists in complete conformity to the world with the only exception being that one leaves "the world for an hour or so on a Sunday morning to go to church to be assured that one's sins are all forgiven" (CD, 42). It is more than clear that the solution of the relation of faith and the world proposed by Cultural Protestantism, being a spatial one, as Bonhoeffer saw it, was again under heavy attack.

These two aspects of the world, namely, that it is an evil world and that Christianity has been "secularized as never before," must be sharply separated from costly grace.

> God and the world, God and the world's goods, are incompatible, because the world and its goods make a bid for our hearts, and only when they have won them do they become what they really are. . . . We are confronted by an "either–or": either we love God, or we love earthly goods. If we love the world, we hate God; and if we love God, we hate the world. (CD, 157)

God and the world are radically opposed. It is, therefore, quite consistent that the last thing said in *The Cost of Discipleship* is that Christians "are dead to the flesh and to sin, they are dead to the world, and the world is dead to them" (CD, 273).

"The first Christ-suffering which everyone must experience is the call which calls us out of the attachments to this world" (CD, 79). During the discussion, above, of the christology of *The Cost of Discipleship* it was discovered that Bonhoeffer rejected every unmediated relationship, and therefore the possibility of an unmediated relation to the world. This is to be looked at more closely now. But first it may be recalled that the mediation to God by Christ and the mediation to the world are fundamentally different. One of the differences is that the latter gives rise only to a negative relation to the world, at least as far as the statements in *The Cost of Discipleship* are concerned.

The mediation to the world is explicated christologically. "We are now deprived of our direct relationship with all the given realities of the world because Christ, the mediator and Lord, has stepped in between us. Baptized Christians . . . belong to Christ alone, their relationship to the world is mediated through him. The breach with the world is complete" (CD, 207).[47] There can be no objection on principle to this assertion as it can call upon the basic Christian affirmation that salvation in Christ signifies a "new creation" for humanity. Yet Bonhoeffer drew from this assertion what seems to be negative consequences, which he did not further explicate, such as the following: disciples "have only him [Jesus], and with him they have nothing, literally nothing in the world, but everything with and through God" (CD, 95). Generalizing a specific statement, one may say that in *The Cost of Discipleship* "the estrangement of Christian life from the world is patently manifest" (CD, 151). The disciple "does not see Christ *and* the world" but "always and only Christ" (CD, 154).

This indicates that the community of disciples is sharply divided from the world. "The separation of community and world is now complete"

(CD, 170). But this separation also brings with it the separation of the world from the community. "Just as sanctification causes the separation of the community from the world, so it causes also the separation of the world from the community" (CD, 260). This mutual separation takes form in the disciples' visible actions "by which they set themselves apart from the world" (CD, 106). Bonhoeffer summed up the matter in this way: "The Christian is attached to the 'extraordinary.' That is why Christians cannot conform to the world's level. . . . The cross is the differential of what is Christian which enables Christians to transcend the world and gives them the victory precisely in that" (CD, 136).

Before we take up the difficulties of this line of thought we must first consider its ultimate conclusion in order that the inherent problems become even clearer. The question raised in the first part of *The Cost of Discipleship,* "Is there any place on this earth for such a community?" (CD, 103), is given an answer which corresponds to the separation of the disciples from the world. One can describe the relation of the community to the world by means of a few texts. The opening statement reads,

> With his incarnation Christ demands space among humankind. He came into his own. But at his birth they gave him a manger, for "there was no space in the inn." At his death they thrust him out, his body hung between earth and heaven on the gallows. But despite all this, the incarnation does involve a claim to a space of its own on earth. (CD, 223)

Demonstrating how non-religious are these opening words is Bonhoeffer's counter-statement: "A truth, a doctrine, a religion need no space for themselves. They are disembodied entities" (CD, 223). It follows from the presupposition that Jesus Christ lays claim to space on earth that "the community of Jesus Christ claims in the world *space for proclamation.* The body of Christ is visible in the community gathered around the word and Sacrament" (CD, 226). The concluding statement reads, "This visible community of complete common life invades the world and robs it of its children" (CD, 230). In the following remarks it becomes plain that an incorporation of the world into the space of the community is intended: "Even the most secular activity takes place in the community. . . . There is no sphere of life in which the member may withdraw from the body nor desire so to withdraw" (CD, 230). But now it is no longer clear how this is different from the "bechurching" of the world.

If one wanted to state the full range of this argument in Bonhoeffer's own words, one would choose the following, highly significant section which appears toward the end of the work:

> Barred off from the world by an unbreakable seal, the community of saints awaits its ultimate deliverance. Like a sealed train traveling through foreign territory, the community goes on its way through the world. Like Noah's ark, which was "pitched within and without with pitch" (Gen. 6.14) so that

it might come safely through the flood, so the journey of the sealed-off community through the world resembles that of the ark through the floods. (CD, 251)

The nucleus of the understanding of the world in *The Cost of Discipleship* has become apparent in all its one-sidedness by now. Everything depends on the total "separation from the world until the second coming of Christ" (CD, 250),[48] on the basis of which it is no longer clear why Christians should not in fact flee from the world.[49] Bonhoeffer attempted to overcome this difficulty by suggesting that the community's activity must be both visible and hidden. The contradiction is to be resolved in the dialectics of visibility and hiddenness. Bonhoeffer also spoke of the reflection commanded to the disciples, namely, to do everything utterly "unpremeditated" (CD, 143). But this comment is of little use even if the concept of reflection were taken in a primarily ethical sense, namely, in the sense of *actus directus*, and not restricted to the cognitive sphere.[50] One cannot clear up the separation of faith or community and world by suggesting that the disciple's journey through the world is as in a sealed train, or that they are in an ark.

Jesus Christ himself is said to be the basis for this separation of the community, that is to say, the church, and the world. Bonhoeffer's christological assertions are equally marked by one-sidedness. Christ did indeed "suffer vicariously for the world" (CD, 81), but of what use is that to the world when the Christians' worldly life consists of reduplicating it in the church (CD, 230)?

Bonhoeffer answered the already cited question "Is there any place on this earth for such a community?" by referring to the cross: "Clearly, there is one place, and only one, and that is where the poorest, meekest, and most sorely tried of all people is to be found—on the cross of Golgotha" (CD, 103). "The place on this earth" is reduced to the cross not only here, it seems. It does not do to assign the cross to the community as its place on this earth with the comment that "Golgotha, too, is a plot of earth" (CD, 100).[51] That only turns the cross, and with it the community, into a ghetto. How is the world to be renewed from there? The way in which Bonhoeffer spoke of the renewal of the world by the cross in this context suggests no genuine relation of the cross to the world. That the world and salvation are separated one from the other and that, consequently, there is no true universality of the cross is manifest in Bonhoeffer's statement which describes the temple in the Old Testament in an analogy to salvation: "The temple is the place where the gracious presence of God condescends to dwell among people. It is also the place where God receives his community. Both aspects of the temple are fulfilled only in the incarnate Jesus Christ" (CD, 222).[52] What meaning is there in the idea that Jesus Christ is the one "who enters into the very midst of the world of sin and death" (CD, 271)? The center which the temple was to the world is placed in opposition to the meaning of the center of the New Testament: whereas the temple related the world to itself, the cross related itself to God and the world!

Following the radical and complete separation of the Christian community and the world and the one-sided view of the incarnation and the cross which is based on that separation, is Bonhoeffer's similarly negative account of the Christian's life in the world, especially life in vocation. Bonhoeffer spoke explicitly of the disciples' "earthly task" (CD, 104), but he interpreted it negatively. For worldly vocation is not seen as a genuine service to the world and for the world; instead its justification is seen in the fact that it "is sanctified only insofar as that calling registers the final, radical protest against the world" (CD, 40). This view of vocation is explained in part four of *The Cost of Discipleship* as follows: Christians are to

> remain in the world to engage in frontal assault on it, and let them live the life of their "secular calling" in order to show themselves as "strangers in this world" all the more. But that is only possible if we are visible members of the community. The antithesis between it and the world must be borne out in the world. That was the reason why Christ became a man and died among his enemies. That is the reason and the only reason why the slave must remain a slave and the Christian remain subject to the powers that be. (CD, 238–39)

Indeed, the community invades "the life of the world and conquers territory for Christ" (CD, 232) in order that Christians do "not contract out of the world" (CD, 238), but rather "bear witness to the world's lost condition and to the new creation which has taken place in the community" (CD, 238). Yet nothing in all of these statements gives evidence of a relation to the existing world, preserved for the sake of and redeemed by Christ, a relation mediated by Christ and for that reason an indirect relation. Otherwise, the meaning of the call into the world could not be exclusively "a call into existence as strangers in this world" (CD, 239).[53]

For this reason Bonhoeffer vigorously recommended that Christians show a passive demeanor in the world and refrain from all violent alterations of the orders of the world. "As a member of the Body of Christ he [the slave] has acquired a freedom which no rebellion or revolution could have brought him" (CD, 233). Such attempts to change human conditions are to be shunned

> not because the order of secular vocation is so good and godly an institution that it would be wrong to upset it by revolution. The truth of the matter is that the whole world has already been turned upside down by the work of Christ, which has wrought a liberation for the free and the slave alike. Would a revolution not only obscure that new divine order which Jesus Christ has established and hinder the creation of his community? (CD, 234)

Bonhoeffer counseled complete abstinence from worldly involvement, because the renunciation of rebellion against the orders of this world "is the most appropriate way of expressing our conviction that the Christian hope is not set on this world, but on Christ and his kingdom" (CD, 234). Otherwise, Christians would become slaves in two seemingly contrary ways: "by a revolution and the overthrow of the established order on the one hand and by investing the established order with a halo of spirituality on the other" (CD, 234).

Even if one takes into consideration the circumstances in which Bonhoeffer wrote these words, one cannot accept what he says without question. This is true even when those words are stated with great sincerity in the face of the not infrequent, facile support either for violent transformation of established orders or for their stabilization.[54] Bonhoeffer was right in asserting that Christian faith as such is admonished to remove itself from both these positions.

Bonhoeffer's words, "The world is growing too small for the Christian community, and all it looks for is the Lord's return. It still walks in the flesh, but with eyes upturned to heaven" (CD, 243), are both a reminiscence of the end of *Act and Being* (AB, 184) and a summary of the view of the world of *The Cost of Discipleship*. The same impression emerges in the reiteration of the petition "Thy kingdom come" and its interpretation: "God grant that the kingdom of Jesus Christ may grow in his community on earth, God hasten the end of the kingdom of this world, and establish his own kingdom in power and glory!" (CD, 148). This statement reminds one more of the one-sided formulations of 1928 than of the much more comprehensive ones of 1932. The basic note of the understanding of the world of *The Cost of Discipleship* sounds the decline of the world and the separation of the disciples from it.

Indications of the 360-Degree Turn

In *The Cost of Discipleship* there are notes on the basis of which Bonhoeffer later said that in that work he had hinted at, but had not elaborated on, a conception of faith in deep thisworldliness. In the context of the latter Christians were said to be "truly free to live their lives in that world" (CD, 47). It is true that this sovereign freedom for life in the world was not spelled out in detail. And it is also quite true that this is quite a singular assertion. Bonhoeffer did say that "the earth is the Lord's and all that is therein" (CD, 252); and therefore he knew that the place where Jesus is is no longer one single place but that he is present in word and sacrament in many places. Bonhoeffer's conclusion from this knowledge was that "the risen and exalted Christ has drawn close to the world, the body of Christ has penetrated into the heart of the world in the form of the church" (CD, 233). Bonhoeffer paints an appropriate picture of the disciples' life in this interpretation of the story of Abraham.

It is a 360-degree turn, Abraham receives Isaac back, but henceforth he will have his son in quite a new way—through the mediator and for the mediator's sake. . . . Christ has stepped between father and son. Abraham had left all, followed Christ and as he follows him he is allowed to go back and live in the world in which he had lived before. Outwardly the picture has not changed, but the old is passed away, and behold all things are new. Everything has had to pass through Christ. (CD, 89)

As a consequence of that 360-degree turnabout there would have had to have been a different view of the disciples' life in the world than the one that envisions only the disruption of relations to the world, protest, even close combat against the world. The overall view of the world in *The Cost of Discipleship* remains, therefore, negative. Bonhoeffer did not succeed in maintaining the positive note that he had sounded earlier; only later did he achieve this. One may relate his own words to his position: it seems difficult today "to walk with absolute certainty in the narrow way of ecclesiastical decision and yet remain in the broad open spaces of the universal love of Christ, of the patience, mercy, and 'philanthropy' of God (Titus 3:4) for the weak and the ungodly" (CD, 32). This vision "for all humankind" was not in fact developed in its positive form in this book. One may even ask whether the "intolerable dichotomy between our lives as workers in the world and our lives as Christians" (CD, 31), which Bonhoeffer wanted to overcome by writing this book, was not introduced again. But one must then also raise the counter-question as to whether the dichotomy can be overcome in any other way than by the measures which *The Cost of Discipleship* set out to prepare.

OTHER STATEMENTS ABOUT THE WORLD FROM THIS PERIOD

If one traces Bonhoeffer's understanding of the world to the conclusion of his middle period one notices a certain change in his point of view even though the number of comments on this subject are few. In his exegetical writings he asserted that

> even though the community of Christ has been wrested from the world this does not mean that it is to despise the world but that it must stand with it. Precisely because only they who have been wrested from the world's tutelage know the world as it really is are they bound to the world in a new way. . . . The community which withdraws from responsibility for the world, for 'all humankind,' and turns in on itself denies the gospel and its ministry.[55]

This statement may well go beyond *The Cost of Discipleship* but it represents no fundamental change as yet. It is still true that "the goal of God's attention in the world is always his community. Whatever he does on earth is done in the end for the sake of the community of Jesus Christ. The community does everything in order to win salvation for the world which is the same as to serve God" (GS IV, 366).[56] What corresponds to

HISTORICAL SURVEY OF BONHOEFFER'S UNDERSTANDING OF THE WORLD

The Cost of Discipleship is that the church is seen to be the sole aim of God's will in the world; what goes beyond it is that the church has a concrete responsibility for the world. There is no doubt that behind this imperceptible change there hovers the turnabout which, not yet clearly understood or put into effect, took Bonhoeffer onto the road toward active participation in the German Resistance.[57] The change in Bonhoeffer's understanding of the world remained just as tentative initially as this turnabout had been.

The emphasis in *Life Together* is no longer the same as in *The Cost of Discipleship*. In the later work the community of believers is said to take part "in the very events that occurred on this earth for the salvation of the world" (LT, 53). Even if work, through which Christians are plunged into "the world of things," serves as a protection against "the indolence and the sloth of the flesh," they are enabled by their prior encounter with the "Thou" of the "brotherly encounter" to enter into "the impersonal world of things, the 'it', and this new encounter frees them for objectivity" (LT, 70). The reference here to objectivity is something new to Bonhoeffer's work, even though it has a quite ascetic sense. For the duality of prayer and work allows a breakthrough in the "continuing struggle with the 'it' ": behind "the 'it' of the day's work, the 'thou' of God" is found, "the real breaking through the hard 'it' to the gracious thou" occurs (LT, 70). Clearly Bonhoeffer had discovered something since the writing of *The Cost of Discipleship*.

Let us summarize again the understanding of the world of Bonhoeffer's middle period. Without a doubt a different note is sounded from that of the dialectical conceptualizations of 1932. It seems that the negative thread of the understanding of the world which Bonhoeffer had developed in Barcelona was being taken up again, a thread which existed without relation to a positive one. When compared to *Ethics* this primarily negative understanding, leading to the bitter, close struggle against the world,[58] is not simply an understanding restricted to the time of *The Cost of Discipleship*. It is to be found in Bonhoeffer's later theology, albeit as only one side of the coin. This is indicated by the fact that Luther's return from the monastery to the world played an important part in *Ethics*, too. In the latter work the return is interpreted not as a failure or a break, but as the ultimate consequence of the entry into the monastery.

Thus we must reject the suggestion that the continuity of Bonhoeffer's theology lies exclusively in his christology, whereas the understanding of the world of his different periods is marked by utter disparity. The continuity in his understanding of the world is not as manifest as the continuity in his christology; indeed, the continuity of the former is not sustained without that of the latter in which it may well be grounded, since the relation to the world is dependent upon obedience to the call to discipleship. This call leads out of the world and only thereby truly into the world. That is the goal to which *The Cost of Discipleship* points when it speaks of those "who have reached the end of the road we seek to tread," and who, "knowing that [costly] grace, can live in the world without being of it," and are thus "truly free for life in this world" (CD, 47). The way through *The Cost of Discipleship* and back into the world is no retracing of steps that had been taken in the wrong direction, and a search for the right direction, but is the continuation along the way in which that book set out.

THE DIALECTICAL UNDERSTANDING OF THE WORLD OF THE LAST PERIOD

THE APPROACH TO ETHICS

In analyzing the next stage of Bonhoeffer's understanding of the world one again discovers his letter to Theodor Litt.[59] Given the overall perspective of our work, this letter belongs to Bonhoeffer's late theology. This is made clear when the latter is set in contrast to *The Cost of Discipleship,* since a christologically-based, positive understanding of the world finally comes to the fore in this letter; only at that point is the world said to be the world accepted in Christ, the world to which Christians have access through Christ's mediation, which itself is fundamental to faith. With this begins the transition from the *Christus pro nobis,* the "Christ for us," which still governed *The Cost of Discipleship* (CD, 216), to the *Christus pro aliis,* the "Christ for others." If, up to this point in Bonhoeffer's works, God's goal had been the community of Christ, it later became the world; community and world were no longer considered mutually exclusive, as contradictory entities, but were related one to the other in Christ, even though the relation of the community to the world was stated with ever increasing insistence. Bonhoeffer's understanding of the world changed in such a way that the world was said to be preserved for the sake of the church; now the church was said to be there for the world. This reversal culminated in the assertion that Christ is Christ only in the midst of the world (E, 206; LPP, 382).

We have come to a crucial point in our study: from here on christology and the understanding of the world will be inseparably related one to the other. A noticeable shift will become apparent in the use of the works that had been chosen for discussion in parts two and three of this study. Of fundamental importance for part two were *Act and Being;* the addresses delivered in the United States; the courses taught at Berlin, especially on creation and fall and on christology; and, finally, *The Cost of Discipleship.* The sermons from Barcelona and the sermons and addresses from 1932 were of similar importance for part three. From here on, however, these same texts will be drawn upon in an identical manner.

The development of the relation of christology to the understanding of the world up to this point leads one to a similar conclusion. In Barcelona Bonhoeffer explained the correlation between God and the world without any christological mediation; his view of the world was either primarily negative or primarily positive. In Bonhoeffer's middle period discipleship and world were diametrically opposed. A lone christological reflection, dating from 1932 but initiated in Barcelona, spoke indirectly of a link between christology and the understanding of the world. At that time Bonhoeffer spoke of Christ as being the *Lord* of the world, from which followed the necessity for the world to integrate itself into his realm, that is to say, the need for the world to become church. The relation Christians have to the world was described by Bonhoeffer, if not in a negative fashion, at least formally as being in the middle between flight from and bondage to the world.

Compared to the separation of christology and understanding of the world prevalent in Bonhoeffer's work, the letter to Theodor Litt clearly reveals new emphases. Bonhoeffer referred to Litt's comments, noting that "the 'otherworldly' has entered into the 'thisworldly' in the sovereign freedom of grace" (GS III, 32).[60] This statement, which could have been made even in *Act and Being,* is explained in terms of its significance for the thisworldly. Because the otherworldly has entered into the thisworldly, Christian faith has been given "a commission by the otherworldly to work in this world" (GS III, 31). One may "with equal justification base one's refusal to work in this world" on the "perennial sameness of human confusion" as one's acceptance of such work, as Litt had argued (GS III, 31).

In this letter is the first explicit assertion that "the ultimate foundation for the relation of Christian faith to the world" in a positive and constructive sense "is given in the name Jesus Christ" (GS III, 31). In and through Jesus Christ Christians find "in this one place in the world God and humankind at one" (GS III, 32). This sentence may well be the basic axiom of Bonhoeffer's late theology. The whole letter is the upbeat for *Ethics* and *Letters and Papers from Prison;* it postulates faithfulness to the earth for the sake of Jesus Christ directly in the knowledge of the destruction of the earth. On account of that oneness with the new earth, the present earth, doomed to destruction, must be taken seriously. In this idea of taking the world seriously lies the turnabout which occurred just at the time when Bonhoeffer became convinced that his Christian responsibility gave him no other option but to become politically active. Reinhold Niebuhr made a most interesting comment once that confirms this surmise. He recounted a conversation that he had had with Bonhoeffer in London in 1939, in which politics and theology had been discussed. In it Bonhoeffer had spoken approvingly of Karl Barth's political engagement.[61]

Bonhoeffer's turn toward the world is seen again in the first circular letter that he wrote, after the outbreak of war, to the students of Finkenwalde and the participants in the collective pastorates. Bonhoeffer stated that the cross of Christ stands in relation to the world: "In cutting across our ways, God comes to us and says his gracious 'Yes' to us, but only through the cross of Jesus Christ. He has placed this cross upon the earth. Under the cross he returns us to the earth, and its work and toil, but in so doing he binds us anew to the earth, and to the people who live, act, fight, and suffer upon it" (WF, 253).

The basis for responsibility is the cross which is firmly planted on the earth. It is no longer the sign of the cross, but, being far removed from any symbolic and figurative sense, the very cross itself that sends Christians to the world. Jesus does not die, as it were, between heaven and earth, as had been suggested in the sermon in Barcelona.

There is a meditation on Psalm 119 which, although put to paper only in 1940, had occupied Bonhoeffer for a long time before then. It is of particular importance to this study at this point, the final stop, so to speak, before *Ethics*. It shows what, in our present context, are clear signs of Bonhoeffer's new insights. Commenting on verse 19a, "Exile though I am on earth" (JB), Bonhoeffer wrote:

> I must not evade the lot that rests upon me, namely, to be a guest and an exile, nor refuse God's call of me into that form of existence by dreaming my earthly life away in thoughts of heaven. There is indeed a very godless homesickness for the other world for which there is certainly to be no homecoming. . . . I am to wait patiently for the redemption announced in God's promises, truly wait for it and not rob it in advance in dreaming and wishing. (GS IV, 538)[62]

One is reminded of a statement that Bonhoeffer made in 1932 in which he declared that Christians are wanderers who love the earth which bears them (PB, 28). The reference to a homesickness for the other world that is quite godless relates this text very profoundly to Bonhoeffer's consistent warning against a false eschatology, which is expressed in a particularly clear fashion in the prison letters.[63] Also related to that warning is his twofold insistence that spiritual or, as he was to put it later, religious forms of Christianity must be rejected. "Christians want to be more spiritual than God himself," talking all the time about "struggle, abstinence, suffering, and cross" while being "almost embarrassed that the Holy Scriptures speak not only of these matters but also—and not really often enough—of the happiness of the believer and the well-being of the righteous. But then they say that such talk belongs to the Old Testament and is, therefore, outdated" (GS IV, 511).[64] Bonhoeffer spoke more and more vehemently against the spiritualization of Christianity from this point on, for he believed that it represented a religious misrendering of Christianity.[65]

It is really quite significant that ideas about an understanding of the world should be expressed within an exegesis of an Old Testament text. It is certainly no coincidence that the most important assertions about the understanding of the world from the period of *The Cost of Discipleship* appeared also in the context of the Hebrew Scriptures.[66] In the last of Bonhoeffer's letters he put forth the idea that it is the function of those Scriptures to guard faith against evaporating into a faith oriented entirely to the other world.[67]

THE UNDERSTANDING OF THE WORLD IN *ETHICS*

When one begins to probe this fragmentary work for its understanding of the world one becomes aware of the fact that the first sections do not explicitly take up the new insights described above. This fact confirms what was said in part two of this study about the retrospective outlook of those sections of *Ethics*. The world is perceived in them much more negatively in such ideas as the decay of the world and the opposition of church and world.[68] Yet there are several points on the basis of which positive affirmations about the world can be developed. "The Christ who was cast out from the world" (E, 59) is Lord of the world. "The more exclusively we acknowledge and confess Christ as our Lord, the more fully the wide range of his dominion will be disclosed to us" (E, 58).

The Form of Christ and the Conformation of the World

Bonhoeffer's statements about conformation to the form of Christ are also a foundation for a positive view of the world, because in Christ we set our eyes "upon God and upon the world at the same time" (E, 69). Jesus Christ has stepped into the middle "between God and the world" (E, 70) in which is revealed not only "the secret of God" but also that of the world (E, 70). That one must not take this to be a reference primarily to the mystery of iniquity is indicated by the reference to Jesus Christ as reconciler of the world, an attribution which itself has quite specific significance for the world. The statement "God loves the world" (E, 71) means not only that God's love has brought about the confrontation with and overcoming of reality by letting the world exhaust "its fury against the body of Christ" (E, 70). It also expresses God's 'yes' to the reality of human beings and of the world: "God loves the world. It is not an ideal human that he loves, but human beings as they are; not an ideal world, but the real world" (E, 71). Even "what we find abominable in our opposition to God" (E, 71) God accepts, for God not only came to stand with us, but became one of us "so that we may become, not indeed God, but, in the eyes of God, human beings" (E, 82). For that reason, all of our endeavors "to grow out beyond our being as humans" (E, 71) have been defeated by God.[69] We can accept the world and let it be on account of the incarnation alone but we may not leave it behind in flights of enthusiastic fancy or set out to improve it with secularistic programs.

The reason for that lies in the cross of Christ, and in the fact that "the failure of Christ in the world . . . led to his success in history" (E, 78); "but this is a mystery of the divine cosmic order and cannot be regarded as a general rule" (E, 78). Every kind of "formation of a . . . world reconciled with God" (E, 79) must set out from the form of Jesus Christ who "confronts the world and conquers it" (E, 79). Therefore, formation of the world is *"conformation with the unique form of him who became human, was crucified, and rose again"* (E, 80).

Bonhoeffer did not, however, develop his remarks about the conformation of the world or the divine cosmic order for his view of the world. In fact, conformation, at first related to humanity, again became restricted to the church in Bonhoeffer's thought (E, 83). The statement "The concept of formation acquires its significance, indirectly, for all humankind only if what takes place in the church does in truth take place for all people" (E, 84) does not alter this restriction. Even though the statement is immediately qualified to the effect that the church is not a model for the world, so to speak, it does not explain what is meant by the mandates of government and labor which, in one way or another, depend immediately on Christ. Bonhoeffer was simply one-sided in his view that humanity has been given its true form, namely, Jesus Christ, but that is has not yet made this form its own; yet humanity is already called by that name, and thus has been "drawn into the church in anticipation, as one might say" (E, 84). *"The church is the place where Jesus Christ's taking form is proclaimed and accomplished"* (E, 88).

This one-sidedness is manifest in the fact that in spite of the duality of church and state, postulated as early as 1932, Bonhoeffer focused on the church only and left the state aside as "the 'restrainer' " which "takes effect within history through God's governance of the world" and as a "remaining force of order" (E, 108). This conclusive separation of faith and world appears as well in the description of the church as the place where the awakening of faith is announced as a "saving act of God, which intervenes from above, from whatever is historically attainable and probable" (E, 108). But what does salvation have to do with the world, and vice versa, in this statement? It would appear, despite several other important and totally acceptable assertions about the world, that the first fragments of *Ethics*, at least as far as they were developed, did not reach the level attained in 1932. Only in 1939 did Bonhoeffer begin to make statements about the world comparable to the level of those he had made in 1932.

The Dialectics of Ultimate and Penultimate

Bonhoeffer expressed his thoughts about a constructive relationship of Christian faith to the world in a novel and impressive manner in the terminology of the "last things" and the "things before the last"; the sequence of these two phrases, one may add, was by no means coincidental.[70] For Bonhoeffer God's justifying word "is final in a qualitative sense, by the nature of its contents. . . . This word implies the complete breaking off of everything that precedes it, of everything that is before the last; it is therefore never the natural or necessary end of the way which has been pursued so far, but it is rather the total condemnation and invalidation of this way" (E, 122). Yet Bonhoeffer went quite decisively beyond this comment, which continues the line of thought of *The Cost of Discipleship,* by stating that "the penultimate . . . remains, even though the ultimate entirely annuls and invalidates it" (E, 124), an assertion which seems initially to be unfounded. Bonhoeffer assumed that "for the sake of the ultimate . . . we must . . . speak of the penultimate" (E, 125); but instead of supporting this idea Bonhoeffer asked why Christians, confronted with the ultimate, so often decide to "remain . . . in the penultimate," and why their silence perhaps points "all the more genuinely to the ultimate, which God will speak in his own time (though indeed even then through a human mouth)?" (E, 126). Behind these questions there stands Bonhoeffer's own experience.[71] Following the questions is an outline of the two false attempts to solve the relation of the ultimate and penultimate: "The radical solution sees only the ultimate, and in it only the complete breaking off of the penultimate," while the other solution, "the compromise," leaves the ultimate "totally on the far side of the everyday"; "the last word is on principle set apart from all preceding words" (E, 127). Both solutions are equally wrong even though both contain aspects which are correct; they are seemingly extreme "because they place the penultimate and the ultimate in a relation of mutual exclusiveness" and view God as either "Judge and Redeemer" or as "Creator and Preserver" (E, 128). These extremes correspond in substance to the provincialism [*Hinterweltlertum*] and secularism against which Bonhoeffer strongly argued in 1932 (PB, 27–47). In both cases Bonhoeffer supported his repudiation of the false alternative with christology, although he argued more strongly in *Ethics*. Both positions are "opposed to Christ" in the same way, Bonhoeffer maintained, "for in Jesus Christ those things which are here ranged in mutual hostility are one" (E, 130). And that is the final step in support of the argument that we must speak of the penultimate, for "only the God-

Man Jesus Christ is real, and only through him will the world be preserved until it is ripe for its end" (E, 129). In him the penultimate has not only become the penultimate on account of the salvation he wrought and made known but has also been placed into a relation to the ultimate. "In him alone lies the solution for the problem of the relation between the ultimate and the penultimate" (E, 130). With the incarnation comes an absolute condemnation of sin but also a relative denunciation of the human orders which sin has disfigured. The penultimate "has become the outer covering of the ultimate"; the cross is "the death sentence upon the world, . . . the judgment upon all that is penultimate," but is at the same time "mercy toward that penultimate which bows before the judgment of the ultimate" (E, 131). The resurrection has dawned "in the midst of the old world . . . as a last sign of its end and of its future, and at the same time as a living reality," even though, "so long as the earth continues, [it] does not annul the penultimate" (E, 131).

In their unity and diversity, incarnation, cross, and resurrection are the foundation of Christian life in the world; that life is "participation in the encounter of Christ with the world," and for that very reason "a certain amount of room must be left open for the penultimate on account of the ultimate" (E, 133).

The Natural and the Penultimate

"It is Christ's gift to us that we should be reconciled with the world as it is" (E, 129). A purely negative relation to the world has been dispensed with in this comment, and a positive outlook toward it established. Christians no longer eschew the world by maintaining emphatic distance from it, as in a sealed train, as it were; no longer is everything to be drawn into the church. Bonhoeffer stated that there must be no "pharisaical denial of love to evil, and the restriction of love to the closed circle of the devout"; nor must "the open church of Jesus Christ, which serves the world till the end," become closed off and locked up (E, 129). One must not foreshorten the penultimate, or its synonym, the natural,[72] for the sake of the ultimate. It is very significant that Bonhoeffer substituted the concrete and substantive term "the natural" for the rather formal and abstract terms "the preserved world" and "the penultimate." It is quite clear, in light of the basic positions of Bonhoeffer's theology, that the natural is not to prevail apart from Jesus Christ, or even against him; yet it takes this substantive, concrete formulation to express adequately the world's positive significance derived from Jesus Christ: "Only through the incarnation of Christ do we have the right to call others to the natural life and to live the natural life ourselves" (E, 145). Compared to the concept of creation, the natural "implies an element of independence and self-development" (E, 145) which is not reduced but qualified through its reference to Christ.

It is to Bonhoeffer's great credit that he reclaimed the concept of the natural for Protestant ethics.[73] He saw clearly that any foreshortening of the natural, or the penultimate, would pose dangers for the ultimate; it was equally clear to Bonhoeffer that "humanity and goodness should not acquire a value on their own account" (E, 143), for the penultimate is "not our way to him but his way to us" (E, 141).[74]

Bonhoeffer's pleas for the natural should not be interpreted as concealed rehabilitation of the kind of natural theology that Karl Barth had attacked with such vigor. Bonhoeffer had himself stated several times that "there is, in fact, no 'method,' no way to attain to the ultimate" (E, 141). Behind this remark stands the theology of *Act and Being* (AB, 93). Every method fails, be it Pauline, that is to say, "legalistic methodism" (CD, 85), or be it Lutheran, that is to say, "the monastery" (E, 123). This is the basis for Bonhoeffer's sustained polemic against all methodisms finally so apparent in the prison letters (LPP, 213). For Bonhoeffer these methodisms smacked of religious Christianity.

The recognition of the natural is no simple "corroboration of the established world," or something merely "preliminary" (E, 145); it is the form of life, made possible by and preserved for the sake of Christ, which Christians live in the fallen world (E, 145).

In this sense the natural, or the penultimate, is truly something before the last, something pen-ultimate (E, 137). It is nothing without the ultimate, and yet, at one and the same time, it is independent and self-developed. Humanity and goodness in the world are to be claimed for Christ "especially in cases where they persist as the unconscious residue of a former attachment to the ultimate" (E, 143).

Having accepted and reflected upon the natural in this sense one must now avoid dealing "with the practical questions of life" as if one were "more or less deprived of the means of orientation," and thus open the way "for every kind of arbitrariness and disorder" (E, 143). To live as a Christian in the real world requires that the incarnation be regarded with such concreteness that life in the world may be seen to be constitutive for the ultimate but not as a way to it, as something penultimate which must be preserved for the sake of the ultimate.

All of Bonhoeffer's theology is incorporated into these reflections: the rejection of a way, or a method, to proceed from the penultimate to the ultimate, leads one to conclude that the distinction between these two concepts corresponds to the distinction between *actus directus* and *actus reflectus*. Furthermore, both sets of concepts are meant to resolve corresponding contrasts. The distinction between *actus directus* and *actus reflectus* was made by Bonhoeffer in order to resolve the conflict between the transcendental and the ontological points of departure, even though the end result of both these points of departure, despite their apparent differences, was the same pseudo-transcendence. In a similar way the distinction between the ultimate and the penultimate was to overcome provincialism and secularism, monkhood and Cultural Protestantism, all of which, despite the apparent difference between them, result in the same failure to build a truly christological understanding of God and of the world. The consequence of that failure is bondage to the world. One may assume that provincialism is related to the transcendental point of departure, while secularism is related to the ontological one. In any case the distinction between the ultimate and the penultimate is used to guard against religious misunderstanding. The statements about the natural are of particular significance, therefore, since they raise the substantive issue for the first time, thereby advancing decisively beyond negative and strictly formal assertions.

The Rejection of Thinking in Two Spheres

For a long time Bonhoeffer had criticized the error of a "religious" understanding of the world in which God had become "the religious rounding-off of a profane conception of the universe" (E, 189), and the cause of Christ "a partial and provincial matter within the limits of reality" (E, 196).[75] Later he sharply rejected the division into sacred and profane spheres (E, 195).[76] We should not think of Christ and the world as "two spheres, standing side by side, competing with each other" (E, 198). Christ is the center toward which history converges (E, 198). In the repudiation of the spatial there is manifest the primacy of the temporal which had already become apparent in the distinction between the ultimate and the penultimate. One can simply no longer ignore the aspect of history, the connection to Christ's becoming reality "today" (E, 195).

Christ and the world do not stand one next to the other; rather, the world is related to Christ, for it is in the process of "realization" toward his "reality" (E, 190).[77] Therefore, there is *"only the one sphere of the realization of Christ"* (E, 197) because in him the world has been accepted (E, 205) and is now "in the movement of being accepted and becoming accepted" (E, 198). It behooves the world "that it remains the world, the world which is loved by God and reconciled with him" (E, 202). The "space of the church" exists in order to announce this to the world and not "in order to try to deprive the world of a piece of its territory" (E, 202).[78] "The world belongs to Christ," for which reason one should not "try to reserve Christ for the church" (E, 205).

The core of this understanding of the world is found in the following assertion:

> Luther was protesting against a Christianity which was striving for independence and detaching itself from the reality of Christ. He protested with the help of the secular and in the name of a better Christianity. So, too, today, when Christianity is employed as a polemical weapon against the secular, this must be done in the name of a better secularity, and above all it must not lead back to a static predominance of the spiritual sphere as an

end in itself. It is only in this sense, as a polemical unity, that Luther's doctrine of the two kingdoms is to be accepted, and it was no doubt in this sense that it was originally intended. (E, 199)

It is precisely in the reality of Christ that the reality of the world is constituted, such that this reality cannot be taken away from the world again. This would be true even if the world did not know about Christ (E, 203), for even the wicked world is no space, no kingdom which exists independently in opposition to Christ; it is the world no less accepted in Jesus Christ.

Bonhoeffer rejected thinking in terms of two spheres because it is static thinking or, theologically speaking, thinking in terms of laws (E, 199). "Thought which is conducted in terms of two spheres regards such pairs of concepts as secular and Christian, natural and supernatural, profane and sacred, and rational and revelational, as though they were ultimate static antitheses" (E, 198). The result of this is that people are torn, for "so long as Christ and the world are conceived as two opposing and mutually repellent spheres," people must decide, abandoning "reality as a whole," between one or the other of the two spheres: "Christ without the world, or . . . the world without Christ." Or they may try "to stand in both spaces at once and thereby become people of eternal conflict, the kind who emerged in the period after the Reformation and who repeatedly set themselves up as representing the only form of Christian existence which is in accord with reality" (E, 197).

Seeing the world as *"the one sphere of the realization of Christ"* (E, 197) must not lead one to the erroneous conclusion that what is Christian is already what is of the world. Despite this oneness, that which "is Christian is not identical with what is of the world. The natural is not identical with the supernatural or the revelational with the rational. But between the two there is in each case a unity which derives solely from faith in this ultimate reality" (E, 199). Bonhoeffer referred to it as a "polemical" unity. Again, this non-identity must not be seen as a duality, an opposition of principles (E, 220), for "in Christ [Christians] find God and the world reconciled. . . . Their worldliness does not divide them from Christ, and their Christianity does not divide them from the world. Belonging wholly to Christ, they stand at the same time wholly in the world" (E, 201).

Liberation for True Worldliness

The polemical unity of what is Christian and what is of the world is the first indicator of what the central affirmation of *Ethics* means. "In Jesus Christ the reality of God entered into the reality of this world" (E, 194). This unity does not speak of an affirmation of the world which is monophysite and one-dimensional but of the affirmation which embraces the negation. That tension must not be relaxed; one must remember that *reality* is first and last not something lifeless, but is the *real one,* the incarnate God. It is from the real one, whose name is Jesus Christ, that all factual reality derives its ultimate foundation and its ultimate annulment, its justification and its ultimate contradiction, its ultimate affirmation and its ultimate negation (E, 228)

One can speak of the world and of reality only in antitheses of this kind, because it is a reality bigger than can be grasped by any positivistic, empirical concept of reality. The world is neither robbed of nor reduced in its reality in those antitheses. "Action which is in accordance with Christ is in accordance with reality because it allows the world to be the world; it reckons with the world as the world; and yet it never forgets that in Jesus Christ the world is loved, condemned and reconciled by God" (E, 230).[79]

Apart from the unity in Christ there is no other unity of God and the world. Every attempt "to achieve some sort of commensurability between Christ and the world . . . leads, in the form of secularism or the theory of the autonomy of the various domains of life, or else in the form of enthusiasm, to the ruin and destruction of the world which in Christ is reconciled with God" (E, 230). This demonstrates anew that the two false positions which at first seemed to be diametrically opposed to each other are in the final analysis identical,[80] no matter whether they are called secularism and provincialism, compromise and radicalism, secularism and enthusiasm, or Cultural Protestantism and monkhood.[81] Both positions attempt to explicate Christian faith and the understanding of the world on the *same* basis or at least in a one-sided fashion either by affirming the world or negating it, a negation which in the end becomes a one-dimensional affirmation of the world (E, 200). The identity of these two initially opposed positions is apparent not only formally in the one-sidedness but also materially in the bondage to the world which they both manifest.

In order to avoid both extremes Bonhoeffer tried to maintain the tension between affirmation and negation consistently throughout *Ethics*. This is indicated by the fact that he went back to his ideas about vocation when he discussed Luther's return from the monastery (E, 255). But in this work vocation is no longer considered to be a "no" uttered to the world and the decision to be dead to the world; nor is remaining in the world called for in order to mount a frontal attack upon it, as had been argued in *The Cost of Discipleship* (CD, 239; E, 255). Vocation is also a "yes" to the world from which arises our responsible action in the world. An important consequence is indicated here. If *The Cost of Discipleship* virtually omitted the "yes" to the world, the "no" which is spoken in *Ethics* must not be overlooked or even eliminated as a mere residual aspect of *The Cost of Discipleship*.

The term "worldliness" must be understood within this tension between yes and no. It is a term that occurs more than just occasionally; indeed, it is used frequently and with emphasis in the final sections of *Ethics*. There is a second, important foundation for a substantive understanding of the world next to that given in the term "the natural." Bonhoeffer had used the term "worldliness" already in 1932. At that time it was applied to the church. It is not clear what he meant by worldliness at that time because he identified the church in a hazardous way with divinity, worldliness and Christianness. The term recurs in *The Cost of Discipleship* with an ironically negative meaning (CD, 36). It is one of the key concepts in *Ethics*. "The worldliness of the world" is used to qualify the world itself; but its reality, that is, the actuality of worldliness, is given not without Jesus Christ but precisely by him and his cross. That which is Christian is directly affected by this: it is neither "an end in itself" nor something "which lies beyond the human element; it requires to be in the midst of what is human" (E, 296).

Among the consequences of locating the worldliness of the world firmly in a theology of the cross is the fact that the world becomes godless; the world rid itself of God when it relegated him to the cross. But since the cross is also the cross of reconciliation it is our liberation "for life before God in the midst of the godless world" (E, 297), that is to say, "for life in genuine worldliness" (E, 297). For the godlessness of the world is not done away with but kept open by the crucified reconciler; all false self-deification of the world is ruled out, since faith radically removed the gods from the world (E, 96). Liberation for genuine worldliness comes only from the proclamation of the cross of reconciliation, because it alone "leaves behind it the vain attempts to deify the world and because it has overcome the disunions, tensions and conflicts between the 'Christian' element and the 'secular' element" (E, 297). Using the Lutheran terminology of the Eucharist, Bonhoeffer declared that there is life in genuine worldliness only through the preaching of the cross and not against it or next to it. "True worldly living . . . is possible and real only 'in, with and under' the proclamation of Christ" (E, 297).

This idea does not amount to usurpation, as far as Bonhoeffer was concerned, since the world's godlessness becomes apparent only in preaching and is guarded by means of that preaching against its self-deification.

> In both these cases the worldly element ceases to be worldly; if it is left to its own devices the worldly element will not and cannot be merely worldly. It strives desperately and convulsively to achieve the deification of the worldly with the consequence that precisely this emphatically and exclusively worldly life falls victim to a spurious and incomplete worldliness. The freedom and the courage are lacking for genuine and complete worldliness, that is to say, for allowing the world to be what it really is before God,

namely, a world which in its godlessness is reconciled with God. (E, 297–98)

The formal aspect of the world's worldliness is now clearly indicated.

Bonhoeffer was prevented from developing the material aspect of the worldliness of the world.[82] This aspect would have had to have shown that Christ "existed not for his own sake but wholly for the sake of the world" (E, 301). It is certain that between these statements about the worldliness of the world and those about the lordship of Christ over the world there was no contradiction for Bonhoeffer.[83] To separate the two groups of statements would imply a "religious" understanding of the world. The community must render a service to the world; it will learn from the world's refusal to accept the word that "the world is in disorder and that the kingdom of Christ is not of this world" (E, 315). The community would become a "religious club" (E, 315), however, were it to stay away from the world on account of that insight. A spatial separation of community and world indicates the presence of religion.[84]

Reference must still be made to the renewed discussion in *Ethics* on the topic of church and state.[85] Sometime before writing on that topic in *Ethics* Bonhoeffer had discussed it in the account of his visit to the United States in 1939.[86] He focused on that country's curious religionlessness and its relationship to the process of secularization. He made the interesting comment that the separation of church and state, as it exists in the United States, solves the necessarily problematic relation of church and state as little as does the association of the two entities in Europe, which there creates its own difficult problems for the churches of the Reformation. "The world threatens to break in on the church as much because of freedom as because of association" (NRS, 109).

Bonhoeffer returned to this train of thought in *Ethics*.[87] But this matter is given less emphasis than is the subject of the mandates, as the doctrine of the two kingdoms or two warrants is increasingly repudiated in this work. Next to the church, marriage, and work there is the mandate of government.[88] There is, finally, a section dealing specifically with the question of church and state; its composition cannot be dated with accuracy.[89] Again, Christ is the foundation of the state, in light of which one must interpret the following comment: "Government is not itself of the world, but of God" (E, 336). That is to say that government, too, is made legitimate in its dependency on God through Christ the mediator. The relation of church and state is not made up by the state pursuing "Christian policy" (E, 347), nor by the church exercising a direct political responsibility in the sense of governmental responsibility. What the church is to proclaim "is not the wickedness of the world but the grace of Jesus Christ" (E, 350). For that reason, there is no warrant for the church to intervene directly in the concerns of government.[90] But that must not become itself a warrant for the recommendation on principle that the church withdraw from the world (E, 351). The relation of church and state cannot be resolved on the basis of principle. One must examine individually every decision of the church to intervene in politics or to refrain from doing so. The same position that Bonhoeffer had maintained ten years earlier emerges in these reflections, albeit in a less acute, more balanced fashion; here too the argument reaches a climax in the discussion of responsibility which must be taken upon oneself, even at the risk of incurring guilt.[91]

In summarizing the understanding of the world in *Ethics* it becomes plain that Bonhoeffer experienced and stated anew things that he had known for a long time, on account of his worldly activities. Drawing on his thoughts of 1932 he developed a view of the world in which, influenced by the distinction between the ultimate and the penultimate and the "yes" and "no" which faith speaks to the world, the foundation for a true worldliness was laid and the concept of the natural was spelled out in its content. Christians can and must live in that worldliness, in that naturalness, for only thus do they meet their responsibility for the world. Under the lordship of Christ the world does not become estranged but rather attains to its proper essence (E, 322). "The purpose and aim of the dominion of Christ is not to make the worldly order godly or to subordinate it to the church but to set it free for true worldliness" (E, 328). The church must see to it "that it does not leave the world to its own devices" (E, 325). The church must also prevent the relative autonomy of secular institutions from being abolished, while protecting "their true worldliness or 'naturalness' in obedience to God's word" (E, 326). Bonhoeffer also noted that "genuine worldliness is achieved only through emancipation by Christ; without this there is the rule of alien laws, ideologies and idols" (E, 330).

At the beginning of part three we noted that Bonhoeffer had developed his understanding of the world in constant dialogue with liberal theology; this is confirmed by comments that he made late in the period of writing *Ethics*. Referring to that theology, Bonhoeffer raised the basic question of *"whether Christian ethics can make statements at all about worldly institutions and conditions or whether these things of the world are, in fact, 'ethically neutral' "* (E, 321). He proceeded to answer this question by rejecting the position taken by Ernst Troeltsch and Friedrich Naumann; he particularly repudiated Naumann's thesis "that he could be a Christian in only five or ten per cent of his life" (E, 321), namely, when he did not have to deal with worldly institutions. In contrast to such a religious separation of things Christian and things worldly was Bonhoeffer's position in which he endeavored to show their oneness in Jesus Christ. Building on that oneness which, as has been noted, one must not misunderstand in a monophysite manner, Bonhoeffer attacked with equal force the opposite position of the "religious–socialist theologians." It, too, was religious, basing itself

> on the socially revolutionary character of the sayings of Jesus about the poor and the rich, about justice and peace, and about the coming kingdom of God on earth. [It] saw in the gospel of Jesus the world reforming power *par excellence*. "God and the soul" and "the kingdom of God on earth"— these were the opposing watchwords. We have already perceived that this is a false antithesis and that the question is wrongly formulated. For both views have failed to discern the central feature of the New Testament, *the person of Jesus Christ as the salvation of the world*. (E, 321)

The concrete figure in the middle between the extremes elucidates Bonhoeffer's practical life at that time.

The structural development of *Ethics* shows that Bonhoeffer initially drew quite heavily on his earlier theology, although it is clear that he did so with his eye on life after Hitler's demise and Germany's collapse. His analysis of the progress of modernity also shows this, as does his outline of a confession of guilt.[92] But in subsequent sections Bonhoeffer went beyond earlier thoughts, especially in his deliberations on the natural and true worldliness. The central elements of the understanding of the world in *Letters and Papers from Prison* arose directly from these thoughts, as shall become evident in the following discussion.

THE RELIGIONLESS UNDERSTANDING OF THE WORLD IN *LETTERS AND PAPERS FROM PRISON*

The analysis of Bonhoeffer's understanding of the world as it appears in the prison letters leads us to the point at which the issue of the unity and development of his theology is most hotly debated. What must be shown, here, is the kind of continuity that exists between these letters and what preceded them. In order to demonstrate the continuous development of Bonhoeffer's theology, particularly in relation to his understanding of the world in *Letters and Papers from Prison*, certain problematic aspects in the areas of biography and reflection must be traced.

The statements about the world in these letters were certainly shaped by Bonhoeffer's personal experience, as had been the case earlier when he had remarked "that those who wish to speak of God's love for the world will face no minor difficulties these days, unless they are content with mere formulae" (GS IV, 498). But here, too, he rejected all attempts to flee from the world by means of an overemphasis on eschatological hope. Hope that was born in the dead end of a historical situation seemed to him no more than enthusiastic apocalypticism[93] and a betrayal of the very faith that seemed to have become so extraordinarily real in that eschatological outlook. Nor should his statements about the world be taken as the self-compensation of a prisoner who, cut off from the world, glorifies it unduly.[94] Bonhoeffer did have positive experiences of the world while in prison; this he expressed in the quotation from Theodor Storm: "and however crazy, or Christian, or unchristian things may be outside, this world, this beautiful world is quite indestructible."[95] But the world also appeared to be "nauseating and burdensome" to him (LPP, 162). The threatening situation may perhaps have been advantageous: Bonhoeffer was able to work out a positive understanding of the world without hindrance, as the danger of falling unawares into bondage to the world was reduced. One must be concerned about falling into such bondage in times of peaceable arrangements between church and world.

Bonhoeffer's Personal "Yes to the Earth"

It is easy to understand that Bonhoeffer, thrown into prison and torn out of his customary life and action, did not deal with theological thoughts right away. For nearly a year he was absorbed by complete isolation, hearings, the struggle to survive, and the hope for imminent release. In the spring of 1944 theological reflections moved into the foreground again, but there is evidence in certain of Bonhoeffer's prison letters that he used the opportunity offered by his incarceration to put some of his earlier affirmations into practice: "I'm learning to practice myself what I have said to other people in sermons and books" (LPP, 29).

Bonhoeffer made some interesting remarks, in this context, about the topic of religionless Christianity. Long before this time he had written to his friend Erwin Sutz, on the occasion of Sutz's wedding, that "in view of these 'end' times (I don't really mean to sound so apocalyptical) marriage is the venture of affirming the earth and its future."[96] The affirmation of the earth which marriage represents, an affirmation to which God adds his own "yes," occupied him again in his "Wedding Sermon from a Prison Cell." It would seem that this sermon was somewhat of a prelude to his assertions concerning religionless Christianity. According to Bonhoeffer, marriage is "not, in the first place, something religious, but something quite secular" (LPP, 41); our desire for happiness on earth "is justified before God and humanity" (LPP, 42). In marriage we "are placed at a post of responsibility towards the world and humankind" (LPP, 43). One must not, however, confuse the love of marriage with that of God (LPP, 43); but they are related, seeing that Christ is the God-given foundation of marriage (LPP, 46). A year later Bonhoeffer explained this relationship between earthly love and God's love in a meditation on the Song of Songs. Using the christology of the Chalcedonian Confession, he stated that, on the basis of the christological interpretation, human love and God's love through Christ must neither be identified nor separated, for together the two loves comprise the "polyphony of life" (LPP, 303).

Not long after the composition of that sermon Bonhoeffer wrote to his fiancée that for him, too, their contemplated marriage "shall be a 'yes' to God's earth. . . . I fear that Christians who stand with only one leg upon the earth also stand with only one leg in heaven." He himself sought to avoid "the faith which flees the world."[97] Therefore, one may apply to Bonhoeffer, too, the warning of the Wedding Sermon: "We ought not to be in too much of a hurry here to speak piously of God's will and guidance" (LPP, 41). This, his own personal "yes" in an apocalyptic world, may be taken as the personal backdrop to his later statements about the world.

Bonhoeffer's correspondence with Eberhard Bethge began on 18 November 1943; from then on the references to religionless Christianity increased in number. Bonhoeffer assured his friend that he would not leave prison as a *homo religiosus,* something which his at times distant relation to the Bible would confirm (LPP, 135). This was not contradicted by Bonhoeffer's other comment that there were times, also, when he was led "back quite simply to prayer and the Bible" (LPP, 149). He warned against being more pious than God because "the main thing is that we keep step with God, and do not keep pressing on a few steps ahead—nor keep dawdling a step behind" (LPP, 169). The admonition that we ought not to attempt more but in fact less is in truth more than a pious exaggeration, and for Bonhoeffer every exaggeration was pious: the world must not be too hastily left aside in favor of the "world above"; instead we are "to love . . . God in our *lives"* (LPP, 168). Bonhoeffer consciously did not want to discuss religious problems primarily or even exclusively during the rare visits of his nearest relatives; he was anxious, instead, to make contact with a piece of real life, for, had he not done so, he would have denied *the natural.*

Personal experiences were clearly not the least among those causes which made Bonhoeffer seek the form of faith which does not leave the world aside for reasons of religion or piety but which affirms the world and, in so doing, becomes religionless. Bonhoeffer's renewed preoccupation with the subject of the world during his incarceration arose from those experiences. On Reformation Day 1943 he remarked that Luther had desired to see "a real unity of the church and the West . . . the 'freedom of the Christian' . . . and the establishment of a genuine secular social order free from clerical tutelage" (LPP, 123), a remark which still has a somewhat negative accent and which clearly reflects the earlier sections of *Ethics.* That history brought those desires to nought, and that, instead, there was "the disintegration of the church and of Europe; . . . indifference and licentiousness; . . . and insurrection, the Peasants' War, and soon afterwards the gradual dissolution of all real cohesion and order in society" (LPP, 123), gave Bonhoeffer much to think about. Some weeks later he spoke positively of the worldliness of the thirteenth century which had established itself despite papal opposition (LPP, 229). These thoughts are precursory to his reflections about the world come of age.

The Transition to the Second Period in Prison

It has proven impossible thus far in the discussion about Bonhoeffer to refute conclusively the idea that something qualitatively new entered into his theology with the notion of a "religionless Christianity in a world come of age." The proposition that continued to be determinative, if not in its material content then certainly in its formal structure, was Hanfried Müller's idea that the most decisive qualitative leap in Bonhoeffer's dialectical development took place in the spring of 1944, or, to be exact, on 30 April 1944.[98] Eberhard Bethge, too, spoke of a "new start" (DB, 762), and with some justification, one might add, since new assertions appeared instead of echoes of the early statements in *Ethics*. Bonhoeffer no longer complained of a decay which set in with modernity[99] but referred positively to the modern movement toward autonomy, thus taking up what had been said in the latter part of *Ethics*.

The question of a new start has had to be approached with great care all along, for a certain change in Bonhoeffer's life and perception did indeed take place over the course of his imprisonment. A reading of the entire correspondence, that is to say, not only the letters that Bonhoeffer wrote in prison but also those he received, shows that a change began to set in by November or December 1943. The cause could be that Bonhoeffer, although he fought valiantly against it, had to give up hope for his imminent release from prison. In addition, it became possible for Bonhoeffer to have an illegal exchange of letters with Eberhard Bethge; the first of these, as we have already seen, was dated 18 November 1943. Bonhoeffer was able to write much more openly to his friend than to his parents and relatives, who were already deeply involved in the situation which had led to his arrest. He seems to have received new stimulation for theological reflection through this renewed exchange of ideas with Bethge, an exchange that he had been accustomed to for years but which he had sorely missed for several months. One can discern how important that contact was for him from his thoughts about friendship contained in his letters. It was clearly more than a gesture of friendship when Bonhoeffer wrote explicitly that his thinking was set in motion again by Bethge (LPP, 160).

Bonhoeffer first told Bethge about the smaller studies that he had begun during the last few months. There is the essay "What Does It Mean to Speak the Truth?" which was an attempt to think through what it means to speak when one is being interrogated.[100] Then there is a story of a contemporary middle-class family which, apart from meeting

Bonhoeffer's personal interests, was meant to be a rehabilitation of the middle class (LPP, 130).[101] As he wrote that story Bonhoeffer found himself again and again referred back to the nineteenth century, about which he tried to become knowledgeable during the first part of his imprisonment through an intensive study of literature from that century.[102]

But there are also those reflections which seek to interpret current events in light of what is to come after them. "The fact that the horrors of war are coming home to us now with such force will no doubt, if we survive, provide us with the necessary basis for making it possible to reconstruct the life of the nations, both spiritually and materially, on Christian principles" (LPP, 146). The current horror meant a preparation for tasks to be fulfilled: "We are being prepared and made ready for them now" (LPP, 146).

As the correspondence proceeded Bonhoeffer clearly turned away from memories and focused on that which lay ahead. It seems that the developmental pattern of *Ethics* was repeated here and prevailed fully. The different assertions that Bonhoeffer made during his imprisonment certainly permit one to conclude that the turn toward the future that Bonhoeffer made in his thinking occurred at the end of 1943 and the beginning of 1944. For a variety of reasons, among them the exchange of letters with Bethge and the futility of expecting to be released soon, Bonhoeffer energetically accommodated himself to his situation and regained thereby a new, that is to say, an old, freedom. He began his work again. He did not try to finish *Ethics,* however, but instead began something new. As of November 18, 1943, there was, in other words, a coherent transition from one period of imprisonment to a new one (LPP, 276).

The Subject Matter of Bonhoeffer's Last Letters in Light of His Theology to That Time

The well-known expressions "religionless Christianity" and "the world come of age" emanate from Bonhoeffer's second period in prison. In the second section of part three we shall try to interpret those concepts in a primarily systematic fashion. But first the historical development of Bonhoeffer's understanding of the world will be reviewed in order to establish the connection of these late concepts with Bonhoeffer's early ideas.

It has already been stated that "religionless" and "worldly" are adjectives of the Christian faith itself. "Religionless" expresses the negative aspect of faith in relation to the tradition that had taken form above all in Cultural Protestantism. "Worldly" expresses the positive aspect of faith in relation to the future. The negative aspect, that is, the critique of religion, had been the subject matter of Bonhoeffer's first course of lectures. When Bonhoeffer framed the question about religionlessness in the form of the question about the penultimate and the ultimate, the latter being related to the problem of arcane discipline (LPP, 281), he explicitly hearkened back to *Ethics*.

Bonhoeffer wanted to describe a "new" understanding of the world when he spoke of religionless–worldly Christianity (LPP, 281), an understanding to which would correspond an understanding of God that would no longer include the old conceptions of God as "working hypothesis," "stop-gap," and "tutor."[103] This desire of Bonhoeffer is important for the analysis of his last letters. The understanding of God and the understanding of the world were closely interrelated for Bonhoeffer. This fact may be traced back to 1932 when Bonhoeffer tried to deal with the "invisibility" of God.

A world aware of its autonomy requires a religionless Christianity.

> People must . . . really live in the godless world, without attempting to gloss over or explain its ungodliness in some religious way or other. They must live a "worldly" life and thereby share in God's suffering. They *may* live a "worldly" life, that is as those who have been freed from false religious obligations and inhibitions. (LPP, 361)

To be a Christian in that way means to be a believer in "profound thisworldliness" (LPP, 369).

In *Letters and Papers from Prison* Bonhoeffer put forth an understanding of transcendence which corresponds to thisworldliness. The "beyond" of God is not confused with "the beyond of our cognitive faculties" (LPP, 282); "the beyond is not what is infinitely remote, but what is nearest at hand" (LPP, 376). Here the central idea of *Sanctorum Communio* is reiterated. The first point of the middle section of the book Bonhoeffer outlined while in prison is entitled "God and the Secular" (LPP, 381) and represents the theme that is common to worldliness and transcendence.

Worldliness and transcendence are brought together in the notion of "Christ and the world that has come of age" (LPP, 327). Here Bonhoeffer sought to leave the understanding of the world as found in liberal theology positively behind him. He gauged the no longer existing alliance of throne and altar to have been just as false theologically as was the alliance of culture and faith; the latter may have been more dangerous simply because it was also more difficult to discern. Bonhoeffer considered it his task to correct liberal theology without becoming a victim of one or the other form of enthusiasm and without maintaining the acosmic position of Karl Barth, which, in some ways, may not greatly differ from enthusiasm.[104] For Bonhoeffer, the issue was encapsulated in the following question: Seeing that "God is absolutely superior and absolutely transcendent to the world, that is to say utterly remote from it, and given that he is the wholly other one and utterly dissimilar to human beings and their nature, unreachable forever to their thinking and willing" (GS V, 147), how is he the God who is present ever anew in an instant but whom people come short of the very moment they have grasped that instant precisely because their faith becomes religion every time? If one gives this question an affirmative tone, it reads: How is God the one who truly came to humankind, who is truly "haveable" in the world because he came into time and history on his own volition (AB, 91)?

If the question "Where do we stand?" was left unanswered in 1932, Bonhoeffer thought that he was close to an answer now. Two wars had sealed the decline of the West; Bonhoeffer knew that "the old country parsonage and the old town villa will belong to a vanished world" (LPP, 295). It was necessary to pay heed to the future, less threatened by liberal tradition, and more at ease in relation to dialectical theology.[105]

The first section of part three of this work is now complete. It began with Bonhoeffer's polemical survey of the "current situation" in which he, influenced by the work of Karl Barth, rejected Cultural Protestantism as a religion. The issue of religion arose again in the last letters from prison where Bonhoeffer expressed his desire to devote a full, academic study to it. He stated explicitly that it would be necessary to say a number of debatable things about religion; as "a 'modern' theologian [he was] still aware of the debt he [owed] to liberal theology." He hoped that he could lead the church "out of its stagnation" into the open air of intellectual discussion with the world (LPP, 378).

In Bonhoeffer's late letters the circle of thoughts expressed in Bonhoeffer's first lecture courses closes itself. It must be shown at the same time, however, that Bonhoeffer was no longer at the place where he had found himself in 1932. Bonhoeffer no longer pointed in a defensive manner to the problematic aspects of the nineteenth century in order to indicate his distance from it; instead, the urgent questions raised by that century were taken up by Bonhoeffer in order to bring them closer to an answer. This is something that he could not have done within the framework of liberal systematic theology but only within the framework of a post-dialectical theology. Such a theology alone could deal with the positive concerns of liberal theology without neglecting the just prospects of dialectical theology. It shall be seen that the twofold description of Christianity as religionless and worldly arose naturally from Bonhoeffer's endeavor to complete under the influence of Karl Barth what liberal theology wanted to accomplish. For that reason christology and the understanding of the world are inseparable for Bonhoeffer, contrary to liberal as well as dialectical theology.

The analysis thus far has shown that from 1932 onward the question about the world became increasingly tied to christology. That fact alone eliminates doubts about at least some form of homogeneity in Bonhoeffer's understanding of the world. Despite the manifest shift of emphasis in that work there are bases for a positive view of the world in *The Cost of Discipleship*, even though Bonhoeffer's self-critical remark is appropriate, namely, that he did not develop this matter correctly. Still, the fact is that there are statements that point forward to a positive view of the world. If one studies the understanding of the world of Bonhoeffer's middle period against the background of christology one can hardly absolutize the constriction of this period. What must be demonstrated now is that no qualitatively new understanding of the world was developed in his late theology. Contrary to previous interpretations,[106] it shall be maintained here that Bonhoeffer's final theology must also be regarded as a continuation extending his earlier theological endeavors. The latter are not to be written off simply as outdated and forsaken but are to be drawn upon for the interpretation of the prison letters and their at times aphoristic formulations.

5

Systematic Synopsis of Bonhoeffer's Understanding of the World

We shall now endeavor to depict the essential elements of Bonhoeffer's understanding of the world in a more systematic fashion. This will be done against the background of the historical survey just completed. The principal terms for this synopsis may be taken from the last letters that Bonhoeffer wrote in prison not only because they contain those statements which, as the culmination of a long development, have great weight, but also because they stand in close relation to the beginning of Bonhoeffer's reflection on the matter of the world. As we have seen, these final thoughts on the world pursue the same enquiry which Bonhoeffer had regarded to be of special importance to him from the very beginning. The meaning and significance of religionless Christianity in a world come of age has to be spelled out, therefore, with a view to all of Bonhoeffer's theology.

BONHOEFFER'S CONCEPT OF RELIGION AND ITS MEANING FOR THE PROBLEM OF RELIGIONLESS CHRISTIANITY

In the letter of 30 April 1944 Bonhoeffer stated his theme in the form of a question: "Who is Christ really for us today?" (LPP, 279). From there he proceeded to a critical discussion of religion; he did not expound a direct critique of religion in the first sentences of that letter, nor did he speak of religion or religionlessness, but rather of "the time of religion" and a "religionless time" (LPP, 279). What is the concept of religion put forth here? What did Bonhoeffer mean when he said that people are becoming "radically religionless" (LPP, 280), when it is apparent that the statement does not simply suggest that people are turning or have turned away from Christianity? For the question is, "How can

Christ become the Lord of the religionless as well? Are there religionless Christians?" (LPP, 280). The point is not that Christianity must coexist with a non-Christian, religionless world in order to make its place in it and announce its message to it. Bonhoeffer's question "What do a church, a community, a sermon, a liturgy, a Christian life mean in a religionless world?" is made more precise by the subsequent query, "In what way are we 'religionless–worldly' Christians?" (LPP, 280). The question about religionless time is acute for faith itself.

It is necessary, therefore, to analyze more accurately what Bonhoeffer meant by religion, as one encounters the problem of religion quite early in his thought. What is quite clear already is that a religionless Christianity is not simply one which no longer exercises what are traditionally known as religious practices, such as prayer, Bible study, sermon, communion, common life, and, not least, confession. One must ask, however, whether the concept of religion rejected by Bonhoeffer is of the same structure as that of Schleiermacher and Naumann, to name the two views most germane to his discussion. Related to this point is the question of whether Bonhoeffer's antithesis is the same as that of Karl Barth, whose lead in the critique of religion he was following at that time. There are some early indications that Bonhoeffer did not fully agree with Barth's antithetical position.

Bonhoeffer had been inspired by Barth's critique of religion; it had been stated with vigor but never in such a form within Christian circles. One must account clearly, however, for the differences between the views of the two theologians. It is necessary for that reason to sketch out the most important aspects of Barth's concept of religion, even though there are available numerous if primarily summary descriptions of it. This will allow an investigation of how Barth developed and changed his concept of religion,[107] and of whether his influence on Bonhoeffer can be explained on those grounds.

Barth's critique of religion was probably inspired by Franz Overbeck and the "outsiders," Ludwig Feuerbach and Friedrich Nietzsche, Overbeck's close friend.[108]

People were confident that one could deal with the critique of religion of the outsiders in terms of apologetics. Barth and Bonhoeffer's critique of religion cannot be regarded as an apologetic which blunts that of the outsiders. By eliminating religion one eliminates the critique. It may be taken for granted that Barth and Bonhoeffer cannot be understood in this way. On the contrary, they were determined to criticize religion in the name of Christian faith.

For the sake of clarity, Bonhoeffer's understanding of Barth's concept of religion will be discussed here without reference to Bonhoeffer. As his "disciple," Bonhoeffer had come to know Barth's position and had studied Barth's new publications with care without relating them to what would be called his own position. Through assimilation of and confrontation with Barth's works, Bonhoeffer tried to develop his own position.

BARTH'S CONCEPT OF RELIGION

Barth's critique of the theology dominant in the nineteenth and twentieth centuries was not merely a critique of religion. For Barth religion was something negative; it was the power through which people set out to find their own way to God. Religion, however, is not something totally negative; rather, it is dialectical. Whenever revelation came to people it turned of necessity into religion, which does not mean that religion is invariably false religion, since false religion canceled by revelation is true religion. What does this mean in detail?

Religion as a Preliminary Step

The meaning of this dialectical concept of religion is not obvious at first, for Barth tried to characterize Christian faith as something that makes all things new and that makes religion possible.[109] Somewhat later the beginnings of a critique of religion emerged.

> Let us start with the proposition that in the Bible we have a revelation of true *religion*, of religion defined as what we are to think concerning God, how we are to find him, and how we are to conduct ourselves in his presence—all that is included in what today we like to call 'piety.'

But if we search honestly "we shall make the plain discovery that there is something greater in the Bible than religion and 'piety' " (Word, 41).

A few years later a more definite position on religion seems to have emerged. The Bible contradicts religion, Barth said; its polemic, "unlike that of the religious, is directed not against the godless world but against the *religious* world, whether it worships under the auspices of Baal or Jehovah" (Word, 70). "Religion forgets that she has a right to exist only when she continually does away with herself" (Word, 67). Instead of justifying its presence in the world by pointing beyond the world, religion "takes her place as a competitive power *over against* other powers in life, as an alleged superior world over against the world" (Word, 67). Barth's comment that religion is a human product, and, as such, takes its place alongside other human products influenced Bonhoeffer. It is interesting that Barth spoke about religion in this article without any further definition.

The discussion of religion is extensive in the first edition of *Römerbrief*. Religion is seen less as the inevitable disfiguration of revelation than as the prefiguration of it, doomed to failure because God alone reveals and saves.

> What is religion? Nothing! One psychological fact among others. But it has to cry out that we belong to God now because of what God has done to us. . . . On their own, divorced from the living movement of God's coming

world circumcision, religion and church mean just as little as does religious–ethical individuality.[110]

Barth asked whether we, given the "world of sin and suffering" in which we must live, "try to reestablish equilibrium in the fashion of *religion*, namely by speaking of a better world to come" (RB1, 108).[111] Religion has practically the same meaning as the law, which is not simply suspended by salvation (RB1, 219).[112] It is no coincidence that religion is often mentioned in connection with circumcision, as it is in Bonhoeffer's thought (RB1, 86).[113] Barth remarked that "of all things, church, religion and morality are *not* serious because under their tutelage we discover so much truth, but not reality"(RB1, 170). Like the law, religion appears to be a sign of salvation but it cannot save (RB1, 86). "What religion set out to do has come about and is coming about, not because of human zeal but solely because of God's zeal: *He* is righteous! *He* justifies! And so God's patience towards religions has run out. They have lost their timeliness" (RB1, 66).[114] Christ is the one "who perfects and fulfills all religions" (RB1, 68). What is said in the first edition of *Römerbrief* may be summarized in this way: Religion, like the law, is a preliminary step that has been superseded by salvation in Jesus Christ; religion, like the law, is not a precondition believers must embrace first for their salvation.

Religion as Radical Contrast

A quick glance at the second edition of *Römerbrief* confirms that Barth's judgment concerning the original edition, namely, "that not one stone had remained in its old place,"[115] holds true for the topic of religion as well. The fact that Barth's comments are now more critical is probably due to the influence of Franz Overbeck.[116] In the first edition Barth could still say that "behind the manifestations of religion and morality is hidden the eternal objectivity of the true and the good" (RB1, 197). However, in the chapter entitled "The Meaning of Religion" Barth explicitly repudiated such a view.

> Why not proclaim ourselves one with the company of "healthy" mystics of all ages, and set forth the secret of a true supernatural religion running at all points parallel to natural religion? . . . The answer is simply—God forbid, [because grace] . . . is never a possibility above, or within, or by the side of, the possibility of religion. Grace is the *divine* possibility of men and women and, as such, lies *beyond* all human possibilities. (RB2, 241)

The Pauline problem of the law is seen entirely in the context of religion. "I must do what I neither can nor ought to do: I have to formulate the relation of God's eternity to my finite existence, and of my finite existence to God's eternity in the utterly inadequate and unworthy terms of 'religion' " (RB2, 245). That necessity indicates the presence of something in religion which inevitably leads to evil. The law and religion are again and again spoken of together; properly understood they would always do away with themselves, but they are powerless to do so. "When people who exercise themselves in the law *hear* the voice of the law pronouncing that God alone is just; when their religion dissolves religion, and their piety completely subdues their piety . . . then it is that there is manifested the eternal meaning of history" (RB2, 88).[117] When God speaks there takes place that which the law, religion, and piety would like to accomplish but simply cannot bring into existence.[118] God's righteousness "is the meaning of *all* religion" (RB2, 95).

For Barth, faith and its righteousness are unique, new, and strange when contrasted with the entire reality of religion. "In its pure otherworldliness we have found it to be the *beginning* and *truth* of religion" (RB2, 126). The question of whether religion "provides the presupposition of and the conditions for the positive relation between God and humankind" (RB2, 128) is to be answered in the negative.[119] "Even in the temporal sphere the call of God in actual fact precedes the contrasts, circumcised–uncircumcised, religious–irreligious, ecclesiastical–secular" (RB2, 128). Religion and the law do not lead us to God; yet one should not speak of religion in an unambiguous negative fashion for the law and, we may add, religion, have their "invisible foundation and meaning from God" (RB2, 184). "The *divine* possibility of religion can never be changed into a human possibility" (RB2, 184).[120]

Religion is itself limited, but, like nothing else, it calls attention to the limits imposed on us (RB2, 231). Religion cannot lead us to God from whom alone it has its meaning. It is limited by the cross; "Golgotha is the end of law and the frontier of religion" (RB2, 233). Golgotha has taken us out of the way of religion; as long as we live "in the flesh," however, we are "woven into the vast ambiguity of religion, enmeshed in the game of 'Yes *and* No' (a dangerous game, but one full of promise), and in the equivocality of pious experience and history" (RB2, 234). Religion is what we can experience of the event of salvation: "Whatever becomes observable in us and in others—that is religion over and over again" (RB2, 238).

What is the meaning, then, of religion? "We have now discovered its meaning to be that our whole concrete and observable existence is sinful" (RB2, 246). The meaning of religion "is to disclose the dominion of sin over the people of this world: even religious persons are sinners, exactly they, exactly as religious persons" (RB2, 257). For that reason, religion is also our greatest enemy. By being a reflector but not a representative of the divine we are made aware of what we lack the most. It is precisely religion, which, calling us to God and offering a possible way to God, does not lead us to God and for that reason tears us apart.

> In religion, dualism makes its appearance. The one who conceals this with the fine sounding phrases of monism is the 'supreme betrayer of religion' (Overbeck), and does the greatest possible disservice to those who are

satisfied with them. . . . Religion breaks people into two halves. One is the *spirit* of the inward person, which delights in the law of God. . . . The other half is the *natural* world of my members; a world swayed by a wholly different law, by a quite different possibility and vitality. (RB2, 268)

This gives religion a radically negative character. In the revised edition of this commentary religion was for Barth the concrete, directly applicable and acute form of Paul's law which came from God but which is now no longer the sign of salvation. It is a sign of great ruin, not least because it heralds salvation. "Religion, though it come disguised as the most intimate friend, *is the adversary*. Religion is the *crisis* of culture *and* of barbarism" (RB2, 268).

> The characteristic mark of true religion is the dismay, the horror of people of themselves. But *Jesus Christ* is the new human being, standing beyond a humanity possible to us, beyond particularly the pious. He is the dissolution of humankind, of *this* world in its totality. He is the one who came into life out of *death*. He is—what I am not—my existential I—the I which in God, in the freedom of God—I am. (RB2, 269)

The basic tenor of Barth's second *Römerbrief* is to be found in this dialectics which eventually becomes an explicit dualism. This will not be pursued any further now; suffice it to say that religion was given a completely negative emphasis. Barth's comments about the church underline this negative note.

> The church confronts the Gospel as the last human possibility confronts the impossible possibility of God. The abyss which is here disclosed is like to none other. Here breaks out humanity's veritable God-sickness: for the church, situated on this side of the abyss which separates humanity from God, is the place where the eternity of revelation is transformed into a temporal, concrete, customary and self-evident thing of this world. In the church, the lightning from heaven becomes a slow-burning, earth-made oven, loss and discovery harden into a solid enjoyment of possession; divine rest is changed into human discomfort, and divine disquiet into human repose. In the church, the "Beyond" is transformed into a metaphysical "something," which, because it is contrasted with this world, is no more than an extension of it. . . . To a greater or lesser extent, the church is a vigorous and extensive attempt to humanize the divine, to bring it within the sphere of the world of time and things, and to make it a practical "something." . . . (RB2, 332)

It would seem that a great distance lies between this statement and the one that Barth made later about "true religion."

The Suspension of Religion

Religion is discussed in *Church Dogmatics* under the heading "The Revelation of God as the Abolition of Religion." In the tradition of the eighteenth, nineteenth, and twentieth centuries, as Barth saw it, religion "is an independent familiar entity over against revelation; *religion has not to be understood in the light of revelation, but revelation in the light of religion."*[121] Barth protested strongly against such a subordination of revelation to religion. "There can . . . be no question of a *systematic* co-ordination of God and humankind, of revelation and religion. For neither in its existence, nor in its relation to the first, can the second be considered, let alone defined, except in the light of the first" (CD, 296). Indeed, God is present in his revelation "in the world of human religion" (CD, 297).

This statement shows the difference between *Church Dogmatics* and the second edition of *Römerbrief* on this issue. As an analogy to the assumption of the flesh, revelation can be referred to only as the abolition of religion. Religion as such is unbelief. "It is the one great concern of the *godless*" (CD, 300). This is because "religion is clearly seen to be a human attempt to anticipate what God in this revelation wills to do and does do. It is the attempted replacement of the divine work by a human manufacture" (CD, 302). And behind it is the intent to attain to "justification and sanctification as our own work" (CD, 309). But here religion is no longer necessarily false religion, even though one can speak of "true religion" only as one does of "a 'justified sinner' " (CD, 325).[122] "We can speak of the truth of the Christian religion only within the doctrine of the *iustificatio impii*" (CD, 337). Just as the only confession of Christians can be that they are sinners even in their best actions (CD, 338), true religion may be summed up in the acknowledgment that Christian religion as a human work is unbelief. True religion is characterized by the fact that, in its false orientation, true religion nevertheless achieves its purpose, because God has made it his own cause.

In summing up one may say that Barth understood religion to be our unending attempt to justify ourselves. But we can be justified only through the grace which is mediated in revelation, the grace which justifies even our self-righteous attempts to justify ourselves, namely, religion. One can speak of true religion only in the sense of the justified sinner. True religion, therefore, is the religion which in God's revelation has been grasped, superseded, and abolished. In that revelation religion and sinners are justified correspondingly. This does not negate Barth's assertion that religion, that is to say, self-justification, is the only possibility that we have, the purpose of which we try again and again to achieve. One cannot say, therefore, that Barth argued in favor of religionlessness; religion, after all, is the antithesis of revelation and is given with revelation itself as the human medium of accepting revelation. The dualistic dialectic of the revised edition of *Römerbrief* is to be overcome by speaking dialectically of religion as being true and false; the dialectic of revelation and religion leads to true religion. Faith is related to religion as gospel is to law.[123] Therefore, religion must not be negated and left behind; nor must the law be negated and left behind, since both are given to us in dialectical unity with the gospel.

The discussion in *Church Dogmatics* undoubtedly led to a more positive view of religion than did the second edition of *Römerbrief*. The latter work depicted the positive only in terms of "a crater" or "a void," in which the gospel reveals itself. All else leads only to "an ineffective peace-pact or compromise with that existence which, moving with its own momentum, lies on this side of the resurrection" (RB2, 36).[124] It would seem that certain aspects of the concept of religion that Barth had held before 1920 reemerged in *Church Dogmatics*.

THE DEVELOPMENT OF BONHOEFFER'S CONCEPT OF RELIGION

The brief survey of Barth's concept of religion has shown that this concept, too, underwent the change that marked all of Barth's theology. This has not been sufficiently noted in the studies which contrast Barth's concept of religion with that of Bonhoeffer.[125] The problem here is to discover which of Barth's views on religion most influenced Bonhoeffer. His early and basic assertions cannot be related to *Church Dogmatics* since they predate that work. Therefore, one must ask whether the change in the concept of religion, as seen in the second edition of *Römerbrief*, was important for Bonhoeffer. A thorough answer to that question requires consideration of more than just one of Barth's works. Bonhoeffer was certainly familiar with *The Word of God and the Word of Man*,[126] and he quoted the revised edition of *Römerbrief*.[127] It would appear, however, that Bonhoeffer was influenced more profoundly by Barth's early addresses than by the radical formulations of the revised edition.[128] These different works by Barth do not really present alternative views of religion in the strictest sense of the word, but more of a shift in emphasis. The dialectic of gospel and law and its dualistic form influenced Bonhoeffer as little as did the dialectic of faith and religion. Quite apart from that, the understanding of religion to which he addressed himself in his prison letters was fundamentally different. This requires detailed analysis.

Systematic Critique of the Religious Understanding of the World

In his first lectures Bonhoeffer spoke, at a crucial point, of a movement against religion, and in so doing referred directly to Barth. It was the religion which was made to serve people and which had become one sphere in their lives next to others.[129] Bonhoeffer acknowledged his indebtedness to Barth but already sought to go beyond him. In those lectures religion was given the outstanding characteristic of particularity and, related to that, the false incorporation of religion into the spheres of the world and the false division between faith and the world. Even there

Bonhoeffer pointed out the special significance of religion as a modern phenomenon.

But Bonhoeffer made statements about religion much earlier than that. The important characteristic of religion in *Sanctorum Communio* is individualism. In the context of the sociology of religion Bonhoeffer defined religion "as the touching of the human will by the divine, and the overcoming of the former by the latter with the resultant free action." It follows "that in religion an intention directed to religious community is not established in principle" (SC, 94).[130] This description of religion is clearly based on Reinhold Seeberg[131] and, most likely in deference to him, is not subjected to detailed critique. Bonhoeffer lifted it from the context of the sociology of religion and applied it to the problem of revelation and the church (SC, 96). The assertion that Christianity is also a religion becomes conditional, for there is "only one religion from which the concept of community is essentially inseparable, and that is the Christian religion" (SC, 92). There is no explicit critique of religion nor any influence of Barth in this passage; yet further on Bonhoeffer begins his critique: "This was not a new religion seeking adherents, which is a picture drawn by a later time. But God established the reality of the church, of humankind pardoned in Jesus Christ. Not religion, but revelation, *not a religious community, but the church:* that is what the reality of Jesus Christ means" (SC, 111).[132] Barth's influence is quite manifest, even though he is not mentioned. Barth's antithesis is taken into the juxtaposition of revelation and religion, although Bonhoeffer saw no reason to develop it in any sense.

After the completion of his doctoral studies Bonhoeffer dealt intensively with the subject of religion. But his comments on this subject are not completely consistent. In relation to the christological address that he had delivered in Barcelona it was earlier noted that Bonhoeffer spoke out against religion. In this action, the influence of Karl Barth is apparent. But Bonhoeffer stressed, long before his initial lectures at the University of Berlin, that the most important feature of religion is its partiality. He also delivered a sharp attack on ethics, religion, and the church as representing human attempts to reach the divine. Bonhoeffer would not have said something like that about the church in *Sanctorum Communio*. The Christian message is "amoral and a-religious," as he put it; he went on to the climactic assertion of the lecture, saying, "Christ does not bring a new religion, he brings God."[133]

Bonhoeffer's sharp critique of religion was not restricted to this lecture; it was, in fact, present in a primary stage in his sermons. In his first sermon in Barcelona he spoke of the alternative between the "lines" drawn from us up to God and from God down to us. Speaking of the former, Bonhoeffer described religion as "the most grandiose and tender of all human attempts to reach eternity" (GS V, 418). Religion, however, "is not what makes us good before God, God alone does that"

(GS V, 419). Further on Bonhoeffer asked, "Does it mean that religion and morality are finished, seeing that they do not lead us to God?" The answer was "Certainly not!" Even if it is true that "religion and morality are the gravest dangers for the knowledge of grace since they bear the seeds for our wanting to find the way to God on our own," we still need them "so long as there is grace, as the feeble endeavor, presentation, or sacrifice to which God can say yes or no, according to his pleasure" (GS V, 421). These thoughts were inspired by Barth's writings prior to 1920. This suggested influence can be supported by certain comments of Bonhoeffer in which he spoke positively of religion without subjecting it to any critique. There is also no critique of Barth. In the arts and sciences as well as in religion "there are times of high excitement and times of routine work and exercise." It follows, therefore, "that we must work at our communion with God" (GS V, 437). "Religion is work, perhaps the hardest but certainly the holiest work anyone can do" (GS V, 437).

But the sermons also show a radical critique of religion that is reminiscent of a much sharper attack in Barth's second edition of *Römerbrief*. For Bonhoeffer, religion was no longer the source of happiness; it was the source of misfortune. God's grace alone, not religion, could bring salvation. Bonhoeffer, using expressions typical of Barth, called grace something "beyond grasping," and the event of salvation, "beyond the world."[134]

Bonhoeffer's critique of religion became most intense in his christological address but was furthered in his subsequent address on ethics. Bonhoeffer declared that "Christianity is basically amoral . . . because [it] speaks of the single way of God to humankind."[135] The result of making such a statement in relation to the question of ethics is that God's way and our ways do not correspond. Thus, the Sermon on the Mount and its significance for life in the world were put so much into question that Bonhoeffer was unable to offer any positive solutions (NRS, 42). Already the Cultural Protestantism represented by Friedrich Naumann and dialectical theology faced each other as opponents. Bonhoeffer stood entirely with Barth, attacking the opposition, but without being able to comprehend its positive concerns. These polemical statements against religion correspond most closely to the harsh polemic of the second *Römerbrief*.

In his *Habilitationsschrift* Bonhoeffer continued to attack the equation of religion and revelation (AB, 41) in idealism and the transcendental identification of revelation with religion (AB, 46). But such an equation or identification requires the presupposition of a religious a priori "wherein the divine content of revelation may pour" (AB, 46). Here transcendentalism changes into idealism.[136] The equation of religion and revelation or revelation and religion is finally the same for idealism and transcendentalism. Bonhoeffer rejected this equation just as he later rejected the religion of secularism and provincialism. There is both a formal and a material correspondence between the early and late polemics of Bonhoeffer.

But Bonhoeffer moved forward decisively in his argument, taking up the question which Barth's polemic and his whole theology left open, namely, how we can envisage the human religious act in conjunction with the divine act of belief without either allotting these acts essentially different spheres or suppressing the subjectivity of God or the existential impact of revelation on people? (AB, 94). Bonhoeffer maintained the distinction between religious acts stimulated by people and the act of belief effected by God (AB, 94); he also accepted Barth's accusation that Schleiermacher confused religion and grace (AB, 176). But Bonhoeffer wondered how to prevent the juxtaposition of revelation and religion from tearing the believer in two, that in faith the new "I" of people is merely a "heavenly double" (AB, 102).

The truth of human justification is that we are justified as sinners; we are not left in our current state but with a new transcendent "I" created for us in faith by grace. Barth's *finitum incapax infiniti* was problematic for Bonhoeffer (AB, 83, 138). He sought, therefore, to establish a new relation between revelation or faith and religion which would have, of course, a different nature than the relation liberal theology had forged. "It must be plainly said that within the communion of Christ faith takes shape in religion, that therefore religion is here called faith, that, as I look on Christ, I may and must say for my consolation 'I believe'—only to add, of course, as I turn to look on myself, 'help Thou my unbelief' " (AB, 176).

On the basis of the dialectic of act and being given in Christ, Bonhoeffer sought to eschew religion as the identification of faith and world and to avoid falling victim to Barth's actualism and its resultant worldlessness, in which faith no longer really touches the world. He already opposed the dualism that ultimately emerged for him in the dialectical theology of Barth. He asked how God, the wholly other, truly comes to us; but it is wrong in one's attempt to give God's transcendence its due place that revelation and faith become transcendent themselves and, as a consequence, have no contact with the world and history.

The first phase of Bonhoeffer's reflections about the concept of religion provides us with a paradigmatic overview of how significant Barth's thinking was for Bonhoeffer. In *Sanctorum Communio* traditional statements, subject already to indirect questioning, are made initially in the same context as some of Barth's polemical statements. In Barcelona the attack on religion becomes more pervasive and radical, ending with the unambiguous adoption of Barth's position. In *Act and Being*, however, there appear the first signs of a critique of Barth, and the critical use of Barth's position is again apparent in the first course Bonhoeffer gave in

Berlin.[137] Barth's concept of religion had been shaped predominantly by such Schleiermacherian categories as experience and morality, whereas Bonhoeffer's concept was characterized quite early by the categories of individualism and partiality and was directed chiefly against the understanding of the world manifest in Cultural Protestantism. Both Barth and Bonhoeffer spoke of religion as a human way to reach God; both depicted it as something partial. But the charge of wordless actualism also applies to Barth. Bonhoeffer, unlike Barth, argued in his polemic against religion on the basis of christology; he was not content to say with Barth that "the *Word of God* is the critique of all religion" (GS V, 304).[138] His critique spoke much more of *Jesus Christ,* and thus was an indirect critique of Barth (AB, 160).

The christological element emerged clearly in the address "Thy Kingdom Come," where Bonhoeffer protested against the religion of secularism and provincialism.[139] In both these forms of religion the relation of Christian faith to the world is debased, because God's kingdom, "the kingdom of Christ as God's kingdom here on the cursed ground" (PB, 32), is rejected. This signals another highly significant characteristic of religion as Bonhoeffer saw it, one that was quite contrary to Barth's concept: a false understanding of, and a wrong relation to the world. Both of these were seen to be aspects of particularity, the latter indicating the division of faith and the world as well as the coordination of religion into all other areas of life (GS V, 218). Bonhoeffer concluded that in view of this division there is no access from the religious sphere to the world, and since such a division is in fact unworkable, it leads inevitably to all areas of life being mixed together. No religious understanding of the world leads us to the real world but at best to a phantom world.

The main elements of Bonhoeffer's early critique of religion, being individualism and particularity, were also present in the middle period of his theological studies.[140] For Bonhoeffer, religious knowledge excluded grace and discipleship in such a way that even a better religion could not bring salvation.[141] In light of Bonhoeffer's understanding of the world at that time it is understandable that he did not stress the false understanding of the world inherent in religion. One may sum up his views of that period in the concluding comment of his report about his second visit to the United States: "God's 'criticism' touches even religion, the Christianity of the churches and the sanctification of Christians. . . . God has founded his church beyond religion and beyond ethics."[142]

The problem of religion did not truly claim Bonhoeffer's attention during that period. His early beliefs on the question remained the same at the beginning of his late theology and during the composition of *Ethics.*[143] There are no obvious signs that Barth's discussion of religion in *Church Dogmatics* had made an impact on Bonhoeffer.

RELIGIONLESS CHRISTIANITY IN A WORLD COME OF AGE

The development of Bonhoeffer's concept of religion leading up to *Letters and Papers from Prison* shall be outlined here. Initially, Bonhoeffer, like Barth, opposed religion as our own self-justification. But Bonhoeffer soon stressed the failure of religion to provide an appropriate understanding of the world, a failure that arises from the disregard of God's kingdom as the kingdom of Christ on earth. Barth had spoken analogously of the relation between revelation and religion, and the dialectic of gospel and law; Bonhoeffer, on the other hand, spoke of religion as the antagonist of Jesus Christ and his church. For that reason, Bonhoeffer did not ask whether or not there is a true religion; he also made practically no comment about the abolition of religion. What is encountered in Bonhoeffer's work is a general systematic polemic against religion;[144] but one cannot really claim that Bonhoeffer's concept of religion is dialectical in the sense of Barth's dialectics, apart from some very early adaptations of that view.[145] Yet religion did claim Bonhoeffer's attention again. But religion is not the necessary form which revelation assumes when it has encountered people. Stimulated by Barth's critique of religion Bonhoeffer used many of its individual assertions; but, after some initial hesitation, he began to criticize the basic position Barth had taken in his critique of religion. This led Bonhoeffer to develop his own concept of religion. On the basis of the formal structure of this concept, but without knowing to what extent Barth had stimulated Bonhoeffer, it would appear that the dissimilarities between Barth and Bonhoeffer were greater than were their affinities.

Religion as a Historically Conditioned and Transient Form of Expression

Because the discussion of religion had diminished in importance since its high profile in the early period, it comes as somewhat of a surprise that the topic emerged again in the late letters from prison. This new discussion was probably not inspired by Barth, as religion appears only marginally in the latest volume of *Church Dogmatics*, which Bonhoeffer read in prison.[146]

It is necessary to analyze the basic structure of Bonhoeffer's late concept of religion, particularly since it appeared so suddenly, and to bring some clarity to the meaning of religionlessness. Only after such analysis is it useful to depict the individual elements of that concept of religion which Bonhoeffer lifted from his earlier theology.

As noted before, Bonhoeffer did not speak of religion as such in that discussion, but of "the time of religion," which he explained in this way:

> Our whole nineteen-hundred-year-old Christian preaching and theology rest on the "religious *a priori*" of humankind. "Christianity" has always been a form—perhaps the true form—of "religion." But if one day it

becomes clear that this *a priori* does not exist at all, but was a historically conditioned and transient form of human self-expression, and if therefore people became radically religionless . . . what does that mean for Christianity? (LPP, 280)

Bonhoeffer's earlier polemic against the religious a priori was made more specific here. Bonhoeffer rejected the idea of revelation being bound to a human precondition, not on systematic grounds but because the a priori is primarily conditioned by history and is therefore transient. Thus, from that time onward, Bonhoeffer considered religion "the garment of Christianity" (LPP, 280).[147] He further asked what it would mean if "the western form of Christianity, too [were] only a preliminary stage to a complete absence of religion?" (LPP, 280).

Religion is the form and expression of the Christian faith which belongs to an age that is disappearing or that has already disappeared, making room for a religionless time. Bonhoeffer searched for a new mode of speaking about God appropriate to that time, namely, "without religion, i.e., without the temporally conditioned presuppositions of metaphysics, inwardness and so on" (LPP, 280). Religion is the direct parallel to temporally conditioned presuppositions. Bonhoeffer wanted to know "how this religionless Christianity looks, what form it takes" (LPP, 282), and thus religion became a subject that interested Bonhoeffer from this point onward. In this letter, the first in which Bonhoeffer raised the question, religion and religionlessness were seen primarily from the perspective of history; his concept of religion was no longer a systematic concept in the sense of Barth's dialectic but a concept of *Geistesgeschichte,* a concept belonging to a specific period of history. Religion is a historically conditioned and transient phenomenon.

One may understand the individual elements of religion only from the perspective of history. Among these elements are metaphysics and inwardness,[148] or a certain view of the world and of humanity in which God is beyond the world, from whence he addresses our subjectivity and our inwardness. But, as the Old Testament and its rejection of nonhistorical, metaphysical myths has already indicated, Christian faith is about historical salvation on this side of the boundary of death (LPP, 336). Instead of suspending history through metaphysics, the Christian message speaks to history itself. The term metaphysics also covers the false conception of transcendence which Bonhoeffer had opposed since *Sanctorum Communio.*[149] That conception is related to individualism, or, as Bonhoeffer put it, to an "individualistic doctrine of salvation" (LPP, 286).[150] Metaphysics and individualism not only stand one next to the other but are themselves materially inseparable. That they are seen to be historically conditioned may be taken for granted.

This is true also for another element of religion: the familiar element of "partiality." Bonhoeffer criticized the endeavors of Karl Heim, Paul

Althaus, and Paul Tillich, "which were all, in fact, still sailing, though unintentionally, in the channel of liberal theology [because they tried to] clear a space for religion in the world or against the world" (LPP, 328). It has already been demonstrated that partiality is the fruit of metaphysics and subjectivity, and that it represents the attempts of Schleiermacher and his followers to overcome the impasse of Kant's philosophy.

Three outstanding characteristics mark this distinct and limited time of religion: metaphysics, inwardness, and partiality. This time has its own concept of God which is shaped by those characteristics; it is the religious concept of God that speaks of him as God, the working hypothesis, God, the stop-gap, and God, the tutor. It is obvious that God is located at the boundaries of the world and of human knowledge. Subjectivity is the counterpart to the absolute and is said to be dependent upon it; it is something not yet of age. This leads to an understanding of "God's omnipotence" which is "not a genuine experience of God, but a partial extension of the world." But, noted Bonhoeffer, "our relation to God is not a 'religious' relationship to the highest, most powerful, and best Being imaginable—that is no authentic transcendence" (LPP, 381).[151] One can see here how much a particular experience of God and a particular relation to the world were bound together in religion and expressed in a particular metaphysics. A concept of God was derived from the experience of the world which became an absolutization of worldly concepts projected into the beyond. The decline of this metaphysical understanding of the world caused its corresponding metaphysical understanding of God to be doomed as well. That is why the world has become godless during the course of history and the time of religion has come to its end. "The religiosity of people makes them look in their distress to the power of God in the world. . . . The Bible directs them to God's powerlessness and suffering; only the suffering God can help" (LPP, 361).

That is the view of the world, of humanity, and of God held by this declining religion. This view represents "one particular stage in the religiousness of humankind" (LPP, 327) which has been left behind by a world now come of age. To continue to buttress that stage of religiousness would be like the attempt to keep circumcision as a condition of salvation. "The Pauline question whether *peritomé* (circumcision) is a condition of justification seems to me in present-day terms to be whether religion is a condition of salvation" (LPP, 281). For Bonhoeffer, circumcision was a phenomenon of the time of the law, that is to say, something which belonged to a particular period of history; it is a phenomenon in light of which one may discuss what is necessary for faith today. Barth had also spoken of circumcision in connection with religion, but he had retained it as a systematic concept, like the question of the law, in his discussion. This reinforces the idea that Bonhoeffer regarded religion as a form of Christian faith that belonged to a certain period in intellectual history. His statement that Pietism was a final and reactionary attempt "to maintain evangelical Christianity as a religion" (LPP, 381) may only be understood in light of that fact. Bonhoeffer differentiated between Christianity or Christian faith and religion, but he could not separate Christianity and church.[152]

The basic structure of the understanding of religion found in those last prison letters should now be manifest.[153] Religion is a phenomenon of intellectual history, the form and garment of the Christian faith of a particular period and of particular historical conditions. But form and garment must be subjected to a biblical critique because they neglect important aims of the faith that they seek to mediate.

The crucial difference between Bonhoeffer's concept of religion in his prison letters and that of Karl Barth is this: Bonhoeffer no longer conceived of religion as being a term of systematic theology but as one of *Geistesgeschichte*. But even at that time Bonhoeffer acknowledged Barth's contribution with gratitude. He referred to him at decisive points in these letters as the first theologian "to begin the criticism of religion" (LPP, 286): "He brought in against religion the God of Jesus Christ" (LPP, 328). But Bonhoeffer later accused Barth of not having gone far enough, even though each time he accused Barth of propounding a "positivism of revelation" he also cited the theologian's merits. That accusation was, then, linked with another charge, the charge of making no more than a restoration, since positivism of revelation was either restoration or was made into restoration.[154]

This again confirms that religion is a phenomenon of intellectual history. The accusation of positivism of revelation clearly shows that Barth had advanced only one step without taking the indispensable subsequent one. Bonhoeffer had stated this on various occasions since his first lecture course. At that time he had blamed Barth for not having developed concrete instructions in his ethics.[155] The critique in Bonhoeffer's last letters proceeded in the same direction when Bonhoeffer said that "the positivism of revelation makes it too easy for itself, by setting up, as it does in the last analysis, a law of faith, and so mutilates what is—by Christ's incarnation!—a gift for us" (LPP, 286). But the issue at stake cannot be a law or, in Bonhoeffer's synonymous terms, generally valid norms, principles and ideas. "In the place of religion there now stands the church [for Barth]—that is in itself biblical—but the world is in some degree made to depend on itself and left to its own devices, and that's the mistake" (LPP, 286). In other words, Barth did not draw the conclusions to the question of the world which his point of departure had provided.

Bonhoeffer charged that Barth's theology had not gone far enough: "For the religionless worker (or anyone else) nothing decisive is gained here" (LPP, 280). This positivism of revelation consists of an abstract state[156] in a worldlessness and an absence of history in which Barth was irrevocably mired. There is a passage in *Ethics* which may be used to support this claim, a passage which also illuminates the initially obscure term "positivism":

> *What is the basis for the concrete warrant for ethical discourse?* Two answers at first present themselves. The warrant for ethical discourse may positivistically, without any further attempt at explanation, be found in reality as it is given. Or else one may construct a system of orders and values within which the father, the master and the government all have this warrant assigned to them. It is evident that the positivistic argument forms a very shaky foundation. . . . It might at first sight appear that more reliance can be placed upon the attempt to construct a rigid system of authorities and subordinations such as has repeatedly been undertaken by Christian philosophers. . . . The difference in principle between this and positivism is obvious; there are now other criteria, beyond the positive data, for the classification of the authorities and of their warrants. These criteria are of a religious, or more exactly a Christian nature. The concrete authorities are divine appointments, *direct manifestations of the divine will* which demands submission to them. By this means there is no doubt achieved a certain independence from the shaky foundation of the positive empirical given reality of a particular time. On the other hand, empirical positivism is now replaced by a metaphysical and religious positivism, and here again this is in itself enough to frustrate any attempt to establish any but arbitrary boundaries between the various authorities and warrants. (E, 274–76)[157]

Bonhoeffer differentiated between empirical positivism and metaphysical–religious positivism. In the latter the warrant for ethical discourse is not given positivistically by empirical reality, but by criteria "beyond the positive data." Exclusive recourse to positive empirical given reality is positivistic in Bonhoeffer's judgment, as is recourse to metaphysical realities of the beyond in order to legitimate ethical discourse. Positivistic is also in that sense direct, and therefore abstract, recourse to God's will since God's will is concretely given only through the mediation of Jesus Christ. Thus, metaphysical–religious positivism does not establish the concrete warrant for ethical discourse.

The basic problem of Bonhoeffer's theology is the question of concreteness, reality, and history; it is again encountered in *Letters and Papers from Prison,* where it is raised in connection with Barth's concept and critique of religion. Bonhoeffer followed Barth in the critique, but not in the interpretation of religion, because Barth's solution was not concrete and because it left the world to its own devices (LPP, 285). What the incarnation had brought together was torn apart again.[158] That is why Barth was of no help to Bonhoeffer in the discussion of how Christ lays claim to the world come of age.

Our analysis has attempted to describe the meaning of Bonhoeffer's concept of religion, particularly as it differed from that of Barth. We saw that Bonhoeffer closely followed Barth's critique at the outset but that he soon began to move beyond Barth. It was only in the prison letters, however, that a basic change occurred in Bonhoeffer's understanding of religion: religion became something that could be overcome, since only a reality shaped by history could be fundamentally altered by a change of epochs. Bonhoeffer's last letters allow for the conclusion that Bonhoeffer went decisively beyond Barth by replacing a systematic concept of religion with one of *Geistesgeschichte*.[159] Bonhoeffer could indeed draw on his earlier views, especially the idea that the concept of religion became the main concept for faith only in the modern age.[160]

This preliminary clarification of what religion meant to Bonhoeffer allows one to draw a conclusion about religionlessness. Convinced by his own experience Bonhoeffer said: "We are moving towards a completely religionless time; people as they are now simply cannot be religious any more. Even those who honestly describe themselves as 'religious' do not in the least act up to it, and so they presumably mean something quite different by religion" (LPP, 279).[161] Bonhoeffer's concept of religion took account of that observation and thus his negatively stated concept of religionlessness stands for something very positive:[162] the form of Christianity in the newly emerging epoch in which there will still be church, sermon, and sacrament, that arcane discipline in which Christ "is no longer an object of religion, but something quite different, really the Lord of the world" (LPP, 281). In a religionless Christianity Christ is no longer the partial object of religion, but Lord of the world; the world is no longer left to its own devices, and God is transcendent in its very midst. For the church this means that it will no longer be a separated region, but a church open to the world, a church for others.

What does it mean for Christians to live a worldly life? In raising this question one may state the positive meaning of religionlessness more accurately: "They *may* live a 'secular' life (as those who have been freed from false religious obligations and inhibitions)" (LPP, 361). Bonhoeffer's term "religionless" was inseparably related to the adjectives "worldly" or "secular." It shall be seen that worldly was not a systematic static category but also one of *Geistesgeschichte* in the sense of a world come of age. In his "Outline for a Book" Bonhoeffer laid out his plan for a discussion of the connections between religionlessness and worldliness in the sense of a world come of age in actual, historical fact. He entitled the proposed chapter "The Religionlessness of Humanity Who Has Come of Age" (LPP, 381).

THE ORIGIN AND MEANING OF THE REFLECTIONS ON THE WORLD COME OF AGE

The subject of the world come of age appeared just as suddenly and unexpectedly as had the topic of religionless Christianity in letters of a few weeks earlier.[163] It is not clear at first how the two subjects are related. Thoughts about the world come of age aroused more interest in Bonhoeffer than did thoughts about religionless Christianity. Religion was an early question for Bonhoeffer and one may relate his work to that of Barth on the same topic; but there are no such points of orientation for the notion of the world come of age. The meaning of religionlessness had been formulated for some time, at least in its negative sense; the concept "coming of age" was indeed quite new in the form and stature given in those letters.[164]

THE INFLUENCE OF WILHELM DILTHEY ON THE PRISON LETTERS

The surprising emergence of the term "coming of age" has led to a number of attempts, albeit unsatisfactory, to explain its origin. The most plausible solution was the reference to the Enlightenment in the work of Immanuel Kant.[165] But Bonhoeffer did not borrow the phrase directly from Kant; nor was the concept, as it appears in Bonhoeffer, derived directly from the ethics of Richard Rothe.[166]

Another suggestion concerning the influences upon Bonhoeffer includes the name of Wilhelm Dilthey, to whom Bonhoeffer owed the essential content and important assertions of his concept of the world come of age. Bonhoeffer knew of Dilthey[167] but only while in prison did he intensively study his works: "I really wanted to become thoroughly familiar with the nineteenth century in Germany. I'm now feeling particularly the need of a good working knowledge of Dilthey" (LPP, 204).

Bonhoeffer had previously read Dilthey's *Das Erlebnis und die Dichtung*.[168] A few days after avowing this desire to understand Dilthey, Bonhoeffer cited Lessing in another letter, the quotation most likely coming from Dilthey.[169] On his birthday, 4 February 1944, Bonhoeffer received another book by Dilthey, *Von deutscher Dichtung und Musik* (LPP, 209). Soon he requested the volume entitled *Weltanschauung und Analyse des Menschen seit Renaissance und Reformation*.[170] He studied this important work very carefully and made extensive use of it, although he did not state that fact explicitly.[171]

In *Das Erlebnis und die Dichtung* Bonhoeffer read about the "autonomy of reason," about the "inwardness" of modernity,[172] as well as about the Enlightenment in Germany, France, and England. In all their diversity these three manifestations of the Enlightenment had one thing in common: "The conviction of the independence of the ethical–religious process in the individual completely carried the day."[173] Bonhoeffer also learned that in the first decades of the seventeenth century the natural sciences taught people to discern an order of reality in nature according to laws.[174] The reading of that book alone caused Bonhoeffer to regret his own ignorance of the works of Dilthey.

Bonhoeffer promised to make a commentary about Dilthey's other work, *Von deutscher Dichtung und Musik* (LPP, 209). A month later he wrote that he had been studying "the mature 'worldliness' of the thirteenth century" (LPP, 229)[175] as he saw it, citing as his witnesses Walther, the Nibelungen, and Parsifal (LPP, 229).[176] "This worldliness is not 'emancipated', but 'Christian', even if it is anti-clerical" (LPP, 229). He wondered where this mediaeval worldliness, so different in essence from that of the Renaissance, had ended: "A trace of it seems to survive in Lessing . . . and in a different way in Goethe, then later in Stifter and Mörike . . . but nowhere in Schiller." He added, "It would be very useful to draw up a good genealogy here" (LPP, 229–30). Then he again turned to the question of the value of the ancient world which he had already addressed in *Ethics* (E, 89).

In *Von deutscher Dichtung und Musik* Bonhoeffer found these issues. Dilthey opened his book with a brief discussion of classical antiquity.[177] The first major section dealt with heroic poetry and national epic, and the beginnings of the German Middle Ages: "In the course of the eleventh century *the real appropriation of the Christian ideal* by large sections of the populace took place. . . . This movement brought about an *inwardness of the religious life* which became and remained in the background for heroic education" (*Von deutscher*, 66). Alongside religious inwardness there "emerged a *free, worldly reflection about life*" (*Von deutscher*, 70). But something like a separation of the worldly from the religious must have followed:

> The religious contrast of the Christian and the worldly kingdom, which pervades the Middle Ages, is deepened and extended. The meaning of life is no longer determined by death. The focus of life shifts from the transcendent orders, fears and desires to this world. Lady World and her needs, demands, possibilities, ethical structures and ideals govern the new society. (*Von deutscher*, 77)[178]

And yet one cannot speak of a complete separation of the religious and the worldly; rather there is a union of the two kingdoms in the worldly one. The Holy Grail serves as the symbol of the union of heaven and earth: "Parsifal's grail comes from heaven and binds together the transcendent world and life on this earth" (*Von deutscher*, 116).[179] Embodied in Dilthey's reflections, which were of great importance to Bonhoeffer in the prison letters, are those concepts essential to Bonhoeffer's concerns: worldliness (*Von deutscher*, 118);[180] metaphysics defined as religious metaphysics (*Von deutscher*, 8–10); and inwardness (*Von deutscher*, 194).[181] In Dilthey's later chapters are references to the emergence of modernity, in connection with which the term "coming of age" is used.[182] One may safely assume that there is a direct connection in Bonhoeffer's cited letter between the statements of Dilthey and about Christian worldliness.

On 30 April 1944, three weeks after he referred in a letter to the second of Dilthey's books, Bonhoeffer spoke for the first time about "a completely religionless time" toward which we are moving (LPP, 279). It is very likely that this remark was influenced by his study of Dilthey, as religion is defined in terms of metaphysics and inwardness.[183] Yet the preoccupation of Bonhoeffer in that letter is chiefly with religion and, to a certain extent, is more Barthian in its conceptuality, although Bonhoeffer's actual concept of religion was now influenced by Dilthey's ideas as well.

Three weeks later Bonhoeffer compared his thoughts on this matter to the ideas of Carl Friedrich von Weizsäcker in his book, *Zum Weltbild der Physik*.[184] This work most likely influenced Bonhoeffer when he described God as a "stop-gap" who is settled at the boundaries of human knowledge and for that reason is in continual retreat (LPP, 311).

A few days later Bonhoeffer again spoke about the thirteenth century, using the concept of adulthood (LPP, 327)[185] which probably came from his reading of Dilthey's *Weltanschauung und Analyse des Menschen seit Renaissance und Reformation* where the terms "coming of age," or "adulthood," are used at the very beginning of the book. There the terms have a much broader meaning than in *Von deutscher Dichtung und Musik*.[186]

This third work by Dilthey certainly inspired Bonhoeffer's letter of 16 July 1944.[187] It may have been Eberhard Bethge's new quarters which stimulated Bonhoeffer's opening reflection on Henry IV's pilgrimage to Canossa, but in the course of the letter Bonhoeffer returned to the subject of "non-religious interpretation of biblical concepts." As on a previous occasion, Bonhoeffer got lost in preliminary reflections after having announced his subject, and, instead of addressing its substance, he explored the historical background for it (LPP, 359).[188]

Bonhoeffer must have been impressed with Dilthey's analyses, because he said, "It is one great development that leads to the world's autonomy" (LPP, 359). The names to which Bonhoeffer referred at important junctures were often found in Dilthey: Lord Herbert of Cherbury; Montaigne; Bodin; Machiavelli; Grotius; Descartes; Spinoza; Nicholas of Cusa; Giordano Bruno.[189] He also discovered Grotius's phrase, "even if there were no God" (LPP, 359) in Dilthey, a phrase which has by now become famous.[190]

It is not only the citing of these figures but also Bonhoeffer's train of thought that shows how much he had engaged in Dilthey's historical assessment of the course of modern intellectual history.[191] Bonhoeffer fully accepted Dilthey's thesis that

> humanity moved out of the theological metaphysics of the Middle Ages and towards the work of the seventeenth century with the help of the spiritual processes of the sixteenth century. [And the work of the seventeenth century was this]: the establishment of human dominion over nature, the autonomy of human knowledge and action, the formation of natural systems in the fields of law, politics, art, morality and ethics. (*Weltanschauung*, 41)[192]

In his own words Bonhoeffer commented that "God as working hypothesis in morals, politics, or science, has been surmounted and abolished; and the same thing has happened in philosophy and religion (Feuerbach!)" (LPP, 360).[193]

This modern movement toward autonomy was based on a "system of natural law, natural morality and natural theology" (*Weltanschauung*, 91),[194] that is to say, "natural religion," a system strongly influenced in its conception by Stoicism.[195] The autonomy of humanity was based on that system (*Weltanschauung*, 91), and behind the movement for emancipation stands the confusion created by the religious wars. Since Christianity could not provide a basis on which the denominations could build a human and political community, one had to look for a natural and, for that reason, neutral basis. This is what Hugo Grotius meant when he spoke of life in this world as if there were no God. Faith not only did not prevent wars but it pushed them, as religious wars, to their most irrational level (*Weltanschauung*, 95). Thus, "the real needs of seventeenth-century society created on the new foundations of a science come of age, prepared by Humanism and the Reformation, a *scientific* system which yielded generally valid principles for the conduct of life and the guidance of society" (*Weltanschauung*, 90).

The neutral basis, the Archimedean point required for a badly needed tolerance was found in natural reason and natural law (*Weltanschauung*, 95). From that basis "the movement towards human autonomy" proceeded, as Bonhoeffer put it (LPP, 325), leading not only toward a science come of age but also toward a world come of age.

The "system of natural law, natural morality and natural theology" provided the foundation for the coming of age of modernity.

> According to this system there are in human nature firm concepts and ordered relations, a uniformity which everywhere leads to the same basic patterns of economic life, legal order, moral law, rules of aesthetics, belief in and veneration of God. These natural structures, norms and concepts of our thought, poetry, belief and social action are unchangeable and independent of cultural changes. They govern all peoples, are effective in all regions. Human autonomy is founded on them. Humanity enters upon the stage of adulthood and enlightenment to the extent to which it becomes conscious of these structures, norms and concepts, makes them the guide

of its activities and places all existing beliefs and institutions before the tribunal of the system derived from them. And there all social institutions and ecclesiastical teachings have to account for themselves. There has never been a greater and more protracted process than that. (*Weltanschauung*, 91)[196]

This was how Dilthey pictured the development of modernity.

There were boundaries that Bonhoeffer could not cross. He tried to accept the autonomy and the adulthood of humanity without reserve. But the decisive question for him was whether autonomy was necessarily the tribunal before which faith had to account for itself or, conversely, whether autonomy was infringed upon by the mere fact that people follow Jesus Christ. Therefore, Bonhoeffer's central issue was "Christ and the world come of age" (LPP, 327).[197] He emphasized that Jesus Christ does not prevent the world from coming of age. In light of Dilthey's analyses he regarded all attacks on the "adulthood of the world . . . pointless, . . . ignoble, and . . . unchristian" (LPP, 327). He tried to accept into theology the

> complete shift of interest . . . in otherworldly matters to thisworldly self-knowledge [which occurred between the fourteenth and seventeenth centuries]. People now were interested in learning about human beings, in the study of nature, the recognition of the independent value of reality, the value of work for them in their vocation; they were interested in uniform, worldly education and in the blessedness and happiness of life in the midst of the orders of reality. (*Weltanschauung*, 322)

Bonhoeffer wanted to participate "in the joyful affirmation of life and the world" (*Weltanschauung*, 246) without reducing it in any way because of faith in Jesus Christ. Instead he sought to establish that joy in its highest level through faith in Jesus Christ.

It is really surprising that Bonhoeffer drew on Dilthey to such an extent in his last letters. One may assume that in doing so he extended the subject of his first lecture course where he had shown, through the works of Dilthey, Troeltsch, and Simmel, that the attempts of Christianity to align itself with culture had failed.[198] Based on the historical insights derived from Dilthey, Bonhoeffer again took up the matter of religion. In the letters, as in the seminars, he continually referred to Barth's critique of religion. Bonhoeffer probably became aware of the issue of religion, again, through Dilthey who himself represented a religious Christianity. Dilthey's description and evaluation of the course of modern history gives proof to Bonhoeffer's thesis that only in the world after Copernicus did the word *religio* take the place of the word faith, filling it with its substance (GS V, 185).[199] Dilthey himself had applauded that process.

All this confirms that *Letters and Papers from Prison* does not speak of a dialectical, and consequently somehow static, juxtaposition of faith and religion, as had been the case in dialectical theology. Instead, the work develops a historical concept of religion which permits Bonhoeffer to move beyond that juxtaposition. Dilthey's argumentation appears to have influenced Bonhoeffer's concept of religion, although it was necessary to accommodate the latter to long-established theological presuppositions. Bonhoeffer's concept of religion is paradigmatic in showing how he adapted and evolved the ideas of other theologians: Bonhoeffer accepted some of Dilthey's analyses and developed his own theories while retaining the constructive thrust of Karl Barth.

Bonhoeffer agreed with Dilthey in his analysis and assessment of the course of modern history and in his opposition to metaphysics. No doubt as a result of his Dilthey studies, and without detailed explanation, Bonhoeffer cited metaphysics and inwardness as elements of religion (LPP, 280). These elements had played an important part in *Von deutscher Dichtung und Musik,* and an even more important part in *Weltanschauung und Analyse des Menschen.*

While attacking metaphysics vigorously,[200] Dilthey spoke positively about inwardness.[201] It was Luther who laid great emphasis on it.

> The "inward" person, the invisibility of the religious process and human freedom do not embody relations of power and obedience in an ecclesiastical entity. Only a political association permits the organization of social activities. Such associations, therefore, become the location of all activities of God's work in this world. *The sphere of the works of faith is human society and its orders.* (*Weltanschauung,* 61)[202]

Since Luther failed to abolish the mediaeval doctrine of the worldly and spiritual kingdoms and since "the transformation of German society in its worldly and ecclesiastical structures" (*Weltanschauung,* 62) did not come about, it would seem that all attempts to do so on the basis of the division of inwardness and worldliness will fail utterly. Yet that division was made, as Dilthey noted with approval, causing something other than our subjectivity to be regarded as the arbiter of our external actions (*Weltanschauung,* 61).[203]

The essence of Reformation religiosity is this, according to Dilthey:

> People as individuals are fully aware of the substance of their total uniqueness. Over against every association they are conscious of their self-worth and the independent power residing in them. This came about as a consequence of an economic, social and spiritual movement. Humanism had made its crucial strides in that direction. The religious expression of this was that people, alone with their God, gave shape to their relation to the invisible in their own way and through their own effort. (*Weltanschauung,* 212)

Dilthey undoubtedly meant this to be a positive assertion; he approved of the course that religion took, particularly in the pantheistic development of Reformation insights.[204] Bonhoeffer turned against such inwardness, as a special characteristic of religion, with the same rigor that he mustered against religion itself.[205]

An interesting example of Bonhoeffer's interest in the theological reflections contained in the rich material of Dilthey's work is to be found in a brief note in which he said, "A confession of faith does not express what someone else *'must'* believe, but what one *believes* oneself."[206] The substance of this is also stated in the "Outline for a Book": "What do we really believe? I mean, believe in such a way that we stake our lives on it? The problem of the Apostles' Creed? What *must* I believe? is the wrong question" (LPP, 382). The context points to the coercive nature of the creeds; that was also behind the comment of Episcopius, which Bonhoeffer had discovered in Dilthey.

Bonhoeffer seriously considered what he had learned in his Dilthey studies. According to Bonhoeffer, the movement of modernity was justified in its basic concern. Therefore, he rejected apologetics just as he had done in his lectures of 1932–33.[207] There was no reason, in his view, to seek shelter in apologetics. Instead, he counseled abandoning religion altogether, thus making sure it would no longer be a condition for faith:

> Only in that way, I think, will liberal theology be overcome (and even Barth is still influenced by it, though negatively) and at the same time its question be genuinely taken up and answered (as is *not* the case in the Confessing Church's positivism of revelation!). Thus the world's coming of age is no longer an occasion for polemics and apologetics, but is now really better understood than it understands itself, namely on the basis of the gospel and in the light of Christ. (LPP, 329)

This statement from Bonhoeffer's prison letters is truly legitimate only in view of the long experiences of his life, even though it can be traced to his 1932 lectures on ecclesiology.[208]

Because of the revelation of Jesus Christ we no longer need to doubt the autonomy of the world but can, in fact, achieve it properly. This is demonstrated in Bonhoeffer's exploration of how the world that has come of age is claimed by Jesus Christ (LPP, 342). The encounter of Jesus Christ with this world come of age is not heteronomous; it is not a denial of its adulthood.

> I therefore want to start from the premise that God shouldn't be smuggled into some last secret place, but that we should frankly recognize that the world, and people, having come of age, that we shouldn't run people down in their worldliness, but confront them with God at their strongest point, that we should give up all our clerical tricks and not regard psychotherapy and existentialist philosophy as God's pioneers. The importunity of all these people is far too unaristocratic for the word of God to ally itself with them. The word of God is far removed from this revolt of mistrust, this revolt from below. On the contrary, it reigns. (LPP, 346)[209]

If one compares the endeavors of the prison letters to Bonhoeffer's whole theology one discovers that something is expressed in the statements about "religionless Christianity" and "the world come of age" that had occupied Bonhoeffer from the very beginning. He had taken it considerably further, however, because the danger of being misunderstood on the matter of the world was no longer as great. Previously he had strongly opposed Cultural Protestantism and liberal theology, basing his opinion on Barth's critique of religion; yet still drawing on Barth's work, he later formulated an understanding of the world in which a one-sided withdrawal from the world was overcome. One cannot say that Bonhoeffer brought together the thrust of Barth's theology of revelation and the understanding of the world characteristic of liberal theology. It would be more accurate to say that he developed an understanding of the world by means of Barth's theology, an understanding which neither fell under the spell of the world at the expense of faith nor ignored the world for the sake of Jesus Christ.

GOD'S ABSENCE AND PRESENCE IN A WORLD COME OF AGE

Nearly two decades before his imprisonment Bonhoeffer had encountered Barth's theology which was impressively conceived, although not fully developed. Bonhoeffer, a theological novice, had taken to it readily. When he later studied Dilthey's analyses he had his own theology to which he could relate them.[210] But one should not question Bonhoeffer's originality on account of his extensive use of Dilthey. As stated in the introduction, that originality does not consist so much in the formulation of individual statements as in the independent development of various ideas for the purpose of answering theological questions.

For a long time the prevailing view among critics was that the ideas about the world come of age had been Bonhoeffer's own creation. That view is now changing. Bonhoeffer is regarded as being deeply rooted in a tradition, the concepts of which he did not simply absorb, but rather developed within the context of his own perspective. Bonhoeffer's attempts to assess the modern movement toward autonomy have become so familiar as to be almost commonplace. But that must not conceal the fact that those ideas were highly unusual for theology in general and for his own theology up to that time. After all, he had regarded the development in modernity somewhat critically, especially where a constructive understanding of the world for Christian faith was concerned.[211] There are indeed numerous indications that he looked upon those ideas as quite new, even for him, and that other people would be surprised or shocked by them.[212]

One of the main aspects of Bonhoeffer's originality is his adoption of Dilthey's evaluation of the development of modernity, in his own endeavor to have an adequate understanding of the world. He gave that evaluation his unique interpretation by refusing to systematize it in the sense of an abstract view of secularization.[213] He affirmed the coming of age and autonomy of the world then taking concrete shape, and became convinced that it did not abolish Christian faith, but instead offered faith the chance to become a reality in a new and deeper way, as a religionless Christianity in a world come of age.

Although one can trace certain important statements of Bonhoeffer back to Dilthey, the problem of understanding what religionless or worldly Christianity means is not yet solved. It has been seen that Bonhoeffer and Dilthey were sharply divided over one issue: Dilthey belonged to the past because he affirmed the "new gospel of the infinite universe" and the inwardness that went with it; Bonhoeffer, on the other hand, was anxious to overcome the division of faith and world precisely in view of the world come of age, a division that Dilthey had signaled and lamented and, because it had not been overcome, regarded as insurmountable. On this issue Bonhoeffer opposed not only Dilthey but also Barth, who, although in a manner contrary to Dilthey, also supported a radical division of faith and world. One only wonders why Bonhoeffer did not criticize Dilthey, in *Letters and Papers from Prison*, from the point of view of theology. Perhaps he thought that his own positive acceptance and simultaneous critique of Barth would be enough to criticize Dilthey, for Barth's own critique was certainly directed at Dilthey's understanding of religion. Bonhoeffer's critique of Barth would, therefore, apply indirectly also to Dilthey.

But despite fundamental theological differences Bonhoeffer relied on Dilthey in order to interpret his own experiences with people who could no longer be religious because they had come of age. Being of age is not a category primarily of individual maturation but one of epochal social emancipation. Such emancipation causes people to cope with their problems, be they scientific, ethical, cultural, or religious, without God; they no longer live in the heteronomy of a certain world view and its corresponding understanding of God. Dilthey had also tried to overcome that heteronomy, not in terms of an appropriate understanding of God, but by absolutizing the universe. Bonhoeffer probably assessed Dilthey accurately: even though he had provided a correct and impressive analysis of the development of modernity he remained captive to an understanding of the world that was religious, that is to say, pantheistic and subjectivistic. Dilthey, too, concealed the godlessness of the world with religion.

Irrespective of Dilthey's critique of the "real church," Bonhoeffer emphatically insisted that such a critique should not be raised to the status of principle and be perverted into a general opposition to the church as such. There was no road for him from the church to a general, rational, natural religion, that is to say, inwardness.[214] On the contrary, "the church must come out of its stagnation" (LPP, 378)[215] and back into the living intellectual discussion with its world and time.

The decisive difference between Bonhoeffer and Dilthey, which is precisely the decisive step that the former took beyond the latter, lies in Bonhoeffer's attempt not to let go of the original proclamation and the relation to the primitive church, as contrary to the world's adulthood, and in his attempt to assume that the proclamation takes a new form appropriate to the time in which the world's adulthood becomes historical reality. On this question Barth and Bonhoeffer went separate ways, for Barth wanted to solve the problem by means of an actualistic and acosmic intervention of God in the present non-historical moment.

The conflict between faith and the world was inevitable, according to Bonhoeffer. But it was not primarily a conflict between an almighty God on one side and a sinful world, subject to death, on the other. It was, rather, the conflict between the God who is powerful in this world by virtue of his powerlessness, and a "hopeless godlessness" in a world come of age. The autonomy of humanity had been initially signaled in the negative term "without God," but Bonhoeffer gave it a theological interpretation. Instead of condemning the entire development of modernity for fear that no room would be left for God, and instead of rushing out by "the various emergency exits that have been contrived," or even performing "the *salto mortale* (death leap) back into the Middle Ages" (LPP, 360),[216] Bonhoeffer related our coming of age to a true recognition of our situation before God. It is not the world but God alone who leads us to that recognition, for we must understand "that we have to live in the world *etsi deus non daretur*. And this is just what we do recognize—before God!" (LPP, 360).[217] Bonhoeffer explained what this meant by referring to the cross.

Only in his late letters did Bonhoeffer establish a connection between the theology of the cross, which by no means renounces but rather embraces the world,[218] and the world come of age. This is the world that has become autonomous and, as a consequence, godless in the sense of hopeless godlessness and promising godlessness. The letter in which Bonhoeffer had spoken extensively about Dilthey's *Weltanschauung und Analyse der Menschen* ended with the reference to that connection. Bonhoeffer must have pondered at length about these ideas before making such theological assertions.

It was the phrase "even if there were no God" that had allowed Bonhoeffer to make a theological response. Grotius had used the words in order to develop a basis for human community life; the phrase provides for our time the interpretation of a Christian understanding of God and the world according to which the godlessness of a social–political entity has become the godlessness of the West. Instead of directing us to God's power in the world, the Bible directs us

> to God's powerlessness and suffering; only the suffering God can help. To that extent we say that the development towards the world's "coming of age" outlined above, which has done away with a false conception of God,

opens up a way of seeing the God of the Bible, who wins power and space in the world by his weakness. (LPP, 361)

Contrary to what the religious expect of God, Christians are "summoned to share in God's sufferings at the hands of a godless world" (LPP, 361). It has already been noted that people may and must live worldly lives now: Christian belief in the world come of age is "participation in the sufferings of God in the secular life" (LPP, 361). Belief is certainly not the seeking of one's own personal salvation (LPP, 361). The *troika* of individualism, inwardness, and piety has now been overcome;[219] given up is the metaphysical view of God which had sought to activate God's power at the edges of life[220] as a compensation for human weakness.[221] But this only leads to a view of the world in which the world continues to be beyond our grasp. Only when such a metaphysics is overcome will the world's godlessness no longer be concealed by religion, but will become clearly manifest (LPP, 362). Bonhoeffer concluded by saying that "the world that has 'come of age' is more godless, and perhaps for that very reason nearer to God" (LPP, 362).

The thesis that secularization was caused by Christian faith must be rejected.[222] That thesis arose from the suspicion that the theological theory of secularization seeks to co-opt the autonomy of humankind. Applied to Bonhoeffer, the proponents of this thesis would suggest that by bringing the emancipation observable in modernity and the godlessness to which it led together with a theology of the cross, Bonhoeffer wanted to give to Christians a better way to faith, and to the godless a deeper way of understanding themselves and the world, than either of these two groups could have on their own.[223] To put it differently, it would suggest that Bonhoeffer wanted to avoid the inevitable conflict with the world by removing God from the world and, in reliance upon God, he wanted to instruct the world about its proper self-understanding.

The first thing to be said about this thesis is that the concept of the limits or the weakness of humanity, as well as the whole subject of the theology of the cross, pervade all of Bonhoeffer's theology, as does the problem of godlessness. These matters are closely interrelated in his entire thinking and do not arise only in *Letters and Papers from Prison*. Bonhoeffer's earlier endeavor to find God at the genuine limit or boundary, and his later attempt to seek God at the center, were correlated, to a great extent, since the power, or the weakness, of the world and the weakness, or the power, of God, which cannot simply be joined, were ambivalent terms from the outset. The power of the world has always been a weakness when seen in relation to God because that power was the attempt to forge a way to God and to establish autonomy; that power was the way of religion, morality, and piety. In opposing that way Bonhoeffer pointed to our weakness, and to death and sin. But he refused in his final letters to make our weakness the point of departure because God's omnipotence did not manifest itself in this worldly power, but in his search for our human weakness.[224]

Bonhoeffer rejected the temptation to lead people to God by reminding them of their weakness. He called that course the way of methodism,[225] since behind it there lurks once again our human power, albeit our alleged power, for forcing others to come to God. God's power always resides in what, in this world, is called weakness, and in his solidarity with the weak. That is why the notion of God's power residing in his powerlessness in this world is not a new one, postulated as a kind of afterthought to the world come of age. The theology of the cross was certainly not introduced in order that the conflict between faith and world could be effectively removed.

There is also a theological version of that interdependence of power and weakness which confirms our thesis about problems relating to the relationship of power and weakness. Bonhoeffer pondered, at length, the problem of God's absence and God's presence; that problem was behind Luther's comment, which Bonhoeffer had used on more than one occasion, that the curses of the godless are at times more pleasing to God than the hallelujahs of the pious.[226] Luther's expression was used by Bonhoeffer in connection with his distinction between *actus directus* and *actus reflectus;* it again appears in *Ethics* precisely where he discussed "the godlessness in religious and Christian clothing" which is "a hopeless godlessness," and "the godlessness which is full of promise, . . . which speaks against religion and against the Church" (E, 103). That distinction stands behind the assertion that "the world that has 'come of age' is more godless, and perhaps for that very reason nearer to God" (LPP, 362).[227] Bonhoeffer's endeavors to describe, most incisively, our experience of transcendence reached their highest point in that assertion.

Bonhoeffer's positive assessment of the historical development in which the world has come of age is now brought together with his fully developed christologically-based idea of God's presence and alleged absence. This brings his occasional thoughts about modern secularization to their conclusion. Bonhoeffer probably did not use that term because it struck him as being too negative in its definition. Instead, he adopted a positive assessment of the movement toward autonomy; that does not mean that he regarded as positive all events and facts related to the movement. On the contrary, even then the ambivalence of history was not overcome but was present in a different way. His "yes" to modernity was not simply a justification of modernity. He affirmed modernity as a command to have positive dominion over the world, particularly since the way to do so has now become apparent.

A new form of Christian faith is not only possible, as a consequence of the course of history, but also necessary. The imperative to have dominion over the world demands it. Just as Christ was there for others, the community of the faithful or the church must also be there for others (LPP, 381). Faith must not concern itself with its self-defense in a world that is now godless; it must attend to its service to that world and participate in God's redemptive suffering for the world in order to protect it against "shallow and banal thisworldliness" (LPP, 369) and "one dimensional" reality (LPP, 311), and therefore against itself. To remain multi-dimensional means, in a Chalcedonian sense, to remain steadfast in the true worldliness which was constituted only in the incarnation and the godlessness of the world which resulted from that worldliness, a godlessness in the sense of eradicating gods. Here the reality that has given shape to history maintains the difference between God and the world and overcomes it at the same time. That is why the godless world can be nearer to God. Here, then, is the basic concern of Bonhoeffer's religionless understanding of God and the world, which must be further developed.

First, one must probe more deeply into the predicaments of the concept of secularization. Bonhoeffer was surely aware of the debate surrounding secularization, although it was more a debate about "secularism" then, the term having negative connotations.[228] There had been a very audible debate about the matter between the two world wars, but Bonhoeffer had stayed away from it almost completely. He called the religion upheld by one side secularism; but that description is much more a characterization of a type than a reflection of what had occurred in the development of modernity.[229] There is a reference to that debate in Bonhoeffer's address on christology which he had given in Barcelona: "What we need to do now . . . is to take Christ out of the process of secularization into which he has been drawn since the days of the Enlightenment" and to oppose the humanism which had led "to morality and religion" (GS V, 136, 150).

Bonhoeffer set out from that point to solve the modern problem of faith and world, bringing it to its conclusion in *Letters and Papers from Prison*. Both the similarities and the differences between those early statements and the final letters are significant. What they have in common is the polemic against religion being understood as a cultural phenomenon. Their differences lie in the fact that Bonhoeffer initially attempted to reckon with the issue without Christ. Later, however, he wished to accomplish the opposite: convinced that the absence of Christ in the discussion of this problem was the mistake of religion, Bonhoeffer tried to avoid the spatial separation of Christ from the world.

Bonhoeffer had spoken quite early about the divorce of Christianity from culture (GS V, 210). He also discussed the issue of secularization in his reports about the visits to the United States.[230] Evidence in his report about the 1939 visit supports the thesis that a close relation exists between an alleged freedom of the church from, and an ingrained bondage to, the world.

> The praise of freedom as the possibility for existence given by the world to the church can stem precisely from an agreement entered upon with this world in which the true freedom of the word of God is surrendered. Thus it can happen that a church which boasts of its freedom as a possibility offered to it by the world slips back into the world to a special degree, that a church which is free in this way becomes secularized more quickly than a church which does not possess freedom as possibility. (NRS, 104)

Bonhoeffer added, referring to American and European secularization, that

> *the secularization of the church on the continent of Europe* arose from the misinterpretation of the reformers' distinction of the two realms; *American secularization* derives precisely from the imperfect distinction of the kingdoms and offices of church and state, from the enthusiastic claim of the church to universal influence on the world. (NRS, 108)

Bonhoeffer reiterated this idea in *Ethics* in a reflection on the French Revolution and the godlessness arising from secularization and revolution (E, 96, 105); this was Bonhoeffer's most extended historical consideration before the prison letters. In *Ethics,* Bonhoeffer referred to the modern process of secularization "at the end of which we are standing today" (E, 96). Contrary to earlier statements, Bonhoeffer spoke here of the end of that process, which had radically removed God from the world and caused a widespread loss of faith in God (E, 96).[231] But even here Bonhoeffer tried to acknowledge the positive results of the process, namely, the intellectual integrity and the use of reason set free, without ignoring the fact that "intellectual clarity is often achieved at the expense of insight into reality" (E, 97). Yet he insisted that "we cannot now go back to the days before Lessing and Lichtenberg" (E, 98). While acknowledging the modern process of secularization and the results of the French Revolution, Bonhoeffer could not overlook the negative consequences. Western godlessness had become a religious godlessness as a result of the French Revolution: "Western godlessness ranges from the religion of Bolshevism to the midst of the Christian churches" (E, 102). Bonhoeffer's thoughts led him to conclude that "by the loss of the unity which is possessed through the form of Jesus Christ, the western world is brought to the brink of the void. . . . It is, once again, a specifically western void, a violent void, and one which is the enemy of both God and humankind. . . . It is the void made god" (E, 105). Continuing his argument in the prison letters, Bonhoeffer began to ponder "the godlessness that is full of promise"! Thus, the subject of secularization leads to the absence as well as the presence of God, that is to say, the absence of God versus the seeming absence or presence of God.[232]

RELIGIONLESS CHRISTIANITY AND NON-RELIGIOUS INTERPRETATION

The Relation Between Religionless Christianity and Non-Religious Interpretation

There have been several references here, already, to religionless Christianity, but almost none to the non-religious interpretation of biblical concepts. This may have caused some surprise to readers, and thus an explanation is in order. Eberhard Bethge has quite rightly called attention to the curious fact that in Germany the discussion focused almost exclusively on non-religious interpretation, whereas in the English-speaking world it focused entirely on religionless Christianity. Whereas Germans were concerned with proclamation, English-speaking people concerned themselves with the problems of practice.[233] The cause of this distinction may lie in the fact that in Germany the hermeneutical discussion simply outweighed all else, whereas practical questions dominated the Anglo-Saxon agenda. In Germany Gerhard Ebeling initiated and also shaped the hermeneutical discussion relating to Bonhoeffer.[234] Bethge insisted, however, that Bonhoeffer discussed both proclamation and practice; to this may be added the comment that Bonhoeffer's primary interest lay in religionless Christianity which is considered in terms of non-religious interpretation. The latter derives from the former, which it must serve. A discussion of that idea will help to explicate the content and meaning of the concept of religionless Christianity.

Bonhoeffer declared in the letter of 30 April 1944 that "the time when people could be told everything by means of words, whether theological or pious, is over" (LPP, 279). He followed this statement with the remark that religion had become the transient form of expression, and the Western form of Christianity its garment. He continued by questioning the status of the church, congregation, sermon, liturgy, and Christian life: "How do we speak of God—without religion?" (LPP, 280). Clearly, this question about our "speaking" of God is one of Bonhoeffer's many queries and statements concerning a particular reality and the practice which pertains to it, and is only indirectly a question about the hermeneutic appropriate to it. In the second half of that letter Bonhoeffer spoke about "mentioning" God's name, and how religious people "talk" of God. But the real topic of the letter is religion as a contemporary synonym for circumcision. The letter concludes with statements about God's transcendence and the form of religionless Christianity (LPP, 281-82).[235] Thus, one may conclude that Bonhoeffer was not primarily concerned with our "speaking," or with interpretation or proclamation, but with the form of religious Christianity and its practice.

The second letter about this topic begins by naming the concept "religionlessness." Simply noting the problem Bonhoeffer here suggests that the whole New Testament would have to be interpreted and proclaimed in a non-religious sense (LPP, 285). He continues by asking, "What does it mean to 'interpret in a religious sense'?" (LPP, 285). Here his ensuing discussion does not touch on the problem of language, but only on the problem of the form of Christianity.

Some time after he had raised the matter that way did he name the issue, the non-religious interpretation of theological concepts (LPP, 328). But again it does not appear to be his primary concern, for he writes: "Let me just summarize briefly again [sic] what I'm concerned about—the claim of a world that has 'come of age' by Jesus Christ" (LPP, 342).[236] That claim does not become actual through proclamation, but, as shall be seen, through our being drawn into the suffering of Jesus Christ.

The relation between religionless Christianity and non-religious interpretation, as described in Bonhoeffer's late letters, embraces a relation discussed in part one: it is the relation between life and thought, praxis and theory, or in theological terms, between faith and theology, *actus directus* and *actus reflectus*.[237] Here the crucial thrust of Bonhoeffer's theology is encountered in its entirety: no action will happen automatically by simply weighing the possibilities in advance (LPP, 298). It will only happen as a consequence of decision; and decision can neither be measured wholly by reflection, nor completely expressed and motivated by it. Bonhoeffer called it the cardinal error of his generation not to have known and heeded that insight (LPP, 298).

These reflections provide guidance for our interpretation of the material significance of religionless Christianity and non-religious interpretation. The latter, being itself dependent upon Christianity, is the endeavor to prepare the religionless form of Christianity. Therefore, we may not expect to find in Bonhoeffer's theological exploration conclusive and final statements about, or a fully developed model of, non-religious interpretation. We are not dealing with a problem which can be solved by thinking; it raises itself, historically, in the praxis of life, and seeks to be solved through action. Of course, thinking makes a contribution that must not be underestimated. One must seriously regard Bonhoeffer's assertion that "we are once again being driven right back to the beginnings of our understanding." Bonhoeffer further declared, "In the traditional words and acts we suspect that there may be something quite new and revolutionary, though we cannot as yet grasp or express it" (LPP, 299–300). Bonhoeffer hoped that "prayer and righteous action among people" would lead to the regeneration of the church's form (LPP, 300). "We are not yet out of the melting-pot"; only when there is real "conversion and purification" will a new language come out of the new form, a language "perhaps quite non-religious, but liberating and redeeming—as was Jesus' language" (LPP, 300).

We must note, therefore, that Bonhoeffer not only spoke of religionless Christianity before he spoke of the non-religious interpretation of biblical concepts, but that he gave precedence to the question of the church's form over the matter of the hermeneutics arising from it.

The Meaning of Non-Religious Interpretation

Before clarifying what is meant by the form of religionless Christianity, the non-religious interpretation of biblical concepts shall be discussed. Bonhoeffer approached this problem, too, through various theological routes,[238] but he was unable to move beyond a few substantive comments. Although his opponent in this discussion was clearly Rudolf Bultmann, one cannot suggest that there was a greater relationship between Bonhoeffer and Bultmann than between Bonhoeffer and Barth.[239]

The non-religious secular interpretation of biblical concepts was designed to be a corrective to Bultmann's demythologizing which, in Bonhoeffer's assessment, was directed incorrectly "only [at] the 'mythological' concepts, such as miracle, ascension, and so on" (LPP, 285). He objected that those concepts "are not in principle separable from the concepts of God, faith, etc." (LPP, 285).[240] Indeed, Bonhoeffer found fault with Bultmann not because he had gone too far, but because he had not gone far enough. Bonhoeffer considered Bultmann's article liberal, meaning that it abridged the gospel (LPP, 285). "Bultmann seems to have somehow felt Barth's limitations, but he misconstrues them in the sense of liberal theology, and so goes off into the typical liberal process of reduction . . . and Christianity is reduced to its essence" (LPP, 328–29).

Behind Bonhoeffer's brief comment may be his conviction that Bultmann was quite justified in attempting an appropriate understanding of the New Testament, but that he went about the task through the false conceptuality of liberal theology which still influenced Barth, though negatively (LPP, 329). Bultmann had made a false peace between human consciousness and Christian faith in his attempt to confront the modern understanding of the world. In order to achieve his purpose, declared Bonhoeffer, Bultmann had separated such concepts as God and miracle, and had labeled the world view of the New Testament as "mythological"; in this way Bultmann had created the impression that he was dividing the New Testament into mythological and non-mythological parts, according to their dependence or non-dependence upon that world view.

We do not need to explore whether or not, or to what extent, Bultmann had intended such a division. Bonhoeffer sensed the danger of such a separation, and therefore insisted that one "must be able to interpret and proclaim *both* [sc. concepts like God and miracle] in a 'non-religious' sense," and that one must "think theologically" (LPP, 285). Here the word "theological" is most likely used in contradistinction to "liberal" or "religious," the latter terms amounting to the same thing. Bonhoeffer thought that Bultmann was mistaken in perceiving "universal truth" behind those mythological concepts; "the full content, including the 'mythological' concepts, must be kept . . . ; this mythology (resurrection, etc.) is the thing itself" (LPP, 329). Demythologizing the New Testament does not necessarily overcome a religious misunderstanding of the Christian faith or the New Testament.

One makes a religious interpretation of a concept when the concept is interpreted metaphysically, that is, interpreted in terms of a purely otherworldly salvation, or when the concept is interpreted inwardly, that is, interpreted in relation to a worldless subject. The price of such an interpretation is the elimination of the offensive statements of the New Testament which are said to be unable to defend themselves before the tribunal of emancipated reason. And that kind of interpretation was done for the sake of the world come of age. But one should have related the offensive statements to the world in order that they could exist for it; "what is above this world is, in the gospel, intended to exist *for* this world" (LPP, 286). There should be no more serious argument as to whether or not Bultmann's existential interpretation guarded the relation of Christian faith to the world and its history sufficiently, when it related faith completely to the subject and interiorized it. Bonhoeffer's charge that Bultmann followed liberal theology is in fact quite justified.[241] Bonhoeffer wondered whether existential interpretation, with its restrictiveness, did not lead to a process of reduction which put the conflict between faith and world "right out of the world"; and was that not a form of flight from the world? In order to overcome such deficiency, Bonhoeffer proposed to interpret all of Christian faith in a worldly fashion.[242] But a worldly interpretation must consider seriously that there is no Archimedean point somewhere outside the world, as the theology of revelation had assumed (LPP, 381). Only "from the resurrection of Christ [can] a new and purifying wind blow through our present world. *Here* is the answer to 'Give me somewhere to stand, and I will move the earth' " (LPP, 240).[243]

Religionless Christianity as a Form of "Worldly-Universal" Christianity

Our reflections have tried to show, through comparison with a position that Bonhoeffer had rejected, that the point of non-religious interpretation of biblical concepts was not to gain "a little 'non-religious' language,"[244] in the sense of language fashionable for that day. This punctuates the question about religionless Christianity, and any further statements about non-religious interpretation would be conjectures. If we are correct in asserting that it is impossible to design a model of non-religious interpretation in the abstract because it is so closely interrelated with religionless Christianity, then such restraint is not of great consequence. The problem of the new "form" of Christianity, however, either cannot be solved, or, if a solution is found, it is inadequate or merely formal.[245] At the time when Bonhoeffer was thinking about that new form there were only a few hints as to what it would be. Whether he would have apprehended more explicit manifestations of it in the restoration period after the war must be left unanswered, but may be seriously questioned. It is simply illusory to speculate how Bonhoeffer would have acted in the rebuilding of the church; such speculation, however, does not belong in a study like this. Suffice it to say that even the notion of a *re*-building of the church would have disappointed him.

Yet we can and must ask whether, next to the formal and negative descriptions of this religionless Christianity, there were also concrete and positive references or indications which would permit a more accurate understanding of the statements from these late letters. The formal thrust of the latter has already become sufficiently clear: Bonhoeffer wanted to establish an open and constructive relation of Christian faith to the world, thereby overcoming and eradicating the previously dominant arrangement between faith and world. In this case even a separation of faith and world has to be regarded as an arrangement between them. In Bonhoeffer's first letter about religionless Christianity he had wondered whether "the Western form of Christianity, too, was only a preliminary stage to a complete absence of religion" (LPP, 280). That letter concluded by reiterating the same thought in a positive formulation: "How this religionless Christianity looks, what form it takes, is something I've been thinking about a great deal, and I shall be writing to you again about it soon. It may be that on us in particular, midway between East and West, there will fall a heavy responsibility" (LPP, 282).[246] Of course, Bonhoeffer was unable to reach "the more constructive part" which he had indeed anticipated (LPP, 393).

What was behind that comment about the Western form of Christianity? It implies the alternative of a real, or perhaps only potential, Eastern form of Christianity. Bonhoeffer, in fact, made reference to such a view in a letter of 22 May 1934: "The fact is that Christianity did come from the East originally but we have so westernized it and so permeated it with the concerns of civilization that we can see that we have almost lost it" (GS II, 182).

It would seem that, for Bonhoeffer, religion is the Western form of Christianity, while religionlessness is the form which, after the decline of the West, will take the place of religion as the dying form of Western Christian faith. This would tend to confirm that for Bonhoeffer religion is indeed a concept of intellectual history. Accordingly, it is a specifically Western phenomenon, and, in that sense, "a historically conditioned and transient form of human self-expression" (LPP, 280).[247]

One may conclude, therefore, that the positive and concrete form of post-Western faith, namely, religionless Christianity and the correlative non-religious interpretation, is a Christianity freed from its Western shackles, and therefore is "worldly-universal," or related to the whole world. Bonhoeffer had hoped that a visit to Gandhi in India would provide him with material illustrating such a form of faith.

Evidence supporting this conclusion is to be found in Bonhoeffer's letter to his grandmother, which is referred to above. "Before I settle down anywhere for good, I am thinking again of going to India. I have given a good deal of thought lately to Indian questions and believe that there is quite a lot to be learned there. Sometimes it even seems to me that there is more Christianity in their 'paganism' than in the whole of our Reich church" (GS II, 182).[248]

One may draw a number of inferences to support this conclusion from Bonhoeffer's numerous comments about his plans for India, and from the late letters. As already indicated, Bonhoeffer regarded religion as a dying phenomenon. The sense that European Christianity as well as the West were on the decline, a view by no means exclusively held by Bonhoeffer, was manifest even in his early period. In 1931 he asked in a letter whether "our time is up and the gospel has been given to another people" (GS I, 61).[249] Six months later, writing to Sutz, Bonhoeffer said: "A year ago I was in Mexico with Lassere. I can hardly think about it without a great urge to go away again, but to the East this time. I do not yet know when. But it cannot be much longer delayed. There must be other people in the world who know and who can do more than we. And in that case it is simply philistine not to go and learn from them" (GS I, 32).[250]

What Bonhoeffer knew about Europe and what he had learned in North America led him to be pessimistic about the future of the West. He shared the not uncommon hope that new powers would radiate from Gandhi's India, which would be of value for Europe and North America as well, particularly in relation to Christian faith.

A second inference may be drawn from the fact that in the prison letters Bonhoeffer spoke of a transient form and its transient interpretation, namely, the religious interpretation. In one of his early letters, written while at his English vicarage, Bonhoeffer remarked to his brother: "Somehow I think of my stay in England . . . as an interlude. I had thought that my next step would have finally taken me to India and the East. And such a step seems more real from here. And since I become more convinced each day that Christianity is coming to its demise in the West—at least in its present form and interpretation—I would like to go East before returning to Germany" (GS II, 158).[251]

The comment about the likely demise of Western Christianity uses the terms "form" and "interpretation,"[252] which were of such importance in the last letters from prison, and uses them in the same sequence in both the early and late letters. A terminological congruence of that kind is no sheer coincidence.

The third and most important inference is to be drawn from Bonhoeffer's christology. Bonhoeffer had begun the whole discussion in *Letters and Papers from Prison* by questioning the nature of Christianity and the role that Christ plays for us today. In 1931 he wrote to Helmut Rössler,

> I want to go to a great country and see whether the great solution is to be found there—India. If it is not there then it is finished, the great demise of Christianity is upon us. Is our time up and has the gospel been given to another people, proclaimed in perhaps very different words and deeds? How do you view the belief that Christianity is everlasting in the light of the world-situation and our own way of living today? . . . I am now chaplain at the Technical Institute but how is one to preach these things to people here? Who still believes such things? The invisibility of God breaks us to pieces. If we cannot see in our personal lives that Christ has come then we shall see it at least in India. But to be thrown back again and again on the invisible God is insane and no one can stand it any longer. (GS I, 61)[253]

Bonhoeffer's search for a concrete, "thisworldly" experience of God in Jesus Christ is related to his thoughts about India.

Given these correspondences between some of Bonhoeffer's early endeavors and his late concerns, one may well use a comment that Bonhoeffer made in 1928 as a motto for the work of his final period: No single person will find the answers to the great questions of Europe today, he said; they will emerge instead only from the combined human efforts of a great Asiatic–European–American process (GS V, 117).

No doubt the process has been initiated, but it is still so much in its early stages today that no results can as yet be foreseen. It is certain that Bonhoeffer had hoped for and expected such a measure, for, in comparison with his earlier, pessimistic statements, his later assessment of the modern development is positive. We cannot determine whether or not Bonhoeffer would have found in India what he was looking for; there is some evidence that he would have been disappointed. It may suffice to say that through his hope to learn something there he came to perceive at least the relativity of the European as well as the North American form of Christianity and life, and to reflect upon it thereafter. The religionless Christianity that he had anticipated would clearly lead to a new freedom upon its release from its Western connections and restrictions, a freedom which, in analogy to the example and counsel of Gandhi, would be marked by active passivity. Bonhoeffer spoke of that passivity in his last letters in terms of our participation in God's suffering at the hands of a godless world, through communal activities and communal life. This is also why Bonhoeffer was anxious to become familiar with the common life of Gandhi's ashram and of Anglican monasteries before introducing a common life to his preachers' seminary.[254]

If our thesis is correct, the conception of religionless Christianity had had a long tradition in Bonhoeffer's theology and its terminology had been formulated even before he turned directly to that subject in *Letters and Papers from Prison*. In those final letters, however, Bonhoeffer no longer looked for help in the salvation of Occidental Christianity and Western culture; his earlier pessimism had also disappeared. Even in his affirmation of the world's adulthood Bonhoeffer knew that God rules; for that reason he was not needlessly concerned about the church's self-affirmation. He was confident that the church would continue to exist, but not because of the possibility of Europe experiencing a regeneration, or because of the presence of other worldly powers; rather, it was because God acts in the history of the world into which he entered through Jesus Christ.

The few concrete points that Bonhoeffer made about religionless Christianity must be combined against the backdrop of his conception of a non-Western form of human autonomy and life. It is necessary again to describe the basic aspects of this concept. God is not to be settled at the boundaries or in the weakness of the world; nor are God, the individual, and the concept of God to be correlated. The nucleus of religionlessness is a new relation to the world, namely, the constructive relationship of the Christian faith to the world in which the world is affirmed in its many dimensions. There are certain features of the community of believers which correspond to a religionless form of Christianity, such as the believers' refusal to regard themselves from a religious point of view as specially favored (LPP, 281), but, instead, as people "there for others" (LPP, 381). To be religionless and worldly means to live in a paradox, for one is called out of the world, and yet one belongs wholly to it (LPP, 281). The only concrete consequences that Bonhoeffer drew from these features of the community of believers were related to the church, which he declared should give away all its property and completely reform its office of the clergy (LPP, 382). Bonhoeffer seemed to think that the whole structure of ecclesiastical offices needed restructuring so that the whole church could become an example again (LPP, 382). Bonhoeffer had something like that in mind when he wrote, "The first confession the Christian congregation makes before the world is its action. It interprets itself" (GS V, 259).

In connection with that statement, Bonhoeffer also spoke of the *arcanum,* which is referred to in the prison letters in the very same connection.[255] Attention has already been called to Bonhoeffer's assertion that the right word of proclamation can arise only from silence.[256] One must remember that, according to Bonhoeffer, even the good which Christians do in the world can be done only as something arcane. This does not and will not separate them from the world at all, but it will spare the world a direct, unmediated confrontation with the Christian message, and especially with the Christian worship of God in baptism, eucharist, and confession. By guarding the world from that confrontation Christians in fact exercise the discretion appropriate for doing good in relation to the world. This does not mean that there are two kinds of sermons now, one for the assembly of believers and one for the world, but that the community's worship of God does not belong in the public square.[257]

It is important to recall that Bonhoeffer related this arcane discipline to the world come of age as well. If this discipline is exercised by a community of people who desire to be obedient in their discipleship in spite of, or perhaps precisely because of, their experience of human autonomy in the world, then it must become part of the melting down, or purification and renewal, that the church must undergo. This much can be concluded from Bonhoeffer's few statements about the reordering of the ecclesiastical office.

A merely external modification in the administration of the sacraments and in preaching is not equivalent to what Bonhoeffer meant by religionless Christianity and the non-religious interpretation of biblical concepts corresponding to it. "Certain forms and traditions will indeed have to be given up so that we may perhaps attain to more felicitous and freer forms. . . . But a radical cure, such as deleting the words cross, sin, grace, etc. from our vocabulary, will accomplish nothing," he wrote years earlier (GS III, 41).[258] Those are the very words that he touched on in the discussion of non-religious interpretation. They need not and cannot be replaced by other words, but they do require new strength through prayer and righteous action.

Arcane discipline and religionless Christianity belong together. They hold in common the non-religious and worldly interpretations of the Christian message. Such interpretations would have to inform the preaching that the community addressed to itself and the missionary preaching it addressed to others. Bonhoeffer made it clear in his question of revising the creeds that the arcane is equally affected by the development toward autonomy. The same question had already occupied him when he was a student of Adolf von Harnack, as had the revision of Christian apologetics.[259] Bonhoeffer was convinced that if such a new form of secret discipline were indeed to be exercised, the church would no longer stand "at the boundaries where human powers give out, but in the middle of the village" (LPP, 282), and would then be the church for others (LPP, 383). One may again see that arcane discipline is not a withdrawal from the world.

For the church to be in the "middle of the village" and to exist for others situated there does not mean that it can rule over subordinate people for its own glorification. That position and existence is made manifest outside the church as service and inside the church as training for that service, namely, as the service of worship with the celebration of the sacraments and preaching. The concrete comments that Bonhoeffer made about the reordering of the ecclesiastical office and theological education in his "Outline for a Book" (LPP, 383)[260] had as their purpose the renewal of that position and existence. Secret discipline is no new form of partiality, or of the withdrawal from the world; it is not a form of provinciality. Bonhoeffer's own practical attempts, described in *Life Together*, were not in the service of an esoteric religious life or a new methodism; they were meant to strengthen the service to the world. "The aim is not the seclusion of a monastery, but a place of the deepest inward concentration for service outside" (WF, 31).

We have now looked, within the context of Bonhoeffer's whole theology, at the relatively few comments that he made about arcane discipline. We have seen what that discipline meant for non-religious interpretation in its new context, namely, in a religionless or worldly Christianity. It is quite clear that Bonhoeffer's religionless Christianity does not mean a Christianity without worship, sacraments, preaching, and prayer (LPP, 280), or that love for God and love for one's neighbor must not be identified, or, again, that the "Christian" and the "ethical," that is to say, real brotherliness/sisterliness, are not the same. Where such identifications are made one attains secularism, which is the denial of the ultimate for the sake of the penultimate. Where love for God and love for the neighbor, where the Christian and the ethical are separated, one attains provincialism, which is the denial of the penultimate for the sake of the ultimate. The tension must be kept up between the ultimate and the penultimate; one must not lose the polyphony and multidimensionality of the world, for they alone establish and protect profound thisworldliness as true worldliness.

This worldly faith can finally overcome Cultural Protestantism and Pietism, those two false developments of religion which are identical in the long run. Liberal theology is at last left behind by a non-religious, worldly interpretation of faith. Religionless Christianity overcomes the double partiality of faith, the partiality which arises when faith and world are separated and the partiality which arises when Christian faith is restricted to the sphere of Western life and Occidental culture. Christians are now able, and are, in fact, obliged, to live worldly lives: "They must live a 'worldly' life and thereby share in God's suffering. They *may* live a 'worldly' life as those who have been freed from false religious obligations and inhibitions" (LPP, 361). Put in a positive way, this means that "it is only by living completely in this world that one learns to have faith" (LPP, 369).

Epilogue

The significance of Christ and the world come of age in Dietrich Bonhoeffer's thought has been demonstrated in the second half of part three. The entire study was intended to further clarity concerning Bonhoeffer's theology and to show that the valuable arguments Eberhard Bethge developed in his biography of Bonhoeffer have theological warrant.

Beyond that goal, this study has not led to any "results" which is calmly acknowledged. It set out to interpret Bonhoeffer's fragmentary ideas, but not to supplement their content so as to "round them off." Some readers may be disappointed at that, but it was not part of the analysis to indulge in clairvoyance about the new form of religionless Christianity. What arises from this examination is the practical task of dealing with those problems which have, in the meantime, become most urgent. The turn toward praxis proceeds from Bonhoeffer's theology because the latter directs us to action, which it cannot do, itself. It is hoped that the interpretation of Bonhoeffer presented in this book will assist in such action.

It has been argued in some circles that Bonhoeffer's view of religionless Christianity in a world come of age is not nearly as radical, not nearly as exciting, and certainly not as troublesome as many of his alleged followers and opponents believe. Quite apart from the fact that it is not possible to judge what is more and what is less radical, it must be said that the transformation of the church's form in a new period of our understanding of the world is presumably more radical when the church reacts positively to that process and embraces its heritage in a positive way as well. Such a response is clearly more sensible than a self-distancing from the world, on the part of the church, in the name of a radical theology of crisis which undoubtedly permits more radical and critical statements. Whatever the merits of dialectical theology were, and that theology was quite justified in its historical situation, it is clear by now that dialectical theology remained between the times. Such a statement is not meant to be depreciative of Karl Barth's contribution to that period. Bonhoeffer understood why he followed him. He also knew that one would have to relate oneself to the world in a new way, precisely on the basis of such a theology, not only in order to proclaim a message to the world, but also because God has accepted the world in the incarnation of Jesus Christ. That acceptance always meant "here and now" for Bonhoeffer. Liberal theology had divided the world from faith and had bracketed it theologically, permitting Cultural Protestantism to enter into a shallow arrangement with the world. Christian faith must ultimately repudiate such a situation, and Bonhoeffer took it upon himself to enter into a positive and theologically balanced engagement with the world. Barthianisms would fail in accomplishing this, as would repristinating liberal theology.

It may be a good thing to chide Bonhoeffer for his intermediate position between liberal and dialectical theology. But on closer study this does not turn out to be an intermediate position at all. Bonhoeffer had no wish to bring those two theologies together, and it cannot be done in any case. If one seeks something original in Bonhoeffer one must look at the fact that he became inspired by Karl Barth and took the positive concerns of the nineteenth century seriously. Bonhoeffer may well have been more radical than Barth inasmuch as he endeavored to accept the heritage of liberal theology and to settle its unsolved problems; this was done on the basis of Bonhoeffer's own origin and upbringing, and even more on the basis of his own way into and through Barth's theology. Barth had tried to divorce himself from the heritage of liberal theology. Today it is generally believed that this heritage must be accepted, although it certainly has not been mastered. The solution is not to fuse both positions, but one may advance the notion that Bonhoeffer was more dialectical than Barth, whose dialectical theology threatened in the end to lead to dualism. Bonhoeffer tried to press beyond Barth's antithesis to liberal theology toward a post-dialectical position in which the correct desiderata of pre-dialectical theology were honored without their becoming pre-dialectical again. That is why Bonhoeffer's remark about being a modern theologian is perhaps more accurate than he himself thought (LPP, 378). Influenced by Karl Barth, who had called his attention to the word of God, Bonhoeffer had encountered the question about the concreteness of Jesus Christ in the world. Now Bonhoeffer wanted to "move out again into the open air of intellectual discussion with the world and risk saying controversial things, if we are to get down to the serious problems of life" (LPP, 378).

The claim of Jesus Christ on the "world come of age" was the theme of Bonhoeffer's life, and to that claim he gave his service. This devotion was borne by the hope *in* the eschatological fulfillment of the world. He had expressed that idea already in his doctoral dissertation through the concept of *apokatastasis* (SC, 201; AB, 183). Later Bonhoeffer spoke more carefully but with greater conviction about the "restoration of all things—*ānakephalaiōsis—recapitulatio*—a magnificent conception, full

EPILOGUE

of comfort" (LPP, 170). He awaited this restoration as *"kainè ktísis* through the *pneuma ágion,* a new creation through the Holy Spirit" (LPP, 170), and he repeated that expectation for himself in the final words we have from him: "This is the end—for me the beginning of life" (DB, 830).

Notes

INTRODUCTION
1. Following is a listing of the works of Bonhoeffer referred to and the abbreviations in terms of which they are cited.

Act and Being, trans. Bernard Noble (New York: Harper and Row, 1962, and London: Collins, 1962); hereafter cited as AB.

Christ the Center, trans. Edwin H. Robertson (San Francisco: Harper and Row, 1978). The British edition is entitled *Christology* (London: Collins, 1978); hereafter cited as C.

The Cost of Discipleship, trans. R. H. Fuller, rev. Irmgard Booth (New York: Macmillan, 1959, and London: SCM Press, 1959); hereafter cited as CD.

Creation and Fall: A Theological Interpretation of Genesis 1–3, trans. John C. Fletcher and the editorial staff of SCM (New York: Macmillan, 1959, and London: SCM, 1959). This work is now published together with *Temptation,* trans. Kathleen Downham (New York: Macmillan, 1955, and London: SCM Press, 1955), under the title: *Creation and Temptation* (same publishers, 1966); hereafter cited as CF.

Ethics, trans. Neville Horton Smith (New York: Macmillan, 1955, and London: SCM Press, 1955); hereafter cited as E.

Gesammelte Schriften, ed. Eberhard Bethge, 6 vols. (Munich: Chr. Kaiser Verlag, 1958–74); hereafter cited as GS.

Letters and Papers from Prison, trans. Reginald Fuller, Frank Clarke and others, and John Bowden (New York: Macmillan, 1972, and London: SCM Press, 1971); hereafter cited as LPP.

Life Together, trans. John W. Doberstein (San Francisco: Harper and Row, 1954; and London: SCM Press, 1954. The pagination of the two editions differs; in this study the American edition was used); hereafter cited as LT.

No Rusty Swords: Letters, Lectures and Notes 1928–1936 from the Collected Works, trans. Edwin H. Robertson and John Bowden, ed. Edwin H. Robertson (New York: Harper and Row, 1965, and London: Collins, 1965. The pagination of the two editions differs; in this study the American edition was used); hereafter cited as NRS.

Sanctorum Communio: A Dogmatic Inquiry into the Sociology of the Church, trans. Ronald Gregor Smith and others (London: Collins, 1963; published in the United States as *The Communion of Saints* [New York: Harper and Row, 1963]); hereafter cited as SC.

True Patriotism: Letters, Lectures and Notes 1939–1945 from the Collected Works, trans. Edwin H. Robertson and John Bowden, ed. Edwin H. Robertson (New York: Harper and Row, 1973, and London: Collins, 1973); hereafter cited as TP.

NOTES

The Way to Freedom: Letters, Lectures and Notes 1935-1939 from the Collected Works, trans. Edwin H. Robertson and John Bowden, ed. Edwin H. Robertson (New York: Harper and Row, 1966, and London: Collins, 1966); hereafter cited as WF.

2. Because Bonhoeffer's life and work are so interrelated, Eberhard Bethge's extensive biography is of great value to us: *Dietrich Bonhoeffer: Man of Vision, Man of Courage,* trans. Eric Mosbacher, Peter and Betty Ross, Frank Clarke, and William Glen-Doepel, ed. Edwin H. Robertson (New York: Harper and Row, 1970, and London: Collins, 1970); hereafter cited as DB. At times, reference is made in this study to the German text: *Dietrich Bonhoeffer: Theologe, Christ, Zeitgenosse* (Munich: Chr. Kaiser Verlag, 1967); hereafter cited as DBG.

3. Hanfried Müller, *Von der Kirche zur Welt* (Hamburg: Herbert Reich Evangelischer Verlag, 1961); hereafter cited as KzW.

4. See William Kuhns, *In Pursuit of Dietrich Bonhoeffer* (Dayton, Ohio: Pflaum Press, 1967), 262. One wonders whether Roman Catholics can correctly understand what Bonhoeffer discovered; see p. 263.

5. Werner Elert, *Der christliche Glaube. Grundlinien der Lutherischen Dogmatik,* 3d ed. (Hamburg: Furche Verlag, 1956), 38 n. 2. See also p. 437. True, Bonhoeffer was clearly aware quite early that he made himself vulnerable to this charge:

> But with this are we now drawing suspiciously near the Roman Catholic doctrine of the *thesaurus* which is accorded a central place in the whole recent Roman Catholic view of *sanctorum communio*? Indeed we are, and we are approaching it quite consciously, as we are seeking, together with Luther, to make sure of preserving in Protestant dogmatics, the sound core which is in danger of being lost. (SC, 130)

PART ONE

1. See Wilhelm Niesel, "From Keelson to Principal of a Seminary," in *I Knew Dietrich Bonhoeffer,* ed. Wolf-Dieter Zimmerman and Ronald Gregor Smith (New York: Harper and Row, 1966, and London: Collins, 1966), 145; see also Julius Rieger, "Contacts with London," on p. 95 of the same volume.

2. See, e.g., Eberhard Bethge, "The Challenge of Dietrich Bonhoeffer's Life and Theology," *The Chicago Theological Seminary Register* 51, No. 2 (1961): 1-38; John Godsey, *The Theology of Dietrich Bonhoeffer* (Philadelphia: Westminster Press, 1960), 19, 80, 195; KzW, 14, 437 n. 1, all of which draw on biography as a backdrop to Bonhoeffer's theology.

3. Karl Barth, "Letters to Superintendent Herrenbrück," in *World Come of Age,* ed. R. G. Smith (Philadelphia: Fortress Press, 1967, and London: Collins, 1967), 89-92. Barth referred explicitly to the earlier writings in his *Church Dogmatics III/1* (Edinburgh: T. & T. Clark, 1958), 194, and IV/2, 533, 641; cf. Hans Pfeifer, *Das Kirchenverständnis Dietrich Bonhoeffers. Ein Beitrag zur theologischen Prinzipienlehre* (Diss., Heidelberg, 1964), 43 n. 3.

4. Jürgen Moltmann and Jürgen Weissbach, *Two Studies in the Theology of Bonhoeffer* (New York: Scribner, 1967), 21-94. See Moltmann's critical questions in *Mündige Welt,* ed. Eberhard Bethge, Richard Grunow, 4 vols. (Munich: Chr. Kaiser Verlag, 1955-1963), III, 9; hereafter cited as MW.

5. John A. Phillips, *Christ for Us in the Theology of Dietrich Bonhoeffer* (New York: Harper and Row, 1967; the British edition is entitled: *The Form of Christ in the World* [London: Collins, 1967]) and Rainer Mayer, *Chris-*

tuswirklichkeit (Stuttgart: Calwer Verlag, 1969) correspond to Müller in the structure of their analyses.

6. Cf. Ernst Feil, "Standpunkte der Bonhoeffer-Interpretation," *Theologische Revue* 64 (1968): 1-14.

7. "Dietrich Bonhoeffer," MW I, 23.

8. See below, note 99.

9. See, e.g., John A. T. Robinson, *Honest to God* (Philadelphia: Westminster Press, 1963, and London: SCM Press, 1963). Concerning the discussion about Robinson's book, see Heinrich Ott, *Reality and Faith* (Philadelphia: Fortress Press, 1972, and London: Lutterworth, 1971), 25; Benkt-Erik Benktson, *Christus und die Religion* (Stuttgart: Calwer Verlag, 1967), 36 n. 2, and 48; J. A. Phillips, *Christ for Us*, 190; R. Mayer, *Christuswirklichkeit*, 291–96.

10. [This passage appears on p. 37 of the German edition of SC but was not translated for the English edition which put in its place material from the appendix of the German edition.]

11. Franklin Sherman surmises that it was the controversy between Barth and Przywara which suggested the topic "act and being" to Bonhoeffer. See "The Methods of Asking the Question Concerning Jesus Christ," in *The Place of Bonhoeffer*, ed. Martin E. Marty (New York: Association Press, 1962), 110 n. 21.

12. See Hans Christoph von Hase, "Begriff und Wirklichkeit," in MW I: 34. This is denied by H. Müller, KzW, 438 n. 85.

13. This phrase is used only four times in a short section of AB (119–26), whereas it had appeared seventeen times in SC and nineteen times in the unpublished text of the *Habilitationsschrift*.

14. This distinction is made only once, in SC, 167. *Fides directa* is spoken of here in the context of infant baptism, the context in which that distinction had originally been made in the formation of doctrine. The distinction is absent from its parallel section in SC, namely, 57, and especially where faith itself is discussed (124, 128, 140). Not only is this distinction cited twelve times in AB but it is one of that work's basic themes.

15. Luther's *Commentary on Romans* is cited at this point. The expression *cor curvum in se* is used quite frequently in AB (47, 72, 89, 156). See also NRS, 60 (dating from 1930), and 370 (from 1931); GS III, 164 (from 1931–32). Cf. DBG, 1092, 1094; C, 31 (from 1931). After that time, use of the expression is greatly reduced.

16. [The English translation reads, ". . . in the strength of Christ, the strength of my faith." The German text (108) reads, ". . . in der Kraft Christi, in der Kraft der Gemeinde, nicht in der Kraft meines Glaubens." The English translation, in other words, is the exact opposite of what Bonhoeffer said!]

17. See GS I, 47. Cf. the material reference in CD, 73, where "exegesis" is used for *Hermeneutik* (DB, 474).

18. "Man in Contemporary Philosophy and Theology," NRS, 50–69.

19. GS III, 91–99. These lectures were given in 1930–31. In CF, 12, Bonhoeffer states that "we think in a circle"; it is a thinking that has no beginning. Not only do we think, we also exist in a circle. For Bonhoeffer the vicious circle is the turn that the *cor curvum in se* gives our cognitive faculties. Indeed, in his address, "The Theology of Crisis and Its Attitude Toward Philosophy and Science," he places *cor curvum in se* and *corruptio mentis* side by side (NRS, 370).

20. Bonhoeffer wanted to familiarize the Americans with Karl Barth. In these lectures and addresses he followed Barth so closely that he not only did away with an otherwise customary critical discussion but even attributed some of his

own views to Barth. He said that Barth could (!) have stated, *reflecte fortiter, sed fortius gaude et fide in Christo,* which is really from AB. See H. Pfeifer, *Das Kirchenverständnis,* 79 n. 7.

21. This was published in *The Journal of Religion* XII, 2 (April 1932): 177–85.

22. The lectures appear in English under the titles *Christology* (British edition) and *Christ the Center* (American edition).

23. On this matter see the important lecture on the Jewish question in NRS, 221–29: "not just to bandage the victims under the wheel, but to put a spoke in the wheel itself. Such action would be direct political action" of the church (NRS, 225). [The translation of the German text here fails to render the force of Bonhoeffer's personal readiness to give himself for this cause. It should read: "the third possibility is not just to bandage the victims under the wheel, but to hurl oneself into the spokes of the wheel. Such action would be direct political action of the church. . . ."] Bonhoeffer repeats the idea of hurling oneself into the wheel in E, 321; there the English text reads, "prevent the wheel from crushing" the victims. A similar expression, made while he was in prison, is recorded in DB, 755. Responding to his reading of that work, Karl Barth wrote Bethge, admitting that he had not spoken clearly enough about the Aryan Clauses; see "Letter to Eberhard Bethge" in Karl Barth, *Fragments Grave and Gay,* ed. H. Martin Rumscheidt (London: Collins, 1971), 119–22, specifically 119; or *Canadian Journal of Theology* XV, 3/4: 201–3, specifically 201.

24. It is possible, for this reason, that theologians fell considerably short of the demands in the Church Struggle. Quite apart from the fact that it was hard for university faculty members, particularly the German Christians, to stand up against National Socialism, most of them simply could not perceive the need for a new relationship between church and state except for those who were prepared to legitimize theologically the ideology of National Socialism by means of the so-called "orders of creation." It is for this reason that Bonhoeffer rejected the concept vigorously in DB, 160; cf. Bonhoeffer's appeal for the seminaries of the Confessing Church in WF, 70. An exception to this theological cooperation of the churches with the Nazi ideology were the clear declarations issued by the faculty of Marburg and by R. Bultmann. See DB, 248.

25. TP, 68. The passage is from a letter written in 1940.

26. For Bonhoeffer's opposition to despisers of theology in his own ranks see GS III, 243 (dating from 1933); his circular letter of Christmas 1939, TP, 28; and from 1940, GS III, 421–25. A comparison can be made when one considers Bonhoeffer's critique of the American assessment of theology (GS I, 111). Similar criticism is made of the lack of interest in theology displayed in the ecumenical movement (NRS, 157–73). On 26 July 1932 Bonhoeffer made the following appeal: "Let there be an end to the disregard of theology on the part of the 'practical people'" (GS I, 159).

27. 2 Chron. 20:12. A sermon on this text, preached in 1932, is found in GS I, 133. Writing to his friend Erwin Sutz, Bonhoeffer mentions that sermon, and adds, "I have given vent in it to my entire despair" (GS I, 31). Cf. NRS, 165, and his letter to Karl Barth of 24 October 1933 (GS I, 234). Cf. E. Feil, "Dietrich Bonhoeffers engagierte Theologie," in *Orientierung* 30 (1966), 31–34, and F. Hildebrandt, "German Address," in *Bonhoeffer Gedenkheft,* ed. E. Bethge (Berlin: Haus und Schule, 1947), 13–16.

28. Writing to Lord Bishop Bell, Bonhoeffer stated that in that church there were held to be "many sources of revelation besides and except Christ, other constitutive norms for the church than Christ himself" (GS I, 190), or, in an earlier letter to Bell, "the famous statement about Jesus being only the exponent

of a Nordic race" (NRS, 270). This sort of thing went as far as a reformulation of the Prologue of John's Gospel uttered during a church celebration at which the bishop of Saxonia, Dr. Coch, was present: "In the beginning was the Nation, and the Nation was with God, and the Nation was God, and the same was in the beginning with God, etc." (NRS, 275). A similar exclamation came from one of the highest members of the German Christian movement, Hossenfelder, who amended Genesis to read, "And God said: let there be Nation, and there was Nation" (GS II, 98).

29. Bonhoeffer made this claim in 1934 (NRS, 282) and again a year later in a letter to Leonard Hodgson (GS I, 231).

30. This was most likely written in 1933.

31. See WF, 75–96.

32. Bonhoeffer makes use of this distinction as made by Karl Barth; see DB, 364 n. 31. If there were no such distinction, every difference separating schools would also be a difference separating churches. Church membership, therefore, should not be determined by theology alone; see DB, 22, 83, and GS III, 425 (dating from 1940) where Bonhoeffer says that "theological factions can become church-dividing opposites (liberals–German Christians) and church-dividing opposites can become school-divergencies." Church membership is not the sum of individual members but "always something qualitatively total" (WF, 82).

33. In addition to the reference already cited see SC, 193, and GS V, 256, dating from 1932.

34. This comment is explicitly made in relation to the Roman Catholic Church and not, as it was four years later, in relation to the ecumenical movement (GS III, 425).

35. See the frequent allusions to this in LPP, e.g., "What will happen to Rome? The thought that it might be destroyed is a nightmare" (LPP, 195, 204, 218, 239, 271). Cf. Feil, "Dietrich Bonhoeffers engagierte Theologie," in *Orientierung* 30 (1966): 31.

36. See Julius Rieger, "Contacts with London," in *I Knew Dietrich Bonhoeffer*, 96.

37. Karl Barth, "Letter to Eberhard Bethge," in *Fragments Grave and Gay*, 119–22.

38. "There are times in which all reality is so mysterious and oppresses us so much that any direct word seems to destroy the mystery of God for us, that we speak about and would like to hear about the last things only in hints. Everything that we can say about our belief then seems so flat and empty against the reality which we experience and behind which we believe there is an unspeakable mystery. It is the same with those of you at the front as it is with us at home: whatever is uttered vanishes in a flash, all formulas no longer make contact with reality. There can be something very real in all this, as long as one word does not vanish within us, namely, the name of Jesus Christ" (TP, 125).

39. Cf. SC, 166.

40. See CD, 142, 154, 162. Already in 1932–33 Bonhoeffer had related these points to one another; see GS III, 163, and GS V, 353.

41. TP, 154; cf. 161. In 1937 a similar point was made (WF, 152). The reference to the prison letters is to LPP, 373.

42. E, 143 or, in a different formulation, E, 191. See also E, 22, 33, 56.

43. E, 103, which corresponds to AB, 183 n. 1.

44. GS III, 461. This is a section of preliminary drafts for E.

45. The polemic against a positivistic-empirical concept of reality does not contradict the designation of theology as a positive discipline. Theology thinks

NOTES

about the mystery made manifest in history, namely, God in Jesus Christ, in the knowledge that it cannot grasp God in thought and thus absorb "the religion made manifest" (*geoffenbarte Religion*) in the "manifest religion" (*offenbare Religion*). It was Hegel who had made this distinction.

46. This empirical-meretricious concept of reality corresponds to what Bonhoeffer called the unmysterious life in the sermon of May 1934. Cf. LPP, 369, where it is called "shallow this-worldliness."

47. This assertion, interestingly enough, is not part of the preliminary draft; see GS III, 458. Cf. E, 128.

48. Regarding the knowledge of good and evil, see CF, 51, 54.

49. [The English rendition "valiantly grasping occasions, not cravenly doubting" does not distort but certainly does not accurately express the German original. Bonhoeffer's point was to assert that action was not to hover among possibilities but to seize bravely what is real in the sense of "the possible" and "the real" as described above.]

50. See, e.g., NRS, 32–33, dating from 1927; 51, 64, from 1930; AB, 60, 98, 118–19, from 1931; CF, 68; CD, 175. Cf. Bethge, "The Challenge of Dietrich Bonhoeffer's Life and Theology," 36.

51. Cf. AB, 80, 118, 138, 148. From the same period is GS III, 160. From 1932 are the passages in NRS, 369, and GS IV, 147.

52. See also AB, 173; CD, 87; GS III, 455; E, passim.

53. [The English text omitted "inasmuch . . . revelation."]

54. Bonhoeffer makes this critique of Karl Barth already at this stage. Even though Bonhoeffer cites Barth's warning against abstraction in AB, 82, he believes that Barth fails in his intention to be concrete. Still, he defends Barth against this accusation when it comes from the other side. See NRS, 356.

55. Cf. GS V, 226, which dates from 1931–32.

56. Bonhoeffer made this statement in lectures in 1932–33.

57. Cf. CD, 166.

58. See also C, 76, 80–81.

59. Cf. GS III, 105, dating from 1931; CF, 68. The same charge against idealism was already laid in SC, 31.

60. GS III, 126. Cf. GS III, 104, 106; NRS, 362–63.

61. E, 227–228; cf. 128–129. Pfeifer argues in his work *Das Kirchenverständnis* that reality finds its opposite not in idea but in possibility (15). But both concepts are parallelized in substance already in SC, 91. Pfeifer's comment on p. 79 referring to NRS, 362–63, is important: Bonhoeffer juxtaposes reality and idea differently than Barth and, in fact, puts his own theological views into Barth's mouth.

62. There are many references one could give here to support this claim, but a few will suffice. Christian principles: NRS, 39–40, 137; eternal norms and law: NRS, 320; principles: NRS, 162, 163; CD, 73, 206; GS IV, 534; E, 68; LPP, 7; the generally valid: E, 84–85; general principles: E, 273–74, 276; system: E, 232 (cf. AB, passim); ideal: SC, 139; NRS, 344; GS IV, 209; CD, 272; LT, 26; ideology: E, 234; GS III, 461; eternal truth: GS III, 28. On the whole point see Kuhns, *In Pursuit*, 160–66.

63. Just before writing the passage cited above, Bonhoeffer, still quite under the impact of his stay in the United States, had written:

> Seen from over there our situation and theology seem to be so provincial and it is difficult to concede that Germany of all places and a few people there should have understood what the gospel is. I really see no message anywhere else. The gigantic work of American missions is inwardly hol-

low, the mother-church itself in the process of dying. And yet it is certain that our current understanding of the gospel simply cannot be accepted over there. Things are split apart as never before. I would really like to visit a great country yet and see whether the great solution might perhaps come from there: India. Otherwise it seems that it is finished, the great death of Christianity is upon us. (GS I, 61)

64. See also NRS, 370–71.

65. Clyde E. Fant, *Bonhoeffer: Worldly Preaching* (Nashville and New York: Thomas Nelson, 1975; hereafter cited as BWP), 140.

66. This is from a letter to Rüdiger Schleicher, dated 8 April 1936.

67. In LPP, 360, Bonhoeffer speaks of God's suffering, but it is clear that he did not mean to neglect or even remove the Trinity thereby, as W. Hamilton and R. G. Smith suggest. See John A. Phillips, "Die Bedeutung des Lebens und Werkes Dietrich Bonhoeffers für britische und amerikanische Theologen," MW IV, 164 n. 58. Bonhoeffer speaks about the Trinity, e.g., in GS III, 109, NRS, 371, and GS II, 96 (all dating from 1931); GS IV, 208 (from 1935); GS III, 341, 363, 367 (from 1936); and up to 1939 in WF, 216, 254, as well as in LT, 20, 58. One cannot conclude that Bonhoeffer meant to forget the Trinity, much less rescind what he had declared earlier. LPP, 139 and 286 would tend to support this.

68. GS I, 64. See the letter in its entirety (62–65).

69. "Here and now" and *hic et nunc* are described already in AB, 145 as characteristics of an existential assertion. See also GS V, 335, dating from 1932–33.

70. Concerning a council, see NRS, 226 (from 1933); GS II, 55 (also 1933); GS I, 219 and NRS, 344 (dating from 1935). These texts supersede SC, 148, and SC, 154. Concerning heresy, see NRS, 178 and GS I, 180 (from 1932); GS I: 228, 230, and C, 75 (from 1933); WF, 87 and WF, 92 (from 1935); GS II, 243, 264 (from 1936); WF, 180 (from 1938).

71. NRS, 329 (from 1935). In this context Bonhoeffer's concept of ministry (*Amt*) is important. See SC, 160–63; CD, 227; E, 293; and (from 1932) GS V, 257. Ministry becomes the permanent possession of the clergy. As long as they possess ministry the promise holds that what they do shall not be in vain. Cf. the distinction between the ministry of preaching and the office of pastor; the ministry of preaching is conveyed by ordination and cannot be removed from the recipient; BWP, 134 (from 1935–39). See also GS IV, 349 (from 1936); WF, 186 (from 1938). Concerning ordination, Bonhoeffer says, "In fact it seems difficult to understand why it should not be a sacrament" (BWP, 135). See also AB, 147, and GS II, 66 (from 1933); TP, 59 (from 1940); TP, 106 (from 1941); E, 346; LPP, 157.

72. "His concern was with the concrete and binding nature of this community, now gathered together in Jesus Christ" (DB, 312). Cf. his discussions about the ecumenical movement's character as church in NRS, 157, and the character as church of the Confessing Church, in GS I, 230–39, and especially NRS, 326–44.

73. Cf. GS I, 31, 34; GS V, 290.

74. NRS, 163. Cf. also NRS, 156 (dating from 1932), and GS V, 335.

75. Cf. E, 194, 232, 276.

76. The danger of turning command into law, which is just as abstract as a principle, is met by Bonhoeffer in his dialectic of law and gospel. See DB, 158 (referring to statements made in 1932), and DB, 47. See also CD, 259; E, 310, 356. Concerning the problem of law and freedom, see E, 261.

NOTES

77. Cf. SC, 156–57; AB, 142–47; the sermon as a public occasion: CD, 194.
78. Cf. SC, 99; C, 46.
79. Cf. C, 51–52; E, 293.
80. Cf. CD, 29.
81. SC, 155, and E, 294. See also note 71 above.
82. CD, 224. Concerning his rejection of Christianity as teaching see GS V, 201; AB, 150; BWP, 133. Jesus Christ is not to be conceived of simply as teacher; see GS III, 104; CD, 52; E, 80, 84.
83. E. Bethge, "Dietrich Bonhoeffer—der Mensch und sein Zeugnis," MW II, 92.
84. Bonhoeffer criticized much North American preaching sharply; see NRS, 86. [Intriguingly, the latter section leaves out the seven and a half pages of Bonhoeffer's comments on preaching.] The orginal is in GS I, 93. Cf. GS I, 108.
85. Cf. LT, 117. The demand for confession is made by Bonhoeffer in the context of the preaching of forgiveness (CD, 259; WF, 150; GS IV, 483; esp. E, 292).
86. See GS IV, 71.
87. He made that plan at a time when the hermeneutical question was not yet on everyone's agenda. See DB, 474, where reference is made to a remark Bonhoeffer made in 1936; see GS I, 47 for that remark.
88. Bethge rightly notes that non-religious interpretation "is more an ethical than a hermeneutical category" (DB, 783), a comment directed against Ebeling's "The 'Non-Religious Interpretation of Biblical Concepts,'" in *Word and Faith* (Philadelphia: Fortress Press, 1963), 98–161.
89. Cf. TP, 29.
90. It is significant that CD ends with a chapter entitled "The Image of Christ." Concerning the image as a category of hermeneutics, see CF, 48; GS IV, 297; BWP, 133; E, 205.
91. Cf. CD, 229. See also BWP, 174 and GS IV, 120.
92. Concerning Holy Communion, see NRS, 164 and CF, 47, dating from 1932; from 1933, see esp. C, 53 and 62–65; from 1937, WF, 153–54; from 1940, see TP, 38–43. Concerning Baptism, see TP, 143–64, dating from 1942, which is one among many discussions on this subject. Bonhoeffer also raises the matter of ordination in the context of sacrament: see BWP, 134, dating from 1935. Bonhoeffer's diary speaks of his understanding of the Roman Catholic practice of the sacraments which caused him to be both impressed and critical.
93. In this statement, dating from 1932, is an explicit reference to arcane discipline.
94. CD, 112–13; E, 26, 43, esp. 45–46. See also CD, 172–73, 175.
95. Cf. LPP, 298, and LPP, 15 with critical comments about his own time.
96. Cf. the central assertion of CD, 54: "Only they who believe are obedient, and only they who are obedient believe."
97. In the study by Ebeling cited in note 88 above, the priorities of language and life, of proclamation and the form of the church are reversed, if seen from the perspective of Bonhoeffer; cf. *Word and Faith*, 110–20, 122 n. 4. An indication of this consistent reversal is found in that study on 128 where, referring to LPP, 298, Ebeling states that the point of the concept of non-religious interpretation was not "in order to play off life against doctrine, action against thought, but to incorporate life really in doctrine and action really in thought." From AB to LPP the exact opposite is the case.
98. KzW, 9, 31. Cf. Phillips, *Christ for Us*, 120, 137.
99. Mayer, *Christuswirklichkeit*, 227.

100. See esp. DB, which argues the case of continuous development throughout.

101. Most scholars speak of the unity of Bonhoeffer in the sense indicated: cf. esp. Bethge, von Hase, Ebeling, Jorgen Glenthoj, Moltmann, Gisela Meuss in her article "Arkandisziplin und Weltlichkeit bei Dietrich Bonhoeffer," MW III, 68–115, Hans Schmidt, D. Müller, Jörg Martin Meier, W. Krause, Ott, (to some extent); John A. Phillips, René Marlé. See also André Dumas, *Dietrich Bonhoeffer: Theologian of Reality* (New York: The Macmillan Company, 1971), 69–76; G. Th. Rothuizen, *Aristocratisch christendom. Over Dietrich Bonhoeffer. Leven, Verzet, Ecumene, Theologie* (Kampen: J. H. Bok B.V., 1969), 309. Corresponding to the view that Bonhoeffer's theology represents a unity are the attempts to indicate what the basic theme of his theology is; e.g., Bethge, von Hase, Marlé, Albrecht Schönherr, Glenthoj, Godsey, Phillips, Weissbach, Meier, Mayer, Krause. One could also count Hanfried Müller and Martin Kuske among this group.

102. The distinction of periods in Bonhoeffer's work is made by Bethge, von Hase, Hanfried Müller, Godsey, Phillips, and Mayer, although there are divergencies regarding especially the second period. Concerning these divergencies, see DB, 763.

103. Cf. LPP, 380, and Sabine Leibholz-Bonhoeffer, *The Bonhoeffers: Portrait of a Family* (London: Sidgwick and Jackson, 1971), 83, the excerpt of Bonhoeffer's funeral sermon for his grandmother.

104. Cf. LPP, 280, 286–87, 325, 344–45, together with the postscripts on 347, 359, and 393.

105. Bonhoeffer thought about death quite early in his life; see Sabine Leibholz-Bonhoeffer, "Childhood and Home," in *I Knew Dietrich Bonhoeffer*, 19; DB, 24. Between 1933 and 1935 he said repeatedly that it should really suffice a Christian to have reached the age of 36 or 37 years; cf. Franz Hildebrandt, "German Address," in *Bonhoeffer Gedenkheft*, 14; Wolf-Dieter Zimmermann, "Vorwort," in *Begegnungen mit Dietrich Bonhoeffer*, ed. W.-D. Zimmerman (Munich: Chr. Kaiser Verlag, 1964), 6. The notion of death stayed with Bonhoeffer: see GS III, 265–68, dating from 1932; GS IV, 163, from 1933; GS II, 529, from 1937; WF, 250, 254–55, from 1939. See also DB, 565; TP, 95–96, and esp. LPP, 163, 272, where Bonhoeffer calmly weighs the ending of his life.

106. See, among others, Albrecht Schönherr, "Bonhoeffers Gedanken über die Kirche und ihre Predigt in der 'mündig' gewordenen Welt," WM I, 77; Hermann Schlingensiepen, "Zum Vermächtnis Dietrich Bonhoeffers," MW I, 97; Ebeling, *Word and Faith*, 100 n. 8; Bethge, "Dietrich Bonhoeffer. Der Mensch und sein Zeugnis," MW II, 93; DB, 766; Meuss, MW III, 68; KzW, 29, 32; Ott, *Reality and Faith*, 65.

PART TWO

1. Cf. SC, 103–4, 128–29, and the numerous references to Christ, 103–36. "The person whose life is lived in love is Christ in respect of his neighbor" (127; cf. 119 and 147).

2. See SC, 135 and 138 concerning the equivalence of being in Christ and being in the church. According to Bonhoeffer, "There is no relation to Christ in which the relation to the church is not necessarily presupposes" (89). The very next sentence, "Thus logically the church presupposes its being within itself" (90), does not explicate its christological implication; cf. C, 33–34.

3. Whether Bonhoeffer would have spoken of "a direct relation" between

NOTES

God and his creature in paradise (SC, 39; cf. 22, 44) in his later work may remain open for now. But he does say later that creation was made through Christ and for Christ, which indicates that he is thinking of a mediation by Christ through creation.

4. See above, part one, section 2b. The term recurs in 1930 (see NRS, and DBG, 1062), but it is absent in texts where one would most readily have expected it to be used: e.g., "What is the Church?," NRS, 153, dating from 1932; "The Confessing Church and the Ecumenical Movement," NRS, 326, from 1935; "The Question of the Boundaries of the Church and Church Union," WF, 75, from 1936; "Statements about the Power of the Keys and Church Discipline in the New Testament," WF, 149, from 1937.

5. On p. 138 of *Das Kirchenverständnis*, Pfeifer notes that between Bonhoeffer's earlier works and those of later stages there is a shift of accent in the use of this formula. A good example of an obviously intentional reformulation of the term is found in GS IV, 309. In a Bible study from 1939, Bonhoeffer said: "The house that God wants to build for himself is the seed of David, is the body of Christ, his son and that body is Christ and his community in him." Pfeifer does not mention the quite extensive elaboration of the term in CD, 217–18. The term is no longer found in E, 87f., contrary to Pfeifer, 175. We just wish to call attention to the (erroneous) title of an article by Prenter, "Jesus (sic!) Christus als Gemeinde existierend," in *Lutherische Monatshefte* 4 (1965): 262; it is not for nothing that the formula speaks consistently of Christ only.

6. SC, 134. Pfeifer provides the bibliographical background to that phrase in Hegel's works (*Das Kirchenverständnis*, 34 n. 3).

7. SC, 103–4, 111–12; cf. 141–42, 149–50, 172–73. Note how Bonhoeffer juxtaposes—at least terminologically and, probably, also materially—"historical" and "established by God" (88; cf. 87). Christ "realized [the church] for eternity" (115); a temporal actualization can, therefore, be separated from it! Cf. 107–8, 110–11, 116–17.

8. SC, 103; cf. 30–31, 37, 110–11, 112–13. How can history, in a real sense, begin only with sin (40), when it has been given "from God to God" (67, cf. 61)? Can "the history of the church [really be] the hidden center of world history" (146)? What about "the dual course of history" which Bonhoeffer seems to have presupposed (243 n. 165)? And finally what does he mean by "every age is in direct relationship with God" (198)?

9. Bethge draws attention to this accusation (DBG, 118). See Pfeifer, *Das Kirchenverständnis*, 75.

10. See SC, 52, 60–62, 103, 145–46, 152–54, 157–58, 179–80, 187–90.

11. See above, part one, section 2b, and esp. section 4.

12. These are texts of later periods in which the *actus directus* is said to be directed on God; see NRS, 61, 65, dating from 1930, and 372, from 1931. There seems to be no obvious contradiction here to the statements of AB. In both texts the issue is primarily the question of how philosophy and theology are related and not the specifically theological question of the relation to God through Christ.

13. See AB, 31–32, 75, 80–81, 91, 94–95, 102–3, 118–19, 121–24, 126–27, 129–30, 135, esp. 144–45, 146–47, esp. 159, 162–63, 168–70, 172, 175–76, 177–78, 180.

14. GS III, 100–109, and *The Journal of Religion* 12 (1932): 177–85. The citations were taken from GS III.

15. [The editor of NRS, for inexplicable reasons, left out the last one and a half pages of that address, the section from which this citation was taken.]

16. GS V, 181–227. The final section is on 225–27.

NOTES

17. GS V, 227-75. The foundational chapter is on 243-49. Cf. DBG, 1061-63.
18. That is how Bonhoeffer put it in a marginal note to a lecture prepared in the summer semester of 1926; cf. Pfeifer, *Das Kirchenverständnis*, 70. Pfeifer shows at the same time that Bonhoeffer agreed with Harnack's critique of the Apostles' Creed. See also DB, 143.
19. Cf. the question concerning the word "suffered" in the Creed in Bonhoeffer's course on preparation for church-membership, GS III, 335-68; the specific reference is to 357: "What does 'suffered' signify in the Creed? It sums up the entire life of Jesus Christ." The answer coincides with that of the Heidelberg Catechism. I owe this notation to Ferdinand Schlingensiepen. Another reminiscence of Harnack's question may well be in LPP, 382: "What do we really believe? I mean believe in such a way that we stake our lives on it? The problem of the Apostles' Creed?" and 383: "the question of revising the creeds (the Apostles' Creed)."
20. GS V, 275-300; the specific reference is to 292.
21. Such a position was maintained, for example, by Wilhelm Stählin (NRS, 181), who went on to add that "there were also extra-Christian beliefs in creation" (NRS, 181). Cf. the dangerous consequences which Eugen Gerstenmaier was to draw from such a position (*Die Kirche und die Schöpfung*, published in 1938). See DB, 464 n. 125.
22. [The English text reads, ". . . preservation of God should be carried out by Christ," rendering the German term "ausrichten" in its other sense, which is not applicable here.]
23. CF, 88; cf. 25, 33, 86. See also GS II, 99f., dating from 1933. The orders of creation spoken of here are cited again, in a different form, in *Ethics*, where they are referred to as mandates. See Tiemo Rainer Peters, *Gebot und Verheissung. Die Ethik in der theologischen Entwicklung Dietrich Bonhoeffers* (Diss., Walberberg, 1969), esp. 195.
24. See GS III, 351, Bonhoeffer's second outline for a catechism.
25. See GS III, 351.
26. This is the subtitle of the book. For Bonhoeffer, theological exegesis is the interpretation which seeks to read the Hebrew Scriptures "in church in the first place only from Christ" (CF, 10). Cf. Martin Kuske, *The Old Testament as the Book of Christ: An Appraisal of Bonhoeffer's Interpretation* (Philadelphia: Westminster Press, 1976), 35. On the relationship between the Hebrew Scriptures and the New Testament, on reading the former in the light of the latter, that is, from Christ, see, for example, GS II, 92, and GS III, 294-302, dating from 1933; NRS, 321-22 n.; GS IV, 294-320, from 1937, 414, 422; LT, 45ff.; *Psalms: The Prayerbook of the Bible* (Minneapolis: Augsburg, 1970), 10-12, 19-21, from 1940. Always Christ is "the centre and the strength of the Bible" (E, 56; see esp. LPP, 156-57). Concerning Bonhoeffer interpretations of Scripture as theological interpretations, see Richard Grunow, "Dietrich Bonhoeffers Schriftauslegung," MW I, 62-76, esp. 64, and Walter Harrelson, "Bonhoeffer and the Bible," *The Place of Bonhoeffer*, 115-42, esp. 117; Phillips, *Christ for Us*, 84-105. It would appear that Bonhoeffer is touching on the matter of "theological interpretation" again in LPP where he criticizes Bultmann and proposes that the concepts "God" and "miracle" have to be interpreted non-religiously (285). There is a connection, apparently, between the interpretations of the course on Genesis 1-3 and non-religious interpretations. See Hannelis Schulte, "In den Tatsachen selbst ist Gott," *Evangelische Theologie* 22 (1962): 441-448; Benktson, *Christus und die Religion*, esp. 36-41 and 80 n. 15; and the work by Kuske just cited which deals with the entire issue extensively.

NOTES

27. Both in E and LPP Bonhoeffer was occupied by the question of truth; see E, 363–72, and LPP, 158–59. Cf. Clifford Green, "Sociality and Church in Bonhoeffer's 1933 Christology," *Scottish Journal of Theology* 21 (1968): 423.

28. Bethge points out that Bonhoeffer adds to the traditional signs of Christ's presence in word and sacrament that of the community (DB, 164).

29. Cf. DB, 133.

30. "Dibelius recently told us in a lecture that the church has two thousand five hundred theology students too many, and that therefore (!) special demands must be made on theologians. As a first point for acceptance he put readiness for martyrdom (in a struggle in which religious and political ideals are so intertwined!). By the nature of things, he said, this thought was hard for the younger ones, but the older men had long (!) grown familiar (!) with it and had become attached to it. The audience stamped their feet like mad. Long live the 'violet church'" (NRS, 141). ("Violet church" is an allusion to the color of the binding of Dibelius's book on the church.) This excerpt is from a letter of 1931. Cf. WF, 42–43, dating from 1935–36.

31. This excerpt dates from 1934.

32. Numerous citations could be given in support of this comment, but it is enough to mention the following: GS II, 314; LPP, 328. Bonhoeffer complained about the lack of personal faith in Christ in the Confessing Church (LPP, 381–82).

33. Phillips states that Bonhoeffer again took up his early "christo-ecclesiology" with its identification of Christ and church: "The church *is* Christ, the revelation" (*Christ for Us,* esp. 110 and 120). Bonhoeffer did not propose such an identification at all; instead it is explicitly denied (SC, 101). [See the German edition of SC, 92, to which Feil refers in the German text. That edition has a truncated version of the section "A Brief Outline of the N.T. View of the Church" in its main body, relegating the original material, used in the English text and appearing on pp. 97–102, to the appendix.] The Church Struggle should not be regarded as having restricted Bonhoeffer's development, as Phillips states (125). This identification is spoken of also by Müller, KzW, according to whom Bonhoeffer "in fact placed the church as the medium between sanctification and existence in the world" (233).

34. See GS IV, 157, 161, 168, 174, 181, dating from 1933–34.

35. See DB, 175. Cf. GS IV, 185, 290–390, 393, 398.

36. DB, 362. See GS IV, 240, 247.

37. See esp. NRS, 308–25, particularly 316, dating from 1935, and WF, 75–96, from 1936.

38. Cf. GS I, 43, dating from 1934.

39. That was written in 1935. Cf. GS III, 26, and WF, 116, dating from 1936.

40. See NRS, 41, 42, 45, dating from 1928; NRS, 147, from 1931; NRS, 159, from 1932. Later on, the Sermon on the Mount drew his attention again and again; see: BWP, 146, from 1935; WF, 151, from 1937; GS III, 35, from 1940; GS III, 464, 470, from 1941; E, 359; LPP, 14, 346. See on the whole matter Jorgen Glenthoj, "Dietrich Bonhoeffer und die Ökumene," MW II, 149.

41. [The English text reads "Jesus Christ himself," although the German does *not* have "Christ." The addition distorts Bonhoeffer's point.]

42. [The translation of CD deals so freely with the German text that an independent translation became necessary at this point. An entirely fresh translation of CD would serve Bonhoeffer studies very well.]

43. KzW, 231, 238.

NOTES

44. The letter is found in GS III, 31–33; the specific citation is on 31.

45. The term "Christian understanding of the world" must not be construed as an inadmissible usurpation any more than such terms as "Christian sociology" or "Christian philosophy." A Christian understanding of the world can be maintained only through Jesus Christ. See esp. E.

46. For the significance of the christology of that time see esp. GS IV. Cf. the comment about the neglect of christology during the Enlightenment and especially the nineteenth century (GS IV, 388–90, dating from 1936). Regarding the eschatological component of christology, see GS IV, 358, and WF, 164, 176, all dating from 1938. Between the writing of CD and E lies Bonhoeffer's second visit to the United States and his decision to take part in the fate of Germany; see LPP, 174. Bonhoeffer's diary for that period confirms the central significance which Jesus Christ and christology had for him. As a personal testimony they show much more than that, of course.

> When the confusion of accusations and excuses, of desires and fears, makes everything within us so obscure, he [Jesus Christ] sees quite clearly into all our secrets. And at the heart of them all he finds a name which he himself has inscribed: Jesus Christ. So too one day we shall see quite clearly into the depths of the divine heart and there we shall then be able to read, no, to see, a name: Jesus Christ. (WF, 217, from 1939)

In his report about the visit to America in the early thirties, Bonhoeffer remarked that "the neglect of christology is characteristic of the whole contemporary American Christianity" (NRS, 116; cf. NRS, 117–18 and GS I, 296). See also GS I, 110.

47. See also GS III, 296, dating from 1935, and GS IV, 367, from 1938.

48. Bonhoeffer had already cited it in CF, 77. It was Elisabeth Zinn who drew Bonhoeffer's attention to Oetinger's words; see DB, 101.

49. See esp. DB, 619–26. A very circumspect judgment is made by Müller, KzW, 43. Phillips, *Christ for Us,* is more explicit (129); his thesis of the liberation of christology from ecclesiology, 137 and 139, and of the "unhappy marriage" of the "two christologies" in *The Cost of Discipleship,* 111, for example, is quite unacceptable.

50. SC, 33; cf. SC, 27–35, 51–52, 128–29. Cf. above, part one, section 2a and part two, section 2a. It was Reinhold Seeberg who suggested to Bonhoeffer that he might explore the problem of ethics, that is, the neglect of ethics, in high scholasticism, in his *Habilitationsschrift*; see NRS, 36.

51. GS I, 33, 63, 65, and NRS, 160. Cf. above, part one, section 5b and part two, section 3a. This idea emerges clearly in *Ethics,* where it is dealt with at length. See particularly "The Warrant for Ethical Discourse," 263. Cf. NRS, 160, dating from 1932; NRS, 155; NRS, 330–31, from 1935. Regarding "commandment," see E, 267–68, and GS V, 275. This idea is treated both terminologically and materially, especially in the notion of the mandates, in E, 207 and 286; cf. LPP, 192.

52. Bethge related that text to CD; see E, 7 and 13, as well as DB, 624.

53. E, 17, particularly 20 and 25; CF, 51. The question of the knowledge of good and evil goes back all the way to the address on ethics in Barcelona (NRS, 41, 43–44), where it is related back to Nietzsche, to whom Bonhoeffer makes surprisingly frequent reference in E. In SC and AB conscience was already dealt with; see SC, 71–72, 84–85; AB, 57ff. The remarkably polemical statements about conscience found in CD, e.g., 62, all the way to E, are eventually changed as work on E proceeds; see E, 25 and 263.

54. CD, 269, 272. In E, 120, 124, Bonhoeffer attacks cheap grace again.

55. See esp. E, 224, 296–97. Dorothee Sölle's comments about Bonhoeffer in her work *Christ the Representative* (Philadelphia: Fortress Press, 1967), 92–97, in no way do justice to him; see Ott, *Reality and Faith*, 213. Helmut Gollwitzer entered the discussion with Sölle in his book *Von der Stellvertretung Gottes. Christlicher Glaube in der Erfahrung der Verborgenheit Gottes. Zum Gespräch mit D. Sölle* (Munich: Chr. Kaiser Verlag, 1968). He showed that her exposition of K. Barth was completely inadequate, a criticism one could apply equally to her exposition of Bonhoeffer. Cf. also Mayer, *Christuswirklichkeit*, 183 n. 89.

56. E, 221–22, 234–35, 248–49. On 234–35 the change from the "I-thou-I-God" scheme of SC is quite apparent. See GS III, 465, concerning the "privatization" of E.

57. See also E, 69–70, and elsewhere. This statement makes too many gradations to allow the conclusion that Christ equals reality; Ott, *Reality*, 167. Therefore, an ontologically expounded christology, as Ott proposes (178), is to be rejected; see 167–91. The term *Christuswirklichkeit* (reality of Christ), as it appears in E, 212 and 288, is unsuitable as a guiding concept, because it is open to an undifferentiated understanding, as Mayer's thesis of a "christological ontology as a system" shows.

58. See below, part three, section 5b.

59. It is Pfeifer who makes that judgment concerning history (*Das Kirchenverständnis*, 75). Similarly, Hans Schmidt, "Das Kreuz der Wirklichkeit," MW IV, 79–108, esp. 99 and 102. A critique of Schmidt is made by Kuske, *The Old Testament*, 142–45, esp. 142 n. 389. The critique that Bonhoeffer had no sensibility for eschatology is made by Joachim Schwartz, *Christologie als Modell der Gesellschaft. Eine Untersuchung zu den ersten Schriften Bonhoeffers* (Diss., Vienna, ca. 1968), 54; Ott, *Reality and Faith*, esp. Martin Honecker, *Kirche als Gestalt und Ereignis. Die sichtbare Kirche als dogmatisches Problem* (Munich: Chr. Kaiser Verlag, 1963), 156; and Gerhard Sauter, *Die Theologie des Reiches Gottes beim älteren und jüngeren Blumhardt* (Zürich: Zwingli Verlag, 1962), 294–300, esp. 297. A critique is found in DB, 60, and, more extensively, in Mayer, *Christuswirklichkeit*, 99–103.

60. The paper was about the historical and pneumatical interpretation of Scripture, given on 31 July 1925.

61. C, 109–13; cf. GS III, 108, and NRS, 364. Later on this idea recurs in its "ethical" form as God's powerlessness or weakness in the world.

62. GS V, 292. Cf. DBG, 260, 1075; DB, 378.

63. See also GS III, 98, where grace is spoken of as "coming grace."

64. See the entire section of that address (NRS, 311–18). In prison Bonhoeffer reflected a good deal on the problem of time because imprisonment is in a particular sense an existence without time; see his note about "passing the time" (LPP, 33). [The translation of *Zeitvertreiben* as "amusement" appears highly inappropriate under the circumstances. The idea of "passing the time" in amusement is quite unlikely in a prison; instead, the German verb *totschlagen* should be translated in such a way as to indicate the "killing" of time.]

65. GS I, 356. Cf. TP, 108–9.

66. "Thinking about the future must not lead to flight into imagination but must become the concrete service of one's neighbor" (GS I, 356).

67. The question is not placed into juxtaposition with the other one: "Who [is] Christ really . . . for us today?" (LPP, 279).

68. Cf. LPP, 176, and John Godsey, *Preface to Bonhoeffer: The Man and Two of His Shorter Writings* (Philadelphia: Fortress Press, 1965; hereafter cited as PB), 62.

69. The opposite concept, *diaboli ex machina*, is dealt with in CF, 64.
70. Cf. LPP, 325–26, 341–42, 344, 359–60.
71. The "death-of-God" theology really cannot claim Bonhoeffer for its foundation. Following him one can only state that we must live in this world "even if God *were* dead." The mistake of Kuhns, *In Pursuit of Dietrich Bonhoeffer*, in translating Bonhoeffer's translation of *etsi deus non daretur* as "to which God is not given" (124), is most likely due to his assumption that the statement is in the indicative. The 1962 edition of LPP deletes Bonhoeffer's conjunctival translation "even if there were no God," which the new, greatly enlarged edition of LPP properly includes; cf. 359.
72. Cf. LPP, 360, 369.
73. To be free in the sense of being free for the neighbor is discussed already in CF, 36. On the same page Bonhoeffer says that God is the one who "in Christ is free for people." Cf. AB, 90.
74. See above, part two, section 4b.
75. Cf. E, 297. The notion of being there *for* or dependent upon the neighbor(s) appears, at least terminologically, already in SC, 32f. It follows for the church that it must "exist for others" (LPP, 382), and for Christians it is to be "a new life in 'existence for others,' through participation in the being of Jesus. The transcendental is not infinite and unattainable tasks, but the neighbor who is within reach in any given situation" (LPP, 381). See also above, part two, section 3b.
76. Cf. E, 83, and esp. 87–88.
77. Cf. Kuske, *The Old Testament*.
78. See GS III, 294–302, esp. 297.
79. Cf. Kuske, *The Old Testament*, 19, and the parallels in GS II, 92; CF, 10, dating from 1933; and BWP, 141, from 1935.
80. Cf. GS V, 137, dating from 1928.
81. See Ebeling, *Word and Faith*, 106. The difference between Barth's and Bonhoeffer's christology was emphasized by Bethge, "The Challenge of Dietrich Bonhoeffer's Life and Theology," 8. A different view emerges from John Godsey, *The Theology of Dietrich Bonhoeffer* (Philadelphia: Westminster Press, 1960), 17.

PART THREE

1. This was written in 1942. Cf. GS II, 375; TP, 88; LPP, 234. On the wish to experience old things anew, see LPP, 3.
2. Cf. LPP, 359.
3. PB, 31. Cf. CD, 110.
4. This applies strictly to Barth's theology! Influenced initially by Blumhardt, Kutter, and Ragaz, Barth became a "religious socialist." Despite his later detachment from it, he maintained an active political-social engagement; he was always ready to become involved with completely worldly and political events.
5. In relation to the development of worldlessness (acosmism) and the parallel development of Cultural Protestantism in Ritschl and Herrmann, see Hermann Timm, *Theorie und Praxis in der Theologie Albrecht Ritschls und Wilhelm Herrmanns. Ein Beitrag zur Entwicklungsgeschichte des Kulturprotestantismus* (Gütersloh: Gütersloher Verlagshaus Gerd Mohn, 1967).
6. GS V, 181–227, given in 1931–32.
7. DB, 27, 35.
8. Friedrich Schleiermacher, *On Religion: Speeches to Its Cultured Despis-*

ers, trans. John Oman (New York: Harper and Brothers, 1958; hereafter cited as *Speeches*), 276.

9. DB, 27.

10. Friedrich Naumann, *Briefe über Religion,* in Vol. 1 of *Werke,* (Cologne: Westdeutscher Verlag, 1964), 609.

11. The following shows how sharply Naumann separated the Sermon on the Mount and life in the world:

> According to Luther one cannot decide about matters of state on the basis of the gospel. Jews and pagans can decide about these as well as Christians since reason alone is required in order to regulate them and not revelation. The Lutheran separation of these areas appeared at times to reduce the sphere of influence of Christianity and its rights. But when one thinks about this deeply enough this impression proves false. We truly follow the old great doctor of German faith when we regard political matters as being outside the sphere of the preaching of salvation. I vote and gather support for the German fleet not because I am a Christian but because I am a citizen and because I have learned to give up looking to the Sermon on the Mount for solutions to questions of state. (*Werke,* 626)

Cf. Hermann Timm, *Friedrich Naumanns theologischer Widerruf* (Munich: Chr. Kaiser Verlag, 1967).

12. Naumann had said that "religion is becoming more and more an inward question of the soul" (*Werke,* 631).

13. Naumann, *Werke,* 589.

14. GS V, 174; cf. E, 321.

15. A letter from Tripolis, dated 9 May 1924, contains these remarkable words: "In Islam everyday life and religion are not kept separate, as they are in the whole of the church, including the Catholic Church. With us one goes to church and when one comes back an entirely different life begins again" (DB, 38). Note the absence yet of any polemics against religion.

16. Karl Barth is the "divide" in which God is no longer confused with religion. See GS V, 216.

17. GS V, 190. The following quotation from Troeltsch will show how little Bonhoeffer could have agreed with Troeltsch's definition of religion:

> Religion is fluid and alive, drawing deeply from God always through direct contact; it is highly inward, personal, individual and abrupt. The times when religion is most alive are not times of the church, they are times of high enthusiasm, allowing the individual and his/her heartbeat to come to the fore. (*Religion und Kirche* in Vol. II of *Gesammelte Schriften* [Aalen: Scientia Verlag, 1962], 148)

18. It is a fact, but only that, that the subject of the world is not explicitly dealt with in SC and AB. To conclude that Bonhoeffer was basically uninterested in the world would be an argument from silence. The subject becomes more manifest in Bonhoeffer's inaugural lecture; see NRS, 50–69. One hears, for example, that humans are "lord of the world" (66). There seems to be a different understanding of the world only in one place where Bonhoeffer said, "Those in Christ are not taken out of the world; they are the people of daily work, of toil, of profession . . ." (67).

19. GS V, 463–468. Bonhoeffer preferred the reading of *Kairō* over *Kuriō* in this text. Cf. SC, 238 n. 123, where this is clearly noted. In SC, 191, where the same text from Romans is referred to, Bonhoeffer said, "For above all the gospel must deal with the present—and that means at this moment the proletar-

ian mass—in a concrete way." It is possible that Bonhoeffer adopted that textual reading from Karl Barth; see his 1919 version of *Der Römerbrief* (Bern: Bäschlin), 363 n. 1, and his defense of that reading in the revised edition of 1922 (Munich: Chr. Kaiser Verlag), 437.

20. These four kinds of need possibly correspond to the four mandates of which Bonhoeffer later spoke: government, work, marriage, and church.

21. See NRS, 47; GS V, 445; SC, 157, 167.

22. GS V, 461, 481, 117, dating from 1928; GS I, 138, from 1932; PB, 34, and GS IV, 69. In his drama, the fragment of a drama, to be precise, Bonhoeffer also spoke of the giant Antaeus. The point is the same: the proletarian conversation partner also struggles to have ground underfoot. Cf. GS III, 494, and E, 339 [where "a solid basis" is the translation of the German "we obtain solid ground under our feet . . ."]. "In Jesus God has said Yes and Amen to it all, and that Yes and Amen is the firm ground on which we stand" (LPP, 391); cf. LPP, 3, 296. In the various ways that this assertion is made there recurs the sense of uncertainty and convulsion of the present time and the desire to find or to have firm ground under one's feet.

23. See PB, 27–47.

24. Bonhoeffer's American lectures were very important for his later lecture course on christology (see above, part two, section 3a), but they refer to the world only as the point to which the incarnation was related; see NRS, 362 and GS III, 108. The point is not developed as such in the American lectures. The reason that Bonhoeffer did not speak about the world while in the United States may be that, in his view, Jesus Christ had been forgotten there and that Christianity had as a result become subject to the world; cf. GS I, 110, dating from 1931. It is certain that the visit to the United States had a sustained influence on Bonhoeffer's question about the world, even though he did not mention it explicitly. One would conclude this from his openness to pragmatism: see NRS, 91 (the full text is in GS I, 90–93); to the social gospel: see NRS, 91 (for the full text, GS I, 101); and to social work: see MW V, 26. That influence is made clearer in Bonhoeffer's report about his second visit: see WF, 213–49, and NRS, 92–118.

25. See GS I, 133–39; GS IV, 69–79, and NRS, 182–89.

26. Cf. NRS, 157–73; PB, 27–47; NRS, 153–57.

27. Cf. the sermons of February to October 1932: "God's way in the world leads to the cross and through the cross to life" (GS IV, 42). This sentence, so reminiscent of the prison letters, recurs almost verbatim several times; e.g., GS IV, 87, 150, 38, 84. The sermons in Barcelona spoke often about the cross, but it was not an event which touched and changed the world. It was the sign which took us out of the world. It is a silent retraction of the Barcelona sermons when Bonhoeffer affirmed that there is "basically nothing else that makes eternity visible in this world" besides the cross (GS IV, 57).

28. Bonhoeffer complains in this connection that the suspicion that "Christians are dreaming about a better world beyond and are useless, therefore, for the revolutionary acts which every generation must carry out," is in fact justified (GS IV, 69). It has to change, however.

> We should not let things come and go as they are. Our faith should not be the opiate which lets us rest content in the midst of an unjust world. Precisely because we look for the things that are above we ought to protest on earth more obstinately and more convinced of our goal. Protest in words and deeds so that things move forward no matter what the price. Must it really come to this that Christianity which had such a revolutionary beginning now stays with its conservatism for ever? That every new movement

must make its own way without the church? That the church always discovers twenty years later what had actually gone on? If it does come to that then let us not be surprised that times will come again when the blood of martyrs will be demanded. But it will not be blood as innocent and radiant as that of the first witness, should we even have the courage and faithfulness to spill it. On our blood would rest our own great guilt, the guilt of the useless servant who will be cast out into the darkness. (GS IV, 71)

Cf. also 79. The call to revolutionary acts is repeated later; see 180 (dating from 1934). It arose from the admonition that we seek the things which are above and do so precisely in our concrete given situation. Christians have the duty "to shock the world" (GS IV, 181). Cf. GS V, 328, dating from 1933.

Bonhoeffer's call for an engagement that may have to be revolutionary is based on the connection between faith and life which Bonhoeffer had begun to make. Faith enables life to change the world without falling into bondage to it; indeed, it is faith which saves life from that, and sets it free. Bonhoeffer modified his ideas about revolution later, e.g., E, 351: "According to Holy Scripture, there is no right to revolution; but there is a responsibility of every individual for preserving the purity of office and mission in the *polis*"; see also 246. Bonhoeffer draws attention particularly to the boundaries of responsibility, something that he had done in speaking about the guilt associated with revolutionary action. The question "Why should only bad people carry out revolutions?" has validity certainly for himself; see Franz Hildebrandt, "German Address," in *Bonhoeffer Gedenkheft*, 15. Cf. E, 152, 338. Throughout his life, Bonhoeffer refused to call Jesus a revolutionary; see his sermon of 3 June 1928 (p. 1 of the manuscript); CD, 115. "The source of all action truly appropriate to reality is the incarnate God Jesus Christ. It is not the pseudo-Lutheran Christ whose task it is to sanction the status quo, nor the radical-revolutionary Christ of the enthusiasts who is to bless every upheaval" (GS III, 460). See also E, 321.

29. See above, I: 5b and the assertions about the concrete commandment.
30. Cf. Bonhoeffer's first two lecture courses of 1931–32.
31. See, e.g., NRS, 167.
32. Christ has commanded the church "to say his word to the whole world. The territory of the one church of Christ is the whole world" (NRS, 161). "God is one, and his kingdom shall be the whole world" (SC, 184).
33. False christianization is attacked again in E, 317, 328.
34. PB, 40–47 and NRS, 153. The first time that this topic emerges is in Rome, where Bonhoeffer was on a visit in 1924. He wrote the following in his diary: "Now, when the official tie between church and state has been dropped, the church is confronted with the truth; it has for too long been a home for homeless spirits, a place of refuge for uninformed edification. Had it never become an established church, the state of affairs would be very different . . . ; it must begin to limit itself and make selections in every respect, particularly in the quality of its spiritual educators and what they teach; in any event it must completely dissociate itself from the state as soon as possible, perhaps even sacrificing the right to religious instruction . . ." (DB, 41). He touches on this subject again in SC, 188, where he speaks of "the conservatism of a Protestant national church." See also C, 96.
35. Cf. GS V, 272, dating from 1932; NRS, 155, from 1932 or 1933; NRS, 222, from 1933; C, 62, and GS II, 114, also from 1933.
36. This explains more precisely what was meant by "the church limits the state, just as the state limits the church" (PB, 43). See also NRS, 156; GS V, 273; NRS, 172.
37. [The text in GS II, 48 erroneously uses the term *mittelbar* while the

translator of NRS follows Bethge's correction, reading *unmittelbar* and translating it as "direct."]

38. This was written in 1933.

39. The two positions of provincialism and secularism are in Bonhoeffer's mind when he writes: "One can take one's stand on the 'not yet' both from the viewpoint of an unbroken worldliness and from that of a pious withdrawal from the world" (GS II, 119). The term "worldliness" has a different tone than before. This becomes manifest in what follows: "Both [sc. viewpoints] are on the same level. Neither can think the thought of the end in Christ and, thus, both think in a basically worldly way" (GS II, 119). Worldly has the sense of "world-like"; only in the last period of Bonhoeffer's theology does it have a different meaning.

40. This was written in 1934.

41. The text of the address, delivered on 28 August 1934 is found in GS I, 216–19. Cf. DB, 312, on the impact of and sequel to it.

42. BWP, 129. Cf. the citation from GS I, 217, above.

43. This raises an objection against Luther.

The consequence of Luther's doctrine of grace is that the church should live in the world and, according to Romans 13, in its ordinances. Thus in his own way Luther confirms Constantine's covenant with the church. As a result, a minimal ethic prevailed. Luther, of course, wanted a complete ethic for everyone, not only for the monastic orders. Thus the existence of the Christian became the existence of the citizen. The nature of the church vanished into the invisible realm. But in this way the New Testament message was fundamentally misunderstood, inner-worldliness became a principle. Therefore today we must be concerned with the witness to its application to the outer world. (NRS, 324)

44. Bethge suggests that the understanding of the world manifest in the period of CD is a negative one (DB, 378). One readily concurs in that judgment.

45. See also CD, 43, where Kierkegaard is mentioned. Concerning Kierkegaard's influence on Bonhoeffer see Wenzel Lohff, "Rechtfertigung und Ethik," in *Lutherische Monatshefte*, Vol 2. (1963): 311–18; Traugott Vogel, *Christus als Vorbild und Versöhner. Eine kritische Studie zum Problem des Verhältnisses von Gesetz und Evangelium im Werke Sören Kierkegaards* (Diss., Humboldt University, Berlin, 1968). There are a number of terms and arguments in the Kierkegaard selection that influenced Bonhoeffer in CD. See Kierkegaard's *The Individual and the Church,* on the opposition to the view which held Christian faith to be a "doctrine," in which many of the terms of CD have their counterparts. It could have been that influence which caused so remarkably many individualistic statements to be made in that book, even though they are broadened out toward the community; e.g., CD, 80. The decisively negative view of worldliness was quite likely framed under the impact of Kierkegaard.

46. Cf. PB, 29.

47. This goes against Bonhoeffer's sermon "Serve the Times," preached in Barcelona; see above, part three, section 3a; also CD, 208, 84–88.

48. Cf. CD, 252:

"The Spirit seals off the church from the world. In the strength of this seal the church must vindicate God's claim on the whole world. At the same time the church must claim a definite sphere in the world for itself, and so clearly define the frontier between itself and the world. Because the church is the city set on a hill and founded on earth by the direct act of God—the *polis* of Matt. 5.14—and because it is as such God's sealed possession, its "political" character is definitely involved in its sanctification. Its "political ethics" has its basis only in the church's sanctification: the world is the world and the church the church. And yet the word of God must go forth from the church into all the world, proclaiming that the earth is the Lord's and all that therein is. Herein lies the "political" character of the church.

The meaning of "the political character of the church" and its message is different from what it meant in 1932. See also CD, 253, 257. T. R. Peters relies strongly on these texts to demonstrate a positive understanding of the world in Bonhoeffer and to refute my interpretation. After careful study I have no reason to change my views. See my review of his book, *Die Präsenz des Politischen*, in *Theologische Revue*, Vol. 73 (1977), 483–85.

49. Bonhoeffer warns against this; see CD, 171 and even more clearly on 139. He is seeking to establish a balanced position; cf. 240.

50. See above, part one, section 4, and part two, section 2b.

51. *Nachfolge*, 85. [For inexplicable reasons, this sentence was left untranslated in *The Cost of Discipleship*. It should follow the sentence, ending ". . . even to the length of the cross," on p. 100.]

52. Cf. CD, 245:

Only God is holy. He is holy both in his perfect separation from the sinful world and in the establishment of his sanctuary in the midst of the world. . . . The holiness of God means his coming to dwell in the midst of the world and to establish his sanctuary. . . . Separated from the world and from sin the body of Christ is made the special possession of God and his sanctuary in the world. God dwells in it with the Holy Spirit.

It is remarkable that in this understanding of the Old Testament Bonhoeffer projects a negative relation to the world. This is quite unique because usually the Old Testament becomes the occasion for Bonhoeffer to speak of thisworldliness, something we shall see especially in the prison letters.

53. "Luther did not return to the world because he had arrived at a more positive attitude towards it. Nor had he abandoned the eschatological expectation of early Christianity. He intended his action to express a radical criticism and protest against the secularization of Christianity which had taken place within monasticism" (CD, 239).

54. The discrepancies between a theology of order and a theology of revolution opposed to it, which are hidden behind this discussion, are discussed in Ernst Feil and Rudolf Weth, eds., *Diskussion zur 'Theologie der Revolution'* (Munich: Chr. Kaiser Verlag, 1969).

55. GS IV, 364; the entire text is thoroughly christological.

56. Bonhoeffer adds that prayer is not for the purpose of pursuing any "political-worldly" aims. See also GS IV, 370.

57. Cf. especially DB, 525.

58. See CD, 238 and E, 255.

59. GS III, 31. See above, part two, section 5a.

60. As far as we know this is the first time "thisworldly" is used in a positive sense.

61. The reference must be to 1939; see DB, 543. Bonhoeffer assured Niebuhr that Barth was right in becoming more political, but . . . criticised Barth for defining his position in a little pamphlet. "If," [Bonhoeffer] declared in rather typical German fashion, "one states an original position in many big volumes, one ought to define the change in one's position in an equally impressive volume and not in a little pamphlet." (DB, 526)

Cf. the whole section, 524–26, esp. 580.

62. In 1935 Bonhoeffer had paid a visit to an Anglican monastery; his strong interest in Psalm 119 arose there; see DB, 335. One wonders whether Bonhoeffer actually wrote down in 1940 "something he had had in mind for years" (DB, 524); it is not likely that he would have spoken about the world in this way in those earlier years.

63. Cf. above, part two, section 5b.

64. This is from the meditation on Psalm 119 referred to earlier. The point is made even more clearly on 559: many earnest Christians "refer to the corresponding prayers in the Psalms as an imperfect and preliminary stage of Old Testament piety, overcome in the New Testament. But in saying so they want to be more spiritual than God." See LPP, 156, where the issue of the Old Testament as a religious primer is dealt with more drastically.

65. See, e.g., GS IV, 541.

66. GS III, 300, dating from 1935; in CD the context was the Abraham saga. It is instructive to note, in this connection, that there are 22 references to the Old and more than 500 to the New Testament in CD.

67. LPP, 286; see also above, part two, section 5c. Beginning in 1935, but quite strongly as of 1940, the Old Testament is seen as the advocate of profound thisworldliness; see, e.g., GS IV, 466, 471, 498; TP, 77–81, 124, 128. Bonhoeffer relates Christ to the Old Testament first and draws the conclusion from that later in his theology.

68. See the titles to parts I and II in E, 17, 57.

69. The ethical consequence is that we may neither despise nor idolize humanity; E, 72; cf. 74.

70. The order of this sequence expresses that there can be no road leading from the penultimate to the ultimate. The first indication of that terminology may well be a letter from 1926, which was lost, see DB, 66. For its usage later, see NRS, 347, 357, dating from 1932; NRS, 203, from 1933. It occurs last in LPP, 157, 281.

71. Bonhoeffer practices this himself in prison: during air raids, when the inmates were quite helpless, he would not speak to them about God but would say that it would be all over in ten minutes; see LPP, 199. He considered it wrong to force religion down their throats just then. The comment about the two thieves crucified with Jesus, which follows after that statement, had already been made in E, 124.

72. E, 143. The consequences drawn from this are on 155. Bonhoeffer's comment that he wanted to restore the concept of the natural to its proper place in connection with preaching has the air of an announcement (GS IV, 281). In E, this idea is then generalized to include other areas.

73. E, 143. Bonhoeffer wrote that chapter in the Benedictine monastery of Ettal; he was most likely not left untouched by his surroundings. The natural is given a much more christological interpretation by him than in the Roman Catholic ethics of the day. Bonhoeffer's charge that original sin was taken too lightly resulted probably from that insight, as did the one that Roman Catholic theology also saw itself too much as a natural theology. Cf. E, 326.

74. Cf. E, 125, 356; the latter text was written most likely in Tegel. In Barcelona Bonhoeffer said that there was no way to God except God's way to us. "The religious way to God leads straight to the idol of our heart, made in our image" (GS V, 148); cf, NRS, 40.

75. See above, part three, section 2b.

76. E, 195; see also above, part two, section 3a.

NOTES

77. Behind the concepts of reality and realization probably stands the distinction between the reality and actuality of SC. Now the terminology is simpler and more appropriate. The problems raised in the concepts of form and formation (E, 84) are taken up in those of reality and realization.

78. The restriction to the church found in SC and present in some form still in E, 82, is now dropped altogether; see E, 190. It is not immediately clear in what way the sphere of the church is conceived of differently now than in CD. "One must bear in mind that the confines of this space are at every moment being overrun and broken down by the testimony of the church to Jesus Christ. And this means that all thinking in terms of spheres must be excluded, since it is deleterious to the proper understanding of the church" (E, 203). The relation of church and world must not be "formulated in too one-sided a way" (TP, 162).

79. Cf. E, 231, and GS III, 459. It is very revealing to juxtapose the assertion "The world remains the world because it is the world which is loved, condemned and reconciled in Christ" (E, 232) with "The world remains the world, and we are still sinners 'even in the best life.'" . . . Well, then, let the Christian live like the rest of the world" (CD, 35). The tone of the two verbally identical openings is fundamentally different. The term used to characterize cheap grace in CD is taken up in E to characterize a positive view of the world.

80. Bonhoeffer states this explicitly in GS III, 471. Cf. above, part three, sections 2a and 3b.

81. See above, part three, section 3b.

82. Bonhoeffer was arrested at this time. See DB, 625.

83. Cf. E, 314. Bonhoeffer rejects the lordship of Christ seen as "christocracy," since that would imply a heteronomy. "The antinomy of heteronomy and autonomy is here resolved in a higher unity which we may call Christonomy" (E, 299 n. 5).

84. Cf. Bonhoeffer's exegesis of 2 Chron. 16:12, "He did not seek guidance of the Lord but resorted to physicians" (GS III, 426, dating from 1941). "In all his piety the man thought in a modern way; he distinguished sharply between the things of religion, in which one turns to God, and the things of the earth, in which one seeks earthly help when needed. . . . That is quite reasonable and perhaps also quite religious. But it is wrong." Bonhoeffer probably had Cultural Protestantism in mind when he wrote that.

85. See above, part three, section 3b.

86. See NRS, 92–118.

87. See E, 104, and NRS, 107.

88. E, 209, 286, 330, 344. The description of the mandates is not always the same. There is no need to reiterate that Bonhoeffer speaks of mandates in order to highlight the dynamic characteristic within which one may speak again correctly of orders.

89. E, 332–35. Bethge believes that this text was prepared for a meeting of the Freiburg Circle of the German resistance, to be held in November 1942. The meeting was to prepare a memorandum about, *inter alia,* the question of church polity; DB, 681.

90. The church is to remind the state of its limits, yes, but it should not, for example, make detailed plans for post-war reconstruction; see TP, 109, dating from 1942. This is reminiscent of what was said on this subject ten years earlier. The state is also to be protected against "the alien rule of the church" (E, 329). See also PB, 37, and NRS, 156. See above, part three, section 3b.

91. Cf. E, 343. Bonhoeffer's own situation is clearly manifest in this statement. We need to refer to an important detail here: Bonhoeffer was concerned

about the fact that an unjustly gained success cannot be permanently repudiated in history (cf. E, 75, 117; also LPP, 6). Since Bonhoeffer addressed that concern from 1940 onward, it would seem that Niesel's interpretation does not hold ("From Keelson to Principal," 146 n. 1). Niesel suggested that in 1940 Bonhoeffer tried to adjust himself to Hitler's successes and supported the idea of a working arrangement with Hitler. Cf. the confession of guilt, written most likely at that very same time (E, 110).

92. For the analysis of the progress of modernity see E, 88–109; for the outline of a confession of guilt, E, 110–19. See also "The End of the Church Struggle," GS II, 433–37, and especially *I Loved This People* (Richmond: John Knox Press, 1965, and London: SPCK, 1965), 45–48, Bonhoeffer's proposal for a proclamation to be read from pulpits after the downfall of Germany.

93. See above, part two, section 5b.

94. Cf. the surmise of Karl Barth, "Letters to Superintendent Herrenbrück" and the even more strongly stated one of Wilhelm Niesel, "From Keelson to Principal."

95. LPP, 118 n. 41.

96. GS I, 50. Cf. DB, 647. A letter to Paul Lehmann, written in 1938, shows that Bonhoeffer was not ready yet to affirm the earth as he does now (GS II, 348).

97. The letter is dated 12 August 1943.

"When I also think about the situation of the world, the complete darkness over our personal fate and my present imprisonment, then I believe that our union can only be a sign of God's grace and kindness, which calls us to faith. We would be blind if we did not see it. Jeremiah says at the moment of his people's great need "still one shall buy houses and acres in this land" as a sign of trust in the future. This is where faith belongs. May God give it to us daily. And I do not mean the faith which flees the world, but the one that endures the world and which loves and remains true to the world in spite of all the suffering which it contains for us. Our marriage shall be a "yes" to God's earth; it shall strengthen our courage to act and accomplish something on the earth. I fear that Christians who stand with only one leg upon the earth also stand with only one leg in heaven. (Maria von Wedemeyer, "The Other Letters from Prison," *Union Seminary Quarterly Review*, Vol. 23, No. 1. [1967]: 26)

The translation is that of Ms. von Wedemeyer.

98. KzW, 9, 31, 354–56. Cf. above, part one, section 1.

99. Cf. "Inheritance and Decay," in E, 88, and the comments about the Reformation (LPP, 123).

100. Bonhoeffer had hoped that he would be released at Christmas time (e.g., LPP, 133). That hope, however, soon fades away (LPP, 166, 173). This is coupled with some critical comments about the speed with which he judged his case being processed (174, as well as 195 and 217).

101. The text of that story is found in TP, 220–35. The Drama Fragment was composed at that time as well (TP, 197–215).

102. See LPP, 78, where he lists Gotthelf, Stifter, Immermann, Fontane, and Keller. See also the list of books Bonhoeffer read in prison, found in DBG, 1103.

103. For God as "working hypothesis," see LPP, 325, 360, 381; God as "stop-gap," see LPP, 311, 381, and PB, 61; God as "tutor," see LPP, 326.

104. Karl Barth answers one of Harnack's questions to "the despisers of scientific theology" as follows: "The so-called 'experience of God' . . . is therefore as different as heaven and earth from the faith awakened by God and is

practically indistinguishable from 'uncontrolled fanaticism'"; see H. Martin Rumscheidt, *Revelation and Theology—An Analysis of the Barth–Harnack Correspondence of 1923* (London: Cambridge University Press, 1972), 32. This correspondence shows clearly the impasses which plague Bonhoeffer's theology. Despite his critical support of Barth's point of view, Bonhoeffer could not deny that liberal theology had a number of strong points; he certainly could not take sides anymore. Instead he set out on his own dialectics of liberal and dialectical theology.

105. Bonhoeffer's charge of positivism of revelation takes up the issue of the ninth thesis defended at his doctoral examination in 1927; see NRS, 33.

106. Bonhoeffer's development is depicted in ways which have a formal resemblance one to the other; this applies to H. Müller, who rejects CD and LT as dead ends; to J. A. Phillips, according to whom the unhappy marriage of christo-ecclesiology based on their first "engagement" in SC and AB, had to be divorced after 1932–33; and to R. Mayer, according to whom the christological ontology broke down as a system after Bonhoeffer had tried so hard to erect it all the way to the *Ethics*.

107. This topic urgently requires an accurate analysis.

108. See Karl Barth, *Theology and Church* (London: SCM Press, 1962), 55–73, where Overbeck is discussed. This text was written in 1920, just after the first edition of *Römerbrief*. Some of Overbeck's critical comments about religion are cited; e.g., 72: "Religious problems must eventually be based in a wholly new area (in contrast to the antagonism between Catholicism and Protestantism) at the expense of what has until now been called religion." Cf. Benktson, *Christus und die Religion*, 59 n. 6.

109. Karl Barth, *The Word of God and the Word of Man* (New York: Harper and Brothers, 1957; hereafter cited as Word), 26. The reference is to an address Barth delivered in 1916.

110. Karl Barth, *Der Römerbrief* (reprint of the first edition of 1919; Zürich: TVZ Verlag, 1963; hereafter cited as RB1), 88.

111. Just before that Barth had stated that one no longer needed to be "religious" (RB1, 106).

112. Cf. RB1, 108. Barth's critique also is directed against the name of a new encyclopedia: *Die Religion in Geschichte und Gegenwart*. He says that "religion had become such a 'powerfully noticeable force' in 1909 that a special 'handbook' about its history and presence became necessary" (RB1, 299).

113. Cf. RB1, 40. Religion seems to be the result of what God does but it has no power to save. After all, religion and morality are assigned to the "age of the flesh" (56). See LPP, 281. For both Bonhoeffer and Barth the question arose about the partiality of religion. Barth asked whether God did not have "a precisely marked sphere in this world, namely in the holy area of explicitly religious and orderly ecclesiastical life" (RB1, 84).

114. The temporal dimension is raised here which was to become very important for Bonhoeffer.

115. Karl Barth, *The Epistle to the Romans*, trans. Edwyn C. Hoskyns (London: Oxford University Press, 1953; hereafter cited as RB2), 2.

116. RB2, 3.

117. The coordination of law and religion is often supplemented by the terms "piety" or "experience," e.g., RB2, 88 or 109: "Whoever speaks of law, religion, experience, speaks of knowledge or feeling or action or experience, all *human* work."

118. "That God speaks, that we, known by him, see ourselves and the world

in his light, is something strange, peculiar, new; and this 'otherness' runs through all religions, all experience, and every human disposition, when these are directed towards God. . . . It is the truth of all religion, but for that reason never identical with its reality" (RB2, 92).

119. This matches Barth's clear rejection of the religious a priori or universal religion of reason, behind or in front of all so-called positive religion (RB2, 386). Bonhoeffer followed Barth in this rejection.

120. We must understand, therefore, that "we encounter the freedom which is ours by grace beyond the humanism which reaches its culminating point in religion" (RB2, 230).

121. Karl Barth, *Church Dogmatics* I/2, trans. G. T. Thomson and H. Knight (Edinburgh: T. and T. Clark, 1956; hereafter cited as CD), 291. The problem of religion recedes from later volumes of the *Dogmatics;* see below, part three, section 6b.

122. It is here that we discern the error in Barth's analogy of true religion and justified sinner inasmuch as he draws the parallel between religion and sinner but not between religion and sin.

123. The dialectics of religion and revelation was not a central issue for Bonhoeffer, nor was that of gospel and law. He did not make much use of Barth's *Evangelium und Gesetz,* although he surely knew it; see DB, 472. We cannot deal with the difficulties or even contradictions of Barth's view of religion now.

124. Bonhoeffer also speaks of a void in his address on christology in Barcelona; see GS V, 153.

125. Regin Prenter, for example, bases his conviction on the second edition of *Römerbrief,* that "the views expressed in that work about God's revelation are not opposed to those found in his later *Church Dogmatics*" (Ronald Gregor Smith, ed., *World Come of Age* [London: Collins, 1967], 106). Benkston does not weigh the differences between Barth's first works, the second edition of *Romans,* and *Church Dogmatics,* which become manifest, e.g., in his *Christus und die Religion,* 59. Both, however, deserve credit for having made the comparison between Barth's and Bonhoeffer's positions.

126. See DB, 50.

127. SC, 121 n. 2 (text on 226-27); GS V, 303; LPP, 328. It is not known whether Bonhoeffer knew the edition of 1919.

128. Already in 1926 Bonhoeffer was worried that Barth was retreating from the stand of the revised *Römerbrief;* see DB, 54.

129. See above, part three, section 2b, and GS V, 218.

130. SC, 90-93, 116 n. 37 (text on 223-24). The characteristic of religion called "an individualism in principle" is not denied by the fact "that religion is a social matter" (SC, 94); cf. SC, 93-97. For the problem of religion prior to SC see DB, the quotations on 38 and 56.

131. See SC, 94 n. 8 (text on 221), and 93 with its reference to Schleiermacher.

132. "This, however, is not to accept but to circumvent God's will, which is to reveal in the church as he did in Christ everything which he reveals by concealing it in the guise (sic) of historical events" (SC, 88). This comment has special significance for the interpretation of LPP.

133. GS V, 154. Many details of this address show Barth's influence.

134. In his sermon of 3 June 1928 Bonhoeffer spoke about God's fire which was to burn on earth. "Whatever we mobilize against that fire will be consumed. We bring up our costliest and purest treasures: our morality and our religion.

But behold! God's fire singes and burns until there is nothing left of our glory" (manuscript, p. 2). Much more pointedly:

> Religion does not fulfill what the world does not give us: religion is not the bringer of happiness. No! Unhappiness, unrest and privation became strong in the world through religion. The word of grace confronts everything that happens in the world. Grace tells of an event beyond the world and seeks to draw us to it and away from our world. (GS V, 460)

The following text points to Barth's 1921 *Römerbrief:* "Nothing of what exists in time is divine, absolutely nothing, not even the church, not even our religion" (GS V, 464).

135. NRS, 40. Cf. GS V, 126. "To be religious means to understand that one will never be religious; to have God means to see that one can never have him. The people of Israel now had to discover that religion led either to salvation or to perdition, that there is no neutrality in it." These sentences remind one of Barth's second *Römerbrief* edition, since religion is related as an ambivalent phenomenon to the Hebrew Scriptures.

136. Cf. the critique of Brunstäd's view of religion. Brunstäd understands religion as experience, like Schleiermacher, and identifies religion and revelation (AB, 40, 108, 161 n. 1). Seeberg especially had identified revelation and religion; his understanding of the religious a priori had let revelation become religion (AB, 45). Bonhoeffer opposes the religious a priori already in his seminar about the difference between historical and pneumatic exegesis. Seeberg himself conducted that seminar in the Summer term of 1925. This repudiation is maintained right into LPP. Cf. above, part one, section 2b and part two, section 2b.

137. In the meantime Bonhoeffer had been in the United States where he had been most anxious to make Barth's theology known; see above, part two, section 3a. That is why there are no critical assessments of Barth's critique of religion. Bonhoeffer said that "the basis of religion and of ethics is here self-justification before god. Grace destroys all those attempts, destroys religion and ethics and experiences of grace . . ." (GS III, 97, dating from 1930). Cf. GS III, 109; NRS, 365; GS III, 125. Concerning religion which has become social ethics, see GS I, 92; religion is a faulty conception of transcendence.

138. In GS V, 306 we read "even *religio caro est*."

139. PB, 27; see above, part three, section 3b.

140. On individualism, see GS IV, 202, dating from 1935; on particularity, see Bonhoeffer's distinction between "church and a 'religious fellowship' " (WF, 47). The division of religion and world is made plain again in GS IV, 389, dating from 1936, and GS III, 426, from 1941.

141. Cf. CD, 50, 269. "A truth, a doctrine, or a religion need no space for themselves. They are disembodied entities" (CD, 223). This does not necessarily contradict the assertion about the spatial separation of religion and the world. In the final analysis this separation, too, implies the dissolution of religion into world.

142. NRS, 117. This is from the report about the second visit to the United States. American theologians have not understood this, in Bonhoeffer's view: "In American theology, Christianity is still essentially religion and ethics" (NRS, 117). His diary of the period manifests his renewed preoccupation with religion. Reporting about the "a-religiosity" of college students, who are "just not interested," he says that the development in America had to go that way "if one doesn't eventually realise that 'religion' is really superfluous" (WF, 230). After a sermon, which was strictly human, that is, humanistic, he asks, "Do

people not know that one can get on as well, even better, without 'religion'—if only there were not God himself and his word?" (WF, 230). And there is a scribbled note about the church as a religious province (WF, 232).

143. Religion is spoken of on several occasions in E: in religion a human being seeks union with God (21); religion is not what matters in the church (84); the church is not a religious community (83); the church becomes a religious society when it struggles for its self-preservation (202); Western godlessness is called religion (102); there is no purely religious preaching which separates the gospel from human existence in the world (316); there is no restriction to any particular religious domain (GS III, 473; a fragment belonging to *Ethics*). And yet, religion is not a governing concept. The term is absent in discussions in which at earlier times it appeared prominently, e.g., thinking in terms of two spheres (E, 196), even though it would suggest itself. Cf. E, 200, on "inwardness."

144. GS IV, 18, dating from 1931; 65, from 1932; 126, from 1933. See also CF, 69.

145. Benktson fails to keep up the dialectics, as is shown in his attempt to salvage the honor of the word religion by turning religion into natural theology (*Christus und die Religion*, 157). R. Mayer goes wholly astray in his comment that for both Barth and Bonhoeffer "religion as a distillation of revelation in time is a legitimate phenomenon" (*Christuswirklichkeit*, 230). He characterizes their critical position toward religion by saying that "their concept of religion is thoroughly dialectical."

146. The volume in question is II/2, published in 1942. The dialectics of revelation and religion is now gone. This discussion about religion is not really a direct discussion with Feuerbach, as was suggested by Henri Mottu, "Feuerbach and Bonhoeffer: Criticism of Religion and the Last Period of Bonhoeffer's Thought," in *Union Seminary Quarterly Review*, Vol 25 (1969): 1–18.

147. Reference has already been made to a comment Bonhoeffer made in 1942, in which he spoke of "clothing things in religious garments" (GS II, 420).

148. LPP, 280, and, used in adjectival form, 286. A comparison of these two citations shows that inwardness and subjectivity mean the same. See also 344, where these terms appear in a specific formulation. They will be dealt with again below, part three, section 7.

149. Cf. LPP, 168, 281, 375. Bonhoeffer refused to locate God at the edge of our knowledge (281, 311, 325).

150. Bonhoeffer believed that this connection was made following Kant's philosophy, which sets out from the human subject and removes God from the human spheres of knowledge and experience into the transcendent; this is stated clearly in LPP, 374.

151. Such a God is a "God, as we imagine him" (LPP, 391). Such a God is always defined in terms of human limitations or weakness. Cf. LPP, 281, 336, 345.

152. LPP, 280, 300, 381; here Bonhoeffer opposes the separation of Christianity and church, whereas religion and church are set in opposition on 286.

153. Eberhard Bethge lists four additional features of religion in addition to metaphysics, inwardness, and partiality; they are *deus ex machina*, privilege, tutelage, and dispensability; see DB, 776–81. Privilege goes with partiality, *deus ex machina* with metaphysics, and dispensability with the historical relativity of religion. Bethge refers to this when he asks about the relation of Barth's systematic concept of religion to the historical one of dispensability (781).

154. LPP, 280, as related to Barth; 382, as related to the Confessing Church;

328, as related to the Confessing Church in following Barth's lead: "The Confessing Church has now largely forgotten all about the Barthian approach, and has lapsed from positivism into conservative restoration."

155. GS V, 225; see above, part three, section 3a.

156. Bonhoeffer modifies the charge that Barth had not given any concrete guidance in ethics.

> He brought in against religion the God of Jesus Christ, "pneuma against sarx." That remains his greatest service (his *Epistle to the Romans*, second edition, in spite of all the neo-Kantian eggshells). Through his later dogmatics, he enabled the church to effect this distinction, in principle, all along the line. It was not in ethics, as is often said, that he subsequently failed: his ethical observations, as far as they exist, are just as important as his dogmatic ones; it was that in the non-religious interpretation of theological concepts he gave no concrete guidance, either in dogmatics or in ethics. There lies his limitation, and because of it his theology of revelation has become positivist, a "positivism of revelation," as I put it. (LPP, 328)

See also his moderate explanations to his brother-in-law Gerhard Leibholz (GS III, 35).

157. It is most significant that authority, be it patriarchal or its extension into the absolute, divine, is already perceived as a positivistic solution arising out of the state of tutelage.

158. This is how one has to interpret the comment which, correctly applied to Barth, is still difficult to understand: " 'Like it or lump it': virgin birth, Trinity, or anything else; each is an equally significant and necessary part of the whole which must simply be swallowed as a whole or not at all. That isn't biblical. There are degrees of knowledge and degrees of significance" (LPP, 285). Everything is equally significant if there is no concreteness. And that is what Bonhoeffer believed was missing in Barth.

159. On the subject of religion in Bonhoeffer see Gerhard Ebeling's essay, "The 'Non-religious Interpretation of Biblical Concepts,' " in *Word and Faith*, 98–161. But he imputes a false concept of religion to Bonhoeffer; religion meant, according to Ebeling, "the supplementing of reality by God" (148). See also the article by Prenter, "Dietrich Bonhoeffer and Karl Barth's Positivism of Revelation," in *World Come of Age;* he did not make the specific difference between Barth and Bonhoeffer clear enough; and Benktson, *Christus und die Religion*, especially 58–76. A dialectical concept of religion is read into Bonhoeffer, but that is wrong (59 n. 2), as is the suggestion that presuppositions of Bonhoeffer, which are conditioned by the time in which he lived, are to be traced back to Barth's "non-historicity" (71 n. 38). He unjustly opposes Bethge's comment that, late in his life, Bonhoeffer regarded religion as something "transitory historical . . . , and therefore perhaps a unique 'Western' phenomenon" (DB, 776). Sigurd M. Daecke argues in *Teilhard de Chardin und die evangelische Theologie* (Göttingen: Vandenhoeck und Ruprecht, 1967), 116–24, that Bonhoeffer had a thoroughly different understanding of worldliness and history than Barth. Finally, we note particularly Bethge's description of religion in Bonhoeffer as a historical phenomenon and his distinction between Barth's systematic concept of religion and Bonhoeffer's historicized one.

160. GS V, 185, dating from 1931–32. At times Barth saw religion as a phenomenon of intellectual history; see above, part three, section 6a.

161. The terms "religionless" and "religionlessness" are found already in Bonhoeffer's report on his second visit to the United States. The United States as a whole and the individual states, as well as public schools, are religionless

(NRS, 106, 110). The term relates, however, to the problem of the false, or insufficient, separation of church and state. That is why the meaning of these terms in the early letters is quite different from their meaning in LPP.

162. Cf. the negative meaning of religious in LPP, 344, "religious blackmail"; "religious compulsion," 280 [the German term actually means "rape"]; "religious method," 362; "explain its ungodliness in some religious way or other," 361; etc. The negative form of religious practice is clearly manifest in these statements and Bonhoeffer attacks it strongly. He does so for the sake of a new form in which people are neither blackmailed nor God co-opted by religion.

163. It appeared in the letter of 8 June 1944, in LPP, 326. Bonhoeffer stresses the temporal aspect in the word "come" or "has come," 327; cf. 341 and elsewhere. This aspect has already occupied us in the discussion of the significant term "today"; see above, part two, section 5b. When Bonhoeffer speaks of the world's "adulthood," e.g., 327, temporal language is, of course, inapplicable.

164. To be of age and adulthood are ideas which are expressed in a variety of ways earlier. E.g., "maturity," NRS, 202, dating from 1933; see also GS IV, 257, 260, 268, 271; LT, 52, 88, all from 1936–37; GS III, 422–24; E, 100, from 1940. It is interesting that these terms are applied in Bonhoeffer's middle period to the community and the Christian but not to the world and humanity.

165. See Jürgen Moltmann, "Die Wirklichkeit der Welt und Gottes konkretes Gebot nach Dietrich Bonhoeffer," in MW III, 54–57, esp. 56.

166. Moltmann, "Wirklichkeit," 56, and Daecke, *Teilhard de Chardin*, 35. Bonhoeffer had purchased Rothe's ethics but, as Bethge informs us, the usual underlining is missing in that copy, a sign perhaps that Bonhoeffer had not worked through the book in his usual depth (DB, 619). Cf. Gerhard Sauter, "Zur Herkunft und Absicht der Formel 'Nicht-religiöse Interpretation biblischer Begriffe' bei Bonhoeffer," in *Evangelische Theologie*, Vol. 25, No. 6 (1965): 283–97. Sauter draws interesting parallels to Ragaz (292 n. 28, see also n. 29). See Bethge, "Der mündige Mensch—der mündige Christ," in *Ohnmacht und Mündigkeit* (Munich: Chr. Kaiser Verlag, 1969), 170–182.

167. There are only scattered references to Dilthey prior to LPP; e.g., AB, 43 n. 1; GS V, 186, 205, 215.

168. See the letter of 14 Jan. 1944 in LPP, 187; cf. 189.

169. LPP, 191. The quotation is from Dilthey's *Das Erlebnis und die Dichtung. Lessing, Goethe, Novalis, Hölderlin*.

170. LPP, 227. The influence of this book on Bonhoeffer has been discussed by Chr. Gremmels, *Mündigkeit—Geschichte und Entfaltung eines Begriffs*. He showed especially that the concept "metaphysics" is "a historically restricted phenomenon" (363 n. 16), referring to Dilthey's collected works, Vol I, 133.

171. Bethge recently discovered a note which had been left in that book; see below, n. 206. Bonhoeffer's reference to Cardano, LPP, 333, has been demonstrated to be indeed a reference to Dilthey's *Weltanschauung*.

172. See 8 and 64 in *Das Erlebnis* about inwardness; Dilthey speaks of Luther in connection with inwardness.

173. *Das Erlebnis*, 151. Dilthey speaks of *disciplina arcani* in this work (97).

174. *Das Erlebnis*, 61. In this context Dilthey also discusses modern autonomy in relation to the endeavors for natural law and natural theology.

175. This is the place in LPP where the term "worldliness" reemerges; it does so clearly conditioned by Bonhoeffer's study of Dilthey. Concerning Bonhoeffer's prior use of "worldliness," see above, part three, section 5b. The first hint that Bonhoeffer is reading the second of Dilthey's books sent to him is in the letter of 2 March 1944 (LPP, 227).

NOTES

176. He adds a comment about the "surprising tolerance of the Muslims in the figure of Parsifal's half-brother Feirefiz."
177. Wilhelm Dilthey, *Von deutscher Dichtung und Musik. Aus den Studien zur Geschichte des deutschen Geistes* (Stuttgart/Göttingen: Teuber–Vandenhoeck und Ruprecht, 1957), 1–15.
178. This goes hand in hand with Walther von der Vogelweide's discovery of the laity's self-awareness (84), as with his warning against "the dark pressure of the church on worldly existence" (135).
179. He speaks of Feirefiz in connection with Parsifal; cf. also 108, 115.
180. Dilthey then discussed Wolfram von Eschenbach.

The determination of the goal of poetry was just as significant as the first phase of its development. The goal was to discern the activity of Christian religiosity in the life of the world. It was an ideal, the form of which was still governed by the class-related, conventional ideas of chivalry. But what future of our spirit he foresees! Hutten's ideal of a knightly struggle for a new Christian society, the ideas manifest in the patricians of the free cities, Luther's view of Christianity as a power in worldly matters—that is the next stage in the transformation of medieval Christianity. At the end of it there stands Faust and his exclamation: we can save those who actively strive forward.

The new ideal of life is said to be contrary to that of "monkish Christian religiosity" characterized by its mystic contemplation of Christ's passion, endeavoring to "grasp this high object and its transcendent state of the soul" (*Von deutscher*, 118).

181. Protestantism "rests wholly in inwardness and on the word" (118). Cf. 66 and 277.
182. *Von deutscher*, 326–36. Here the idea of "being of age" is raised in connection with the natural sciences (332). The extensive discussion of Schiller may have caused Bonhoeffer's comments about him. On 2 April 1944, he refers to the Klopstock biography of K. Kindt (LPP, 246); Dilthey had discussed Klopstock quite extensively (*Von deutscher*, 301).
183. It would appear that these concepts are not yet shaped by the ideas of the third work of Dilthey which Bonhoeffer was to read.
184. LPP, 308, 311. Earlier Bonhoeffer had complained that he knew so little about the natural sciences (LPP, 204): "It's a matter of great regret to me that I'm so ignorant of the natural sciences, but it's a gap that cannot be filled now."
185. In the letter Bonhoeffer states with regret that he is still "very much in the early stages; and, as usual, I'm being led on . . . by an instinctive feeling for questions that will arise later" (LPP, 325).
186. Wilhelm Dilthey, *Weltanschauung und Analyse des Menschen seit Renaissance und Reformation, Collected Works*, Vol. II (Stuttgart/Göttingen: Teuber–Vandenhoeck und Ruprecht, 1960), 91. Bonhoeffer's reference to a movement toward autonomy suggests his use of this book (LPP, 325). His reference to Cardano leads one to conclude that he had finished reading the book, because he is mentioned there only at the end of *Weltanschauung* (429–32).
187. LPP, 357. Bonhoeffer's father comments to Bethge that Dietrich was studying Dilthey (LPP, 377): "He will be suffering very much from his isolation in this fast-moving time and have trouble concentrating on Dilthey, which he is studying now for his ethics."
188. He had made a very similar comment earlier (LPP, 327), which is followed by his reflections on liberal theology.

NOTES

189. See LPP, 359. In *Weltanschauung*, Dilthey refers to Machiavelli and Montaigne on 24–39; to Herbert of Cherbury and Grotius on 248–57 and 276–83; to Bodin on 145–53; to Bruno on 297–311 and 326–42, with particular reference on 330 to the infinity of the world; to Spinoza and Descartes on 342–58. The two citations from Bruno and Spinoza in LPP, 375, are from *Weltanschauung*, 341, 209.

190. It occurs in Dilthey, *Weltanschauung*, 280. Dilthey records a very similar phrase from the writings of Gabriel Biel, 279 n. 1. Wolfgang Schweitzer has shown in his *Der entmythologisierte Staat. Studien zur Revision der evangelischen Ethik des Politischen* (Gütersloh: Gütersloher Verlagshaus Gerd Mohn, 1968), 145 n. 2, that the phrase as it stands did not come directly from Grotius. Grotius said that there would have to be a natural law *"etiamsi daremus, quod sine summo scelere dari nequit, non esse Deum"* (Schweitzer, 145). It can be shown that the shorter version Bonhoeffer used came from Dilthey, although it is not clear yet how he came to the Latin *etsi deus non daretur,* for in Dilthey the phrase occurs only in German.

191. Bonhoeffer certainly did not make Dilthey's theological position his own; it was probably in line with modern, generally "reasonable" natural religion.

192. There are many other references one could cite in support of this perception; cf., e.g., 283: "All of these movements in theology, the natural sciences, morality, jurisprudence and politics strove for the establishment of a *natural system* based on naturally evident concepts and statements. Reason [Vernunft] was regarded now as being capable on its own to understand nature and to provide order for life and society." Cf. also 348.

193. Cf. LPP, 325. The term "working hypothesis" was already used in E, 98.

194. For natural law, see *Weltanschauung*, 276–82; autonomous morality, 261, 265, 276, 447; natural religion or theology, 90, 99, 105–7, 151–53, 248, 261 n. 1.

195. On the influence of Stoicism, see *Weltanschauung*, 153, 260, 285.

196. The concept "being of age" is found, e.g., in *Weltanschauung*, but the concept "the autonomy of reason" is much more prevalent.

197. That Bonhoeffer could not accept the notion of unchanging and suprahistorical norms and principles has already become evident; see above, part one, section 5.

198. See GS V, 215.

199. Concerning Dilthey's religious Christianity, see below, n. 204.

200. *Weltanschauung*, 236; see also 1–15, 90, 214, 494. These references have most likely shaped Bonhoeffer's rather summary concept of metaphysics. He thinks of the metaphysics of the Middle Ages which, according to Dilthey, "is still the substratum of our popular and religious metaphysics" (16).

201. Inwardness has its roots in the Middle Ages, according to Dilthey (*Weltanschauung*, 19).

202. See also 216. It was Zwingli who completed the "transformation of Christianity into the independent inwardness of the individual made one in the will" (63). See 79 on the continuation of this process. Dilthey then speaks of the "splendid, progressing tendency to develop, in the sense of the Luther of 1520, the personal inwardness of the religious-ethical process, the moral capacity of people, and the reforming power of true faith over against existing society" (66).

203. This alone represents for Dilthey "the complete abolition of the notion of work as maintained in the church" (*Weltanschauung*, 61).

NOTES

204.

I consider the statements by Bruno, Spinoza and Shaftesbury a justified, valuable and promising reshaping of European religiosity. We shall pursue its history as a living faith which will capture some of the greatest minds. The conclusion of that process came with Schleiermacher. . . . The Christian religiosity to which we belong nowadays is the faith which developed from its historical origin in the church within European humankind but which *cannot go on being dependent* on its origin, the religiosity of primitive Christian communities." (339)

This shows plainly what Dilthey meant by the religiosity which began with Bruno, namely, "the new gospel of the infinite universe" (*Weltanschauung*, 342).

205. Inwardness as a characteristic of religion was more important to Bonhoeffer than metaphysics. Cf. LPP, 344–47, and GS V, 304, dating from 1932–33 (!), where Bonhoeffer criticizes it in the context of the critique of all religion. See also CD, 252, in connection with the "pious wishes of the religious flesh," and E, 200, regarding the "cultivation of a Christian inner life, untouched by the world." Religion, piety and inwardness belong together. Bonhoeffer had opposed them for long, but did so under the influence of Dilthey.

206. LPP, 343. He adds in parentheses, "Episcopius at the Synod of Dordrecht for the Arminians," citing Dilthey (*Weltanschauung*, 102). On that page one reads,

It was Episcopius, representing the Arminians at the Synod of Dordrecht, who uttered the important sentence: "If we consider the oldest traditions of the church we note that the aim and intent of those who drew up creeds, spiritual canons, confessions and confessions of faith was none other than to declare what they themselves believed and not what one had to believe."

207. In connection with Troeltsch's critique of Christianity's claim to absoluteness, Bonhoeffer wrote: "It takes courage to say such a 'No.' Apologetics is always the product of anxiety" (GS V, 202). Cf. LPP, 326, the attack on method in the context of his polemics against apologetics.

208. Cf. CD, 98, and GS V, 271.

209. It is plain that religion and adulthood are in contradiction, and not adulthood and the word of God. Bonhoeffer's aversion to psychotherapy was influenced by his father as well as by Barth, who had raised strong objections against the notion of "experience" and, indirectly, against Schleiermacher.

210. This is why we did not describe Barth's theology directly in relation to Bonhoeffer's theology in part three, section 6a, above. We did describe Dilthey's position, however, as seen from Bonhoeffer's occupation with it.

211. Cf. SC, 65. Other early texts are NRS, 308, dating from 1935; GS IV, 388, from 1936; note the tendentious, German-Christian summation of that address in WF, 73. E, 96–109 paints a primarily negative picture, as does LPP, 123. E, 273 is both critical and appreciative. His critical relation to natural law (e.g., GS II, 101, and GS III, 34, as well as E, 360) does not change, nor that to natural theology. His changing perception of modernity may have been initiated by Nicolai Hartmann's book *Systematische Philosophie*, published in 1942. He read it with much appreciation (LPP, 121).

212. Cf. LPP, 229, 280, 325.

213. That Bonhoeffer's view of secularization is different from that of Gogarten is evident from the difference in the reception accorded to each. At times they are said to be closely related and, indeed, there were some early similarities, since both depended on Griesebach's work. It is noteworthy that Gogarten

used the work of Troeltsch, Dilthey, and C. F. von Weizsäcker in formulating his view. He cites *Zum Weltbild der Physik*, relies on Dilthey's essay on Lessing in *Das Erlebnis und die Dichtung*, and on his *Weltanschauung*, in the book *Der Mensch zwischen Gott und Welt*. Reference is made again to *Weltanschauung* in the work *Verhängnis und Hoffnung der Neuzeit*. Despite their recourse to the same authors, fundamental differences remain in relation to the concepts of subjectivity, inwardness, and worldlessness.

214. That is why Bonhoeffer begins with the question of what religionlessness means for the church (LPP, 280).

215. Cf. GS V, 234.

216. Bonhoeffer went on to say: "But the principle of the Middle Ages is heteronomy in the form of clericalism" (LPP, 360). It would appear that that comment is a reminiscence of Dilthey's *Von deutscher Dichtung und Musik*. The reading of that book led Bonhoeffer to speak of anticlerical, but clerical reality; see above, part three, section 7a.

217. "Before God and with God we live without God" LPP, 360 is, as we have already seen, a reversal of the statement that Adam has "to live before God without life from God" (CF, 90).

218. The specific citations are given above, part two, section 5c. It has to be emphasized that this theology of the cross cannot be isolated, since it is borne by the hope for the new creation. See below, Epilogue.

219. Cf. on individualism, in addition to SC and AB: GS I, 100, dating from 1930–31; GS I, 64, from 1932; NRS, 193, from 1933. In his middle period, Bonhoeffer relates "individual" mainly to "pious"; cf. PB, 36, dating from 1932, and especially GS IV, 202. Individualism, piety and inwardness are interrelated; it is a relatedness to which Schleiermacher had provided the theological basis and had given currency. Bonhoeffer was consistently opposed to individualism, piety, and inwardness.

220. We have already stated that the question of limits is raised throughout Bonhoeffer's theology. His polemics against the view that we must live through the limit situation (AB, 87 n. 1, and NRS, 58) may be behind his critique of Tillich in LPP, 327.

221. Bonhoeffer's reflections on weakness go together with those on limits. One can trace them through his theology in a twofold way. He asks about human weakness, in which we are or are not to search for God, and asks about God's weakness in the world. God's revelation in weakness completely contradicts religion. Two functions are served by religion: it is the sign of our alleged strength and it seeks to prove God in our weakness to be the one who is strong and able to do everything.

222. This has been argued most elaborately by Hans Blumenberg, *Legitimität der Neuzeit* (Frankfurt: Suhrkamp Verlag, 1966). The chief aim of his polemics is most likely Gogarten's theses.

223. Bonhoeffer's assertions about multidimensionality in LPP are part of this discussion, as are those against a one-sided view of reality in E; see above, part three, sections 5b, c.

224. This holds true for the christological address of Barcelona and LPP.

225. This is one of the elements of religion discussed as early as AB; see above, part three, section 5b.

226. AB, 183 n. 1; GS V, 265; E, 103. See above, part two, section 3a. Bethge reports that Bonhoeffer used that sentence in one of Karl Barth's seminars (DB, 132).

227. LPP, 362. On the presence and absence of God, see, e.g., GS IV, 67, dating from 1932; GS IV, 398, from 1935; TP, 52; and especially E, 259. This

coinciding of God's absence and presence determines the difference also between an alleged and an actual presence or absence of God or godlessness. See GS V, 225, dating from 1931-32. On the question of an unconscious Christianity, see E, 143. Relating to the concept of unconscious Christianity in Rothe see DB, 771 n. 182. Often Bonhoeffer brings the cross together with this ambivalent godlessness; e.g., CD, 81; GS IV, 420; LT, 118 [the word "wickedness" is used for the German "godlessness"]; NRS, 146.

228. Cf. as indirect evidence Helmut Rössler's letter to Bonhoeffer in NRS, 74, where popular religion is said to be "completely secularized." See Friedrich Karl Schumann, *Der Gottesgedanke und der Zerfall der Moderne* (Tübingen: J. C. B. Mohr, 1929), and Hermann Lübbe, *Säkularisierung. Geschichte eines ideenpolitischen Begriffs* (Freiburg: Karl Alber Verlag, 1965), 86-108. The attempt to desecularize (97) is very instructive.

229. See PB 28-40; NRS, 114; GS III, 471; E, 230.

230. NRS, 91, dating from 1931, and WF, 239, from 1939.

231. The parallel development in Roman Catholicism is discussed in E, 96. In 1944 Bonhoeffer wrote about the world from which the gods were removed; see GS IV, 604.

232. Bonhoeffer discusses the process of secularization apart from its manifestation in intellectual history or the social-political sphere. Kant's ethics of duty is described as a secularization of the Protestant experience of grace (GS III, 94, dating from 1930); cf. SC, 152, speaking of Kant's secularized notion of the kingdom of God. Hegel's philosophy of religion is a secularization of Christian truth in relation to the doctrine of the eucharist (GS III, 32). The philosophy of existence and psychotherapy are called "secularized offshoots of Christian theology" (LPP, 326).

233. DB, 774. Cf. Ernst Feil, "Religionsloses Christentum und nicht-religiöse Interpretation bei D. Bonhoeffer," in *Theologische Zeitschrift*, Vol. 24: 40-48.

234. See the works by Ebeling, Sauter, and Ott cited above.

235. LPP, 280-82. Ebeling fails in his attempt to show that *speaking* has predominance (*Word and Faith*, 122 n. 4). It is not a coincidence that he speaks first of proclamation and then of form. He has removed quotations several times from their context and introduced them with expressions used in relation to proclamation, that is to say, in relation to speaking and interpretation, without heeding the fact that they are in the context of religionless Christianity, its form and practice.

236. What Bonhoeffer deals with here is not chiefly a problem of proclamation; see also LPP, 361, 369.

237. See above, part one, section 6, where this point was elaborated in connection especially with the relation of sacrament and preaching and with the hermeneutical function of action.

238. He speaks of "being able to interpret and proclaim . . . in a 'non-religious' sense and to 'interpret in a religious sense' " (LPP, 285); of reinterpreting concepts in a worldly sense (286); of non-religious intepetation of theological concepts (328), or of biblical concepts (344); of worldly interpretation of biblical concepts (361). The terminology is still not firmly fixed.

239. Thus, Gerhard Krause, "Dietrich Bonhoeffer und Rudolf Bultmann," in *Zeit und Geschichte. Dankesgabe an Rudolf Bultmann zum 80. Geburtstag*, ed., Erich Dinkler (Tübingen: J. C. B. Mohr, 1964), 439-460. Bonhoeffer knew of Bultmann quite early but he became no central figure for him. In his last period he read Bultmann's works, especially his article "The New Testament and Mythology." Cf. GS III, 45, and DB, 615-17, 761.

NOTES

240. Other concepts listed are creation, fall, reconciliation, repentance, *vita nova*, the last things, justification, rebirth and sanctification (LPP, 287, 382).

241. On 23 or 25 July 1942 Bonhoeffer wrote:

"I am one of those who welcomed this treatise [sc. The New Testament and Mythology], not because I agree with it; I regret the double line of approach in it . . . ; so up to this point I may perhaps still be a pupil of Harnack. To put it crudely: B. has let the cat out of the bag, not only for himself, but for a great many people (the Liberal cat out of the Confessional bag) and for that I am glad. He has ventured to say what many people inwardly repress (I include myself) without having overcome it. (Cited in DB, 616)

242. Barth is a victim of positivism of revelation because he lacks concreteness, which is the same as the absence of a relation to the world; Bonhoeffer raises this in connection with non-religious interpretation (LPP, 286, 328–29). This is also where the only references to Tillich occur; he "set out to interpret the evolution of the world (against its will) in a religious sense" (327); the world rejected this attempt to understand it better than it did itself. This critique shows that Tillich and Bonhoeffer are not to be confused with one another. Bethge confirms this (DB, 770, 777, 782); but see DBG, 1080. Neither J. A. T. Robinson nor B. E. Benktson show this difference clearly enough.

243. Cf. NRS, 309.

244. Karl Barth, *The Humanity of God* (Richmond, Virginia: John Knox Press, 1960), 59.

245. The term "formal" reflects E, 297; see above, part three, section 5b.

246. Bethge is quite correct in saying that for Bonhoeffer religion was "a transitory historical [phenomenon], and therefore perhaps a unique 'Western' (sic!) phenomenon that would not return" (DB, 776).

247. LPP, 280. See E, 90, about "the Occident," or western Europe. In 1932 Bonhoeffer remarked that "the tradition and values, especially our so-called Christian values, are falling apart" (GS IV, 150); see also 28 and 62. Later, however, he feels less worried that the end of the Constantinian age in church history, to which we are witnesses, would put Christian faith in doubt; see above, part three, section 4a.

248. See GS II, 180, with its remark about India and the monastery. Even as a student, Bonhoeffer had been interested in India and Gandhi. In 1928 his grandmother advised him to travel to the East; three years later, while in the United States, he seriously planned to travel to India. In 1935 it seemed finally feasible to go, helped by recommendations from Bishop Bell; see NRS, 295, or Bonhoeffer's letter to Reinhold Niebuhr (GS IV, 297). But he was called back to Germany to direct the preachers' seminary. That those plans were well known but also misunderstood is shown in a letter Barth wrote to Bonhoeffer. He said that he had not heard anything of late from or about Bonhoeffer, except: "the strange news that you intend to go to India to take over from Gandhi or some other friend of God there a spiritual technique, for the application of which in the West you promised great things!" (WF, 119).

249. Bonhoeffer made numerous very pessimistic statements at that time. See NRS, 139; GS I, 32, 61. There are some rare comments reflecting the opposite (GS I, 37, or GS II, 79, dating from 1933). It is this hope for something new and positive to come *after* Hitler's time which pervades LPP.

250. From that comes a comparison of India and the European–American world. "In that faraway, fruitful and sunny country of India which is so rich in forms and ideas," a solution has been found "to feed the body easily with goods,

leaving the soul free to roam and submerge itself in itself" (surely a text not without its problems!). There is another great solution, that "of the civilization of Europe and America, the solution of the wars and industrialists" (GS III, 261–63). Cf. also LPP, 340, a similarly positive remark, and 1934, GS I, 219, about the "pagans from the East." On the subject of India and America, see William J. Peck, "The Significance of Bonhoeffer's Interest in India," in *Harvard Theological Review*, Vol. 61: 431–50.

251. GS II, 158. Cf. GS I, 41.

252. See the comment about the antithesis of God's word and our human word, of grace and religion, of a purely Christian and a general religious category, of reality and interpretation in Barth (NRS, 366). The juxtaposition of reality and interpretation is clear—made, incidentally, in analogy to *actus directus* and *actus reflectus;* the juxtaposition returns in LPP. Interpretation falls short of reality as does the word of action.

253. GS I, 61, again influenced by his experiences in the United States.

254. Bonhoeffer had visited Anglican seminaries and monasteries prior to his establishment of the preachers' seminary and the community house (DB, 335). LT is his account of those ventures. The aspect of sociality has now fully returned.

255. Concerning the arcane see also CD, 45, GS IV, 239, WF, 151, all dating from 1937; TP, 42, from 1940; and GS IV, 606–9, from 1944. See also Gisela Meuss, "Arkandisziplin und Weltlichkeit bei Dietrich Bonhoeffer," MW III, 68–115; DB, 784–86; and Bethge, "Gottesdienst im säkularen Zeitalter," in *Ohnmacht und Mündigkeit*, 114–34.

256. See especially his christology lecture, C; also above, part two, section 3b.

257. E, 303, 311; cf. CD, 194.

258. This was probably written in 1940.

259. LPP, 383; see also above, part two, section 3a; cf. the question, "What *must* I believe?" (LPP, 382, and part three, section 7a, above).

260. Cf. LPP, 382, against the background of what Bonhoeffer had concluded concerning the changes in our lives, the chief problem of which lies not only in nature but especially in organization (380). See 296 and 299.

Index of Subjects

Actualism, 170, 171, 187
Antaeus legend, 112, 113, 222 n. 22
Apologetics, 184, 200, 237 n. 207
Autonomy, 13, 15, 18, 50, 103, 119, 122, 148, 151, 155, 178, 181, 182, 184, 185, 187, 188, 189, 199, 200, 227 n. 83, 234 n. 174, 236 n. 196

Barmen, 20, 23, 41, 77
Bethel Confession, 125

Chalcedon, Confession of, 19, 47, 83, 94, 106, 153, 190
Church Dogmatics (Barth), 165–67, 171, 172, 230 n. 125
Church struggle, 17, 20, 21, 22, 23, 24, 25, 45, 76, 77, 209 n. 24, 217 n. 33
Circumcision, 163, 164, 174, 192
Confessing Church, 20, 21, 22, 23, 24, 25, 47, 77, 184, 209 n. 24, 212 n. 72, 217 n. 32, 232 n. 154
Cultural Protestantism, 78, 101, 106, 107, 108, 131, 146, 148, 156, 158, 169, 171, 185, 201, 204, 220 n. 5, 227 n. 84

Dahlem Synod, 20, 23, 41, 77
Demythologizing, 194
Dialectical theology, 34, 48, 102, 107, 158, 169, 170, 182, 203, 204, 229 n. 104

Ecumenism, 20, 22, 23, 41, 42, 209 n. 26, 210 n. 34, 212 n. 154
Enlightenment, 51, 178, 190, 218 n. 46
Eschatology, 12, 72, 89, 94, 108, 109, 119, 140, 152, 204, 218 n. 46, 225 n. 53

Exegesis, 73, 141, 208 n. 17
Existential(ism), 12, 13, 14, 15, 34, 47, 66, 170, 184, 195, 212 n. 69

German Christians, 16, 23, 24, 42, 124, 209 n. 24, 210 n. 32

Humanism, 69, 181, 183, 190, 231 n. 142

Idealism (idealistic tradition), 5, 6, 7, 33, 36, 38, 45, 61, 63, 64, 124, 169, 211 n. 59
Ideology, 21, 29, 34, 50, 151, 211 n. 62
India, 37, 38, 197, 198, 212 n. 63, 240 nn. 248, 250

Jewish people, the, 121, 209 n. 23, 221 n. 11

Kingdom of God, 101, 108, 114, 118, 119, 120, 121, 122, 135, 151, 171, 172, 223 n. 32, 239 n. 232

Liberal theology, xiii, 54, 101, 103, 105, 106, 107, 151, 157, 158, 170, 174, 184, 185, 194, 195, 201, 204, 210 n. 32, 229 n. 104, 235 n. 188, 240 n. 241

Mandate(s), 43, 120, 142, 150, 218 n. 51, 222 n. 20, 227 n. 88
Marxism, xv, xvi
Metaphysics, 6, 9, 31, 33, 39, 90, 92, 102–3, 165, 173, 174, 176, 179, 180, 181, 183, 188, 195, 232 n. 153, 234 n. 170, 236 n. 200, 237 n. 205

INDEX OF SUBJECTS

Methodism, 145, 189, 201
Mysticism, 69, 163

Natural reason, 80
Natural theology, 145, 181, 226 n. 73, 232 n. 145, 234 n. 174, 236 n. 194, 237 n. 211
Nibelungen, 179

Orders of creation, 71–72, 79, 93, 209 n. 24, 216 n. 23
Orders of preservation, 71–72, 85, 89, 93, 120, 121, 123

Pietism, 101, 175, 201
Positivism of revelation, 34, 53, 104, 175, 176, 184, 229 n. 105, 233 nn. 156, 159; 240 n. 242
Provincialism, 117, 118, 119, 143, 146, 148, 170, 171, 201, 224 n. 39

Revolution, 54, 116, 134, 135, 152, 191, 193, 222 n. 28
Rome, 25, 26, 210 n. 35, 223 n. 34

Sacrament(s), 15, 21, 42, 45, 48, 49, 50, 74, 75, 76, 81, 132, 177, 200, 201, 212 n. 71, 213 n. 92, 217 n. 28
Secularism, 117, 118, 143, 146, 148, 170, 171, 201, 224 n. 39
Secularization, 150, 185, 188, 189, 190–91, 225 n. 53, 237 n. 213, 239 n. 239
Sociality, 6, 8, 9, 10, 12, 34, 41, 74, 75, 76, 86, 96, 119
Solidarity, 112, 116, 119, 125, 189
status confessionis, 23
Stoicism, 181

Theodicy, 17, 18
Two kingdoms (realms, spheres, doctrine of) 101, 104, 113, 123, 124, 146–47, 150, 232 n. 143

Index of Names

Althaus, Paul, 173–74
Augustine, 18

Barth, Karl, xii, xiii, xix, 4, 12, 13, 14, 26, 34, 48, 70, 76, 85, 96, 102, 104, 106, 107, 108, 119, 140, 145, 157, 158, 161, 162–67, 168, 169, 170, 171, 172, 174, 175, 176, 177, 178, 180, 182, 184, 185, 186, 187, 194, 203, 204, 207 n.3, 208 nn.11, 20; 209 nn.23, 27; 210 nn.32, 37; 211 nn.54, 61; 219 n.55, 220 nn.81, 4; 221 n.16, 222 n.19, 225 n.61, 228 nn.94, 104; 229 nn.108–13, 115; 230 nn.119, 121–23, 128, 130; 231 nn.134, 135, 137; 232 nn.145, 153, 154; 233 nn.156, 158, 159; 237 n.209, 238 n.226, 240 nn.242, 244, 248; 241 n.252
Bell, George K. (bishop), 209 n.28, 240 n.248
Benktson, Benkt-Erik, 208 n.9, 216 n.26, 229 n.108, 230 n.125, 232 n.145, 233 n.159, 240 n.242
Bethge, Eberhard, xi, xii, xiii, xvi, 4, 52, 53, 61, 126, 154, 155, 156, 180, 192, 203, 207 n.2, 209 n.23, 211 n.50, 213 nn.83, 88; 214 nn.100, 102, 106; 215 n.9, 217 n.28, 218 n.52, 220 n.81, 224 nn.37, 44; 227 n.89, 232 n.153, 233 n.159, 234 nn.166, 171; 235 n.187, 240 nn.242, 246; 241 n.255
Biel, Gabriel, 236 n.190
Blumenberg, Hans, 238 n.222
Blumhardt, Christoph, 220 n.4
Bodin, Jean, 180, 236 n.189
Bruno, Giordano, 180, 236 n.189, 237 n.204

Brunstädt, Friedrich, 231 n.136
Bultmann, Rudolf, xii, 34, 194–95, 209 n.24, 216 n.26, 239 n.239, 240 n.241
Busch, Eberhard, xiii

Camus, Albert, 113
Cardano, Geronimo, 234 n.171, 235 n.186
Cherbury, Lord Herbert of, 180, 236 n.189
Coch, Friedrich (bishop), 210 n.28
Copernicus, Nicholas, 182
Cox, Harvey, xv
Cusa, Nicholas of, 180

Daecke, Sigurd M., 233 n.159, 234 n.166
Day, Tom, xvi
Descartes, René, 180, 236 n.109
Dibelius, Otto (bishop), 76, 114, 217 n.30
Dilthey, Wilhelm, xii, 178–84, 185, 186, 187, 234 nn.167, 169–75; 235 nn.177, 180, 182, 183, 187; 236 nn.189–91, 199–203; 237 nn.204–6, 210; 238 nn.213, 216
Dumas, André, 214 n.101

Ebeling, Gerhard, 192, 213 nn.88, 97; 214 nn.101, 106; 220 n.81, 233 n.159, 239 nn.234, 235
Elert, Werner, 207 n.5
Episcopius, Simon, 184, 237 n.206
Eschenbach, Wolfram von, 235 n.180

Fant, Clyde, 212 n.65
Feil, Ernst, xi, xii, 208 n.6, 209 n.27, 210 n.35, 217 n.33, 225 n.54, 239 n.233

INDEX OF NAMES

Feuerbach, Ludwig, 161, 181, 232 n. 146
Fontane, Theodor, 228 n. 102

Gandhi, Mahatma, 197, 199, 240 n. 248
Gerstenmaier, Eugen, 216 n. 21
Glenthoj, Jorgen, 214 n. 101, 217 n. 40
Godsey, John, xi, 214 nn. 101, 102; 219 n. 68, 220 n. 81
Goethe, Johann Wolfgang von, 179
Gogarten, Friedrich, xix, 237 n. 213, 238 n. 222
Gollwitzer, Helmut, xiii, 219 n. 55
Gotthelf, Jeremias, 228 n. 102
Green, Clifford, xvi, xvii, 217 n. 27
Gremmels, Christian, 234 n. 170
Grotius, Hugo, 91, 180, 181, 187, 236 nn. 189, 190
Grunow, Richard, 207 n. 4, 216 n. 26

Hamilton, Kenneth, xi
Hamilton, William, 212 n. 67
Harnack, Adolf von, 71, 105, 200, 216 nn. 18, 19; 228 n. 104, 240 n. 241
Harrelson, Walter, 216 n. 26
Hartmann, Nicolai, 237 n. 211
Hase, Hans Christoph von, 208 n. 12, 214 nn. 101, 102
Hegel, Georg Wilhelm Friedrich, 63, 102, 105, 211 n. 45, 215 n. 6, 239 n. 232
Heidegger, Martin, 32, 34
Heim, Karl, 173
Herrmann, Wilhelm, 102, 220 n. 5
Hildebrandt, Franz, 209 n. 27, 214 n. 105, 223 n. 28
Hitler, Adolf, 77, 84, 152, 228 n. 91, 240 n. 249
Hodgson, Leonard, 210 n. 29
Holl, Karl, 66
Honecker, Martin, 219 n. 59
Hossenfelder, Joachim, 210 n. 28

Immermann, Karl Leberecht, 228 n. 102

Kant, Immanuel, 7, 102, 105, 174, 178, 232 n. 150, 239 n. 232
Keller, Gottfried, 228 n. 102

Kelly, Geffrey, xii, xvii
Kierkegaard, Sören, 46, 224 n. 45
Klopstock, Friedrich Gottlieb, 235 n. 182
Krause, Gerhard, 239 n. 239
Krause, W., 214 n. 101
Kuhns, William, xi, 207 n. 4, 211 n. 62, 220 n. 71
Kuske, Martin, 214 n. 101, 216 n. 26, 219 n. 59, 220 nn. 77, 79
Kutter, Hermann, 222 n. 4
Kwiran, Manfred, xii

Lassère, Jean, 197
Lehmann, Paul, xiii, 228 n. 96
Leibholz-Bonhoeffer, Sabine, 214 nn. 102, 105
Lessing, Gotthold Ephraim, 51, 178, 179, 191, 238 n. 213
Lichtenberg, Georg Christoph, 51, 191
Litt, Theodor, 83, 138, 139
Lohff, Wenzel, 224 n. 45
Lübbe, Hermann, 239 n. 228
Luther, Martin, 11, 15, 25, 28, 49, 66, 104, 122, 128, 129, 130, 137, 146, 147, 148, 183, 189, 207 n. 5, 208 n. 15, 221 n. 11, 224 n. 43, 225 n. 53, 234 n. 172, 235 n. 180, 236 n. 202

Machiavelli, Niccolo, 180, 236 n. 189
Marlé, René, xi, 214 n. 101
Marquardt, Friedrich-Wilhelm, xiii
Mayer, Rainer, xi, 207 n. 5, 208 n. 9, 213 n. 99, 214 nn. 101, 102; 219 nn. 55, 56, 59; 229 n. 106, 232 n. 145
Meier, Jörg Martin, 214 n. 101
Metz, Johann Baptist, xvii
Meuss, Gisela, 214 nn. 101, 106; 241 n. 255
Moltmann, Jürgen, 4, 207 n. 4, 214 n. 101, 234 nn. 165, 166
Montaigne, Michel Eyquem, 180, 236 n. 189
Mörike, Eduard Friedrich, 179
Mottu, Henri, 232 n. 146
Müller, D., 214 n. 101
Müller, Hanfried, xi, xvi, xx, 4, 155, 207 n. 3, 208 nn. 5, 12; 214 nn. 101, 102; 217 n. 33, 218 n. 49, 229 n. 106

INDEX OF NAMES

Naumann, Friedrich, 104, 105, 151, 161, 169, 221 nn. 10–13
Niebuhr, Reinhold, 139, 225 n. 61, 240 n. 248
Niesel, Wilhelm, 207 n. 1, 228 nn. 91, 94
Nietzsche, Friedrich, 106, 112, 113, 161, 218 n. 53

Oetinger, Friedrich, 84, 218 n. 48
Ott, Heinrich, xi, 208 n. 9, 214 nn. 101, 106; 219 nn. 55, 56, 59; 239 n. 234
Overbeck, Franz, 106, 161, 163, 164, 229 n. 108

Parsifal, 179, 235 nn. 176, 179
Peck, William J., 241 n. 250
Peters, Tiemo Rainer, xvi, 216 n. 23, 225 n. 48
Petrarch, 126
Pfeiffer, Hans, 4, 207 n. 3, 209 n. 20, 211 n. 61, 215 nn. 5, 6, 9; 216 n. 18, 219 n. 59
Phillips, John A., xi, 207 n. 5, 212 n. 67, 213 n. 98, 214 nn. 101, 102; 216 n. 26, 217 n. 33, 218 n. 49, 229 n. 106
Prenter, Regin, 215 n. 5, 230 n. 125, 233 n. 159
Przywara, Erich, 208 n. 11

Ragaz, Leonhard, 220 n. 4, 234 n. 166
Ranke, Leopold von, 111
Rieger, Julius, 207 n. 2, 210 n. 36
Ritschl, Albrecht, 102, 220 n. 5
Robinson, J. A. T., 208 n. 9, 240 n. 242
Rössler, Helmut, 198
Rothe, Richard, 178, 234 n. 166, 239 n. 227
Rothuizen, G. Th., 214 n. 1
Rumscheidt, Martin, xvii, 209 n. 23, 229 n. 104

Sauter, Gerhard, 219 n. 59, 234 n. 166, 239 n. 234
Schleicher, Rüdiger, 212 n. 66
Schleiermacher, Friedrich Daniel Ernst, 102, 103, 104, 105, 161, 170, 171, 174, 220 n. 8, 230 n. 131, 231 n. 136, 237 nn. 204, 209; 238 n. 219

Schiller, Friedrich von, 179, 235 n. 182
Schlingensiepen, Ferdinand, 216 n. 19
Schlingensiepen, Hermann, 215 n. 106
Schmidt, Hans, 214 n. 101, 219 n. 59
Schönherr, Albrecht, 214 nn. 101, 106
Schulte, Hannelis, 216 n. 26
Schumann, Karl Friedrich, 239 n. 228
Schwartz, Joachim, 219 n. 59
Schweitzer, Wolfgang, 236 n. 190
Seeberg, Reinhold, 105, 168, 218 n. 50, 231 n. 136
Shaftesbury, Earl of (Anthony Ashley Cooper), 237 n. 204
Sherman, Franklin, 208 n. 11
Simmel, Georg, 182
Smith, Ronald Gregor, 212 n. 67
Sölle, Dorothee, 219 n. 55
Spinoza, Baruch, 180, 236 n. 189, 237 n. 204
Stählin, Wilhelm, 216 n. 21
Stifter, Adalbert, 179, 228 n. 102
Storm, Theodor, 153
Sutz, Erwin, 153, 197, 209 n. 27

Tillich, Paul, 105, 106, 174, 238 n. 220, 240 n. 242
Timm, Hermann, 220 n. 5, 221 n. 11
Troeltsch, Ernst, 105, 151, 182, 221 n. 17, 237 n. 207, 238 n. 213

Vogel, Traugott, 224 n. 45
Vogelweide, Walther von der, 179, 235 n. 178

Wedemeyer, Maria von, 228 n. 97
Weissbach, Jürgen, 207 n. 4, 214 n. 101
Weizsäcker, Carl Friedrich von, 180, 238 n. 213
Weth, Rudolf, 225 n. 54
Woelfel, James, xi

Zimmermann, Wolf-Dieter, 215 n. 105
Zinn, Elisabeth, 218 n. 48
Zwingli, Huldrych, 236 n. 202

www.ingramcontent.com/pod-product-compliance
Lightning Source LLC
Chambersburg PA
CBHW031411290426
44110CB00011B/343